D0778692

Frontiers of History

DONALD R. KELLEY

Frontiers of History

HISTORICAL INQUIRY IN THE TWENTIETH CENTURY

Yale University Press
New Haven &
London

Published with assistance from the Kingsley Trust Association Publication Fund established by the Scroll and Key Society of Yale College.

Set in Sabon by Keystone Typesetting, Inc.
Printed in the United States of America.

Library of Congress Cataloging-in-Publication Data
Kelley, Donald R., 1931–
Frontiers of history : historical inquiry in the twentieth century / Donald R. Kelley.
p. cm.
Includes bibliographical references and index.
ISBN-13: 978-0-300-12062-2 (cloth : alk. paper)
ISBN-10: 0-300-12062-1
1. Historiography — History — 20th century. 2. History — Philosophy. I. Title.
D13.K43 2006
907.2 — dc22

                                                        2006003783

A catalogue record for this book is available from the British Library.

The paper in this book meets the guidelines for permanence and durability of the Committee on Production Guidelines for Book Longevity of the Council on Library Resources.

10 9 8 7 6 5 4 3 2 1

This book is for Bonnie,
who made the whole trip with me,
and for our children, J., P., and P.

A man sets out to draw the world. As the years go by, he peoples a space with images of provinces, kingdoms, mountains, bays, ships, islands, fishes, rooms, instruments, stars, horses, and individuals. A short time before he dies, he discovers that the patient labyrinth of lines traces the lineaments of his own face.

— *Jorge Luis Borges*

Contents

Preface   ix

Introduction: Horizons, 1914   1

1   Before the Great War   5

2   Reevaluations   46

3   After the Great War   89

4   Modern Times   135

5   After the Good War   170

6   Circumspect and Prospect   206

Conclusion: Millennium   243

Notes   253

Index   285

Preface

The idea of this project came to me over fifty years ago, and the reading and research have continued fairly steadily since then, though the writing began less than ten years ago during my third sojourn at the Institute for Advanced Study and was finished just as I retired both from Rutgers University and from my editorship of the *Journal of the History of Ideas*. For me at least this marks indeed the "end of history" and may account for some of the indulgences in this book.

Most of the people I have to thank for encouragement and for expanding my horizons have been listed in the first two volumes, and indeed some appear in the present volume, though I would like to single out again Anthony Grafton, Peter Paret, Daniel Woolf, Perez Zagorin, Joseph Levine, David Sacks, Peter Burke, Georg Iggers, John Pocock, Paul Hunter, Jerry Schneewind, Donald Verene, Constance Blackwell, Allan Megill, Edoardo Totarolo, Ulrich Schneider, Martin Mulsow, Michael Carhart, and Lorraine Daston, as well as my late friends Charles Schmitt, Felix Gilbert, Paul Kristeller, Jack Hexter, Richard Popkin, and John Salmon. My best collaborator remains Bonnie Smith, who has also worked in the tradition of historiography. These friends, colleagues, and collaborators in my researches into lost time constitute my own Republic of Letters.

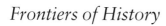

Frontiers of History

Introduction

Horizons, 1914

What is characteristic of the present situation is that the two rivals of antiquity — Herodotus and Thucydides — have become the acknowledged founders of historical research. Herodotus would not have minded, but Thucydides must be horrified at the association.

— *Arnaldo Momigliano*

The first volume of this narrative began with the conceit of these two faces, those of Herodotus and Thucydides — cultural history and political history, anachronistically speaking — and added a third, a Livian (or Eusebian) national (or confessional) and by imperial extension universal history from a European and ethnocentric center; and these forebears still haunt historiographical practice. What Momigliano suggests is that Herodotus, in a world still being explored and charted, would have continued going about satisfying his curiosity and seeking local meanings, while Thucydides would have thrown up his hands at the unanalyzable chaos which his posterity has brought. As for the national-ethnic traditions, these continue to predominate despite the intellectual imperialism reaching out to embrace the whole globe of human occupation. The second volume, overlapping with the first in the Enlightenment, followed the fortunes of history in periods of accumulating erudition and controversy, as authors, with the help of secondary and tertiary literature, auxiliary sciences, interdisciplinary contacts, demographic expansion, and institutional organization, carried historical inquiry down these diverging paths into modernity, philosophies and theologies of history, state-inventing, empire-building, and colony-founding. Enticed by the passing fashion of the "post-modern," I had first thought of calling this third volume "Fragments," or even "Follies," of History but then decided that "Frontiers" better suggests its orientation, since the line of inquiry takes up the post-European story, or stories, in the early twentieth century and carries them down to the world horizons of the future, at least as seen from my own parochial point of view, ending with some ego-historical reflections about the current state and prospects of the Herodoto-Thucydido-Polybio-Eusebio-Bodino-Herdero-Rankean-Huizingian project in an age of enthusiastic but anxious and undirected globalization.

From the beginning my focus has been not on ideological claims but on historiographical themes, language, and methods which have persisted down to the present, despite intrusions of ideology and repeated efforts to find and to advertise novelty. Despite the Copernican revolution, the marvels of technology, the exploding universe, and flights of imagination deriving from these, we still *live* and perceive within small geocentric horizons. "We have never been modern," Bruno La Tour has argued, and this applies to most of the writing of history. "New histories" come and go, but history continues its quest despite unfamiliar conditions and changes in targets, values, and goals. For Herodotus nothing human was alien to *historia;* and hardly anything, "human" or not, is alien to his successors following the dream, or nightmare, of a "total history." Yet our categories and vocabulary have preserved semantic continuity despite (or perhaps because of) rhetorical invocations of rupture, revolution, rebirth, and renewal.

My second volume began with the setting sun of Enlightenment and ended with the "crisis of historicism" and of culture in general associated with the experience of the First World War, and the present sequel reviews the predicament produced by this global cataclysm, when Europe ceased to occupy the center of the world or at least to monopolize the attention of scholars, and when, through easy transportation and the media, the "world" became an object of daily experience — which, as Martin Jay has recently suggested, has undergone its own "crisis." Local knowledge was still necessarily privileged, and in many ways national histories continued to be the rule, but increasingly nationalism became a problem rather than an ideal — a question about and not an answer to political, social, economic, and cultural problems, an occasion not for political or ethnic celebration but for critical historical inquiry. The old call for a "new history" followed the familiar shift from power and politics to questions of peacetime culture — spiritual and material, high, middle, and low, masculine and feminine — and the lives of all the inhabitants of the biosphere. Not that "world history" was new, since it had at least nominal roots in Polybius, Eusebius, Otto of Freising, and many eighteenth-century textbook writers, but its attraction became more urgent in an imperialist and global age. On this level historical inquiry became increasingly divorced from old-fashioned archival research and dependent on secondary sources, and was turned, with the help of the modern human sciences and the problem of "information overload," into a version of the "conjectural history" of the Enlightenment.

In this age of fragmentation the "great powers" remained dominant, conceptually if not politically; and German and French scholars and theorists, especially, concerned themselves with the practice and theory of history in an age of post-nationalism, post-Marxism, post-masculinsm, post-colonialism, and globalism, while British scholars stayed in more conventional channels, Italians and Spanish looked to the Germans, and Americans to the French and more derivatively to the Germans for methodological and theoretical guidance — this at least from my limited intellectual horizons. In many ways anthropology has replaced the more reductionist and abstract fields of political science, economics, and sociology as the discipline of choice for large-scale interpretation. Yet Eurocentrism, despite growing awareness of exotic, especially Middle and Far Eastern, influences, remained in place for the understanding not only of local but also of world history, for which cosmopolitanism, as in the Enlightenment, represented a geographic rather than a conceptual or ideological orientation.

Like other human scientists, historians have had to accommodate themselves to extremes of war and ideological conflict, although their search for patterns and institutional regularities has often dismissed or avoided such as aberrations. Yet war, too, has been continuous in Western — and indeed global — civilization; and national focuses and the search for causes and guilt among the elite leadership have reinforced the belief that war is an exceptional cultural condition, with the result that economic exchange, social structures, and cultural patterns have been largely founded on tacit assumptions of a stable, peaceful, progressive order. Some of this complacence (not shared by ancient and early modern historians) did not survive the experience of (so far) two world wars, but it is still embedded in academic traditions and the premises of world history. European historians of all nationalities have looked for their place in the world and have interpreted their pasts as processes of maturing and adaptation to the spread of humanity around the globe and beyond. Under the impulse of the new histories of the past century, historians have also turned their attentions to the peaceful arts and acts of civilization, especially domestic, sexual, symbolic, scandalous, representational, and ornamental aspects. Disillusioned with Enlightenment ideals of unlimited progress and "perfectibility," recent historians have nevertheless embraced the values of civilization and culture, low as well as high, capitalist as well as communitarian, above the repetitive headline stories of public life, international conflict, and affairs and scandals of state.

This work covers just about a century, though in increasingly fragmentary fashion and without the benefit of judgments about the shelf-life of books. The first chapter reviews the state of the art of history on the eve of World War I, considering the "mini-national" traditions as well as historiographical practice in France, Germany, Britain, and the United States, although to the West the untranslated master historians of these traditions remain little more than names. Chapter 2 takes up the "ideas of 1914," the immediate legacy of the war, the study of prehistory and the "new past," and varieties of the philosophy of history, while chapter 3 deals with the controversies and revisionisms, in America as well as in Germany, Britain, and France, between the wars, and chapter 4 continues this discussion through the Second World War (or is it the remainder of the past century's Thirty Years War?). Chapter 5 treats the attempts to reconstruct and to revise history after 1945, including the enlarging of horizons beyond Europe to an updated and intellectually post-colonial and post-imperialist world history; and chapter 6 surveys the newer "new histories," interdisciplinary encounters, the "linguistic turn," the question of the "end of history," and various "postmodernisms," and offers a more personal critique of the state of history at the start of the third millennium within deepening perspectives and expanding horizons in an age when historical information is accumulating logarithmically beyond the limits of the field pioneered, as it still may seem to us epigones, by Herodotus and Thucydides. Simply adding more information cannot provide satisfactory answers, and history cannot be, as Nietzsche saw, "a final closing out of the accounts for the history of mankind" — though it may invoke Joyce's "nightmare of history" to put an end to generations of utopian dreams. In any case this is a book about books, a subject with no end in sight; but for me this particular book is indeed "closing time" — the last stop on the Vico Road.

I

Before the Great War

The scope of history has gradually widened until it has come to include every aspect of the life of humanity.

— G. P. Gooch (1913)

The Condition of History

The year 1910 was marked by the appearance of Halley's comet, the deaths of Leo Tolstoy, Mark Twain, and William James, James Joyce's departure from Dublin for "civilization," the organizing of the Psychoanalytical Association, growing nihilism and a remarkable incidence of suicide, the birth of the concept of the "death instinct" later adopted by Freud, George Simmel's reflections on "the metaphysics of death," a continuing flood of expressionist, futurist, and surrealist art, cultural "dissonance" across the arts, music, and some of the sciences, and the fictional setting for the German invasion of Europe described by William Le Queux's *The Invasion of 1910* (1906).[1] It was also the year when, as Virginia Woolf wrote facetiously in 1924, "human character changed."[2] As Henry Adams wrote to Barrett Wendell in 1910, "It is a scientific demonstration that Socialism, Collectivism, Humanitarianism, Universalism, Philanthropism, and every other ism, has come, and is the end."[3] As Charles Olson wrote, "Draw it thus: ( )1910(" and also, "the present is prologue, not the past."[4] Or maybe it was just the way that some humans looked at the world, for that acute observer Arnold Bennett could find nothing more important to write than "this year I have written 355,900 words" — more, probably, than most historians could boast.[5]

Despite the prevailing faith in progress in the early twentieth century, humanity was intellectually and culturally oriented in the opposite direction. As Rilke asked,

> Who has twisted us around like this, so that
> no matter what we do, we are in the posture
> of someone going away?[6]

So it was with historians, who were struggling with a huge burden of accumulated Western scholarship before being plunged into a series of political, social, and moral catastrophes. At the same time historical inquiry grew up in a world shaped by cultural forces which we have learned to call modernism, which wanted, among others things, to change the backward-looking position of thought and writing. It is fairly easy, if laborious, to trace the scholarly heritage of historiography, harder, if more arbitrary, to judge the impact of wars and revolutions; but there have been no sustained attempts to relate historical thought and writing to the modernist environment of the early twentieth century. The condition of "modernity" has a long history, going back indeed to the time of its opposite, "antiquity"; but the modernism of the past century was a product of nineteenth-century discontents and provocations by middle-class values, including the notion of the free and autonomous subject, historical continuity, universally valid scientific method, and an open horizon of unending progress. For tradition modernism substituted what Wyndham Lewis called the "demon of progress in art," and so it was also in literature. In the human sciences modernism questioned and subverted Enlightenment ideas of reason, history, philosophy, and mastery of nature and society — and in this way perhaps the meaning of history itself.

Friedrich Paulsen, dead two years in 1910, was a good representative of the old school, teaching the history of philosophy at the University of Berlin in the generational cohort of Ranke, Mommsen, Droysen, et al.; and he expressed his fears of the views of their younger rivals. One of his last essays was on the legal status of women in the past and in the future, and this assignment made him "realize once again how far I had gradually moved from the outlook of our 'modern' writers." Was it the result of old age, he wondered? "Or am I right in thinking that they have lost all contact with the world of reality and are building their airy utopias in cloudland?"[7] He felt uncomfortable traveling with "exotic figures," such as the Hungarian Jew of "a truly terrifying apparition" whom he had to dine with during a train trip to Munich. The experience made him understand the contemporary "anti-Semitic mood of resentment" and conclude that if he were Austrian, he would prefer Roman rule to that of the Jews. He overcame his hatred of the automobile, but he was losing his strength, and looking back on a life rich in accomplishment Paulsen, "with a thankful heart," died less than three weeks after giving his last lecture.

One younger witness to the anxieties of modernism was Franz Kafka, who in 1910 was all of twenty-eight years old, though in his diary he pretended to be in his forties as he reflected on his cultural condition. "I must say that my education has done me great harm in some respects," he wrote.[8] He should have preferred, he continued, to have lived not in the middle of a city but rather in a place of ruins in the mountains or beside a lake, where he could have avoided the evil influence of all the people he had known. It is perhaps not inappropriate to extend Kafka's hyper-urban, self-conscious, self-enhancing, and self-deprecating insight to the condition of Europe of that time. European society, too, had fallen victim to bad influences, its members addicted to reviewing and analyzing their predicament by thinking and writing about it. Moreover, as Kafka's diary was the only place where he could "hold on," so the tradition of European historiography was the only place that people of that time could connect themselves to their past. The difference was that, in the spirit of his own brand of modernism, Kafka hoped to repudiate or transcend the past, while historians struggled to understand connections and continuities, recognizing that they could not escape from their "education," their "old culture" — though neither could they anticipate the soon-to-come nightmarish consequences which Kafka fore-sensed and wove memorably into his fiction.

"One must be absolutely modern," wrote Arthur Rimbaud in 1871. "Modernism" is the word which emerged to cover all sorts of anxiety, perversity, subversion, and ingenuity that arose in the generation of the turn of the twentieth century. For Hugo von Hofmannsthal the "modern" was either the analysis of life or a flight from it, but in either case new perspectives were opened on what Burckhardt called "the culture of old Europe." A product of the cities, modernism reached beyond the world of everyday "reality," middle-class life, and a complacent European society devoted to the unreflective pursuit of wealth and global expansion. Breaking with this tradition, modernism sought new horizons across which to extend what Friedrich Karl has called the "sovereignty of the artist" into the future, especially through various movements, manifestos, and magazines which activated the intellectual avant-garde of the new century.[9]

Central to these movements was the human — observing, interpreting, and creating — subject, which had been overshadowed by science and "scientism," from which champions of the arts wanted to be liberated. In 1910 in his *Revue de Synthèse* Henri Berr used his review of the last volumes of Lamprecht's German history to underline the central importance of "le subjectivisme moderne" and the impressionism *(Reizsamkeit)* which accompanied it. "It is true," wrote Charles Seignobos in that same issue of the review, "that the historical method has invaded everything."[10]

In this way of looking at things the modernist is Wallace Stevens's "man with the blue guitar," who unsettles his hearers with his performance:[11]

> They said, "You have a blue guitar,
> You do not play things as they are."
> The man replied, "Things as they are
> Are changed upon the blue guitar."

Difficult it is to render life in such an indirect way,

> to play man number one . . . ,
> to nail his thought against the door . . .
> to bang it from a savage blue,

and impossible it is to

> bring a world quite round.

Yet such is the mission of the artist:

> So that's life, then: things as they are?
> It picks its way on the blue guitar.
> A million people on one string?
> And all their manner in the thing,
> And all their manner, right and wrong,
> And all their manner, weak and strong?

This vision is that of Ranke, to present things as they really are, but within the restriction of Kant, who denies accessibility of "the thing in itself" and privileges the intervening human medium.

This attitude toward interpretation made its way into historical writing, too, as authors came to realize that their own apparatus and performance had to intervene between the objects of their study and its rendition into intelligible and meaningful form. Hermeneutics implied a sort of relativity that required the observer and interpreter to take part in the field of exploration which, as Wilhelm Dilthey wrote, is life experience in time or, in the phrase of Gadamer, the "experience of tradition." So the historian enjoys an equivalent of "the sovereignty of the artist," meaning not the pose of the omniscient observer, as in the Victorian novel, but rather the self-aware search for meaning from an authorial point of view. The condition is that of Nietzsche's "'Interpretation,' the introduction of meaning — not 'explanation.' . . . There are no facts, every-thing is in flux, incomprehensible, elusive; what is relatively most enduring is — our opinions." The inference is that not only art but historiography is also, in its modernist guises, a variety of the Nietzschean "will to power."

Modernism in a backward-looking historiography — Nietzsche's "anti-quarian history" — was marked by the siren song of "novelty" being answered by a younger generation in the early years of the century. In the arts Hermann Hesse remarked that "one ought not to take the revolutionary antics of a portion of the younger generation too seriously, except in one respect: They have a deep need to find new ways of expressing worries and emotions that are indeed new."[12] A variety of "new histories" were proclaimed if not always practiced in Germany, France, Italy, Spain, the Netherlands, and America (if not in England). Among many other scholars Karl Lamprecht, Kurt Breysig, Henri Berr, Benedetto Croce, José Ortega y Gasset, and James Harvey Robin-son rode the crest of an international wave of novelty which they believed would raise the science and philosophy of history to new heights. Not that such "new histories," though they revived the old complaints about narrow political and military history, opened up many unfamiliar sources, since the old cultural history had already pioneered such efforts for over a century.[13] Nor, remarkably, did they have much to do with the experimentalist and subversive "modernisms" flourishing in literature and the arts, where the gen-erational divide was more pronounced, perhaps because the weight of profes-sional authority could more easily be avoided or rejected. What novelty meant in historical studies was establishing cordial relations with other human sci-ences, including sociology, economics, anthropology, archeology, paleontol-ogy, and histories of philosophy, literature, science, art, and mathematics — relations which then yielded new specialties and syntheses.

The truth is that the larger questions about the turn being taken by the historical process in the early twentieth century were posed for the most part by scholars in other disciplines, especially philosophers, sociologists, econo-mists, geographers, anthropologists, linguists, and even theologians, who were joined by a common, if not always admitted, commitment to "histor-icism," which emerged in the first quarter of the century as a central problem of European thought and of the self-definition of cultures.[14] Historicism ap-peared as a problem first in economics and then in theology, especially as a threat to the universalist ideals of social science and Christian religion. Like "modernism" and "naturalism" and (later) "psychologism" and "sociolog-ism," historicism was rejected by ecclesiastical authority, which feared the reduction of the transcendent to the merely human, and by the consensus of liberal economists like Carl Menger, who attacked the "errors of historicism" in 1883.[15] Philosophers, too, had suspicions about the anti-theoretical intrusions of history into their domain, and in 1912 Rudolph Eucken was lamenting "enervating historicism."[16]

The economic, theological, and philosophical aspects of the question converged in the work of Ernst Troeltsch, who as historian turned his attention to *The Social Teachings of the Christian Churches*, who as theologian established *Religionsgeschichte* as a distinct field of study, and who as philosopher explored more general questions of *Historismus*.[17] His articles were gathered into a volume titled *Historicism and Its Problems* (1922), which provoked criticism by Otto Hintze, Karl Mannheim, and others and which underlay the larger efforts both of Karl Heussi, who surveyed the whole arena of debate in his *Crisis of Historicism* (1932), and of Friedrich Meinecke, who projected the topic back to the seventeenth century in his *Rise of Historicism* (1936). Nor has the debate subsided even in this new "postmodern" millennium, as indicated by the international volume published in 1997 on "historicism at the end of the twentieth century" — not to mention the self-proclaimed "new historicism" of recent times.[18]

Twentieth-century historians measured the progress of their craft not only by the quantity of new information but also by the growth of critical acumen and ideological propriety. They were more aware than their forebears of the bad habits that the genre of history had produced, especially careless subjective and partisan generalizing. One of the founders of modern sociology, Georg Simmel pointed to the historiographical convention of relying, usually unreflectively, on concepts such as the group mind or social psyche in their explanations. Ranke had tried to eliminate this procedure, but for Simmel it was humanly impossible for historians not to project their own mental states onto their materials. In his *History of Rome* Theodor Mommsen had written that "A cry of rage was heard throughout all of Italy," and "The factions breathed a sigh of relief," while in his *Civilization of the Renaissance in Italy*, Burckhardt concluded that "Florence had always acknowledged its Guelphic sympathies for the French with a dreadful naivete." Now Burckhardt was the epitome of impressionistic historical writing, and the "scientific" side of Mommsen appeared in his constitutional and epigraphic researches which, rather than the early book for which he received the Nobel Prize, won him the adulation of colleagues and posterity. But Simmel wanted to open the study of history to speculative lines, including "laws of history," if only in the sense of "provisional synthesis."[19] This was the aim especially of cultural historians like Lamprecht and Breysig, who, in the style of eighteenth-century "conjectural history," followed an interdisciplinary and "scientific" path in search of the various stages and laws of history.[20]

At the turn of the twentieth century, while historians were expanding their analytical inquiries into the historical — and prehistorical — past or improving on the received narratives of national history, other scholars were asking questions about the meaning of history in more synthetic and conjectural terms. The ancient view that philosophy dealt with universals and history with particulars was given a new twist by German thinkers at this time. The basic premise was established by Wilhelm Windelband, who distinguished the natural sciences (*Naturwissenschaften*) from the human sciences (*Geisteswissenschaften*), corresponding to the distinction between the "nomothetic" and the "idiographic" disciplines, a point which was reinforced by Heinrich Rickert, though he preferred the more fashionable term "cultural sciences" (*Kulturwissenschaften*).[21] In any case the point was a distinction between phenomena that could yield natural laws and those bound to the individual, to human values, and to history. Historicism was in a sense a general inference drawn from the condition of the human sciences, which raised the threat of relativism and which was therefore unacceptable to many philosophers and persons in authority.

This was the case with all the major social and historical thinkers of the early twentieth century, including Simmel, Weber, Troeltsch, Mannheim, and Dilthey. Though still a Kantian, Dilthey took the path rather of critics of Kant like Herder, "founder of the Historical School," as he called him, in search of the missing dimension of critical philosophy, which was a "critique of historical reason." He did this with the help of hermeneutics and an epistemological shift of perspective from metaphysics to "life philosophy," and while he drew on cultural history, he reformulated it as "cultural systems." Dilthey was drawn to historical experience (as well as poetic insight) as foundational for philosophy, but he never overcame the paradox — the "crisis" — of historicism, which, while liberating thought from dogmatic premises, nevertheless led to an unacceptable relativism about not only historical phenomena but also philosophy and religion. Dilthey aspired to combine analysis, especially "analysis of special domains" (*Einzelanalysen*)[22] with synthesis, especially in the form of "life philosophy" (*Lebensphilosophie*) and that union of human and scientific knowledge which provided meaning, a "world view" (*Weltanschauung*).[23] Yet despite his vision of a post-Kantian synthesis, much of Dilthey's work was devoted to the question of how to "make the past present"[24] through the pursuit of intellectual history (*Geistesgeschichte*); and his systematic work in this field was a distillation of this scholarly work even more than a working out of the implications and deficiencies of Kantian epistemology.[25]

Dilthey had a conventional view of the history of history. For him Greek historiography reached perfection in Thucydides but then unfortunately lost its way, following a rhetorical rather than a philological path; and even when the critique of the Donation of Constantine reawakened criticism, rhetoric triumphed once again, not to be set aside until the time of Voltaire and the Göttingen school in the eighteenth century. From this issued nineteenth-century historical scholarship, which Dilthey came to know at the University of Berlin, and the transcending of old-fashioned chronicles and "pragmatic" (political) history, according to which "the universal historian has the task of reconstructing the whole of inner life, so that something like a second self-consciousness of history is achieved." Historical experience had been accumulating for centuries, but it is the interests of later ages that "serves to select which of these facts will reach us" — from which comes the fundamental importance of philology and hermeneutics and which permits the reconstruction of this process of selection and the recovery of this collective memory lost in the shift of presumed historical "interests."[26]

In France the scientific and metahistorical drift of history, traceable back to Comtean Positivism, was apparent especially in the work of Emile Durkheim, who (illustrating the argument of Simmel) focused not on individual agency but on "collective conscience" and "collective representations," which also reflected his public agenda based on the ideal of "social solidarity."[27] In his methodological writings this was given theoretical justification by his concept of "social facts," which — again relying on the dichotomy between the individual and the social, between psychology and sociology — elevated the principal empirical and individualist category of history to a social level. In *The Elementary Forms of Religious Life* (1912) Durkheim drew on anthropological studies of Australian totemism and projected his social and sociological theories back into prehistory, or what has recently been called "the prehistory of the mind."[28] This was also the interpretation of Durkheim's colleague Lucien Lévy-Bruhl, who wrote a biography of Comte and adopted Durkheim's concept of "collective representations" as forces, common to a group and impressed on individual members, which generated feelings of adoration, respect, and fear and which were transmitted from generation to generation. Exploring "primitive mentality" represented a sort of conjectural prehistory designed to extend the range of historical interpretation and speculation, and both Durkheim and Lévy-Bruhl had a powerful influence on young historians who wanted to venture beyond the confines of a narrow, political, and unreflective positivism.

Of course interest in diplomatic and military history was enhanced by the experience of war, but so were special fields of historical study, including economic, social, and cultural history, geohistory, and prehistory, together with archeology, anthropology, and sociology, all of which had emerged into prominence before 1914. These fields were all called upon to raise history above its old narrative function, provide insights not available in the written records, and assist in the pursuit of a more justifiable sort of "conjectural history" than that which appeared during the Enlightenment. The larger context of this pursuit was the philosophy of history, and with it quasi-religious efforts at prophecy, which still attracted many scholars. During the war intellectuals were for the most part too close to — or far from — the action to find historical perspective, except by emphasizing useful aspects of the national pasts, as in the debates over the two German traditions, one stemming from Kant and Goethe and pointing toward universal peace, and the second from Fichte (the Fichte of "Orations to the German Nation") and tied to national expansion.

Another polarity was defined by the mood swings between optimism and pessimism, illustrated by Oswald Spengler, who in late 1914 was "following the war with great optimism" and predicted that it marked "the beginning of a tremendous epoch," but who in 1918 deplored "the "base, stupid, infamously prosaic quality of the war," waiting for later events to reveal its meaning even as he was publishing his *Decline of the West* to show the larger meanings of Western history and to rise about the contemporary tragedy.[29] Despite his lack of credentials and scholarly caution Spengler, and in his wake Arnold Toynbee, forced himself on the attention of a whole generation (and more) of historians, though without diminishing the fragmentary character of the modern sense of history. Spengler cast a gigantic shadow on the next generation, though he was never welcomed into the academy or the seminar room except as a curious specimen of the old-fashioned apocalyptic philosophy of history or as an eccentric pioneer of a self-proclaimed "new history."

British Continuities

British historians were less sensitive to this fragmentation even as anxieties about their national and imperial tradition increased, and they managed to keep up a good front through two major wars. At the turn of the twentieth century British scholars were very busy researching, writing about, and teaching the history of their national and imperial traditions, publishing short histories after the fashion of J. R. Green, long histories in the style of Hume and Lingard, biographies, studies of particular reigns, of institutions, of economic activity, of social life, and even of cultural matters. What Herbert Butterfield deprecated as the "Whig view of history" was in full flower, and there were as yet no serious doubts about the virtues of parliamentary government or even the imperial mission, except from fairly a minor and professionally excluded intelligentsia with socialist, though not strongly Marxist, leanings, who would inspire the critical historiography of a later generation. Not only before but through and after the Great War English historians carried on their "grand narrative" without, moral judgments aside, serious doubts about its fundamental veracity. In the wisdom and isolation of their bachelorhood (most of them) they carried on the unfinished labors of the great Victorian generation — Stubbs, Macaulay, Carlyle, Froude, Freeman, Green, and Lecky — in celebrating the national heritage, but in more specialized ways and with greater attention to the sources which were being collected and published more voluminously and more systematically than ever.[30] As in Germany and France the results of historical research were published in a number of cooperative textbook series, including the histories of England edited by William Hunt and Reginald Lane Poole (12 volumes, 1905–10) and by Charles Oman (7 volumes, 1904–13) and especially the last word in modern scholarship, *The Cambridge Modern History* edited by Lord Acton (14 volumes, 1902–12) — the work, all of them, of the epigones of the master Victorian historians, who likewise clung to most of the ideals and illusions of their academic forebears.[31] "Study problems, not periods," was one of Acton's often-quoted aphorisms, but the *CMH* followed the reverse of this formula. In any case all of these have been supplanted by later, successively updated, if also inflated, diluted, and less confident, series.

The generation of historians coming of age after 1900 preserved and to some extent enhanced the national project of the great Victorian scholars even as they sought to establish their own identity in a world waiting for war. Their work represented both a continuation of and an improvement on their forebears — "revisionism" being the catch-word of this phenomenon of criticizing and perhaps replacing the work of the scholarly ancestors (derived from much older religious and philosophical controversy). The scholar faced the same question as the poet, which was, in the neo-Romantic words of Walter Jackson Bate, "What is there left to do?" — the answer being at the very least to improve on the predecessors.[32] Thus Stubbs's great classic was modified by the work of F. W. Maitland, J. H. Round, William MacKechnie, and C. H. McIlwain, and by foreign scholars like Paul Vinogradoff, Felix Liebermann, and Charles Petit-Dutaillis, while Maitland and McIlwain shifted emphasis from the legislative and representative to the judicial and conciliar functions of Parliament.[33] The constitutionalist line was modified more severely by the rise of administrative history at Manchester under T. F. Tout, while legal history, such as William Holdsworth's magisterial work, came to admit unprofessional social matters into its professional jurisdiction. In terms of method, however, it was mostly business as usual for British scholars, although the division between amateurs and professionals continued. The old-fashioned scientific history practiced by Samuel Rawson Gardiner, with his storied attention to documents and to detail, and his protégé and continuator Charles Firth, contrasted with public- and pedagogical-minded history in the old literary manner of Macaulay's devoted nephew George Macaulay Trevelyan. The opposition between Tory and Whig ideologies continued, but it was muted by the conciliatory liberalism of authors like Trevelyan and Pollard, who sought a national — and indeed imperial — grand narrative that would include all parties and classes. For the most part intellectual novelty came piecemeal from the continent, but it hardly changed or challenged the venerable channels cut by traditional Whiggish history — it's all about "Us."

The study of English medieval history, unlike that of the modern period, had long been informed by continental scholarship and thinking. Stubbs had drawn on the work of Waitz, Maurer, Savigny, and Grimm, for example, while Maitland was responsible for establishing important connections with Felix Liebermann and Paul Vinogradoff and for introducing the corporatist historical ideas of Otto von Gierke to English readers. Liebermann published the major collection of Anglo-Saxon laws between 1903 and 1916. Vinogradoff, who opened the study of Bracton which Maitland continued and who succeeded Maitland's coauthor Frederick Pollock as professor of jurisprudence at Oxford, wrote on many aspects of European legal tradition, including his pioneering sketch of the history of Roman law in 1910, which was written in the spirit of Stubbs but with the aim of rescuing Romanist ideas from the assaults of Germanists. R. L. Lane-Poole, who was a member of a distinguished scholarly family and for many years was editor of the *English Historical Review,* took his doctorate at the University of Leipzig before publishing a standard work on the Exchequer in the twelfth century in 1912 and later a valuable study of medieval historiography.[34]

Maitland is still the idol and the icon of English medievalism, though unlike many colleagues he drew on continental scholarship, especially the Historical School, including Savigny, Grimm, Gierke, and Brunner. Like his German antecedents Maitland insisted on the continuity of English legal history despite a "confluence" of other traditions, especially that of canon law, and on its long-established exceptionalist status.[35] Though he brought Gierke's work on corporatism to the attention of English scholars, Maitland had little use for political theory and, anticipating the "linguistic turn," believed that language was the central concern for historians, "for language is no mere instrument that we can control at will; it controls us."[36] So Maitland's historiography was source-driven, and in England his scholarly example has outlived newer fashions of historical interpretation. In his work the Whig view was reinforced not by the vagaries of political ideology but by the solid evidentiary foundations left by the self-enclosed tradition of English common law.

Maitland himself, who turned down the offer of the regius professorship of history at Cambridge, wanted to stay in the field of legal history, but his influence was felt far outside this professional specialty, to the extent indeed that later observers have seen a "Cambridge School" as part of his legacy. Among his students was John Neville Figgis, who wrote on the divine right of kings (1896) and early modern political thought (1907). For Figgis the divine right of kings was not an academic theory but a deeply rooted popular idea with theological associations, although it was later given statutory form and tied to sovereignty. A product of the conflict between church and state, it was joined to the debates of the Reformation and to the emergence of modern politics; it was also the root of the "priceless legacy," which was "a deep sense of the majesty of law and of the duty of obedience." Figgis's work on political thought from Gerson to Grotius focused on the obverse of this principle, that is, the theory of resistance to sovereignty, likewise the product not of theorizing but of religious, social, and political conditions in the transition from medieval to modern times—and was designed to show "how near the present is to the past, and how slow is the growth from seed to harvest."[37] This suggests how easily the "Whig view" was accommodated to English views of the continent.

Another divergence from traditional constitutional history was the exploration of administrative history led by T. F. Tout and his students at the University of Manchester, a line of research in keeping with Maitland's empirical model but motivated also by modern awareness of the continuing force of bureaucracy beneath the surface of noisy politics. Tout deplored the fact that England had no "schools of history" such as Germany had, and he sought to create a distinctive one for medieval studies.[38] In 1913 he delivered the Ford lectures at Oxford around the question of "the extent to which the English king's court and household remained a chief centre of national administration and finance, even after the development of the constitution had brought about the beginnings of the parliamentary system."[39] Such a study required the investigation of the various small and great seals of the crown and other technical aspects of the government of the crown and its dependent institutions. For Tout the reign of Edward II marked a turning point through the appearance of the distinction between court and national administration. Tout's seminal researches were pursued in his monumental *Chapters in Medieval Administrative History* (1920–33), which inspired later generations of historians down to the time of S. B. Chrimes and G. R. Elton, who carried the project into the early modern period to counterbalance the overemphasis on parliamentary history, which indeed formed the grand narrative of British history down to the postwar period. It seems likely that this administrative orientation prepared the way for the later "revisionist" school of history to which Elton attached himself.

Among modern historians of the early twentieth century Pollard and Trevelyan were the leading figures, Pollard working in a field dominated, unfortunately, as some thought, by Froude, while Trevelyan was the acknowledged heir in more than one sense to his great-uncle Thomas Macaulay. Pollard began his exploration of Tudor history with a revisionist study of the Protector Somerset, who, despite his ambition, rapacity, and ultimate failure, was a man of vision, and "his visions were visions of the future," not only in his repeal of the heresy and treason laws but also in his sympathy for the poor and promotion of religious and civil freedom, which "became the cornerstone of the British constitution." Pursuing toleration, Somerset "added at least one stone to the temple of liberty."[40] This book was succeeded by a biography of Henry VIII, which was standard for over a generation, drawing on the sources published since Froude's time, which "contained at least a million definite facts relating to the reign of Henry VIII." Pollard was critical of Froude, deploring his violation of "the sanctity of inverted commas," but Pollard himself did not bother much with manuscripts, preferring to rely on calendars.[41] Like Froude, moreover, Pollard was aware of the malleability of facts, and here again employed them in a revisionist portrayal of the second Tudor king, who, through all his contradictions, was a seminal figure in parliamentary government. Unlike Somerset, Henry was no dreamer, for he followed efficiency rather than principle: "He sought the greatness of England, and during the unavoidable storms of the Reformation," Pollard wrote, his actions and influence, including the Machiavellian break with Rome, probably "averted greater evils than those they provoked."[42] This ushered in the modern world, defined above all by the appearance of the "New Monarchy," of which Hobbes was the premier theorist.

In 1906 Pollard gave a series of popular lectures on "factor in modern history," in which he sketched the larger framework of his researches, and which received new notoriety in J. H. Hexter's sharp and satirical critique published a half-century later. Besides the New Monarchy (a concept borrowed from J. R. Green) Pollard, following nineteenth-century convention, emphasized, in the emergence of modern Europe, the phenomenon of nationality, the advent of the middle class, the (English) Reformation, Parliament, and the "social revolution" together with the subsequent colonial expansion. He did not present these in any dogmatic fashion, for "History is not an exact science, and nothing that is real and concrete can be exact."[43] But if history had no laws, it was governed by the principle of organic continuity (Leibniz's *natura nihil facit per saltum*), and even the "jump" accomplished by the

French Revolution was not far, only high — and of course it had to include other aspects of life beyond politics. This principle of continuity also informed his long-contemplated history of Parliament and little textbook of English history, which celebrated the modern national state as "the most powerful political organism ever known, because it is the conscious or unconscious agency of a people's will."[44]

Pollard's major effort was his book on the "evolution of Parliament," published in 1920 but begun before the war. He began by quoting from one historian's biography of another (Froude's of Carlyle), in which the latter declared that nothing good would ever come out of a democratic Parliament. Pollard's message was of course quite the opposite, for "Parliamentary institutions have, in fact, been incomparably the greatest gift of the English people to the civilization of the world" — far beyond the pale imitations or analogues of the Anglo-Saxon creation, such as "reichstag and duma, riksdag and storthing, sobranje and meiljiss."[45] But Parliament — and what he called "political communism," that is, the rise of the commons — was also the chief means by which the English people achieved their national unity beginning with the reign of Edward I and the eventual rewards of liberty. In its original form Parliament — here Pollard followed Maitland and anticipated McIlwain — was a council and a "high court," only later adding the foreign "myth of the three estates" and the representative and legislative functions so dear to the hearts of Victorian scholars. The Commons was well established by the reign of Edward III. "Then, as now," Pollard wrote, "the essence of Parliament was parley between crown and commons, the government and the governed." Parliament was the locus of three of the "factors of history" which for Pollard constituted the foundations of the modern world: the growth of the commons, the rise of the middle class, the quest for individual liberty, and the emergence of nationalism, all of this occurring under the aegis of the modern state, of which Henry VIII was the first architect. Pollard traced the fortunes of this seminal institution, with the principle of separation of powers and relations to the crown and imperial realms, down to the "crucial test" of the Great War — which (as Pollard defiantly wrote in August 1915) will end in the defeat of the enemies of the "parliamentary peoples."[46]

Despite Maitland's influence, Pollard was an insular scholar, although in a very long career he ranged over the whole span of British history beyond his Tudor specialty. So did Trevelyan, but he also ventured into continental areas, beginning with his popular trilogy on Garibaldi (with whom his own father, George Otto Trevelyan, had attempted to serve) and modern Italy published between 1907 and 1911. The three volumes took Garibaldi's story from his attempt to defend the Roman republic in 1849 through his return to Italy in

1854 and his association with Cavour, to his triumphant march through Italy and retirement in Caprera. It was a celebration of "the most romantic life that history records" lived by a poetic "man of destiny" who symbolized humanity and liberty as well as heroism—and who combined the mixture of liberalism and military virtue that Trevelyan tried to keep in balance. But even before the war Trevelyan was retreating from the liberal idealism of this youthful work and turning to his true lifework, which was the story of the English people— not unlike Green's colorful and still popular history but relying on more specialized studies. Though much admired, Trevelyan was an old-fashioned gentleman scholar who worked on the edges of professional history with equally old-fashioned aspirations to literary art.

Trevelyan was an ambitiously literary historian, seeking—and finding—a large reading public, as his famous great-uncle had done.[47] In 1899 at the age of twenty-three, he published his first book, composed originally as a thesis for a Cambridge fellowship, and republished several times. *England in the Age of Wycliffe* was not an analysis of a problem but a comprehensive portrait of an age, "a general picture of English society, politics, and religion at a certain stage in their progress," drawing on the work of André Reville and Charles Petit-Dutaillis on the peasant wars and acknowledging his debts to, among others, Bishop Stubbs and Dr. Gasquet ("however much we may differ," he added, from this Catholic scholar). England in Chaucer's times did not correspond to the images of this "jolly poet," since it was dominated by the decay of medieval society. Yet—the Whig message is proclaimed—"though medievalism is sick almost to death, the ideas of the modern world are forming in the greatest minds of the day."[48] It was a dark age of decline, although the peasant uprisings eventually brought reforms and Lollardy marked (Trevelyan invoking here the views of Erasmus and Cuthbert Tunstall) the prelude to Lutheranism, and with it not only the "downfall of the governing church" but also, thanks to Wycliffe, the beginnings of "free thought."

The seminal period of English constitutional liberty, however, was that of the Stuarts, whose struggle with Parliament in the seventeenth century corresponded to the Reformation in sixteenth-century Germany and the Revolution in eighteenth-century France. Trevelyan's balanced study of England under the Stuarts, published in 1904, surveyed English society and culture before turning to the conflicts between church and state and between crown and Parliament and the rise of parties leading up to civil war, "the decisive event in English history."[49] For Trevelyan the Civil War was a war not of classes but of sections, of North and West against South and East, and it was succeeded by a conservative reaction under a series of revolutionary governments, then the restoration of monarchy and "reigns of terror," before the beneficent revolu-

tion which established parliamentary sovereignty at a time when "the necessities of the moment coincided with the strongest tendencies of the age and the
best possibilities of the future." What emerged finally, in this age of bigotry in
Europe, was the principle of religious toleration, if not equality. Yet Trevelyan's adherence to a Whiggish "grand narrative" was, like that of Pollard,
tempered by a sense of relativism and even pluralism; for he concluded that
there were hundreds of other stories "no less noble and significant than the one
story which, being famous in its own day, was enshrined in some superficial
and imperfect record, whence now we drag it out and make it into history."[50]

Trevelyan's idea of history was expressed most dramatically in the famous
exchange between him and J. B. Bury. In 1902 Bury, in his inaugural lecture as
Acton's successor in the regius chain at Cambridge, proclaimed history to be
not a branch of literature but "simply a science, no less and no more," and
eleven years later Trevelyan — who in 1927 would succeed Bury in the same
chair — published his response, "Clio a Muse." By "science" Bury did not mean
the search for general laws but rather the philological (and more recently
archeological) tradition exemplified best by the Homeric scholar F. A. Wolf,
whose methods were joined and enhanced by the national exploration of the
remote past according to ideas of development and were now being carried on
most promisingly by British scholars. The model was the Mommsen not of the
youthful *History of Rome* but of the *Corpus Inscriptionum*. By contrast Trevelyan rejected the essentially German ideal in favor of an updated version of
what Bury regarded as the old "political-ethical" approach, which involved
(though he did not put it this way) another Germanic point of view, that is, the
inevitability of interpretation, as distinguished, he believed, from the misleading model of physical science. History did not follow "laws" nor issue verdicts,
he argued, but was shaped by the intellects and imaginations of historians (like
himself). It was "the tale of the thing done," not the inference of causes, and was
justified by its aesthetic and educational value — and here Trevelyan did not
scruple to invoke the example of Walter Scott in defense of mere "literary
history," which some scholarly critics had begun to use in a pejorative sense.
Among other things this debate reflected the English controversy over the relative merits of research and teaching in the historical profession, but Trevelyan
was especially concerned not to deprive posterity of enjoying classical literary
narratives — "modern Gibbons, judicious Carlyles and skeptical Macaulays."

The distance between Bury and Trevelyan was not great conceptually and
really had to do more with their chosen fields. While Trevelyan operated in the
political, institutional, and social traditions of (still mainly Victorian) England, although unlike his great-uncle he avoided a public career, Bury devoted himself to ancient Greece and the later Roman and Byzantine Empires,

drawing not only on literary tradition but also on recent archeological discoveries regarding Troy and especially those of Arthur Evans in Crete. Still, Bury's story remained the Whiggish one of Greek cultural achievement, above all showing mankind's "fearless freedom of thought."[51] He also speculated about the Greeks' own insights into the process of history — "whether Aristotle divined before his death that the Hellenic cities were not to have the last word in the history of men" — but decided that they did not anticipate the perspective created by modern historicism.

Nevertheless, Bury took special interest in Greek historiography and in 1908 delivered a set of lectures on the topic at Harvard. Among the contributions of the Greeks to Western culture was the theory and practice of history — beginning with the poetic prologue to historiography, the logographers, and other precursors, including the "founder," Hecataeus, but concentrating, as always, on the classical narratives of Herodotus and Thucydides. Herodotus shows the influence of the epic, Thucydides that of the drama. Herodotus it was who introduced rules of criticism, including suspicion of miracles, keeping an open mind, and insistence on first-hand information (*autopsy*); and these principles were extended by Thucydides in his turn to contemporary history and "rationalism."[52] Yet neither author, Bury added, paid sufficient attention to economic factors, being concerned with causes in the sense of "grievances." Of particular significance for historical inquiry were philosophy and antiquarianism (*polypragmosyne, curiositas*). Among the epigones of the founding fathers the most significant was Polybius, whose history "contains the material for a handbook of historical method."[53] Latin historians worked in the shadow of the Greeks, but they extended the study of history to national tradition, especially in the works of Livy, Sallust, and Tacitus. For the ancients history had a variety of uses — practical, antiquarian, and philosophical (as for example in Polybius's theory of constitutional cycles) — and they even had a certain sense of historical and moral relativism, perhaps progress, and certainly the idea of history both scientific and humanistic. In any case the rise of historical studies and criticism was for him an element in a late stage of an evolutionary process, and so indeed it remained in the twentieth century.

Progress was the key to Bury's conception of history, and it became the subject of what became perhaps his most famous book, *The Idea of Progress*, which was published two years after the end of the First World War and which was dedicated to the memories of the Abbé de Saint-Pierre, Condorcet, Comte, Spencer, "and other optimists mentioned in this volume."[54] Bury's retelling of the story begins with universal history in the Renaissance and in particular with Louis Le Roy and Bodin, who went far beyond Machiavelli in their vision of human experience in time. Their message was "that the world has not degenerated; that the modern age is not inferior to classical antiquity; and that the races of the earth form now a sort of 'mundane republic' "; and they were followed by the more elaborate agenda of scientific advance by Bacon and Descartes.[55] The idea of progress was addressed more directly in the quarrel of the ancients and moderns in the seventeenth century and more especially by the "revolutionary speculations" of Saint-Pierre, followed by the new conceptions of history of Montesquieu, Voltaire, Turgot, Condorcet, and the encyclopedists and physiocrats. After this Bury traced the fortunes of the idea in England, Germany, and France and the search for a scientific law in the work of Saint-Simon, Comte, Buckle, Renan, and especially Darwin. Yet even this idea and the laws it suggested might be subject to more fundamental patterns of historical change; for as Bury did not fail to ask, "does not Progress itself suggest that its value is only relative, corresponding to a certain not very advanced stage of civilisation?"[56] In Bury, despite his "scientific" stance, we can see the insular confidence underlying the Whig view slipping toward uncertainty and indeterminism.

French Patterns

In France, where the doctrine of "progress" still prevailed in the twilight of positivism, intellectual fragmentation took the relatively benign form of interdisciplinary rivalry. "Reality," in the form of the historical event, still ruled, and the profession of positivist history itself has continued to thrive.[57] The study of history had become almost a secular religion under the Third Republic, with a remarkable growth both of professorial chairs and students, and in 1896 French higher education had achieved full "university" status comparable to — and in competition with — that of Germany. The old guard of professors, headed by Gabriel Monod (founder of the *Revue Historique*), Ernest Lavisse, and their students Charles Seignobos and Charles Victor Langlois, prided themselves on having escaped the vices of traditional literary and moralistic history (exemplified by the work of Daunou a century earlier) and wanted not only to train historians according to their "scientific" methods but also, somewhat paradoxically, to educate the larger public according to their anti-clerical vision of history and the material and cultural progress of the French nation. The ambitions of Lavisse (invoking Michelet as his "master") were to some extent realized in the two series he edited with Alfred Rambaud, which remained standard textbooks long after the war. The purpose of these volumes was pedagogical, and despite generous citation from original sources, they were even more dependent on secondary literature. For modern history it would be impossible to read all the documents for a single country, admitted

Langlois. "It is therefore impossible, in the nature of things, to write a contemporary history of Europe that shall conform to scientific principles."[58]

Lavisse's *History of France* (like the general history of the West which he edited) was a cooperative enterprise and a legacy of the prewar generation, a descendant of a long line of official histories stretching back to the chronicles of St. Denis and Paolo Emilio and including those of Michelet and Martin but also incorporating the extensive researches into institutional and social history of the previous century as well as the history of civilization urged by Guizot and others. Yet as Langlois's statement suggests, it was not intended to be definitive, and indeed comments were often made about the need to explore further, or collect more documentation about, certain important topics. Contributors to the eighteen volumes included Lavisse, Langlois, Seignobos, Luchaire (successor in Fustel's chair), Philippe Sagnac, and other prominent history professors. The first volume included a "tableau of the geography of France" by Paul Vidal de la Blache, similar to but much more extensive than that of Michelet, and a study of Gallic "origins" by Gustav Bloch, who drew on recent archeological and epigraphical researches. The next volumes followed the conventional periodization based on political and military events and reigns, though attention was paid in separate chapters to culture, that is, the arts and sciences and French education.

The interpretation of history of these scholar-teachers remained Euro- and indeed Francocentric, but they were affected by internationalist, pacifist, democratic, and even socialist values to a greater extent than their German colleagues, and it is perhaps not surprising that the enrollments in German universities far surpassed those of their French counterparts. During the Dreyfus affair they were caught between right- and left-wing turmoil, which invaded not only French society but also "the Republic of Professors." They were also caught between "scientific" history, with its emphasis on objectivity, documentary research, and monographic publication, and the new interdisciplinary approaches, which sought more meaningful—and socially useful—patterns of understanding. Lavisse and Seignobos especially were involved in pedagogical theory, practice, and policy, while Langlois devoted himself to publishing reference works on bibliography. During this period there was an increased emphasis on "contemporary" history, encouraged by Alphonse Aulard and his students Pierre Caron and Sagnac. However, the teaching of history was still not up-to-date (or nationalistic) enough for many members of the "generation of 1914."[59] In 1912 "Agathon" (pseudonym for Henri Massis and Alfred de Tarde) published a manifesto, "The Young People of Today," denouncing the old guard of the Sorbonne—Lavisse, Seignobos, and Aulard —not only for pedantry but also for the invasion of foreign influences such as

Germanic sociology; but the Great War overwhelmed this generational conflict with more urgent issues. Yet there were already signs of a "new history"
moving to challenge French historiographical orthodoxy.

This orthodoxy — the common attitudes and standard practices of professional historians in early twentieth-century France — was in effect codified in
the great manual published by Lavisse's former students Langlois and Seignobos in 1897 and translated into English the following year and reprinted
several times afterwards. These men took their conceptual stand on positivism
not by seeking Comtean "laws of history" but by determining "facts" drawn
from empirical, that is, documentary or monumental, foundations. Unlike the
earlier treatises by Droysen and Bernheim their handbook avoided philosophical questions and addressed not a specialized elite but a general public, though
not in the popular style of Michelet and Lavisse. Their starting point was the
old principle that without documents and the facts inferred therefrom there
can be no history. Thus archival and library research is the main access to
critical historical knowledge, and what the Germans called "heuristic" and
associated "auxiliary sciences" are the basis of the historian's professional
training. An unspoken corollary was that government documents were privileged, as were the political and legal institutions which produced these re-
positories. Yet they were not narrowly political, for they recognized six classes
of the external conditions of historical facts: material (including biology, geography, and demography), intellectual (arts, sciences, philosophy), social (food,
clothing, private life), economic (transport, commerce), and institutional
(family, education, classes) as well as public (state, church, administration).[60]
Of these only the last was "obligatory," while the second and third were "not
obligatory"; and — with a curious lack of historical sense — they argued that all
of these features of the science of history had been developed only in the
previous half-century.

After heuristics came "hermeneutics," the interpretation of documentary
sources — the truth and the meaning of the facts, and then "synthetic operations" based on the selection and grouping of facts. Criticism of Langlois and
Seignobos to the contrary notwithstanding, they acknowledged that the history of civilization and "battle-history" were both needed, but in neither case
could metaphorical interpretation be admitted (referring to Lamprecht's cultural history), and care had to taken in filling in the "gaps" in the record. Last
and least problematic of all comes "exposition," which again had risen from a
literary to a "scientific" level only in post-Romantic times. As for "the causes
of the solidarity between the different habits of one and the same society" and
larger patterns of historical change and evolution, "this is a branch of study
that is not yet fully established." This was an allusion to contemporary social

science in a Durkheimian mode, which in fact was already a major presence. Several years earlier, in fact, Paul Lacombe had published his *History Considered as Science,* which rejected unreflective empiricism and called for historians to search for social laws.[61] There was a difference between historical "facts" and historical "meaning," and in pursuit of the latter historians had to seek regularities and causal connections. Like Lamprecht, Dilthey, and Henri Berr, Lacombe sought the key to scientific history in psychology, though he drew this not from German idealism but from French rationalist tradition. Here he differed from Alexandre Xénopol, who turned to a biological model in seeking to establish the scientific autonomy of history.[62] Another conjectural historian was Alfred Fouillé, who sought to determine the psychology and national character of European peoples through "anthroposociologique" method and an "applied psychology of ideas" (*idées forces*), which, drawing on anecdotal literary sources, made possible the understanding not only of the self but of others.[63] All these scholars pursued historical inquiry beyond the simple search for facts through the "hunt for documents," which defined the traditional art and science of history.

Seignobos himself carried on a running critique of social theory, including the cultural history of Lamprecht as well as the sociological arguments of Durkheim and François Simiand, opposing the "psychological method" of historians, who investigated particular causes of historical change, with the collective methods of sociologists, who — in the old spirit of Comtean Positivism — sought general and abstract laws. Seignobos presented a criticism in particular of the abstract and deterministic "rules" set down by Simiand, who, captive to scientific theory, refused to recognize the (temporally as well as spatially) local character of historical facts and their inseparability from "documents."[64] Moreover, "all the terms needed to define social phenomena, including intention, goal, beliefs, fear, desire, motives, opinion, feeling, are psychological in nature and designed for individual conscious representation accessible only by internal psychological observation."[65] As for Durkheim's "collective conscience," it was a mere "spiritualist" "play on words, a hypothesis incapable of being proven in any concrete or historical way. The same went for the idea of a social organism, a mystical theory derived from the German Historical School and brought to France by Taine.[66] For Seignobos the basic category of the factual past was the individual "event," which through repetition and beyond artificial juridical terms, was the source as well of social customs and institutions — a position which laid Seignobos open to charges of positivist narrowness and naivete.[67] "In any case," he added, "history is still in a state too rudimentary to try to assimilate its method to other established sciences, even the most imperfect and rudest, such as zoology and geology."

Seignobos's critique applied also to the study of prehistory, which could investigate the traces and objects left by primitive man but could not determine motives and meanings.[68] Here the best known culprit was Lucien Lévy-Bruhl, who from 1908 published a series of books on "primitive mentality" which, on the basis of work done by anthropologists and ethnologists, sought to define the collective conscience of prehistorical humanity as an expression of "the solidarity of the individual with his group."[69] His discussions of the "pre-logical mentality" were instrumental in undermining naive views of the superiority of modern humanity and moreover gave currency to the notion of *mentalité,* which was so alien to Seignobos and the older generation but which was embraced enthusiastically by younger scholars such as Lucien Febvre and Marc Bloch, who chose Lévy-Bruhl to review his venturesome book on the thaumaturgic kings.[70]

It is clear, then, that there were other paths to historical understanding being explored besides the straight and narrow old road mapped anew by Langlois and Seignobos. This included historical specialties established before the war, such as the work of economic historians like Emile Levasseur, art historians like Emile Mâle, historians of science like Pierre Duhem and Alexandre Koyré, and even philosophers like Charles Renouvier, Emile Boutroux, and Henri Bergson; but it also has to do with parallel and peripheral lines of research, among them geography, archeology, anthropology, sociology, and other disciplinary efforts to find meaning in human experience across time and space; and these efforts indeed found at least a marginal place in modern syntheses like Lavisse's collection and figured centrally in the self-proclaimed "new history" of the following generation.

For Paul Vidal de la Blache France was a "geographic being" underlying the superficial "centralization" imposed on it by human agents: "neither the soil nor the climate have changed despite various human 'revolutions' " Man himself, a "disciple of the soil," was a product of its fundamental "influences" — a term itself associated with astrology and medicine — beyond the effects of phenomena of shorter duration. This was a truth recognized by ancient authors such as Ptolemy and Pausanias, acknowledged by early modern historians, and formulated more comprehensively in Jean Bodin's "geohistory"; but it was not until the later nineteenth century that, through the efforts of German pioneers like Alexander von Humboldt, Karl Ritter, and Friedrich Ratzel, "human geography" (with its more notorious sister, "geopolitics"), or "anthropogeography," as Ratzel called it, emerged as a discipline associated with history in the circle of modern human sciences.[71]

Archeological discoveries and attempts to interpret them in a large chronological framework extend several centuries into the European past, but, coming thick and fast in the half-century before 1900, established both the principle of the "antiquity of man" and "prehistory" as another distinct discipline. In France the Museum of National Antiquities was founded in 1867, and in 1872, at the International Congress of Prehistory in Brussels, Guillaume de Mortillet proclaimed tertiary man (living up to 70,000,000 years ago) as a "precursor" of *homo sapiens.* In 1904, six years after the death of Mortillet, the Prehistorical Society of France was founded. The scattered remains of humans and proto-humans thus produced theories and then stories that were incorporated, in continually updated forms, into the old narrative of world history.[72] To this were added the ideas, if not discoveries, of anthropologists like Lucien Lévy-Bruhl, whose work on "the mental functions of primitive societies" appeared in 1910, and sociologists like Emile Durkheim, whose *Elementary Forms of Religious Life, which* tried in a conjectural way to show how conceptual thought arose out of an essentialized "society," appeared in 1912.

For Durkheim sociology, aided by ethnological research, was the "science of institutions"; and he was himself indebted to the work of historians, especially Monod and Fustel de Coulanges, although set in a different conceptual frame-work. His *Elementary Forms of Religious Life,* as Steven Lukes said, reversed the argument of *The Ancient City,* "explaining social organization by religion, instead of *vice versa.*"[73] As a system of explanation of social change Durk-heimian sociology was also a radical sort of conjectural history which was tied not only to social policy, especially promoting social "solidarity," but also to social prophecy; but it also served as an aid to historical interpretation, as in the case of Gustav Glotz, whose thesis (read and criticized by Durkheim) dealt with "the solidarity of the family in the criminal law of ancient Greece." At his thesis defense, it was noted, "M. Durkheim [was] pleased to observe that historians are taking more and more account of the truth that between history and sociology there is no watertight division."[74]

In general these parallel and peripheral approaches to history were intended to give meaning, depth, and coherence (*solidarité* — which was also a politi-cally inflammatory term at the turn of the century) to historical reconstruc-tion.[75] Even Seignobos recognized the importance of "synthetic operations" in history, but by this he meant only the classification and linking of facts in a literary and explanatory way for purposes of education, and he specifically denied that there was direct relevance to present (and "presentist") concerns — in other words, business as usual for professional historiography. Nor, curi-ously perhaps, did the experiences of the First World War change fundamen-tally either professionals' adherence to "science" or their historical interpreta-tions, except in some cases to intensify the nationalist and xenophobic tone of their arguments.

But there were more ambitious view of what "synthesis" involved for history, and here the work of Henri Berr and friends was central, even though it fell outside the terrain of professional history. In 1898 Berr defended a thesis on "the future of philosophy" and the goal of "synthesis," two years later he founded the journal *Revue de Synthèse*, and in 1911 he published his best-known book, *La Synthèse en histoire, son rapport avec la synthèse générale*, republished in 1953. The major target of this manifesto for history as "science" was the stance of Seignobos and Langlois and of Monod that ranked erudition and monographs above his philosophical view. "For one day of synthesis," Fustel had commented, "one needs years of analysis"; but Berr thought it was time, in the face of an avalanche of monographs, to turn to the former. In pursuit of his vision Berr reviewed earlier conceptions of science since the time of Comte, Renan, Taine, and Cournot, the "precursor" of synthesis, including philosophies of history, anthropology, German *Völkerpsychologie*, Lamprecht's cultural history, Bergson's "creative evolution," and American Pragmatism, contemporary sociology, and ethnology; and indeed he planned a history of the theories of history, though he never completed this; for his real interest was in "the future of history."

What was history, that is, what had it been to other scholars? To this question Berr, drawing on the history of history, reviews a variety of answers: "History is the study of *hazards* (Eduard Meyer), of singular *phenomena* (Rickert), of *facts* (B. Croce, Adrien Naville); it is opposed to *laws* (Naville) or to the *universal* (Rickert), or it is the study of a *succession of facts* as opposed to a *repetition of facts* (Xénopol). It is very different from a science that is *systematic* (E. Meyer), *theoretical* or *conceptual* (Croce), *theorematic* (Naville), *nomothetic* (Windelband), or *natural* (Rickert)."[76] Berr is in general agreement with these definitions and distinctions, which are all in line as well with the medieval and early modern concept of history, that history deals only with the particular, with "events," while science treated the universal, though not in an idealistic or a priori sense. But he was not satisfied with this common-sense dualism, which relegated the study of history to an analytical and unreflective empiricism. What he wanted was to transcend this division through the new science he called "historical synthesis," which would draw on the work of social scientists like Durkheim, Simiand, Mauss, and Lévy-Bruhl, and which "situate the individual in Humanity and Humanity in the Real."[77] And this was a goal and a faith which he preserved for over half a century, essentially undisturbed by two world wars. Berr represents a central link between the old science of history and the "new histories" not only of his but also of our own time — and even, perhaps, between the "old" and the "new" historicism.

German Ways

Filled with philosophical and political anxieties, German scholars were more troubled than their counterparts in other countries about the nature and value of history. At the turn of the twentieth century, too, German "historical science" was divided by a polemic over method (*Methodenstreit*) between the followers of Ranke, who were educated and pledged to preserve the political history of their master, and Karl Lamprecht and the champions of a new cultural history, which Georg von Below denounced in a review of 1898 and continued to attack for another generation. In a way it was the reverse of the ancient contrast between the old cultural history of Herodotus and the new political history of Thucydides — between looking at humanity in broad compass and deep time and investigating the nature of politics and the causes of war.

In fact the twentieth-century controversy had begun earlier with a dispute between Dietrich Schäfer and Eberhard Gothein.[78] In 1888 Schäfer had defended the primacy of politics over "so-called cultural history," which lowered its gaze from the nation to the trivia of everyday life. "Without political life," Schäfer declared, "there is no growing historical consciousness and no historical process," so that "the true territory of history is political history." In his autobiography he confessed, "The ultimate aim of both my political and my scholarly work has always been to contribute to the emergence of a strong German nation-state."[79] Schäfer was answered the next year by Gothein, a historian of Italian culture, who set about explaining "the tasks of cultural history," especially as exemplified by Burckhardt (and Ranke and Treitschke).[80] "Political history," he argued, "should accept the expansion resulting from the careful study of cultural history, if it wants to reach its goal of establishing the general causal process of political life."[81]

The great practitioner and theorist of *Kulturgeschichte* was Karl Lamprecht, whose controversial *German History* (19 volumes, 1891–1909) combined concerns for material culture and a Burckhardtian sort of art history featuring "spiritual" factors.[82] He carried on his campaign for "an alternative to Ranke" not only in articles and in his seminar at Leipzig but also in the Institute for Cultural History, which he managed to establish over much orthodox opposition. During the 1890s the *Methodenstreit* around cultural history reached a crest, as Lamprecht's work came under fire from a succession of Neo-Rankeans (*Neurankeaner*), including Below, Felix Rachfels, Heinrich Finke, Max Lenz, Hermann Oncken, and Friedrich Meinecke (as editor of the *Historische Zeitschrift*), with Eduard Bernheim and Otto Hintze taking more moderate positions, and Steinhausen, Kurt Breysig, and Walter Goetz carrying on the mission of *Kulturgeschichte* in less dogmatic ways.[83] The result, according to Roger Chickering, was the complete destruction of Lamprecht's professional reputation by the time of his death in 1916 and the undermining of his students' careers. The "new history" in Germany came to a halt, as the conflict between German *Kultur* and French and English *civilisation* was drawn into the national rivalries leading to the Great War of 1914–1918, when military and political matters again took precedence. The exception to this marginalization was the transformation of *Kulturgeschichte* into the tendentious and often racist *Volksgeschichte,* which was restored to popularity during the Third Reich.

In the early twentieth century German historiography was, despite the challenge of the cultural history issued by Lamprecht, dominated by the Prussian school, and indeed this *kleindeutsch* orientation was intensified by the "Ranke-Renaissance" of this generation and by the influence of Treitschke, who also enjoyed a revival, though not an admiring one, during the war years.[84] Friedrich Meinecke, Otto Hintze, Hans Delbrück, Georg von Below, and Theodor Mommsen (as well as Schäfer, Erich Marks, Erich Brandenburg, Max Lenz, and Johannes Haller) all taught and published books on ancient, medieval, and modern history in the old political style, and perhaps even more tied to the political establishment in Berlin.[85] Like Ranke they moved away from narrow classical precedent and indeed were not wholly indisposed to the insights offered by a philosophical outlook. Though far from the vulgar pseudo-Rankean "objectivity" which had notoriously gained currency in that age, they were aware of the complexities of historical interpretation — if not through the idealism of Hegel then at least through the hermeneutics of Droysen and the need to confront the challenge of sociology and historicism.

The standard expression of the German historiographical model was the handbook of Eduard Bernheim, published first in 1889, which hearkened back to earlier works in this genre, including Droysen, Chladenius, Köhler, Vossius, and Bodin, but which was also informed by the contemporary literature of philosophy and the natural and human sciences — Windelband, Rickert, Simmel, Durkheim, Croce, Berr, Flint — and the "so-called cultural history" represented especially by Lamprecht. Bernheim recognized three stages of historical science: narrative, or "referring," which included myth, inscriptions, and memorials, and was represented by the Greek *logographoi* and Herodotus; "pragmatic" history, which had to do with political utility and civic life, and was represented by Thucydides and Tacitus; and "genetic," or developmental, history, which introduced selection and criticism of sources, organic ordering of materials, and philosophical reflection, that is, *Historik,* and problems of geographical and chronological division.[86] The question of "periodization" (*Peri-odisierung*) had progressed from the Four World Monarchies concept to the ancient-medieval-modern convention fixed by Conrad Cellarius in the seventeenth century; but it had become more complex with the addition of a "pre-historical" (*prähistorisch*) stage.[87]

This "encyclopedic" genre, in the tradition of Boeckh and Droysen, also opened up questions of "method" (in a modern, scientific, and not pedagogical, Bodinian sense) and the relations of history to other sciences — philology, politics, science, art, anthropology, ethnography, etc. These contacts had enriched history, and historical method, drawing on philological "inner" and "outer" criticism, was a itself protection against skepticism and the "hyper-critical panic" that had seized some extreme practitioners of *Heuristik* and *Quellenkritik*; but historical method had not expanded to the extent that made "universal history" really possible. History could be objective as well as subjective — as represented respectively by Ranke's first great work on the Roman and German peoples and Schlosser's study of the eighteenth century, both appearing in 1825 — but it could not reach beyond the particular cultural circle of the inquiring and interpreting historian.[88] Even Mommsen, speaking of scientific objectivity, added that this was an "ideal goal which every scientist sought but never reached or could reach."[89] Within those limits, however, scholars could move toward "comparative history" and the philosophy of history in a modern sense, though with awareness of providentialist precedents and "prototypes" in Augustine and Otto of Freising as well as Voltaire, Condorcet, Schlegel, Hegel, Marx, and many others.

At the turn of the twentieth century, however, it was the past and the future — the heritage and the destiny — of the new German Empire that preoccupied these scholars. Just before his death in 1931 Stefan George's disciple Friedrich Gundolf began a study of the origins of German historiography in which he celebrated the literary and nationalist tendencies of history since Herder, Ranke, and other followers of the Herodotean muse, whose purpose was not only to uncover unknown facts and show new meanings but also to celebrate the German tradition in the *völkisch* manner of Luther and not the Catholic and in retrospect grossdeutsch way of Charles V.[90] According to Gundolf, Petrarch, Machiavelli, Joinville, and Commines all supported their national traditions, as did Spanish and English authors, following the model of Rome and Caesar; and German historians continued to promote the national-imperial ideal over the false universalism of Humanism and Enlightenment. This vision of the political past and future revolved around the old Germanism associated with Tacitus and the new Prussianist version of Frederick the Great, the heroes of the *Freiheitskriege,* and Bismarck. Examples of this prewar literature include Delbrück's *History of the Art of War* (1900–1927), Meinecke's *Age of the German Uprising, 1795–1815* (1906) and *Cosmopolitanism and the National State* (1907), Hintze's *The Hohenzollern and Their Work* (1915), Schäfer's *History of Germany* (1910) and *Colonial History* (1903), Brandenburg's *Founding of the Empire* (1916), the biographies of Bismarck by Lenz (1902) and Marcks (1909), and Below's *German Political, Constitutional, and Economic History* (1900), *The German City* (1914), and *German Historical Writing* (1916), which all celebrated the struggle for national unity and the unique virtues and power of German statecraft and culture. The last of these works treated what Below pejoratively called the "new history" of Lamprecht, which deviated from these sanctified national traditions and which was inclined to universalism and pacifist weakness.

Lamprecht was not the only purveyor of novelty, for there was also the "new" military history of Hans Delbrück, though it pointed in the opposite political direction: the arts not of peace (and the pacifist implications of Lamprecht's brand of *Kulturgeschichte*) but of war. Delbrück was the scholar who aimed most directly at the source of German pride and success—and ultimately, as he came to realize, tragedy—which was the military and militarist traditions of the Prussian monarchy. He was admittedly a Rankean epigone: "I am only a historian and wanted to write a book for friends of history and a manual for historians in the spirit of Leopold Ranke."[91] Combining academic and political careers, Delbrück was not eminently successful in either despite his masterwork on the art of war and his successorship to Treitschke in Berlin (though he had broken with that elder scholar).[92] He clashed with military experts over strategy and, during "the greatest of all wars," the policy of "peace through victory," with medievalists over the primitive order of the ancient German tribes, with national historians over his revisionist interpretation of Frederick the Great, denying that he was a "strategist of annihilation," and more generally with conventional scholars such as the Caesar-enthusiast Mommsen over the emphasis on the social, economic, and technical conditions of warfare, implying as this did a subversive receptivity to the new social sciences and a divergence from the Rankean model maintained by Schäfer and Below. In fact Delbrück was closer to his moderate and eventually republican (*Vernunftsrepublikaner*) friends Hintze and Meinecke (who was also, however, a monarchist at heart—*Herzenmonarchist*).

Coming out of a Prussian and Lutheran background, Meinecke had studied with Droysen, Sybel, and Treitschke, worked under Sybel in the Prussian archives, and took his doctorate in 1896 just three days before Ranke's death.[93] In the same year he became editor of the *Historische Zeitschrift*, succeeding Treitschke, who had succeeded Sybel, and kept the post until forced to retire under Nazi rule. Meinecke was long an admirer not only of Ranke but also, more personally, of Treitschke, comparing the relationship to that between Christ and Paul, who (like Treitschke) had the ability to reach the masses.[94] During the *Methodenstreit* over Lamprecht, Meinecke sided with Below (who had known Lamprecht as well as Meinecke from their days in Bonn) and Lenz in support of the Rankean tradition, though in a more moderate way that accommodated economic, social, and cultural aspects of national history.[95] As he told Below in 1896, "Economists, philosophers, and jurists think more about general historical problems than do average historians."[96] Moreover, Meinecke turned increasingly to idealist aspects of historical experience and to the history of ideas (*Ideengeschichte*). Such was the teaching of what he called the "new history" that, aspiring to join German culture and German politics, arose in the period of the rise of the German nation toward a unified state.[97]

This was the line taken in Meinecke's first major book, which celebrated the emergent German nation through its poets, philosophers, and historians before Bismarck brought the ideal and the real—the German nation and the Prussian state—into a vital and expanding combination. *Cosmopolitanism and the National State* is built on a number of dualities, or polarities, beginning with that between the (political) universal and the (psychological) individual but including also that between nation and state, between power and freedom, between peace and war, between the ideal (Hegel?) and the real (Bismarck), between ideas and actions, interests and ideals, and later between cultural history (Burckhardt) and political history (Ranke); and indeed Meinecke himself moved between these poles in the course of his very long life under two empires and two republics. Working, like Ranke, within the framework of world history, Meinecke saw a general pattern, "a massive interweaving and crossing of national and universal developments."[98] In Germany in the Napoleonic age there was a convergence, under the aegis of a new class of civil servants, between the ideal as expressed in literature and philosophy—as in the work of Wilhelm von Humboldt, Novalis, Schlegel, and Fichte—and the real embodied in the Prussian concept of the state and the activities of Stein, Gniesenau, and (again) Humboldt. At the same time "historicising Romanticism" brought the individual into collective national development, encouraged by the experience of war and yet in a liberating way that contrasted with French despotism. By 1905 Meinecke was already moving beyond the Ranke paradigm as conceived by colleagues like Schäfer, Hintze, and Below, turning to the "human sciences" (*Geisteswissenschaften*) associated with his friend Ernst Troeltsch as well as Dilthey, Rickert, and Windelband, and reflecting on the theme that he took up thirty years later, that is, the "rise of historicism."

A central theme of Meinecke's book was "the liberation of political thinking from nonpolitical, universalistic ideas," and here "the three great liberators of the state" before unification were Hegel, Ranke, and Bismarck, who marked a progression from the ideal to the real.[99] Hegel and Ranke were both indebted to Savigny and the Historical School for their conception of nationality, but Ranke, especially in his "epoch-making advance," joined this more firmly to ideas of the "nationalized state" in its full individuality and autonomy. Meinecke followed the views of his friend (and Bismarck's biographer) Lenz in associating Ranke with that "great reader," Bismarck, on the same agenda. For Lenz "the historical ideas of Ranke had become second nature in the politics of the great founder of our empire" — although he was even more admiring of Treitschke, "one of the greatest of the champions of our unity and architects of our state."[100] For both Meinecke and Lenz, Bismarck realized in himself the convergence between the ideal and the real — the cultural nation and the national state developed out of enlightened European values and Prussian tradition, including of course the military dimension. The progression from Prussia to a greater Germany became clear after the experiences and the errors of 1848, and Ranke in particular — in contrast to the "political" historians Droysen and Max Duncker — had the foresight to see this process from an elevated, prophetically national perspective.[101] So the old master "continued to spin the thread of world history" (through public action as well as academic scholarship), and Meinecke obviously hope to embrace and emulate this duality, too.

Meinecke's argument moved not only "from historical study to political interpretation," as he said, but to retrospective prophecy, for his design was indeed teleological in a sort of secular version of Hegelian philosophy.[102] Writing with the vision of German unification in mind, he was concerned to point out failures, wrong turns, and mistaken policies and to judge both actors and intellectuals in the light of this goal. The story was not new, having been told by numerous German historians, but Meinecke's selection of protagonists was original, joining as it did the old political narrative with intellectual history, and, at least before 1914, the Prussian legend, reinforced by archival research, which continued to serve as the master narrative of German history. But Meinecke's story was not completed in the years that saw the beginning of another world crisis, and he had continually to review and to revise his interpretations in the later editions of his book and in other postwar writings.

Prussianism, or Borussianism, in its military if not in its cultural aspect, did not fare well in the First World War, at least among historians. The common nationalist euphoria — the "spirit of 1914" — felt by all of the great powers, illustrated by Meinecke, testifying to "one of the most beautiful moments of

[his] life," and still another (after 1813, 1848, and 1870) "German liberation," was succeeded over the next four years by a long slide into disenchantment, despondency, and social revolution — from the "iron age" to the "iron cage."[103] Prussianist pride turned into sad nostalgia: "Only one who lived before 1914," he remarked later, "knows what living is like."[104] At first Meinecke and his colleagues, especially Hintze, Troeltsch, and Delbrück and later Ernst Cassirer and Alois Riegl, joined the effort enthusiastically, comparing the events of 1914 to the wars of liberation a century before — and the Allies to the Napoleonic threat at that time — and favoring continued expansion of the empire. Moving to Berlin in that year, Meinecke was elected to the Academy of Sciences. At that time, too, he succeeded Lenz as a member of the Wednesday Society of classicists, which had included Droysen, Mommsen, Curtius, and (later) Hermann Diels and Karl Holl; and he took part in other classicist circles of discussion with Troeltsch, Delbrück, and Willamowitz-Moellendorf.[105]

But it could not be scholarship as usual — most of his students, Meinecke lamented, were women — and the prospect of defeat became ever more evident. Historians changed their views about the "Prussian legend" but could do little to resist the course of events; and even those close to power could only protest indirectly as they watched the coming defeat. Military strategies were criticized by Delbrück and the idea of "peace though victory" was deplored by Meinecke, among others. They were forced, too, to answer the severe assaults on German national politics and culture by other Western scholars, who were likewise conscripted into the international conflict with nationalist sentiments that were hardly less virulent than those of Treitschke, who became a major posthumous target for French and English counter-propaganda.[106] It was in this connection, too, that Meinecke, writing popular essays on the world war, became more aware of the diabolical nature of power (*die Dämonie der Macht*) and conceived his plan for a book on "reason of state."[107] By the summer of 1918 the war was lost, the idea of further annexation a false dream, and as "world war was perhaps turning into world revolution," what was called for was a complete review of the view of history taken by Meinecke and his friends — though without surrendering the old belief in national unity. Meinecke himself, monarchist at heart but republican by reason, shifted increasingly from a national to a cosmopolitan point of view.

Meinecke's old friend and colleague Otto Hintze, who had also worked for years in the Prussian archives, cultivated much the same territory as Meinecke in the years before the war, though in a more conventional fashion.[108] He published articles on the German nobility, Prussian reform movements before the Wars of Liberation, constitutional development, military and political organization, a comparative study of administrative history, and — after criticizing Lamprecht's cultural history, "the individual and collective approach to history"—his own comprehensive interpretation of German history, *The Hohenzollern and Their Work* (1915). In this book Hintze played down geographical factors and emphasized the Prussian state, set in the Mark of Brandenburg, and the German empire as the creation not of nature but of dynastic, royal, and imperial will. Like Meinecke and others of the Prussian school, of course, he wrote according to a national teleology, with Germany's world-destiny in mind; but as one of the moderate neo-Rankeans (*Neurankeaner*) he avoided vulgar partisanship and, though eschewing footnotes and criticism of secondary literature, based his narrative on his extensive archival work; much more than Meinecke he emphasized the social, economic, and institutional foundations of the "modern-sovereign" state-to-be.

But this new state, which arose after 1648 in the "iron age" of national rivalries and which after 1740 became a "great power," differed from the other powers in the emergent European state system in that it achieved unity not in cooperation with the assembly of estates but through the actions of its rulers, by the employment of its military, and by "historical necessity."[109] Hintze spoke briefly of "intellectual life" in connection with the founding of the University of Berlin, and he referred to cultural matters — "the inner life of the state"—in the wake of the revolutions of 1848, referring briefly to the *MGH* and the dictionary of the Grimms; but for the most part he concentrated on political, military, and constitutional matters. Surveying in detail the conflicts underlying the process of unification down to Franco-Prussian War, which finally ended the French dominance that for centuries had counted on the weakness and divisions of Germany and opened a "new epoch in the history of the European state system," Hintze ended his story with the age of the ruler, "the Kaiser of Peace," and an afterword about the challenge of 1914, which, as in the days of Frederick the Great, would decide whether or not Germany would continue to be a "great power." "May this illustrious dynasty give leaders to our Fatherland," Hintze concluded, "who will lead us to power and well-being."[110]

Two other members of the "Ranke-Renaissance" deeply involved in national history were Max Lenz and Erich Marks. The latter had a "fifty-year friendship" with Meinecke, who in 1915 discussed the Belgian question with him, Schäfer, and Hintze, and a year later, with him and Schäfer, a possible source collection to be published by the Berlin Academy. Meinecke backed Lenz in the crusade against Lamprecht but had doubts about his exaggerated concern with the sources (the opposite of Schmoller, another target of the Rankeans).[111] Both Lenz and Marcks were Protestant historians, whose work started with the emergence of the great powers, in Ranke's classic interpreta-

tion, and like Meinecke, but more radically, emphasized the agreement between the cultural and ideological sides of German history. Both also celebrated the cultural traditions of Germany by celebrating the achievement of
Treitschke as well as Ranke and by linking intellectual forerunners with the
man of action, Bismarck, Lenz pairing him with Ranke and Marcks with
Goethe.[112] Reinforcement of the belief in cultural- (religious-) political continuity came from the academic habit of celebrating centenaries of key figures
and events—the Lutheran Reformation, of major importance for Ranke
(1917), Luther's birth (1883), the Diet of Worms (1921), and Bismarck's birth
(1915), marked by a volume edited by Lenz and Marcks.[113] In the spirit perhaps more of Treitschke than of Ranke, Lenz (who was Bismarck's official
biographer) celebrated not only triumphant nationalism but also "the wonderful power of war," which likewise enhanced political unity.[114] For Germany
they saw the progression as one "from Luther to Bismarck," and the religious
element was preserved not only through the *Kulturkampf* waged by Bismarck
against Catholicism but also in the "ideas of 1914"—and the temptation for
some old Rankeans was to extend the progression from Bismarck to Hitler.

Georg von Below, determined opponent of Lamprecht, likewise began his
career as a social and economic historian of medieval Germany, especially
eastern Germany, investigating the patrimonial state of the later middle ages in
eastern and northern Germany, which contrasted with the Catholic south (as
Prussia contrasted with the Habsburg empire). In his study *The German State
of the Middle Ages* (1900) he offered a critical review of the vast literature on
German economic, legal, institutional and constitutional history, including the
work of jurists and political theorists as well as historians, adopting at points a
comparative approach, and looking forward always to the fruition in the
monarchy and German empire. By this time he was more interested in critical
historiography and polemic than in original research, and he devoted much of
his time to exposing the errors and misconceptions of Lamprecht, following the
critiques of Lenz, Hintze, and Oncken; the war intensified his ideological
preoccupations. In 1916 Below published a survey of German historiography
and in 1924 an expanded version in a series edited by him and Meinecke.[115]
Here Below, emphasizing the "unity of German historiography" stemming
from of its Rankean tradition, followed in an invidious way the categories set
up by Meinecke. For him cosmopolitanism, together with the rationalism and
abstract individualism, naturalism, and mechanism of the Enlightenment, positivism, liberalism, and contemporary pacifism, were all opposed to the Romantic values of the historical schools, organic society, the *Volksgeist,* and the
concomitantly emergent national state which had attained its own unity.[116]

Below's interpretation obviously drew on conservative politics and the ideological premises of the Prussian school of historians, but it took more definite shape in the overheated context of the "ideas of 1914," when national unity was fulfilled in the experience of a war that was defensive, yet also pursued in an expansionist and more explicitly xenophobic spirit. His arguments were also reinforced by contemporary philosophy, especially the ideas of Windelband, Rickert, and Dilthey concerning the separation between the natural and the human sciences. For Below cultural history as practiced by the late Karl Lamprecht was tainted by its association with Enlightenment scientism and French positivism, which relied on biological and physiological analogies; and he rejected it, as he rejected sociology, in favor of the Rankean tradition of political history — and indeed "historicism" — which drew its strength not only from documentary research but also from the scholarship of legal, institutional, and especially economic historians. Cultural history was indeed essential, but only in the context of its highest expression, which was — as Ranke had endlessly emphasized — the national state as celebrated especially in the work of Treitschke, whose German history appeared in 1879 in the high tide of Bismarckian *Realpolitik*. In this connection, too, Below denied that Ranke's dictum of describing the historical process "as it really was" entailed "contemplative science, or abstract, scientific 'objectivity'"; and he quoted Luther's view that "one understands not in cold blood but in emotion and passion." In any case history had to be the history of the state, and indeed the "power-state" (*Machtstaat*), for "without the state all is lost." Unlike Meinecke, Below seemed to have learned little from the war experience to change his views of the meaning of German history since 1870.

It might be added that there was also a sort of anti-"Ranke-Renaissance," to the extent that the Catholic (and Austrian) tradition of historiography preserved and intensified a totally different conception of modernity and German history than the Lutheran interpretations of the Prussian school. The central figure here was Ludwig Pastor, whose history of the popes from the close of the middle ages (1886–1930) was intended to supplant and to correct Ranke's history of the popes on the basis of the information accumulated since the 1830s. Though following Ranke's methods of massive and critical investigations of sources, Pastor's book, sponsored by the papacy, was even more unashamedly apologetic than Treitschke and other members of the Prussian school, whose anti-Catholic position was reinforced by Bismarck's *Kulturkampf*. Pastor agreed with Ranke than the late middle ages and Renaissance marked the beginning of the modern world, but he denounced the heathenism and subversive ecclesiastical views of humanists like Valla, who celebrated pleasure and who assaulted the authority of the papacy. "It will be seen," Pastor commented, "that it is Valla, not Machiavelli, who started the often-repeated assertion that the Popes are to blame for all Italy's misfortunes."[117] For Pastor what was significant about the Renaissance was Christian humanism and, despite admitted corruption, the piety of the monastic orders. But as Prussian historians wrote with the vision of German unification before their eyes, so Pastor remained within the tradition of papal authority.

Cultural history did not fare well in the postwar period. "Did cultural history come to an end after 1918?" asks Stefan Haas.[118] Books continued to appear — including popular ones like Egon Friedell's cultural history of the modern world — as indeed did the bibliographies published by Georg Steinhausen, but little in a theoretical or methodological way appeared, except in interdisciplinary terms. The peripheral character of cultural history was suggested by the work of Max Weber's brother Alfred, whose *Kulturgeschichte als Soziologie* (1935, 1950), despite pretensions of being a "world history," treated the West as the only "primary culture," while seeing, after centuries of domination by religion and science, a "third" type dominated by a (non-transcendent) social religion and perhaps a fourth, a technocracy (*Funktionarismus*), which was a sort of further extension of the "bureaucracy" conceptualized by his brother.[119] One reason for this may have been the rise of a racist *Volksgeschichte,* which came into its own after 1933, stemming from the conservative *völkisch* — and nonprofessional — "cultural history" as practiced by the likes of Friedrich Hellwald and Wilhelm Riehl, whose work found new life in the Nazi period. The German historical profession was as conflicted and divided against itself as much as was the nation in these postwar years.

Mini-National Traditions

This is a very old story, A. L. Schlözer back in the eighteenth century counting twenty-four "national histories" within the Germanic sphere.[120] The nineteenth century, however, was the great age of national awakening and — besides the expansive unifications of Italy and Germany — of the liberation of ethnic groups from political domination by the great states and empires, especially in the wake of the French Revolution, the revolutions of 1848, and later diplomacy.[121] The social and cultural story behind these shifting boundaries is more complicated, but politically some of the milestones are familiar: Finland declared its independence in 1809 (under Russian control) and again in 1917; after the Congress of Vienna in 1815 Belgium was founded, formalizing a separatist movement started after 1789, while Norway, though part of Sweden, became independent; in 1867 Hungary became a partner in the Dual Monarchy and in 1919 was granted independence; in 1878 Romania, Serbia, and Bulgaria achieved it; and in 1918 so did Czechoslovakia, Latvia, Lithuania, and Estonia. Many of the national insurrections in 1848 were abortive or temporary, but they served as inspirations for continuing national-liberal movements against the counter-revolutionary European settlements. Beneath these legal expressions of the wills of the great powers the national revivals and search for cultural identity in a European context were driven above all by the study of history, the ransacking of national memories and the researching and inventing of national pasts — and mythologies — which had to be done without the Western-style connections with Roman imperial foundations. The vehicles of such revivals began with language and literature, which meant in general the movement from oral to written discourse, sometimes involving the recovery of ancient literary works, especially poetry, and the reconstitution of languages that were on their way to extinction.

The major powers had long established their national vernaculars with attendant cultural and political traditions, and the mini-nationalities paralleled or followed these developments, often in opposition to the hegemony of expanding and absorbing modern states. Some of these (mini-) national literatures emerged in the later middle ages and Renaissance, especially in the form of poetry and Bible translations, and then were promoted more actively by intellectuals in the Enlightenment and Romantic period before taking more organized, political, and sometimes xenophobic form in the later nineteenth century. This was the case with Finnish, Swedish, Danish, Hungarian (Magyar), Polish, Romanian, Serbian, Czech, Lithuania, Latvian, and Estonian (promoted by the "Young Estonia" movement in the early twentieth century). All of these languages were often placed on the cultural defensive — Norwegian, for example, being an oral idiom subordinated to Danish hegemony, while Danish struggled against repeated German intrusions. Norwegian was elevated from an oral, rural form through the efforts of Ivan Aasen and his grammar (1864) and dictionary (1873) and was given official sanction by 1900.[122] Serbia had a rich tradition of oral literature, which was celebrated in the eighteenth century by Herder and Goethe and later received written form, some of the poetic cycles being edited by Bartok in the 1930s. A recent creation of international diplomacy, Belgium was divided by the rivalry of Dutch and French, which produced not only bilingualism but the later Flemish-Walloon conflicts. In these literary movements journalists, novelists, and poets were usually in the lead, but some authors also turned to the writing of history, often in ways not far from the imaginative writings of literary figures, although their work was preceded and sustained by diligent collections of sources and documents — on the model of the *MGH,* Rolls Series, and the French collections inaugurated by Guizot — which supplemented the literary traditions also being edited and published. Among others Hungary and the Baltic states published their retrospectively national "Monumenta," and such series became a state concern in the later nineteenth and twentieth centuries. Other essential elements in the professionalization of historical studies in the mini-national traditions, which paralleled or imitated the processes in Germany, France, England, Italy, etc., begin with the many societies of history, folklore, and antiquarian studies preceding the professional historical associations — for example, those of Riga (1840), Utrecht (1845), Norway (1869), Denmark (1877), Sweden (1880), Hungary (1867), and Romania (1910), with attendant publications.[123] They must include, too, the founding of national historical periodicals (on the model of — but many preceding — the *Historische Zeitschrift*, the *Revue Historique*, the *English Historical Review*, and the *American Historical Review*), most founded in the second half of the nineteenth century; the assembling of national bibliographies (on the models of Dahlmann-Waitz, Monod, and Charles Gross), such as those of Pirenne for Belgium (1895), Sanchez-Alonzo for Spain (1919), Hans Barth for Switzerland (1914–15), Ludwik Finkel for Poland (1889–96), and many others covering most of the mini-national traditions; the compiling of national biographical dictionaries and other reference aids; the organization, opening, and cataloging of the archives; the publication of standard modern historical series such as the *Allgemeine Staatengeschichte* edited by Heeren et al. (1829ff.), the *Histoire générale* by Lavisse and Rambaud (1893–1901), and the *Cambridge Modern History* planned by Acton (1902–12); the establishment of museums; the writing of historiographical surveys; the emergence of academic leaders and schools after founding figures, such as Robert Fruin in the Netherlands, followed by Blok, Palacký in Czechoslovakia, who left no school but was succeeded by Jaroslav Goll, and Godefroid Kurth, followed by Pirenne, in Belgium; divisions between liberals and conservatives (such as the conflict between the Cracow and Warsaw schools in Polish scholarship), Catholics and Protestants (or secularists), "scientific" and "literary" historians, and champions of Rankean political history and the "new" cultural and intellectual history; the generational patterns dividing masters and students (especially after 1870, when students from smaller states went to Germany and to France to study, and around 1900); and attempts to reform higher education and give history a more central, if not controlling, position in public culture and politics.

To this must be added, too, the convening of international congresses (modeled on great diplomatic conventions like the Congress of Vienna) in various scholarly disciplines, beginning especially in anthropology and prehistory, notably that held in 1866 in Neuchâtel, followed by thirteen others down to that of Geneva in 1912, and many other international conventions on ethnology, folklore, archeology, oriental studies, the history of science, and the history of art. All this represented a modern form of the Republic of Letters of the old regime, as did the establishment of the great series of international historical congresses, beginning with that held in the Hague in 1898, which, appropriately enough in an age of imperialism and fears of war, centered on diplomatic history, and including those in Paris (1900), Rome (1903), Berlin (1908), and London (1913).[124] In Paris major topics were comparative history and "historicism," and increasingly interdisciplinary studies made their appearance, in keeping with the cosmopolitan and peaceful rhetoric of many participants — although the spirit of cooperation and "entente cordiale" was broken by national controversies, such as the opposition of Otto Hintze, Max Lenz, Eduard Meyer, Dietrich Schäfer, and Theodor Mommsen (in the last year of his life) to the Berlin congress of 1903, the conflict between the Germans and the Italians in Rome, the echoes of Lamprecht's *Methodenstreit* in Berlin, and the controversy between Pirenne and Dopsch in London. Yet the international character of these well-attended meetings was publicized by the reports in the major historical journals — Monod in the *Revue Historique,* Below in the *Historische Zeitschrift,* and C. H. Haskins in the *American Historical Review* as well as notices in Italian, Swedish, and Dutch periodicals. These meetings were broken off by the war, but they resumed again in Brussels 1923 in part with the help of American money (especially for the collecting and publishing of documents), and continue down to the present day.[125] Of course the war undermined the old spirit of cooperation, as, for instance, in 1919 Below received resignations from Pirenne and Espinas from the editorial board of the *Vierteljahrschrift für Sozial- und Wirtschaftsgeschichte,* whose place after the First World War was taken by the French *Annales.*[126]

By 1900, in any case, these national and mini-national states had become part of this scholarly network, its values, fashions, issues, and polyglot style of discourse (limited obviously to the major languages). However derivatively, they all produced their own "grand narratives," that is, magisterial multi-volume national surveys, which in some cases reached a popular readership comparable to works appealing more directly to literary sentiments and tastes for entertainment in printed forms and envisaging a program of national education as well as cultural enhancement like the historical writings of Michelet, Macaulay, Bancroft, Droysen, Treitschke, Balbo, Pirenne, Blok, Kliuchevskii, and Menéndez Pelayo. Many of the national histories had been studied in the nineteenth century by German, French, and Anglophone scholars — most notably in the sixty-volume series edited by Heeren, Ukert, Giesebrecht, Lamprecht, and Oncken, which featured works by major scholars of England, France, Italy,

Spain, the Netherlands, Austria, Germany, Russia, Poland, Denmark, Switzerland, Bohemia, Finland, and Turkey. For many mini-national traditions there are scholarly studies in (or translated into) German, French, and/or English, such as the work of E. G. Geijer on Sweden (1832–36), Palacký on Czechoslovakia, Constantin Jireček on Czechoslovakia (1876); Johannes Steenstrup et al. on Denmark (8 volumes, 1876); Rambaud on Russia (1877), and various works on the Baltic states, most notably the three-volume survey in German by E. and A. Seraphim (1897–1904). However, others attracted magisterial histories never translated into any of the major languages, such as that on Norway by Johan Sars (4 volumes, 1873–91); Sweden (11 volumes, 1903–10) by Emil Hildebrand, editor of the *Historisk Tidskrift* (founded 1881), and others; Hungary by Sándor Szilágyi (10 volumes, 1895–98); Romania by Alexandre Xénopol (6 volumes, 1888–93); Serbia by Stanoje Stanojeviç (1908); Czechoslovakia by Jaroslav Goll (1897), and others, including Croatia and Slovenia. These studies were often absorbed into later scholarship, but their literary value remains concealed in languages which are inaccessible to all but specialists, and so unfortunately they are also lost to mainstream historiography and even to later bibliographies.

The outpouring of national and mini-national historical scholarship in the early twentieth century reinforced and intersected with the aspirations of the corresponding cultural groups before and after the war, complicated as always by putative "racial" groups (still a major category among historians, whether or not informed by modern anthropological or "scientific" research) and especially by linguistic minorities with their own political agendas. During the war scholars were drawn into the political arena not only to champion or to attack national traditions along conventional lines but also to envision a postwar redrawing of national boundaries to alleviate or even to put an end to classic political and ethnic clashes. Here science and politics established another alliance, as the descriptive and "scientific" study of boundaries—natural, linguistic, ethnic, and cultural—was joined to projected diplomatic prescription for a closer approximation between the frontiers of language and those of political domination, as linguistic geography was made the basis for geopolitical adjustments. A good example is Leon Dominian's work of "applied geography" on "the frontiers of language and nationality in Europe," published in 1917, supported by the American Geographic Society, and introduced by the racialist writer Madison Grant, who celebrated the triumph of the major national languages over the declining local dialects.[127] For him Erse, Gaelic, Cymbric, and Armorican would certainly be engulfed by French, just as Quebecan French (!) would be overcome by English. In any case Grant was confident that Dominian's survey would be invaluable after the end of fighting in making linguistic/cultural and political boundaries as identical as possible, perhaps even in the Serbian-dominated Balkans.

In this effort historical study offered a legitimizing foundation for the post-war designs of the major powers, which were increasingly drawn to the support of national (and mini-national) aspirations against the ancient divisions preserved in Scandinavia, Austria, Russia, and the Balkans. For Dominian the basic premise was Eurocentrically—or Euroasiaocentrically—constant: "Looking over the stormy centuries during which French, German, and Russian nationalities were elaborated," he wrote, "we behold the formative influence of language everywhere"; and this included the brutal linguistic imperialism of France and Germany. The historical movement from language and culture to politics was the natural pattern of historical evolution, and the same principle should apply after the Great War. So Dominian joined history not only to prophecy but also to international policy and on this basis projected his "scientific" analysis into the political future of Europe, or rather Eurasia. As in the case of France and Germany, "The final supremacy of Italian language is already in sight," and the Slavic invasion of Scandinavia and the Baltic states seemed irresistible, although it remained to be seen what preference would be expressed by the inhabitants of Alsace-Lorraine. Other destinies would be resolved by a combination of natural and historical—that is, geographical and linguistic—factors given political "application." Belgium, despite the linguistic division, should remain intact; for practical reasons Poland must be based on natural more than linguistic frontiers; the "national enfranchisement" of Bohemia on linguistic lines was in keeping with restoration of the old crown lands; Romania's national claims were validated by history and geography as well as language; despite the linguistic division Switzerland must also preserve its sovereign status; Hungary had already achieved national identity by force of will in the face of Germany and Austria; and even the Balkans were open to this sort of optimistic, geo-linguistic, and historical analysis: "Whatever be the name applied to Croats, Dalmians, Slavonians, Bosnians, or Serbs, all speak the Serbian language. All have striven for centuries to promote their individuality as a nation. To help them realize themselves as a political unit merely implies furthering the process begun by nature." As for Turkey, the crux of the Eastern Question, Dominian argued that because of its tri-continental position, "it belongs more to its neighbor than to itself," and that "in this respect its future will resemble its past." He could not foresee the extraordinary revival that succeeded Turkey's almost total defeat —nor indeed many of the consequences of President Wilson's dogmatic version of a peace settlement on the basis of nationality.[128]

After 1918 fragmentation became the theme of the world itself, with the end of three empires, the emergence of mini-nationalities to political status, and the replacement of Darwinian continuity by notions of rupture and perhaps revolution. Across Europe historians of the "generation of fire" picked up their tasks where they had left them before the catastrophe, or the realization of catastrophe, and did so without losing faith in a world order of some sort. Yet they did, many of them, lose confidence in political explanations for the condition of the European world, and they turned to more searching and subtle studies of the life and rivalries of peoples, whether or not in the old national terms. In any case their inquiries took differing directions in the wake of miscalculations, misconceptualizations, and mispredictions, and operating, as Huizinga put it, "in the shadow of tomorrow," when history seemed to be getting out of control — yet again.

Reevaluations

There is no world view, no ideology, no religious doctrine, no fad or fancy that does not find itself confirmed and justified by the war.

— *Thomas Mann*

The Ideas of 1914

Life in the summer of 1914 was without meaning, Robert Musil wrote, and it was for this reason that for many people the war had the effect of an almost religious experience, especially in Germany, when, on 3 August 1914, "the day" to which German naval officers had dedicated many a toast finally came and war was declared on France.[1] The world would never be the same, nor would scholars, old or young, pressed into national service while trying to maintain their professional standards and careers. Leaving Trieste and already embarked on *Ulysses*, Joyce went into a second exile, this time to Zurich, not moving on to Paris until 1920. For Musil the "Great War," despite initial euphoria, confirmed his view that history had no essential meaning beyond the chaos confronting all human beings. Yet within a year or two a terrible negative meaning seemed to emerge in the face of what Thomas Mann, in his soul-searching reflections during the war, called "this purely fateful process that is truly taking place beyond good and evil."[2]

These were the reactions of novelists to what Peter Gay has called "the war psychosis."[3] But what about historians? What was the impact of the war on their inquiries and interpretations? In one way it intensified existing trends, especially in reinforcing the principles of nationality and national culture — and the xenophobic obverses. In another way it undermined formerly unquestioned premises, especially in subverting ideas of progress and universal peace. In the early twentieth century historical study had been placed in large part in the service of the state — not only of the large members of the "European state system" but also of the minor and would-be states that likewise founded their aspirations on the belief in deep national traditions and destinies. Through their historians France continued its defense of a "nation" born in early medieval times and living continuously through multiple dynasties, revolutions, and republics; England celebrated its insular "Gothic bequest" and an unbroken continuum of representative government; Germany and Italy, though they attained statehood late, traced their "national traditions" back to German and Roman antiquity, if not to prehistory; and so it was for Spain, the Scandinavian states, even Holland and Belgium, and the countries of Eastern Europe and the Balkans. Romanian historians carried on a long controversy over their alleged continuity with the Dacians of the ancient Roman empire and their modern condition as an "island of Latinity in a Slavic sea," opposed by skeptical scholars invoking methods more critical of national myths and prejudices.[4] Expecting war, most historians accommodated their nationalist premises to the fact of world conflict and shifted their emotions from the ideal of political progress to the goal of military victory. Some, especially in Germany, celebrated the positive, invigorating, and enhancing aspects of war. The war was being waged, wrote Erich Brandenburg in 1916, for "the future of our *Volk*," to give Germany a place in the sun next to the other powers.[5] Karl Brandi made the same argument in his greetings (November 1918) to his "comrades at the front."[6] "In human terms," exalted Erich Marks, "there is nothing greater than war, nothing more manly, but also nothing more inspiring for the inner soul."[7]

In the course of the war such perverse optimism faded, and yet historians clung even more enthusiastically to their national sentiments, and indeed enhanced them with a concomitant xenophobia.[8] All sides agreed on the central role of nationalism, and even on the fact that historically this phenomenon had arisen first in England and France — such being the message, for example, of J. Holland Rose's lectures on nationality given at Cambridge in 1915. Rose found no trace of the idea, at least after Machiavelli, until the idea of "national pride" (*Nationalstolze*) was recognized by an anonymous eighteenth-century Swiss author, which he associated with the spirit of William Tell. To this tradition the contribution of Germany, though it began with idealist philosophy, was late and destructive — "Fichte's celestial arc ends in a Prussian drillyard," Rose concluded, and the final scene of the drama came in the disaster of 1914.[9]

Militarism demonized the ideals of nationality, and the notorious formula in General Bernhardi's *Germany and the Next War* (1912), "world peace or decline," set the tone for the coming debate.[10] The exchanges between English and French scholars on the one side and the Germans on the other showed how history could be swept up in the cause of military violence as it had been in the missions of state-building. Behind a façade of conventional scholarly citation and rhetoric, the historian of political thought J. W. Allen gave a course of lectures on "Germany and Europe" at the very outset of the war, addressed to the questions of the causes of — which also meant responsibility for — the outbreak of war. He noted the theories of the state and militarism which German historians like Treitschke had developed.[11] For Allen not only German politics but also German "culture" underlay the train of actions that led Germany to start war, a war that England never wanted. Germany fought for conquest, which — "Treitschke's illusion" — was "good for humanity"; England fought for "home and liberty," and a peace consonant with the new political realities of "global civilisation." The purpose of "the great treaty that is coming"(here Allen cites Churchill) was "to rearrange the map of Europe on national — I suppose that means social — lines." To this extent the national principle emerged from four years of bloody conflict stronger than ever and would be applied to the "mini-nationalities. Others joined the campaign, and in 1917 A. F. Pollard published *The Commonwealth at War*, lamenting the "military party" in Germany and the "crass and crude philosophy" that regarded war as a natural part of history.

Such English propagandist history was pursued by other distinguished scholars who, too old to fight and forced to mourn the loss of many young students of that generation, were drawn into the war effort with little experience or direct recollection of what a major war involved. In 1912 the periodical *History* was founded under the sponsorship of Tout, Hearnshaw, Hodgkin, Ward, and other scholars as a sort of pedagogical supplement to the more technical professional journals; and "ironically" it published an issue on the peace settlement of 1814 just as the hostilities began a century later. During the war it featured articles on the teaching not only of military and naval history but also of "patriotism," as well as inflammatory essays on Nietzsche, Treitschke, Delbrück, and others. In 1914, too, Oxford University issued a series of pamphlets devoted to the "causes" of the war and the guilt of Germany. Ernest Barker invoked Nietzsche as well as Treitschke as the evil spirits behind the German belief that (in the formula of the professor of English literature Walter Raleigh) "might is right." "It is Germany," he declared, "with its antiquated ideas, its stupidly brutal government, its blindness to what now must constitute political progress for Europe, that has forced Europe to arm, and to keep arming since 1870."[12] Paul Vinogradoff even contributed an essay in praise of Russia and its coming "regeneration" and contrasted it with German barbarism; for the Slavs, too, "must have their chance in the world." Pollard agreed, and added that such chances would not come from a scientific approach, for this "will not help in doing justice to the aspirations of Russians and Poles, Germans and Danes, Czechs and Magyars, Serbs and Italians, Bulgars and Greeks."[13]

In 1915 the medievalist H. W. C. Davis published selections of, with adverse commentary on, Treitschke's *Politics* and its charges of English "decadence" and comparisons with Moslem fanaticism ("The Musselmans alone are men; despise all other nations, they are impure").[14] Perhaps the best official statement by a scholar was James Bryce's collection of essays written during the war, contrasting English love of liberty to the German "worship of the state" and adding that it was not Hegel and Treitschke but "facts," that is, three successful wars, which accounted for Germany's policy.[15] The world advances not by fighting, Bryce added, but by Thinking, and such idealism informed much Allied propaganda. Between 1913 and 1931 F. S. Marvin published five editions of his popular survey of Western history, and although he made some changes during and after the war, for him none of the post-1914 disappointments "affect either the general argument or the ultimate truth of the forecast" — by which he meant the increasingly bright future of Europe.[16]

In France nationalist enthusiasm was rampant, and so for example Fustel de Coulanges's student, the historian of Gaul, Camille Jullian, diverted his energies from the Gallic past to the *patrie* in crisis, contrasting the venerated "soul of France" with that of Germany, whose only motive was conquest — and this even in scholarship: "Those people have done altogether too much history and too much science."[17] War could be just, as history impartially taught, but only in terms of the French mission for "universal liberty"; and here Jullian made an invidious contrast between Fichte's narrow nationalism and the French defense of the rights of man. Among many others, Charles Seignobos carried on the posthumous denunciation of Germanism with the primary defendant being Treitschke and his Machiavellian notion that the state, which he identified with power, was above morality and was an end in itself. The great Catholic historian of the Reformation Pierre Imbart de la Tour sought explanation in the German philosophy of history, but other historians turned more particularly to contemporary behavior. With Lavisse, Boutroux, Bergson,

Durkheim, Gustav Lanson, and Charles Andler, Seignobos formed a Committee for Studies and Documents on the war, which published pamphlets in
French and English, including Lavisse and Andler's *German Theory and Practice of War*, which documented German atrocities.[18] In 1915 Durkheim attacked "the German war mentality," again taking Treitschke as the target,
though his concern was mainly with the current problems of the violation of
Belgian neutrality and "the systematically inhuman war" begun by Germany
and continued by its "morbid mentality."[19] And Alphonse Aulard published a
running commentary on the war, drawn from popular articles published in
France and the United States, which exhorted "imitation" of the French Revolution in the period of the German invasion of 1792.[20]

In Germany scholars tried to defend themselves, their nation, and their
culture from the assaults of their colleagues in the study of world history. In
October 1914 there appeared the German "Appeal to the Civilized World," or
"Manifesto of 93," signed by Karl Lamprecht, Wilhelm Wundt, Ernst Haeckel,
Gerhart Hauptmann, and others German scholars and men of letters, which
provoked reactions not only from French scholars like Christian Pfister and
Charles Bémont but also from Americans like Arthur O. Lovejoy.[21] Otto
Hintze, Friedrich Meinecke and Hermann Oncken — Ranke's epigones all —
published a volume on "Germany and the World War" in 1915, in which they
protested their devotion to the common ideals of "science" and defended
German *Kultur* as no less universal than that of France or England.[22] In that
year, too, Dietrich Schäfer published a collection of earlier articles on the
Anglo-German political and naval competition which he connected to the
war.[23] Hintze also invoked the hard necessities of geopolitics, that is, Prussia's
"desperate position" and need for war in its struggle for unification, yet denying
that this policy was like the "imperialism" of Germany's enemies and comparing England ("God's chosen people") to Napoleonic France. Erich Marcks and
Paul Darmstädter supported this argument by attacking the "policy of force"
displayed by both England and France, and to show England's long-standing
hostility Oncken (who had written a chapter on the German Empire for Acton's
Cambridge Modern History) quoted from the *Saturday Review* of 1896 the
remark that "Germania est delenda." Troeltsch , likewise condemning the
traditional belligerence of England and its "unscrupulous determination to
make use of every weapon," including historical scholarship, provided an old-
fashioned celebration of "the spirit of German culture" and its "inner being," as
reflected in its poetry, art, and religious life.[24] Felix Gilbert, in a chapter in his
memoirs entitled "Why I Became a Historian," recalled that as a boy in Berlin
he had to learn in school a "Song of Hatred Against England."[25]

After 1914 some American scholars remained sympathetic to Germany, or at least German culture and scholarship, but for the most part they were anti-German; and Arthur O. Lovejoy (who was born in Berlin and leaned heavily on German scholarship and who was later a colleague of Gilbert on the editorial board of the *Journal of the History of Ideas*) lamented that Germans, who had taken the lead in the theory and practice of "objectivity," had rejected the ideal at the most crucial point in their history.[26] The "pied pipers of Prussianism," in the phrase of Guy Stanton Ford, were targeted by American historians mobilized by the government (Committee for Public Information) for official propaganda, and other collections were published for the benefit of students and professors who lectured and wrote on behalf of military intervention. As in Germany such involvement seemed contrary to the canons of historical science. Indeed some of these "Star Spangled Men," as H. L. Mencken called them, later regretted their involvement; and "revisionists," beginning with S. B. Fay in 1920, turned against this invidious line of argument.[27]

For Germany the most extreme case perhaps was made by the great ancient historian Eduard Meyer, who in 1915 (and the next year in English translation) published an attack not only on England's political traditions, social policies, "moral decadence," and criminal behavior but also its "deficiency and backwardness in science and the arts," adding that even if defeated Germany must preserve its military and economic organization and "a virile monarchical government placed above party strife, and wholly independent to act, that it may be free to utilize and in creative activity all the forces of which the nation is capable."[28] With the analogy of the Punic wars in mind, Meyer foresaw the decline of Western civilization as Germans understood it. In 1917 J. M. Robertson responded to Meyer's "worthless book," denying German cultural superiority and emphasizing Germany's "stupendous crime" and responsibility for causing the war.[29] Not that Germany was without friends abroad; for J. W. Burgess of Columbia urged his countrymen to sympathize with the Central Powers, "to break through this vast and vicious Colonial Empire Trust and give the world the freedom of the seas and the open door. . . ."[30]

In a very different defensive mode Delbrück defended German military culture, its pedagogical, social, and political value; indeed, having spent his life on a multivolume history of warfare he could not resist carrying this over into his personal view, which was that "If Italy joins the enemy, it means that Germany cannot win the war. But on the other hand, we will show that Germany cannot be conquered."[31] What Delbrück did for warfare, Gustav Schmoller did for the more peaceful traditions of German institutions and self-government. Meinecke deplored the vicious statements of scholars like Raleigh, who compared the Germans with the Zulus ("Kill them all. It's the only thing they understand") and denied the invidious coupling of militarism and culture attributed to the Germans, for "Our modern German historical writers follow in Ranke's footsteps, not in Treitschke's." And again came the argument which he had offered in his first great book, *Cosmopolitanism and the National State*, that Germany's mission was to combine, or balance the political individual with the universal: "We want to found a new balance of power in the world system of states."

Some scholars seemed to learn from their misplaced optimism. "How greatly have I erred," wrote Delbrück in December 1918, turning back to the past to see where he had been wrong, at least in strategic terms.[32] Of course historians of all nations had their ideas about the causes and results of the Great War, and they all revolved about the same fixed principle and value that had dominated their writings before 1914, namely, that of nationality and ethnicity. Arguments about war guilt were based not only on determination of political and military decisions but also on deeper factors of national character and aspirations, such as Gustav Le Bon's doctrinaire *World in Revolt* of 1915, which drew invidiously on renewed concepts about "national character" and the "national soul," which determined the defeat of Germany and the success of France and her allies and which, shaped by proper educational methods would determine the future of Europe.[33] After the war projects for organizing the peace were likewise tied to questions of national self-determination and prominent destiny. According to the Treaty of Versailles, Germany accepted responsibility for causing the war and the damage issuing from it; and the postwar debates centered on this apparently answered question — another kind of "revisionism," seeking to look deeper into the problem of causation obscured by the legal problem of guilt. A larger question is the extent to which the theory and practice of history were affected by this traumatic experience: did historians learn anything about the process of history from this "war to end all wars" — or even about the foolish optimism that encouraged such a formulation? Some did, but in other ways the old historical thinking and myth-making, as Gay has said, "went underground and emerged in disguised form."[34]

Many American historians were drawn into the business of war, especially through the National Board of Historical Service founded in April 1917, in which John Franklin Jameson played an important part, as did James T. Shotwell of Columbia, Frederick Jackson Turner of Harvard, and others. Some also participated in negotiations for peace, Shotwell serving as head of the history division of the American Commission to Negotiate Peace led by President Wilson and being joined by colleagues brought in to give expert advice about the new global settlement.[35] Besides Americans such as C. H. Haskins, G. L. Beer, William Lunt, Robert H. Lord, Wallace Notestein, William L. Westermann, Archibald Carey Coolidge, Dana Munro, James Scott, and

James T. Adams, there were many Europeans, including Ernst Lavisse, André Tardieu, Ferdinand Lot, G. W. Prothero, and J. W. Headlam-Morley, who offered technical advice and, in many cases, reflections about the successes and failures after the conference. Headlam-Morley, who had served in the British foreign office with Toynbee, Lewis Namier, and Alfred Zimmern, had already published a book on the causes of the war in 1915, and he was in close agreement with Shotwell and Haskins during the negotiations.[36] After the war he was involved in the publication of the documents of the conference, edited by G. P. Gooch and Harold Temperley, and in launching the *Annual Survey* of international affairs, edited by Toynbee from 1924 and later by Geoffrey Barraclough.

Nationalism remained a prominent principle not only in the "Punic peace" imposed on Germany and in the principle of self-determination but also in Wilson's plan for a League of Nations, although global ideals and "social justice" were also present, as in the International Labor Organization which Shotwell put together. Shotwell also gave a day-by-day account of the conference, including his impressions of Paris, the terrible destruction of French battlefields, and cities like Rheims, and like Haskins he accepted an invitation to give a lecture at the Sorbonne in the field of medieval history. But the major concern of historians beginning in 1920 was the old question of war guilt, which of course had preoccupied them from the first days of mobilization and fighting but which now was addressed in the wake of unprecedented national traumas and with the benefit of massive and growing (though still not adequate) documentation. The national positions were fixed during the war, but so were "revisionism" and its critiques, which became virtually a cottage industry in the 1920s and which supply material for revisionist historians even today who still hope for "closure."

Legacy of Defeat

The German historical profession emerged from the war disenchanted but unshaken in its resolve to find meaning in the national past. The generation of historians who had made their names before the war, including Meinecke (d. 1954), Brandenburg (d. 1946), Brandi (d. 1946), Oncken (d. 1945), Hintze (d. 1940), Lenz (d. 1932), Meyer (d. 1930), Schäfer (d. 1929), Delbrück (d. 1929), Troeltsch (d. 1923), Moriz Ritter (d. 1923), and Haller (d. 1947), were deeply affected by the tragic conflict; but while they changed their views about the process and even direction of history, they preserved their nationalist values for the most part, whether or not they supported the republic that emerged eventually from the revolutionary chaos following the war and severe peace settlements. After 1914 these scholars constituted a small intellectual community which argued over the twists and turns of the political and military process. Meinecke, Troeltsch, Hintze, and Delbrück were especially close, discussing the "crisis" not only of their fatherland but also of "historicism."[37] They also deplored the lack of male students — "Männerarm" was Meinecke's term — and the postwar flight of young minds away from the academy to careers in commerce and science and technology. Yet even as they in various ways answered the "call to war," especially through journalism, the old generation of historians continued to pursue their "science." In the midst of those "hard times" Meinecke followed his vision of a documentary collection, an *Acta Germanica*, planned with the anti-Weimar historian Erich Marcks, which recalled the patriotic *Monumenta Germanica Historica* inspired by an earlier war a century before. There continued to be a nationalist edge, too, in their scholarship, as in Meinecke's essay contrasting the German and Roman "spirit" and defense of freedom and individuality against the collectivist and organic ideas accompanying the threat of imported revolution at the war's end.

Conservative neo-Rankeans like Lenz celebrated the "wonderful holy power of war" and abiding support of the "German God," and in 1914 Johannes Haller denounced anyone who doubted that victory was a "cure." In the course of time, however, the progress of the war eroded the optimism and confidence of these aging scholars.[38] In 1915 Meinecke, believing that the war was drawing the nation together, could still think Germany was on the brink of a "new epoch"; but by 1917 his hopes were dashed, and all he could think about was a fair peace. He admitted "our stupidity." "We are all sinners," he wrote; and in 1918 his friend Troeltsch expressed his agreement: "the old system has collapsed under its sin."[39] Meinecke became increasingly critical of the Rankean ideas of the "great powers." His reviews of Treitschke's correspondence, which appeared between 1912 and 1920, defended this great precursor from the unfair criticism of English historians, though without justifying his nationalist excesses, which, however understandable in the 1870s, had outlived their value.[40] He tried to preserve a position of national moderation above party divisions, quoting a poetic lamentation: "Prophets to the right, prophets to the left, and in between this poor child of the world" (*Weltkind*). But by September 1918 he realized that all was lost; he could see the beginning of the end, the "dam breaking" in November, and the future darkened further by the specter of revolution; and he turned to "national self-criticism." Yet even if it meant social democracy and republicanism, the remaining task was the restoration of national unity; and all of his writing was based on this premise.

The writings of Meinecke and his generation spanned the pre- and postwar years and were concerned with a number of sensitive topics related to national politics, foreign and domestic, and the role of war, on which they published documentary collections and monographs: especially the Reformation and Luther (Lenz, essays "from Luther to Bismarck," 1920), the wars of liberation and Napoleon (Lenz, 1904; Meinecke, 1905); the University of Berlin (Lenz, 1910–18); Bismarck and the Franco-Prussian war (Lenz on Bismarck, 1902; Marcks on Bismarck, 1909; Oncken on Napoleon III, 1926); national unification (Brandenburg on the foundation of the Empire, 1916; Oncken's collection of sources on the Zollverein, 1934; Marcks on Germany before unification, 1936); and imperial conflict before 1914 (Schäfer on colonialism 1903, 1921; Brandenburg on Bismarck to World War I, 1924), and larger surveys of German history (Schäfer, 1910, 1922; and Hintze, 1915) and world history (Delbrück, 1896–1920). They also published a variety of polemical works relating directly to the war, such as Oncken on the "ideas of 1813" and the possibility of another European war, Delbrück, Schäfer, and Gustav Wolf on the national goals of German historiography, 1918; Hintze, Oncken, and Meinecke on Germany and the war (1915); and many other articles by Meinecke, as well as contributions to the debate over war guilt (*Kriegschuldfrage*). Most of these national historians also treated questions of methodology, following for the most part the Rankean tradition, whether in positivist or idealistic form, against the incursions of cultural history as promoted by Lamprecht (d. 1915) and his students. Among the many contributions to the debate in the wake of Bernheim's handbook were Schäfer's initial assault on cultural history (1888); Lenz's celebration of Ranke (1912); Below's many polemics against Lamprecht, discussions of sociology, and survey of German historiography (1915, 1924); similar surveys by Ritter (1919) and Brandi (1922); Delbrück on Lamprecht, Spengler, and philosophy of history; Hintze on Droysen, Troeltsch, sociology, and comparative method; and Meinecke on many questions and authors relating to "historicism."

Otto Hintze, who was editor of the Prussian Archives (*Acta Borussica*) from 1894 to 1936, wrote extensively about the deep history of Prussia in the perspective of the great world empires, but unlike Ranke emphasizing domestic affairs as well as foreign relations. For Hintze it was German particularism as well as its geographic vulnerability that delayed Prussian political development; and he emphasized the role of the military in terms of society and nation as well as foreign relations. As he wrote in 1908, "German political development is almost three hundred years behind that of Western states; and even though the original lag in the level of political culture seems to be rapidly lessening, an impartial observer cannot avoid becoming aware that the population of the German Empire, and likewise of Prussia and the other Federal States, has not by a long shot achieved that measure of national solidarity, of practical conciliation of the social and religious conflicts, by which a people becomes capable of determining its own fate."[41]

Yet until the war Hintze foresaw a convergence between German political development and the representative institutions of the other Western European states. He was never as rabidly nationalistic as some of his contemporaries, a breadth of view illustrated by his pioneering work in the comparative study of institutions and bureaucracy. In 1919 he focused on the office of the commissary, which Jean Bodin had first analyzed in the sixteenth century, although without any sense of the large and varied future history of this European institution, and then on a global analysis of the "preconditions of representative government."[42] Characteristically, Hintze attributed this to a historical process which had to be studied in terms of archival evidence and not some putative sociological "law"; and this attitude was preserved by his students, including Americans like Gordon Craig and Walter Dorn, who gained his reputation writing on German bureaucracy in the eighteenth century and who finished his career at Columbia.

Hintze carried on his critique of sociology and the philosophy of history in his early writings on the collective vs. the individual approach and his later writings on Troeltsch and historicism. In the early work Hintze's target was Lamprecht and his biological and socio-psychological "laws," which he associated with the similarly conjectural history of Spengler — who had a low reputation among most of these scholars, although Meyer, who late in life turned from ancient to world history, took him more seriously. About Troeltsch's work Hintze had many reservations, commenting that "Historicism is a relatively new term, and its meaning is not quite clear."[43] Troeltsch's concept, comparable to Einstein's theory of relativity (Hintze suggested), was associated with "life philosophy" (*Lebensphilosophie*) and took this into account; but it also led down the dangerous path to relativism and skepticism, which Hintze rejected. Like Spengler, Troeltsch drew on the organic ideas of Romanticism (Vico, Herder, and Rousseau as well as Goethe) and the historical school of jurisprudence, which had led, and not by accident, to the current fashion of cultural history. He drew also on the work of Meinecke and the disciplines of economics, sociology, theology, philosophy, and art history, and he contrasted the historicism emerging from this eclectic field to naturalism, as Rickert had done. The keys to this historicism, as Meinecke argued more systematically and more historically a few years later, were historical individuality and organic development. What Hintze did not like was the theological, if not cyclical, character of Troeltsch's conception of history as well as his skeptical and unhistorical denial of the universal nature of humanity. Among other things, he thought, this view makes impossible both comparative history and the sort of global vision displayed by H. G. Wells (!).[44]

Troeltsch's reflections on the question of historicism were central to the postwar debates pursued by Hintze, Meinecke, Heussi, and others; but his aims were radically different. In the first place, avoiding the pejorative connotations of the term imposed by earlier theologians, philosophers, and social scientists, he denied that historicism implied relativism, and with Harnack he insisted that the new, or renewed, sub-discipline of the history of religion (*Religionsgeschichte*) was autonomous like history itself because its function was "normative."[45] He never denied the paradox, remarking even that compared to dogmatism historicism bore "a certain similarity to the devil."[46] Yet religion was not absolutely absolute, for Christianity, resting on a sort of "evolutionary absoluteness," was "the focal point and culmination of all religious developments" — though he admitted that this attempt to balance the relative and the absolute, between the human and the divine, between the historical and the theological (material base and superstructure), was full of "problems" which could only be resolved through historical inquiry. In any case Troeltsch, opposing the intrusions of naturalism into the social sciences, was always fascinated by the problem of the intersection between human values and historical experience, of the sociology of religion, expressed above all in his monumental study *The Social Teachings of the Christian Churches* (and "groups," as the German original adds). "Historicism" had been a problem not only for religion (as one aspect of the threat of "modernism" denounced by the Church in 1892) but also for classical political economy, as in the attack by the classical economist Carl Menger in 1883 on the "errors of historicism," and for philosophy, where Troeltsch sought answers in the philosophy of history — in which historicism, resting on a "sixth," that is, a historical sense, not only posed the question but somehow suggested the answer.

Troeltsch was part of the European-wide conversation about historicism and its crisis, a conversation in which Karl Mannheim, Karl Heussi, Benedetto Croce, and many others were involved. Mannheim virtually identified historicism with the *Weltanschauung* of the postwar age, and so it itself had to be "historicized," as indeed Troeltsch had begun to do. According to Croce, historicism was a "logical principle" and philosophy was itself "absolute historicism."[47] He was followed in his line of argument by R. G. Collingwood, who joined it to the tradition not only of historiography going back to Herodotus and Thucydides but also of Western philosophy as partners in the pursuit of "self knowledge."[48] But of course it was Meinecke who represents the culmination of modern historicism with his *Rise of Historicism* (1936), which offered a critical review of the tradition inherited from the school of Ranke, defining it in terms of the Romantic principles of "individuality" and "development," which he associated especially with "Herder's pupil" Goethe, and (despite his earlier hostility to Lamprecht) he granted a place for cultural history at least equal to that of political and diplomatic history, eventually even giving precedence to Burckhardt over Ranke as the master historian.[49] "History," he remarked in 1928, hyperbolically and in bitter hindsight, "is nothing else than cultural history."[50]

For Meinecke the way to modern historicism was prepared by the idea of reason of state (*Staatsräson, raison d'état, ragione di stato*), which represented the condition of the European state system before 1914 but which was not revealed in all its "frightfulness" until after the collapse of Germany in 1918. In this idea again Meinecke saw the intersection between politics and history; and in 1924 he published a survey of the theme, which he dedicated to the memory of Ernst Troeltsch, whose contrast between naturalism and historicism Meinecke adopted for his own purposes. In particular Meinecke traced "reason of state" back to Machiavelli and the shift from utopian and natural-law concerns with the "best state" to the pursuit of practical policies suited to the interests of existent states, as seen in the work not only of scholars from Bodin to Ranke and Treitschke but also of statesmen like Richelieu and Frederick the Great, whose anti-Machiavellian posture was belied by his public career. Frederick hoped to join humanitarian ideals with reason of state, though he could not succeed in this plan. On another level Hegel tried likewise to join the rational and the real, though he, too, was incapable of bringing them into unity. With Treitschke, moving away from Ranke, the shift moved even further from political and moral ideals to national power and to the confusion between political and military action.

In the mid 1920s Meinecke was still caught between the extremes of "cosmopolitanism and the national state" (the title of his reputation-making book of 1908) and, like so many of his colleagues, trying to peer into the postwar future. Absorbing the bitter pill of defeat, Meinecke rejected the idealizations of pure power preached, indirectly and directly, by German intellectuals from Hegel to Spengler and even Croce, nourished as he was by the spirit of Machiavelli and Hegel; and he concluded that the best thing was "to strive honourably for a genuine League of Nations," though he was prepared for an international order based on Anglo-Saxon hegemony, which would be at least better than "the scourge of the French continental hegemony," thinking of the Napoleonic experience out of which the German nation had been born. Not that he expected an era of perpetual peace; for the "naturalistic forces" of life did not need the Machiavellian "daemon" — the ambivalent doctrines of power and militarism — to insure conflict in the future.

In the 1920s Meinecke was deeply involved in the Historical Commission for the Imperial Archives (following a plan which he had discussed earlier with Marcks) , along with Marcks, Goetz, Oncken, Brandenburg, Fritz Harting, and others. This project, which became the target of controversies between nationalists and moderate republicans like Meinecke himself, focused on sources relating to political, diplomatic, and military history according to the old Rankean habits of privileging foreign affairs above economic, social, and cultural history; and it underlay the Imperial Institute for the Study of the History of the New Germany, headed by Walter Frank during the Nazi period. Another controversy relating to the official control of history was that between the champions of political (and, in Meinecke's case, intellectual) history, right or left, and the new generation's interest not in "outer" but in "inner politics" (*Innenpolitik*), exemplified especially by the work of Eckhart Kehr, under the influence of Marx and Weber, on the relations between finance and political and military history. But the modern pursuit of economic and social history in Germany had for the most part to wait until the aftermath of the second war and another age of even deeper crisis, reflection, and revision, which Meinecke tragically lived to see.

The Russian historical profession was even more deeply divided than the German, and the émigré community was equally important and widespread, finding refuge especially in Berlin, Eastern Europe, and, in the cases of Karpovich and Vernadsky, the United States.[51] Emigré scholars, who saw Russian history as a series of disruptions and a convergence between attempts at reform and revolution, tried to throw new light on their old regime beyond Marxist stereotypes, for instance in the work of the intellectual historian Florovsky and in the ideas of the Eurasianists. The Marxist construction of Russian history, beginning especially by M. N. Pokrovskii, joined the traditional emphasis on social and economic factors to revolutionary and Stalinist ideology, and its career lasted down to the end of the Soviet Union, which upset the grand narrative of twentieth-century global history, opening the way to a vast new project of revision and reconstruction. In general the contributions of over a century of Marxist scholarship are in danger of being buried in the aftermath of the events of 1989, and indeed I have not found it possible to resist this ideological amnesia from the twenty-first-century perspective of this work. Yet if Marxism has followed Marx himself to the grave at the end of the past century, their "specters," as Jacques Derrida reminds us, remain.[52]

Prehistorical and Ancient Frontiers

The idea of progress had been put in doubt long before the Great War, and it sank further in the bloody years of the conflict itself as well as in the disillusioning aftermath, when dreams not only of the good old days but also of a bright future of a reconstructed Europe began to fade. This was the atmosphere of pessimism that inspired the interpretations of Oswald Spengler and Rudolf Pannwitz. Yet historical knowledge (if not wisdom) continued to increase in these depressing times despite wartime xenophobia, in terms of international cooperation, with scholars around the world joined in efforts to expand the horizons of historical perception in both time and space. Errors and prejudices, old and new, distorted these labors, but the expanding historical record was at least open to criticism and correction through public exchange and debate, and the long-term result might arguably be characterized as a form of "progress" in a conventional sense. The learning and teaching of history were subject to extraordinary demographic growth in these years, as the institutional supports of pedagogy, research, publication, professional organization, and international exchange were expanded to accommodate this growth through journals, source collections, monographs, textbooks, university chairs, academic and professional associations, and international conferences — during the early decades of the twentieth century.

In the restricted perspective of old-fashioned European historiography, as modern history began with Charlemagne, so ancient (and "civilized") history began with the Greeks (and in effect with Herodotus). Such, for example, was the message of Werner Jaeger's monumental *Paideia* (1933). Not that the oriental background of Western history was entirely ignored, but aside from the biblical story, which also shaped the narrative, and the Egyptians, Babylonians, Assyrians, and other Near Eastern nations, "barbarism" was associated largely with fabulous, alien, and infidel traditions that were marginal to the grand narrative of the West. In the Renaissance Pico's motto that "all wisdom came from the east" was discarded except for peripheral, or underground, traditions, of "occult philosophy" (and to this extent Martin Bernal's controversial arguments about anti-orientalist bias seem valid, at least for the nineteenth-century phase of European historical scholarship).[53] However, with the archeological discoveries that began especially in the wake of the Napoleonic expedition to Egypt, it became impossible to ignore or to exclude this earlier phase.[54]

During the first generation of the past century, then, the shape of Western historical narrative (as preserved in the old and still thriving genre of universal, or world, history) was transformed on many levels — though to be sure such transformations had been going on for a century and more in terms of geography, chronology, and subject matter. Joined to geology, evolutionary biology, paleontology, anthropology, and archeology, the study of history was naturalized (as well as secularized) and globalized; and in the form of "prehistory" it turned again to large questions of origins, direction, and destiny. Investigating the life of humanity in the ages before writing no longer depended merely on linguistics, mythology, and historical conjecture and analogies; for now there was a growing body of information about material culture in the amazing discoveries of archeologists around the world; and indeed later periods of history were also illuminated by the same sorts of organized research. Not that old theories of human unity and racial ideas could be purged entirely from such research — indeed they were intensified by the passions generated by the war — but again intrusions of ideology and national prejudice were increasingly eroded by criticism from scholars driven more by professionalism than by politics. As Jacques de Morgan wrote in his synthesis published three quarters of a century ago (and it still holds true), "What we know to-day is very little in comparison with what remains to be learned."

Prehistory (*Vorgeschichte, préhistoire, preistoria*, etc.), as distinct from archeology and anthropology, arose in the prewar age of rampant nationalism, Heinrich Schliemann's sensational discovery of the site of Troy symbolizing the potential of the newest of the human sciences. The true "revolution" of the field, however, occurred during the first quarter of the twentieth century, that is, from the investigations of Arthur Evans at Knossus in 1900 to those of Howard Carter, opening the tomb of Tutankhamen in 1923, and those of Leonard Wooley at Ur in 1926. In this period archeology progressed from crude digging in the style of Schliemann to scientific excavation, and the Hittites and Sumerians, among other lost peoples and extinct languages, found a place in the historical record beside Egypt and Israel. Although a number of talented archeologists were killed in the war, discoveries and interpretations continued to accumulate and to demand the revision of universal history — although the old theory of diffusionism was preserved by scholars like G. Elliot Smith, W. J. Perry, W. H. R. Rivers, and V. Gordon Childe.[55]

The transition between the old and the new past can be seen in François Lenormant's *Ancient History of the East* (1868), which began with the biblical account and included the story of the postdiluvian peopling of the three continents by Noah's sons, but which emphasized the longer perspective opened up by the "completely new science" of "prehistorical archeology," the study of ancient languages, and the idea of the "antiquity of man."[56] Another sign of the attempt to give a scientific foundation to the study of ancient history was the introduction of statistics by Julius Beloch, but the science of historical chronology, founded over three centuries earlier by J. J. Scaliger, was central.[57] Scholars like Silvestre de Sacy had long before denied that there was a real "biblical chronology," and while the biblical problem remained, scholars in effect relegated it to the arena of myth and poetry.[58] The evolutionary scheme, already apparent in the eighteenth (and indeed sixteenth) century, was given a scientific foundation in Darwinian biology, and from the later nineteenth century it entered into the works of Max Duncker and George Rawlinson — as well as Ranke — who, however, worked without knowledge of oriental languages. For the next generation of scholars this gap was filled by the great dictionary of the hieroglyphic and demotic scripts published by Heinrich Brugsch in 1867–82, followed by that of Adolph Erman (1926ff.).

Yet historians always lagged behind the archeological pioneers. "Textbooks of history are a legacy of the past," wrote one champion of archeology and anthropology in 1921. "They are modeled on larger works which were written (in an epoch of enthusiastic nationalism) before the discoveries of prehistoric man had been made. . . . They are as a rule completely out of touch with current ideas and are 'survivals.' Worse than that . . . they are anachronisms, well calculated to jeopardize the fortunes of a project like the League of Nations," which, like universal history, depended on a global outlook (as illustrated by H. G. Wells!).[59] So historians needed to extend their horizons to include those whom J. L. Myres called "the peoples which have no history."[60] This opened a window to what James Breasted called "the new past."

Eventually, however, archeological knowledge was incorporated into the classical historical surveys and textbook histories of antiquity and especially of Egypt by Eduard Meyer (from 1884), C. G. C. Maspero (also from 1884), and James Breasted (from 1896). Maspero succeeded to the chair of Champollion in the Collège de France and was also a founder of the Egyptological Institute in Cairo, while Meyer was professor of ancient history at Leipzig, Breslau, Halle, and finally (1902) Berlin, retiring the same year that Erman left the directorship of the Egyptological Museum in Berlin. Breasted, who held the first American chair of Egyptology at the University of Chicago, published the first version of his Egyptian history in 1905 and worked to import knowledge of the "new past" into history. In 1916, after offering conventional praise to the "miraculous genius of the Greeks," he celebrated the "vast new outlook" produced by archeology. After the productive inquiries into the classical past, he wrote, "There is another similar step to be taken, and that is to discern behind Greece and Rome an additional great and important chapter of the human story." And contemporaneously, the British ancient historian J. B. Bury indeed supported just this step by including the oriental prelude in the planning of the Cambridge Ancient History, which, delayed by the war, began to appear in 1923.

This transformation had already been prepared for a generation earlier, as historians like Victor Duruy, Max Duncker, and George Rawlinson, brother of the great archeologist Henry Rawlinson, included accounts of this chapter in their surveys. Of course these scholars lacked grounding in the relevant ancient languages, and moreover they could not know of civilizations yet to be uncovered. The progress of such discoveries is suggested in the work of George Rawlinson, whose book on the "five great monarchies" (Chaldean, Assyrian, Babylonian, Median, and Persian) was followed by volumes on the sixth, seventh, and eighth monarchies (Parthian, new Persian, Phoenician); but as Bury remarked in the preface to the 1923 CAH volume, Rawlinson did not live long enough to add the Hittite, whose records were then being deciphered and studied. Much more "scientific" was the work of the new generation of ancient historians, including Maspero, Meyer, Breasted, and H. R. Hall, as well as the contributors to Berr's great series, "The Evolution of Humanity," planned before the war (in 200 volumes) but not launched until the 1920s (in 100 volumes). The writings of all of these scholars spanned the period before and after the war and began the attempts to produce a cooperative synthesis — although they all realized that a full account was not possible in the present state of knowledge and uncertainties.

The extraordinary progress in knowledge of the ancient history of the Near East may be seen in the changing editions, from 1912 to 1932, of the standard textbook by H. R. Hall, Keeper of the Department of Egyptian and Assyrian Antiquities of the British Museum. Discoveries came too fast to be incorporated into the text, and so from the fifth edition (1920) Hall appended critical "Addenda," pointing out errors and new information, including the Babylonian excavations at Ur, the tomb of Tutankhamen, the work by Evans at Cnossus, the Mycenaean or "Helladic" art, and the newly uncovered "Indus" civilization of northwest India.[61] The Noahan "Flood" was restored, this time being borrowed from a Babylonian source; the decipherment of the (Indo-European) Hittite language, continuing reports of improvements in chronology, a fuller understanding of the first populations of Greece, and many other details were added to the record — including, even then in progress, the decipherment by Samuel Noah Kramer and his colleagues studying the language of Sumer — where, in the words of a French scholar imposed on Kramer's book of 1956, "history begins."[62] Nevertheless, there are more questions than answers remaining in the wilderness of prehistory.

Actually, as G. Renard wrote in 1929, there were two prehistories. One was "ancient prehistory," which was the old universal survey of the life of humanity from its beginnings, which (like Renard's own book) depended on the pattern of stages, geological, evolutionary, and archeological, and which drew on conjectural sources even including the imaginings of Lucretius; the other was "modern prehistory," which was "sectional, local, and ends at different dates for different races and peoples and extends in some remote corners of the globe to our own day." In historical terms increased specialization led to the discrediting of the old universal, evolutionary, diffusionist (ultimately Christian) narrative — and with it the idea of a "master race" — replaced by a plurality of cultural traditions, or "circles." Like Vico and Herder two centuries earlier, prehistorians came to accept, at least provisionally, the notion of a multiplicity of historical traditions, whose origins could not be determined from the material, mythological, or even linguistic record and certainly not by anthropological conjecture. In any case prehistory had become not only a well-established field but also a regular feature of ancient, world, and national histories, whether in "ancient" or "modern" form.

In German archeology prehistory became a "national discipline," assisted by local associations (*Vereine*) as well as public organizations, and a support both of Germanist, anti-Romanist tradition and of imperial expansion. After unification the study of antiquities (*Altertumskunde*) was encouraged by the government and taught in the universities. Mommsen himself publicized the new field of prehistory, which became entangled in ideological conflicts associated with Germanic origins, Near Eastern diplomacy before World War I, and early history, especially relations with the Romans. Gustav Kossina, whose book on "German prehistory" appeared in 1912, was one of those who sought to "bring together patriotic archaeology and history," and to connect the career of the nation with its Indo-Germanic roots.[63] All this was also part of Germany's prewar celebration of its tradition of *Kultur*, often in invidious contrast not only to the uncultivated *Naturvölker* but also to the effete civilization of France and England, and which reached a high point during the war itself, many of the ancient historians signing the famous "Manifesto of 93" in aggressive defense of national culture. But hyper-Germanic culture also turned against the classicist orientation of the German mandarinate. "The war may not have killed philology," concludes Suzanne Marchand, "but it did administer the dose of humility that the classicist professorate had been unwilling to receive from the school reformers."[64]

The study of ancient history in the early twentieth century, set apart from prehistory only by the fetish of writing which historians preserved, was carried on between two poles, that of deep, source-driven research and the old aspiration for synthesis; and Eduard Meyer illustrated both of these tendencies. Having mastered the major oriental as well as classical languages, Meyer set about to extend the frontiers of historical science in Egyptian chronology and the cultures of the Hittites, Assyrians, and Sumerians as well as the Greeks, Romans, Jews, and Islam, especially in areas of economics and religion, including the origins of Christianity. Some of this work, especially his larger surveys, was premature, but he continually revised his views and struggled to keep up to date in these areas. Thus Meyer's ambitious history of antiquity (*Geschichte des Altertums*) added a progressively expanded and changing section on "anthropology," which was tied to the idea of the state as a universal cultural form, directed against the controversial interpretations of cultural history of Lamprecht and opposed to the philological approach of Willamowitz-Moellendorf, who deemed Meyer's work as superficial (if not as amateurish) as Nietzsche's. The story he told of Greece, in vast detail, was a tragedy, in which classical culture matured and was perfected even as the political fortunes of a democratic, divided, and contentious Greece fell to much larger imperial powers. Meyer also wrote significant books on the origins of Judaism (using Aramaic documents) and of Christianity, placing both in a large Near Eastern context. For him politics was the "center" of history, but he also recognized the role of ideas, created by individuals in the historical process. He rejected ideas of natural law and social contract and turned to the notion of the state, on the analogy of Aristotle's *polis*, emerging from the patriarchal family; and he joined this convention with the conclusions of contemporary ethnologists. He carried his work, along with his convictions, through the First World War and continued efforts on his history of antiquity until his death in 1930.

Meyer was also concerned with general patterns in history and the role of "ideas," indeed looked with some favor at the metahistorical speculations of Spengler, and (as noted) prefaced his history of antiquity by a survey of "anthropology" (which—a sure sign of the times—he considered calling "sociology"). Yet his views were criticized both by contemporary social scientists and by historians for his conservatism, which was scholarly as well as political. Although Max Weber venerated and drew on Meyer's work for his sociology of religion and ideas of charismatic authority, he also objected to his methodology, which downplayed social theory—as well as theology—at the expense of the individual, subjectivity, free will, accident, empirical research and historical experience. "History is not systematic science," Meyer wrote in his *Theory and Method of History* (1902), and for this he provoked criticisms from Bernheim, Beloch, Durkheim, and Troeltsch as well as Weber.[65] In effect Meyer upheld the old doctrine of Rankean individuality and politicocentric history, although he did not deny the subjective element in the complex and many-sided historical process and he insisted that history was to be judged in terms of consequences and effectiveness. In any case he believed that the subject of history was those peoples which had risen to the level of high civilization—namely, the Western tradition.

In 1900 classicism still dominated European education and historiography, with prehistory forming a prelude and extra-European areas relegated to the edges, and to this extent Martin Bernal is not off the mark in his controversial views. In the generation after the standard works on Greek history by George Grote, Ernst Curtius, and Julius Beloch classical studies could boast an extraordinary "scientific foundation," reflected in monographs, textbooks, journals, academy publications, source collections, critical editions of texts, inscriptions, and papyrae, encyclopedias, atlases, and other works of reference as well as historiographical studies. Greece and Rome were also overrepresented in such standard series as Berr's "Evolution of Humanity," Gustav Glotz's "General History," and the Cambridge Ancient History (12 vols., edited by J. B. Bury and others). In retrospect only a few scholars in this overflowing ocean of scholarship are still much recalled, even in footnotes of modern works.[66]

Among the most remarkable French historians of antiquity was Gustav Glotz, who studied with Durkheim and, influenced by contemporary issues of French social conflict and "social solidarity," published his thesis titled *The Solidarity of the Family in the Criminal Law of Greece* in 1904. Glotz was appointed professor at the Collège de France in 1913 and continued to work on Greek social and economic history, notably his study of Aegean civilization, of "Greece at work," and especially, in the shadow of Fustel de Coulanges, the Greek city (1928). For the Greeks the cities were a source both of greatness and of weakness, of growth and decline, leading as they did to revolutions as well as to federative experiments. Glotz proposed to emphasize not only historical development but also geographical context, which had been neglected by Fustel as well as Aristotle, and (like Meyer and contemporary sociologists) to consider not only the family and the *polis* but also the individual. Glotz followed the story down to the end of the city state and unification as a dependency of the Macedonian kingdom. "Was this a good thing or a bad?" he asked. Both, he concluded prudently, since Greece was able to take refuge in philosophy in place of the shorter-lived political success of Philip and Alexander.

In England J. B. Bury carried on the great literary project of Gibbon, though in a more "scientific" spirit as befit the post-Rankean age; and, after his first major work on the later Roman Empire from the fifth to the ninth century, produced an edition of Gibbon's work in 1914, adding to his already overindulgent notes with corrections and bibliography. Of course Gibbon lacked professional training and methods, and his philology left something to be desired; yet Bury commended him for emphasizing, as Freeman and Bryce did later, the continuity of Western history, between Rome and Byzantium in particular; and he at least tolerated Gibbon's didactic excursions, which — against, Bury noted, the famous advice of Ranke, whose work he cited in the notes — were paralleled by the partisan theses of other classic historians, such as "the indictment of the Empire by Tacitus, the defense of Caesarism by Mommsen, Grote's vindication of democracy, Droysen's advocacy of monarchy." Bury made other tangential comments, such as wondering why Gibbon, in his discussion of Rienzi, did not mention the political program of Dante; but for the most part he concentrated on improving the factual and bibliographical content by adding modern adornments to Gibbon's Enlightened toga. But Bury also deplored Gibbon's unfair treatment of aspects of Byzantine history, which was his own special province.

In 1913 Bury published the second edition of his own great survey of ancient Greek history, having had to revise his views of Greek civilization and thus to rewrite the earlier version, which had appeared in 1900, just as Arthur Evans's discoveries at Cnossus were appearing.[67] In this work Bury relied on the older authorities (Grote, Freeman, Droysen, Meyer, and Willamowitz-Moellendorf) but also employed evidence from coins, maps, vases, inscriptions, and museums. He was quite aware of the new questions being provoked by prehistory; and he often departed from earlier views, as from Freeman's classification of Greek and Roman with Teutonic institutions as "Aryan," though he was not receptive to notions of significant Semitic influence. He was aware of the distortion caused by overemphasis on Athens and Sparta and ignorance of other areas — "Les absents ont toujours tort" — especially of the provisional nature of prehistory, still emerging from the darkness of myth and literary conjecture; and he warned that the received story of the Greeks' history might be changed "at any hour." Bury pursued his work on the history of the Christian Empire down to the death of Justinian, admitting the "culminating" time of Constantine, but insisting on the "continuity" between the Greek and Roman Empires and regarding the "Byzantine" period as the last phase of Hellenism culture. But he did not hesitate to differ from older authorities, finding unconvincing, for example, Mommsen's view that women were admitted to public office.[68] He pursued the old Gibbonian question of the Empire's "barbarisation," again in terms of modern scholarship. As Acton, his predecessor in the regius chair, had begun editing the Cambridge Modern History, so Bury took over editorship of the Cambridge Ancient History, which began to appear in 1923, though already falling behind the controversial discoveries that were continuously changing the picture of history and prehistory.

Rome continued to fascinate Western scholars; perhaps, as Guglielmo Ferrero told an American audience, they "find there more than elsewhere what has been the greatest political upheaval of the hundred years that followed the French Revolution — the struggle between monarchy and republic."[69] In the generation after Mommsen the whole range of Roman history was invaded by

many original scholars, including Gaetano de Sanctis (4 vols., 1907–22), Ettore Pais (1898–1920), Guglielmo Ferrero on its "greatness and decline" (5
vols., 1907–09), André Piganiol on origins (1917), Léon Homo on primitive
Italy (1925, trans. by Gordon Childe), Franz Cumont (from 1896) and W.
Ward Fowler (from 1899) on Roman religion, Gustav Bloch on the Republic
(1913), Eduard Meyer on Caesar (1917), Camille Jullian on Gaul (8 vols.,
1907–26), Tenny Frank on Roman imperialism (1914), Samuel Dill (3 vols.,
from 1896) and Ludwig Friedländer (4 vols., from 1908) on society in the
Empire, Michael Rostovtzeff on social and economic history (from 1899), and
Otto Seeck on the decline of the ancient world (1895–1920). And this again
was accompanied by a large outpouring of source collections, encyclopedias,
reference works, new journals, international conferences, and the like. In the
early twentieth century Greco-Roman history, and classical studies more generally, rivaled national historiography both in higher education and in scholarly publication — although there was growing opposition to this old tradition, which many intellectuals were coming to regard as a distraction or
burden, if not worse. Nor did the First World War significantly alter this
process.

Roman history had always provided political models for European scholars, Machiavelli and Montesquieu being only the most celebrated examples,
with Gibbon, Niebuhr, and Mommsen following a historiographical tradition
going back to Livy and Tacitus. Interest had attached especially to questions of
origins (especially with Niebuhr) and decadence (Montesquieu and Gibbon),
but in the early twentieth century scholarship had turned from these classical
treatments as outdated — thanks in the first case to archeology, which carried
further Niebuhr's more conjectural efforts to separate legend from fact, and in
the second case to empirical and conceptual sophistication, which sought to
avoid the anachronistic, moralizing accounts of older historians. The debate
over the early period, which had received archeological evidence and anthropological conclusions and which fully accommodated the fourfold periodization of the prehistorians, was carried on between the "hypercritical" views of
Pais and the "temperate criticism" of De Sanctis, which would keep as much of
the traditional narrative as credible.[70] On the other hand, at the other end of
the story of Rome and the question of "corruption," as Ferrero admitted, the
new views with which he was associated were in another way a turning back
to the arguments of Livy about the destructive effects of luxury, ambition, and
avarice; this was generally the line taken, too, by T. R. Glover, the better to
celebrate the virtues of Christianity.[71] Samuel Dill told the story of the decline
of Rome in conventional intellectual and cultural terms but also noted the
disorganization of public services and the decay of the middle class as conditions of the process — as, under pressures of the Russian Revolution, did Ros-

tovtzeff.[72] In many ways Gibbon remained a presence in the question of "decline and fall," though a much broader range of "causes" was recognized by scholars like Seeck, for whom history, even the succession of a great empire by a number of independent states, was a flowing stream or unbroken chain of connected events.[73]

Gibbon's problem was reviewed by Rostovtzeff in the 1920s with critical reference to modern discoveries and interpretations, physical, economic, political, moral, cultural, and spiritual, but he found no simple key to the "decay of ancient civilization" in the wake of the "social revolution of the third century."[74] He rejected or qualified the theories of Ferrero, who emphasized the accident of Commodus's succession to Marcus Aurelius and consequent undermining of the Senate, the narrowly economic views of Weber and others, the racialist notions of Tenny Frank, and the arguments from purely physical causes such as soil exhaustion, and especially from the rise of Christianity. In line with the Marxist distinction between material base and superstructure current in his native Russia, Rostovtzeff distinguished two parts of the question — the politico-economico-social and the intellectual-spiritual aspects. The first concerned the orientalization of the eastern Empire and the second the barbarization of the western Empire, although he rejected the naive military explanation that relied exclusively on the Germanic invasions. For Rostovtzeff the most significant development was the decline of the cities, that is, the displacement of the "bourgeoisie" by the masses, and more generally the failure of ancient civilization to absorb the peasant class. Indeed this was the basis of his concluding comparison between ancient civilization and the revolutionary age which had sent him into exile.

As for Christianity, which for Gibbon had been so destructive of the Roman Empire, it continued to accumulate its historiographical studies, mainly triumphalist in character — in the grand tradition of Eusebius, Orosius, and both Catholics and Protestants (Cardinal Baronius and Flacius Illyricus, Döllinger and Mosheim, Pastor and Harnack) in the modern period — tracing the miraculous origin, martyrly endurance, missionary expansion, heretical divergences, persecutions, organizational successes, emergence as a political partner of the Empire, and eventually foundation as an independent (secular as well as spiritual) power. The intersection between a world empire with a proselytizing, monotheistic, book-bound religion shaped the destiny of the Roman Church and its own later sectional struggles and confessional and national defections.[75]

Among later scholars who continued the tradition of ecclesiastical history, Louis Duchesne based his narrative on the great corpus of Christian texts, following Eusebius especially in his careful citation of authorities, many preserved only through the ancient author, who "knew everything." Duchesne

traced in fine detail the fortunes of Christianity in its foundational and formative period; one major strength — in contrast to its imperial host and rival —
was its democratic inclinations, based on what he called "the brotherliness,
the sweet and deep affection which bound together all the members of the
Christian community."[76] Despite the last-ditch efforts of the Emperor Julian,
"Greek sophist" as well as "defender of the Roman fatherland," Christianity
continued its holy, universal mission through patristic, conciliar, and papal
agendas. As for the end of the Empire, Duchesne wrote, it "was not a catastrophe." Nor indeed was the break with the Eastern Church, instigated by Felix
III, of whom Duchesne remarked, in the conclusion of his book, as he might
have said of other popes: "God took his side."[77] This was also a "Whig view,"
but now in a transcendental mode and in the face of terrible opponents, including not only paganism and Judaism but also the Roman state, which all
had their histories and historiographies.

Gibbon's work is in fact as much concerned with ecclesiastical as with
political history, and his project of surveying the fortunes of "barbarism and
religion" has been reviewed most recently in an almost Gibbonian way by J. G.
A. Pocock, who retraces Gibbon's epic journey through various historiographical contexts from the Roman republic down to the European Enlightenments
and the first volume of the master work, published in 1776.[78] Passing through
the Gracchan, Tacitean, and Augustinian historiographical models, Pocock
makes an extended tour of Renaissance scholarship (Bruni, Biondo, Machiavelli, Carlo Sigonio, Pedro Mexía, Justus Lipsius, and James Harrington) and
revisits his own theoretical sites (post-Baronian "civic humanism," the "Machiavellian Moment," and the "ancient constitution") to give shape to his own
commentary. What happened in the wake of the Renaissance, as Arnaldo
Momigliano suggested, was the parallel rise and intermingling of three distinct
modes, narrative, philosophical, and antiquarian, which informed Gibbon's
great project. The end product was a matchless display of learning wedded to
a vast dramatic narrative rivaling Milton's *Paradise Lost* in power and ele-
gance. For many contemporary scholars such as Pocock, Gibbon remains in
the front rank of historical inquiry and interpretation.

Philosophy of History

As Paul Klee wrote,

Yesterday's holy
stones, shorn of their riddle.
Today
there is meaning.[79]

Some thinkers, impatient with slow historical inquiry, sought conclusions, if not closure. By the twentieth century the philosophy of history had enjoyed a long and complex career, descended variously from the history of philosophy (*historia philosophica*, as it was called in the seventeenth century), from Voltaire's coinage (*philosophie de l'histoire*), Scottish conjectural history, the German idealization of history, grander efforts associated with post-Augustinian theology, and later spiritualized evolutionism as well as modern attempts at historical forecasting. In the wake of Hegel, Schlegel, and Schelling if not Kant, history was restored to the orbit of philosophy, and indeed the "philosophy of history" became a distinct field of study and speculation, pursued in this idealist style, too, in Italy, Spain, Russia, and to a lesser extent in France and England. The alliance between history and philosophy was also reinforced by Auguste Comte's Positivism, which like German idealism traveled across national borders from France to the rest of Europe.[80] The philosophy of history gained its own history in works such as the survey of Robert Flint, first British biographer of Vico, who sketched a global survey of speculations about history before tracing its modern career from Bodin down to the later nineteenth century.[81] Except in its Anglophone "analytical" form, the philosophy of history also drew on other disciplines, including prehistory, geography, psychology, anthropology, and sociology, in its desire for global reach and conceptual depth. It even spilled over into historiography, to the extent that European cultural historians in the tradition of Herder looked beyond "what really happened" (in the classical as well as Rankean formula) to the larger, underlying patterns and meanings reflected in recorded human experience — not to mention the work of Brooks Adams, who in 1895 extrapolated his gloomy economic retrodiction into historical and cyclical "laws."

These transcendent goals appeared, or reappeared, in the wake of the traumatic experience of the Great War, especially in the work of Spengler, Troeltsch, Löwith, Berdyaev, Kahler, Voegelin, Huizinga, Ortega y Gasset, Ernst Bloch, Sorokin, Teilhard de Chardin, Toynbee, Wells, Voegelin, Niebuhr, and all kinds of Marxists, from keepers of the faith to heretical revisionists. They also appeared in less historical form in the work of Weber, Durkheim, Pareto, Parsons, and many other contributors to grand theory in the social sciences. What these speculators had in common, whatever their attitudes toward research and revelation, was the desire to transcend history through some sort of metahistorical system or intelligible pattern that would permit prediction, prophecy, mythologizing, or some sort of secular revelation. In their hands history turned from inquiry to prediction, from investigation to reflection, from openness to closure, from innocent questions to positive (or negative) answers. The result of these enterprises, though informed by religious motives and residues, was a certain loss of humility preserved even by a scientific historian like Droysen, who, invoking John the Baptist, urged that history was "not 'the light and the truth' but a search therefor, a sermon thereupon, a consecration thereto."[82]

In the twentieth century the philosophy of history became a separate genre, or discipline, which was, in its quasi-theological and quasi-scientific as well as its analytical forms, largely divorced from the practice of historical research and writing. The first two assumed the "unity" of history from a human perspective, while the third disregarded the question of time except as absolute chronological calibration of a field in which to determine the process of cause and effect. None of these approaches really confronted the problematic character of history in terms of the sources that made it accessible, which were taken mainly as a repository of determinable "facts" that could be known and subjected to logical or literary arrangement in the interests of solving a problem or telling a story. It is true that at least since Droysen a hermeneutical tradition was available to historians, but the problems of the interpretation of evidence — the fundamental movement from reading texts or examining artefacts — to formulation were not pursued reflectively, and conjectural historians and philosophers of history were too intent on arranging and manipulating the materials of history derived from the uncritical reading of secondary sources to worry about such epistemological distinctions — or else, like Collingwood, they set these apart from the business of speculation, diagnosis, and prophecy, which in Western tradition represented the main justifications for "self-knowledge." Concerned as it has been with the great questions of the "nature and destiny of man" (in Niebuhr's phrase), the philosophy of history has survived on the margins, the interstices, and largely beyond the sight and tolerance of professional historical inquiry.

At the center of twentieth-century philosophy of history has been the "Vico Renaissance" led by Giorgio Tagliacozzo and spurred by a wealth of new editions, translations, concordances, monographs, conferences, reviews, Web pages, and several periodicals, including *New Vico Studies*, which keeps tabs on the still-growing bibliography.[83] The interest in Vico has been interdisciplinary, although it is the area of historical thought that has attracted most attention. As I noted earlier, "Vico's *New Science* was the end product of a life journey in quest of a full and historical understanding of humanity throughout all its stages from genesis in nature to decline and fall in civil society — a complete 'philosophy of history' in the modern sense of this phrase";[84] and this philosophy has been viewed and criticized from many disciplinary angles — almost as many as Marxism, perhaps, except that in the perspective of the new millennium Vico's posthumous life seems to have outlasted that of Marx.

In a long perspective Marxism may be seen as a leftist, yet quasi-theological form of the philosophy of history, despite its materialist inversions of the conventions of idealism (just as atheism cannot be conceived except within a theocentric framework) and its associations with a revolutionary agenda. Marxism owed its drawing power to its activist claims and to its metahistorical pretensions to be a totalizing philosophy of history, but for historians it also had its methodological uses — their concerns in the twentieth century being rather to extend and to deepen the study of economic and social history and attendant problems than to impose Marxist categories and periodization upon Western historical experience in the name of class consciousness or revolutionary action. In a sense, despite their reception of a view of history "from below" (as Georg Lukács hoped to find in the novel) the position of academic historians was the reverse of the famous eleventh thesis on Feuerbach, for they held that the point for them, in practice at least, was not to change the world but to *interpret* it.[85]

Marxist influence on historical thought was associated, along with economic and cultural historians, geohistorians, and racial theorists, under the general rubric of materialism, which had its own deep tradition, as Karl Kautsky pointed out in his philosophical defense of the doctrine published in 1927.[86] Five years before this Georg Lukács had published an even more orthodox (and party-oriented) defense of dialectical — and of course revolutionary — materialism to resist the rising tide of revisionism, to which historians were prone.[87] The main contributions of Marxism were in the field of grand (and pseudo-scientific) social and economic theory, especially ideas of class conflict, ideology, and the relations between the material base and the superstructure of society; yet the questions provoked by Marx's views had a profound impact on concrete historical research and interpretation, and there is a tremendous bibliography, if now largely defunct (at least in the mainstream) in many languages generated by Marxist scholars, including revisionists, in the twentieth century, especially in Eastern Europe. Britain came late to Marxist theory, but in the twentieth century historians like Christopher Hill, E. P. Thompson, and Eric Hobsbawm made significant contributions to historical inquiry in trying to view historical change "from the bottom up," as did other European historians, such as Georges Lefebvre, Albert Soboul, Georges Rudé, Pierre Vilar, and many scholars of the former East German state. Indeed the best of Marxist scholarship turned away from the macro-theoretical baggage of the Victorian systems, of which Marx's was the most influential, joining life-philosophy as it did with social and political activism — "praxis" — in ways that other philosophies of history could not hope to do.

Marxism drew historical scholars away from their traditional business of interpreting the world. Yet, while historians are normally preoccupied with the immediate problems of research, sometimes they cannot avoid the larger, transcendent questions, that occasionally move humanity on all parts of the political spectrum. The world war which broke out in 1914, declared F. S. Marvin in the very midst of the conflict, was simply "the greatest tragedy in history," and it was to history that one had to appeal for understanding and perhaps remedy.[88] Of course this was not without precedent, for other periods of world crisis and macro-events such as the fall of the Roman Empire, the Protestant Reformation, or the French Revolution had likewise inspired historical reevaluation. Most scholars of all nations agreed with Marvin's characterization, although they took radically different positions on the nature of this understanding. For Marvin and his fellow dons—as well as moderate German defenders of "culture" like Georg Simmel—the question (in part begged) was how to preserve the assumed "unity of Western civilization" in the face of a new barbarism (as Freud regarded it), and in the long run they were still, most of them, inclined to optimism, but at the other intellectual and emotional extreme were authors like Spengler and Theodor Lessing, who, while drawing on the same traditions of learning, took a much darker view. Yet no one seemed to doubt that the early twentieth-century world was in a state of deep "crisis." For many historians after the experience of war it might be academic business as usual, although shifting the focus from political progress to problems of responsibility and guilt; but for more philosophical scholars history "itself" needed reevaluation. This meant not only reviewing old assumptions about unity and progress but also about the intellectual and scientific claims of historical study. Even before the war doubts had been expressed about the "scientific" status of history, but afterwards the criticism was resumed in epistemological as well as political and moral terms.

What sort of knowledge and understanding, or even consolation, could history offer? Not the objective conclusions envisioned by Ranke, Simmel argued in his neo-Kantian study of the problems of the philosophy of history (1892); for the writing of history necessarily involved a subjective element (as indeed had been pointed out a century before Droysen).[89] History dealt not with empirical facts but with mental processes, which, much more than the natural world, were the "subject matter" of the philosophy of history—as Croce and Collingwood would also argue. What a historian could observe was merely external, while the internal meaning had to be established by a kind of human empathy, or "intuitive recreation," which had somehow then to be made objective—although how this could be accomplished Simmel (as Collingwood pointed out) never made clear.[90] Nor did Simmel give up the hope of a "nomological" sort of history in which laws, at least in the form of preliminary or "provisional speculations," could be determined. Indeed it is this line of thought that led him from "content" to form—from the philosophy of history to its systematic and abstract incarnation, which was the discipline of sociology. Like Marvin, Simmel was a champion of the unity of Western civilization, at least in the form of German "culture." Even before the war he saw reasons for pessimism in the "disharmony of modern life," which arose from the eclipsing of spiritual by material culture; and the war itself, which marked "a high-water mark of history" because the disintegration and perversion of cultural life had reached an extreme, seemed to fulfill his historical diagnosis, though he clung to the values associated with the "idea of Europe." For Simmel the crisis revealed and intensified by the international conflict was "the crisis of our own soul." The problem, however, was that spiritual values were personal, while material culture and the "conflict of culture" were in a world beyond the horizons of the individual. This was another reason for shifting from the philosophy of history and its concern for psychology and "mental processes" to sociology, the would-be science of the collective.

Another German thinker who deserves to be counted among the philosophers of history was Karl Mannheim, founder of the sociology of knowledge, and as such often associated with Marxism. Besides his classic treatise on "ideology and utopia," Mannheim took up several essential issues of historical thought, including the questions of "historicism," of "generations," and of "Weltanschauung." For Mannheim history was "the matrix within which man's essential nature is expressed."[91] A key to the coherence of history is the concept of mentality, of *Weltanschauung*, which, Mannheim insisted, following Dilthey, is "not produced by thinking" but is manifested on many levels of "pre-theoretical" culture, especially the artistic (referring to Riegl and Spengler).[92] Moreover, historicism offers the only access to the world of changing values and points of view. Essential to understanding the dynamic patterns of historical change was the concept of "generation," which had come alive in the postwar world but which had a deeper prehistory, including the insights of Hume, Comte, Dilthey, and examples drawn from art history and which was surveyed in the book of F. Mentré on "social generations" (1922).

The sociology of knowledge was, at least in vulgar form, a way of deriving intellectual activities from a social base and so attractive for many unreflective historians seeking a larger vision than mere positivism could offer. Yet the spiritual approach to the philosophy of history persisted, as in the speculations of the conservative philosopher Nicholas Berdyaev, who, driven less by credulity than by a sense of the transcendent character of human existence in a measureless time, sought the "meaning of history" the old-fashioned way, through religious, providential, and even mystical speculation.[93] Berdyaev knew that there could be "no purely objective history," for "History is not an objective empirical datum; it is a myth" — although myth in the sense not of an illusion but rather of a reality of a different order than that of Rankean science. Berdyaev's "interpretation," a product of the "catastrophic" moment of 1914 and its aftermath, stemmed not from Nietzschean insight but from a counter-revolutionary response to the Russian aspect of this catastrophe and a conviction (opposed to the "anti-historical message of the Enlightenment) about the spiritual continuity and "organic reason of history," reinforced by a higher reason and a belief not in secular sciences like economics or sociology but in "the mystery of the 'historical.'" The philosophy of history was "a sort of reversed prophecy" reaching into the future as well as past and concerned less with provenance than with destiny. He deplored the "crisis of humanism" marking the anti-humanist "decadence" of the Renaissance (apparent especially in Renaissance art and its Cubist offspring) and the links to modern socialism and Marxist materialism. Berdyaev deplored, too, the descent, recently traced by Spengler, from healthy "culture" to materialistic, bourgeois, and imperialistic "civilization" and a debased "religion of progress," which was actually a new form of barbarism. This decadence, culminating in the war, signaled a "failure of history," and for Berdyaev the only remedy was a return to the spiritual values of tradition.

A more sensitive and poetic attempt at a philosophy of history, inspired in part also by war experience, was Theodor Lessing's interpretation of history as the act of "giving meaning" to a process that was essentially "meaningless." His views were totally at odds with the assumptions of conventional historians, such as Maurice Powicke, who rejected the speculative views of a champion of historicism, Alois Dempf, who, in his *Sacrum Imperium*, "does not wish to be led [but] wishes to explain." This was the most elementary fallacy according to Powicke's idea of history, which "gives rather than receives."[94] This was exactly the opposite of Lessing's formula, which was that "History does not find meaning in but rather gives meaning to history," and that "History is not life . . . but the realization of the realm of value through humanity."[95] Rejecting the "false starts" both of Descartes and of Vico, Lessing turned rather to the ideas of Husserl and denounced the "mechanical" view of history from Rankean historical science. He also challenged the distinction made by Windelband and Rickert between nature and culture because it violated the unity of human consciousness, though he also invoked Einstein's theory of relativity to indicate the role of the observer — the point of view of the "historical subject" as determining the shape of this world and the idea of non-Euclidean geometry as suggesting the chaotic, non-linear character of historical experience, which had to be subjected to human will in order to receive intelligible form. Lessing's own starting point, a "three-sphere theory of existence" (life, reality, truth), allowed neither for "cultural pessimism" (*Kulturpessimismus*) nor for the idea of unlimited progress, but for a privileged sphere of freedom. For him history was not a science but rather a modern form and descendant of myth, being likewise designed to give human meaning (citing the ancient motto, "man the measure") to an alien world.

Lessing's indulgent pronouncements and the early twentieth-century debate over the nature of history in general were carried on against the background of the old and then renewed distinction between history and nature — historical studies and natural science. For centuries history had been distinguished from philosophy as the particular was distinguished from the general (analogous to the medieval problem of "universals"), but through Dilthey, Windelband, Rickert, Troeltsch, and others the distinction was reframed as the separation between natural science (*Naturwissenschaften*) and the cultural, or spiritual, sciences (*Kulturwissenschaften, Geisteswissenschaften*), the second being defined by its concern with the human point of view and values and thus being (in Windelband's terms) "idiographic" rather than "nomothetic." Dilthey in particular was a key figure in the turn, or return, of philosophy to history, as he devoted his life to the unfinished Kantian project (the analysis of pure, practical, and aesthetic reason) with a fourth installment, namely, a "critique of historical reason," or historical critique of reason. The results of this methodological debate included not only a foundation for the conceptual autonomy of history but also a larger space for the alliance between history and the other human sciences.

Like its conjectural forebears, philosophical history in the early twentieth century was fascinated by the question of periodization, especially in the effort to make history more of a science on the analogy of sociology. This was the project, for example, of the cultural historian Kurt Breysig, who sought, following a comparative method, to establish not only "stages" (like Condorcet's "epochs") but also historical "laws" (like Comte).[96] Like Simmel and Alfred Weber, he applied general categories to historical analysis, which he pursued in evolutionary terms, and virtually identified the philosophy of history with sociology. In dozens of books and articles German scholars like Breysig sought to identify the ages of humanity, the generations, and the rhythms, regularities, and even cycles of the historical process as the basis for a definitive philosophy of history and also for projecting this analysis into the future.[97] In other words the philosophy of history expanded not only in cultural content, in geographical and temporal depth and in aspirations for scientific and systematic structure but also in prophetic and even theological ambitions, harking back to its religious and Augustinian origins.

This is also the context in which the debate over historicism and its own "crisis" was carried on in the postwar years. Here the key work was Ernst Troeltsch's *Historicism and Its Problems* (1922), written in part during that "world catastrophe" that provoked, or exacerbated, the post-Rankean "contemporary crisis of history" (*heutige Krisis der Historie*).[98] From the standpoint of history and philosophy of religion Troeltsch traced the division between "the two great scientific creations of the modern world," naturalism and historicism, and with them the philosophy of nature and the philosophy of history, back to the seventeenth-century opposition between the new science on which Descartes built his philosophy and the newer "new science" of Vico, which Croce also associated with modern historicism. In such terms Troeltsch surveyed the intellectual history of Europe and questions of objectivity, individuality, value, and other European doctrines, including those of Marxism and positivism, and concluded with a critical review of cultural history in a stage of deep crisis and a general periodization of world history.

The question of historicism lay at the center of the philosophy, and besides Troeltsch and his interlocutors, Croce was perhaps the most radical commentator, going so far, indeed, as to identify philosophy with "absolute historicism." Having served his apprenticeship as a historian of Italy, and later of Europe, Croce prepared the way for his philosophical system with studies of Hegel (1906) and Vico (1911) and then, relying for details on the historiographical handbook, unphilosophical as it lamentably was, by Eduard Fueter, of the theory and practice of history more generally — which he followed up, many years later, with his study of "history as the story of liberty."[99] As the subtitle of his book on Hegel suggested, what concerned Croce was "what was living" rather than "what was dead" in earlier authors; and he summed this up in the in many ways conventional and "presentist" insight that all history, since it was conceptualized and formulated after the facts, or residue of the facts, was contemporary, "living" history: not "what really happened," as it were, but "what really matters."

Following the old *ars historica* tradition while at the same time claiming new insights, Croce took up a series of conventional issues: the difference between history and chronicle (the former being the contemporary and "living" incarnation of the first), the role of "philology" (for Croce representing the fetishism of a dead past), the possibility of a systematic, or "universal," systematic history (a Rankean project beyond our comprehension), the "philosophy of history" (a contradiction in terms, since history and philosophy were not separate genres, not form and content, but were fused in Croce's "historicism"), methodological doubt (which rejected pseudo-scientific determinism), the idea of progress (false in its moralistic, from "good" to "bad," form), the human value of history (which is concrete and resists philosophical abstraction and social theory), periodization (varying with contemporary points of view), the divisions of history (special histories, including biography, disciplinary histories, and "philosophies of history"), and finally the history of historiography (an offshoot of the "art of history" going back to Italian and French treatises, such as those of Bodin and Patrizzi) — all of which Croce traced, and in his idealist fashion, though going beyond "the abstractness of Hegel," made present, from the Greeks and the Romans down to the "new historiography" of Meinecke and other contemporaries.

Another example, though more remote from historical practice, is Henri Bergson, whose "creative evolution" represented a sort of idealization of life patterns, establishing a principle of "harmony" behind and not in front of human experience and dissolving the philosophy of history in speculations about the nature of time and of biological nature.[100] In fact Bergson's concerns with history as such were tenuous to an extreme, as he moved directly to the intuitive analysis of inner experience, offering not a "philosophy of history" but rather a "philosophy of life," though in a more general sense than the *Lebensphilosophie* of Dilthey and his followers, after the model not of culture but of individual psychology and evolution, which were conceived in a spiritualist fashion. For Bergson the interest of history was not as a record of human actions but rather as a spiritual realm of memory and free will and a dimension of time existing apart from calendars and human records.

The most common, grossest expression of the philosophy of history was the many-sided idea of progress, which had ancient and medieval roots but which was tied to the processes of economic expansion and secularization. Reviewing the Enlightenment background and the contributions of sociology, Christopher Dawson emphasized the spiritual aspects of the idea which had been lost in modern secularism, when progress had become a sort of surrogate religion and then went into decline.[101] He argued that culture needed a religious as well as a material base and that it was essential to return to the established traditions, culminating in the medieval "unity" overseen by the Catholic Church, which was involved in the original "making of Europe" before humanism and material values reversed the development. Dawson joined his philosophy to Catholic apologetics and a Eurocentric vision; but secular-minded scholars like Robert Nisbet, and J. B. Bury before him, told much the same story without holding out the hope of restoring the old verities in the wake of twentieth-century crises. A still more speculative view, though grounded in scientific knowledge, is the bio-theological extrapolations of Pierre Teilhard de Chardin, who combined the sciences of life and death — paleontology — in his metahistorical conception of the "phenomenon of man," although the process of history was subsumed in a grandiose vision of spiritual evolution that accommodated not only culture but also religion and "universal love."

One of the most ambitious philosophies of history was that fashioned by the Viennese political theorist Eric Voegelin, who taught in England, France, and the United States and from the 1920s published scores of reviews, essays, and lectures on the history of political thought before launching, in 1956, into his five-volume treatise *Order and History*, beginning with Israel, and designed to improve on Spengler, Toynbee, and perhaps the Bible,. He offered a penetrating critique of the dominant ideologies of Nazism, Communism, and racism as modern expressions of "Gnosticism," which for him meant a "dream reality" pursued through pseudo-scientific theory and forcible implementation. "The Gnostics have to speak about it," Voegelin wrote of this dream reality, "as if they have experience of it; and they have to act as if they were capable of bringing it about."[102] The result of such groundless self-confidence was terrible destruction as well as misguided ideas of what history was actually about (not only from the extremes of left and right but also from high-minded champions of "Man" like Erich Kahler, who, after as well as before the second war, held out the holistic hope of "gaining control" of the world through science).[103] Yet Voegelin himself was no skeptic and constructed a vision of a humanity (recalling but claiming to transcend those of Augustine and the Enlightenment) seeking self-understanding and unity through philosophy, which is not gnosis but diagnosis and remedy — that is, "order." He also addressed the old question, "What is History?" and pointed out that modern views that history does not exist except through subjective interpretation can be seen as a revival of old notions of atheism (the gods do not exist, or anyway do not care about men, or can be propitiated by gifts) or pyrrhonism (nothing exists, or anyway is not comprehensible, and certainly not communicable) and are of little use in the endless project of understanding the human condition.[104] Although Voegelin died in 1985, his disciples have kept his teaching alive with a massive program of publishing and commenting on all of his writings.

The culmination of the old philosophy of history came in the work of R. G. Collingwood, whose posthumously published *Idea of History*, deeply indebted to Croce, especially his *History, Its Theory and Practice*, presented a conventional system of historical thought and at the same time reviewed the whole Western tradition in a hybrid, interpretive survey that included not only the mythical, Herodoto-Thucydidean origins of historical writing and the Christian, Renaissance, Enlightenment, Romantic, positivist, and "scientific" extensions and the contributions of Vico and Herder, but also the major figures in the philosophical canon, including Descartes, Kant, Hegel, and Marx, as well as modern thinkers, including Windelband, Rickert, Simmel, Dilthey, Meyer, Spengler, and especially Croce, sharing with the moderns the conviction of a fundamental difference between historical and scientific knowledge.[105] Like Croce, Collingwood took the purpose of history to be not "pragmatic" political insight but a form of self-understanding, arising from the fact that history is not a natural process but an "imaginative re-enactment of past experience."[106] For Collingwood, Vico and Herder were the first to glimpse this insight, and neo-Kantians like Windelband, Rickert, and Dilthey went further, with Croce supplying the link with Collingwood's own philosophy of history and its potential to help solve the world's problems.

The most famous effort of the philosophy of history after the old pattern was surely Arnold Toynbee's *Study of History*, which was conceived of vaguely before the war, acquired shape in the 1920s, and began to appear in 1930. Toynbee's "nonsense book," as he called it, drew inspiration not only from Thucydides and other classical sources but also from Toynbee's own war experience (as journalist and propagandist, for to his embarrassment he never saw active service), from his reading of countless books, such as that by F. J. Teggart, and especially from the intellectual shock he received from reading Spengler's *Decline of the West*, which Lewis Namier lent him in 1920. Toynbee designed his book as a comparative study of the civilizations recognized by Spengler and others. No less than Spengler, he had recourse to such "poetic inventions" (as William McNeill has called them) as "challenge and response," "withdrawal and return," "internal and external proletariat," "mimesis," and others. Toynbee's monumental series generated even more publicity than Spengler's had done and was treated with much the same condescension, or even scorn, that his German predecessor had received. Yet in many ways these two dinosaurs remain the standard for the controversial, bombastic, antiquated, sometimes self-righteous, and much maligned genre which, relying on the published efforts of historical inquiry, has presumed to assimilate the whole range of human experience in time and to reduce this to intelligible and explicable patterns and trajectories perhaps extrapolatable into the future.

There is one other attempt to think philosophically about history and also to respond to the globalizing impulse of modern historiography, and that is Karl Jaspers's notion of an "axial age," roughly the first millennium B.C., which involved (as with Toynbee) several of major civilizations or religions — Greece, Israel, Christianity, Zoroastrian Iran, Imperial China, Hinduism, Buddhism, and later, perhaps, Islam, and which featured a "revolution of ideas" as well as attempts to reorder the world.[107] This conception privileges philosophy, emphasizing the emergence of an intellectual (that is a clerical, priestly, and prophetic) elite and a vision of transcendence beyond the tasks of coping with a material world. With this elevation to a spiritual level came new forms of political organization and internal tensions. In a drive to a transcendent, and in some cases monotheistic view of the world, these civilizations also produced "great traditions" and visions of self-centered history which helped shaped the common historiographical practices, conventional philosophy of history, and secular but still idealistic concepts of social organization and change in a post-Hegelian, proto-Whiggish, crypto-Marxist, though religious mode.

Prophets of Decline

Incredibly different as these philosophies of history may appear, they were for the most part celebratory and triumphalist — "Whiggish" — preferring long-term hope over short-term disappointment and disillusion; but other scholars and speculators had more skeptical views about the direction of change in the modern world and more generally about the inadequacy of historical study for the purposes of life. Among the most radical and eccentric of these critics was perhaps Max Nordau, notorious prophet of "degeneration," that black death of the intellect. As for the philosophy of history, Nordau pointed out its remote origins (the term itself being derived not from Voltaire's ostensible coinage but from Bodin's characterization of Philo Judaeus as "philosophistoricus") and its continuing theological basis. Nordau rejected the views of writers like Simmel, who had the arrogance to argue that history was only the representation of historians; and he dismissed the pretensions of most of the great nineteenth-century historians, especially interpreters of contemporary history like Trietschke, Sybel, Thiers, Blanc, and Hanotaux. For Nordau history was something quite beyond historiographical grasp, as inaccessible as Kant's *Ding an sich*, and so the philosophy of history was not science but theology or myth.[108] No more persuasive to him than the providentialist philosophers of history from Augustine to Bossuet to Vico and Hegel were the humanistic "naturalistic-materialistic" varieties of metaphysical speculation and naive theories of progress. Moreover, historical memory was evanescent, extending over no more than three generations, and in any case written history was always in the service of the ruling elite and designed for the subjection of the lower classes (though Nordau had little use for Marxist simplifications). Nor again was Nordau impressed with the turn to sociology, which had been urged by Paul Barth in 1897, or indeed the claims of social psychology.[109] For him only the individual was "real," and the road to historical understanding was the study of "fundamental instincts" within the assumptions of human evolution. The philosophy of history was an expression of degenerate hubris, "the sign of ill-humour or weakness, sickness or old age," and the search for higher meaning in history than as a "life-force" was hopeless.[110]

Sigmund Freud took a dim view, too, of Western ideas of progress, especially in the face of the Great War which brought disillusionment, a new appreciation of death, and confirmation of his own notions of the destructive potential of the unconscious dimensions of human nature. The hopes inspired by the "white nations" of an international union were dashed, as xenophobia broke out in a new and virulent form and showed that "the primitive mind is, in the fullest meaning of the word, imperishable." The human species cannot escape from its deepest, that is, biological, history. The historical lesson drawn by Freud from the global experience of war was not only for nations, that if they hoped for peace, to prepare for war, but for humans more generally, that, if they would endure life, to prepare for death. Like Enlightenment historians Freud offered insights about "civilization and its discontents" that were always projected from ideas of human psychology, but with a very different view of the origin, course, and direction of the life of humanity — denying his ability to see the future and leaving open the question as to whether humanity could overcome its instincts of aggression and self-destruction which had so far, from a psychoanalytical standpoint, dominated the course of European history. Yet Freud was himself only peripherally a philosopher of history, and his greatest influence was in the arena of individual experience and subconscious and in psychohistorical extrapolations from his conjectural depth psychology.

Oswald Spengler, though he looked more to the humanities — to poetry, art, music, and mathematics — than to natural science for his theories, was less willing to assume the role of prophet or micro-historical mind-reader except on the speculative level of humanity. The second Moroccan crisis and Otto Seeck's history of the decline of the ancient world started Spengler on his speculations about the coming of the war and the larger human trajectory of which it was a small part. *The Decline of the West* was published in 1918, the year of Germany's defeat. Influenced by Goethe and Bergson as well as Nietzsche, the book was more than a comparative history of world culture and indeed more than a philosophy of history; it was a "philosophy of the future." Spengler claimed to make a shift from the parochial or "Ptolemaic" — Eurocentric — to a Copernican or universal point of view. Like Vico he sought to follow the "morphology," the homologous life cycles, of the eight major civilizations — Egyptian, Chinese, Semitic, Indian, Mexican, Greco-Roman, or "Apollonian," late Roman, including Jewish and Arabic as well as Christian, and European, or "Faustian" — in terms of a synthetic view of all aspects of culture, and in his later years he expanded his horizons by turning to the study of prehistory. Like Freud, Spengler was pessimistic about the future of the

West and saw further decline—and wars—in the future. His work, though seldom taken seriously by professional scholars, was a storm-center of controversy among intellectuals who regarded prophecy as a legitimate function of historical inquiry.

Among Spengler's followers was the popular historian Egon Friedell, who adopted the mode of Lamprechtian cultural history as well as Spenglerian pseudo-prophetic history. Friedell's main inspiration, however, was Nietzsche, who "left the earth trembling" and heralded the new age.[111] For Friedell imagination was the motor of history, referring to artists like himself but also to movers like Bismarck; but in his own century Friedell saw the excess of this view, including not only the "decline of logic" but also the "collapse of reality" and the "suicide of art." He broke off his unfinished work with a suggestion that this reality was represented not only by the Kantian *Ding an sich* but also by the Freudian "It" (*sic*), both beyond time and space and beyond the collapsing reality of his age. Like Spengler, Friedell saw a possible light only in the coming age, into which his ranting survey did not extend.

Another German writer deeply affected by the war, in which he indeed served proudly and even passionately, was Carl Schmitt. Among his many works *The Concept of the Political* (1932) took as its target the fundamental unity of modern historical inquiry, the sovereign state, as a way of defining political relations. For Schmitt the "political" was not to be understood in merely juridical or institutional terms, for it was to be opposed (as Burckhardt and in a way Machiavelli had done) to the religious, cultural, economic, legal, and religious spheres. The "political" was to be defined through the "friend-enemy antithesis," the opposition (in a public, not private sense) between friend and enemy, that is, the foreigner, or the "other." It was not Schmitt's intention to glorify war—at least in this theoretical context—and yet he did regard war as an unavoidable part of history, as an institution and not an aberration; and he rejected the notion of an end to the state either through pacifism, the "pluralism" of Cole, Laski, Figgis, and other British theorists, or a League of Nations—not to speak of radical revolution. "A world in which the possibility of war is utterly eliminated, a completely pacified globe," he wrote, "would be a world without the distinction of friend and enemy and hence a world without politics."[112] Schmitt did not predict war in particular, but he naturalized—or historicized—it in general; and his line of argument led him, along with Spengler, to a part in what critics called a "conservative revolution," which converged with the parallel but differently motivated movement of National Socialism.

José Ortega y Gasset was more positive about the human condition and the value of what he called "historical reason" but not much more sanguine about the direction of history. Ortega turned to the philosophy of history as early as 1910, when he "almost drowned in German science."[113] He regarded himself as a herald of a new generation in Spain, the generation not of 1898 but of 1914, positioned on the "edge of history" and of modernity. He was widely read in classic European historiography, as historians in turn were influenced by his work; but his interests remained conjectural, speculative, and synthetic. For him history was "the *systematic* exposition of events or conditions past," given unity through ties to the times and concerns of generations past. Ortega translated the works of Hegel and Spengler and in general remained in the tradition of such philosophers of history, including Dilthey, Simmel, Rickert, Breysig, and Scheler, but also Comte and Vico (via Croce) and later Johan Huizinga, Wells, and Toynbee.

Among the "historiological" ideas developed by Ortega, sometimes originally, were "perspectivism," "generations" (analyzed also by Karl Mannheim), "crisis" (associated with Husserl and Paul Hazard), "point of view," and "modernization." Like Dilthey, Ortega carried on the pursuit of "historical reason"; like Croce, he took a historical and "historicist" (and "historiological") turn in his pursuit of life philosophy, and he concluded that "Man *is* not; he 'goes on being' this and that," and more famously, that "Man, in a word, has no nature; what he has is . . . history."[114] What Ortega celebrated was "life philosophy," the idea of "vital reason," centered on a Heideggerian "I and my circumstances," and a humanistic culture threatened by "the revolt of the masses," which left Europe "without a moral code." Unlike Spengler and others, however, he stopped short of specific prophecies, concluding that "the life of the world has become scandalously provisional."[115]

In 1935 Huizinga gave a series of lectures, invoking Spengler's work as a sign, if not a proper analysis, which agree with his own reflections on the condition of humanity in a "demented age" and "in the shadow of tomorrow." The current "crisis" (which Huizinga realized was a medical metaphor) was not unique — he compared it to the state of Europe before the Reformation and after the French Revolution, but he could not help wondering if the road ahead was not like that of Rome in its decline. Like Ortega, Huizinga deplored the loss of standards of critical judgment accompanying the rise of mass civilization: "the brakes of criticism are slipping."[116] Not that he placed faith in the old rules of "tyrannically consistent rationalism" and the misuses which it produced, but he did lament the current (in part "existential") inclination to set "life" above reason, blood above spirit, will above knowledge, and being above knowing.[117] "Life is battle," he acknowledged, but he disagreed with Carl Schmitt that history should be defined as a drama dominated by friends and enemies, with Freud that human nature should be defined in terms of its lowest, most infantile manifestations ("puerilism"), with Mannheim and Meinecke about their favorable view of reason of state, and with Spengler about the inevitability of war.[118] Like Burckhardt, Huizinga celebrated the culture of "old Europe," lamenting its passing but refusing to surrender to pessimism: "History can predict nothing," he admitted , but still, he protested, "I am an optimist"—invoking, as did so many others, the promise of a new generation.

None of these thinkers, except to some extent Spengler, was really a historian, but they all took world history as their "intelligible field of study" (Toynbee's phrase). They did not try to transcend it (like Kant) or to rationalize it (like Hegel), yet they also did not take it as an object of naive positivist inquiry into the facts. In various ways they tried to accommodate it, as did Heidegger, Troeltsch, Croce, and others, who wanted to assimilate the ideal to the real (though in a very different way than Hegel's), to command a full view of, if not to master, the flow of history, and in this way to approach a prophetic understanding as far as personal experience, knowledge, reason, imagination, and the limits of their twentieth-century horizons would permit.

Of course the philosophy of history drew protests from many sides—not only those of religion and of skeptics but also of Marxist defenders of old-fashioned rationality, who all objected to the indulgent speculations that seemed no more than expressions of ideology in a decadent and confused age. The most extensive indictment came from the great Marxist theorist—and anti-theorist—Georg Lukács, whose *Destruction of Reason* rejected the whole canon of "irrationalism," which for him began with Schelling and included, among others, Nietzsche, Dilthey, Simmel, Tönnies, both Webers, Mannheim, Schmitt, Spengler, Scheler, Jaspers, Heidegger, and a number of sociological, racialist, and fascist theorists, all of them conspiring to produce National Socialism. To this dishonor roll Lukács added the names of Wittgenstein, Sartre, Camus, Kafka, and other champions of the absurd and of "life-philosophy" and ideologues of modern (American) imperialism, direct or indirect supporters of Hitlerism. Here indeed was a panoramic view of decline to set beside that of Spengler's more "primitive" speculations. Yet both Lukács and Spengler were caught in the same obsession with the philosophy of history associated with historicism and modern priests of progress.

Even more negative, perhaps, were the old-fashioned positivists and empiricists who denied the possibility of a "philosophy of history"—or indeed who did not regard the question as worth thinking about. An extreme example was C. V. Wedgwood, who was a master narrator but who did not think that "the historian, like the old fashion writer for the young, [must] for ever be pointing out the lesson as well as telling the story." Not that she questioned the "existence" of history, for the stone moved by Doctor Johnson's foot was enough to dispose of such nonsense; but following the suggestion of Trevelyan, she did not think it constituted more than a field for the narrative art. Creative writers had too much respect for the intelligence of their readers to make this mistake; and admirer of Gibbon as she was, Wedgwood herself was content to pursue the classical — vulgar Herodotean or vulgar Rankean — line of historiographical inquiry leading "towards that always retreating horizon where truth and opinion meet."[119] In her volumes on Charles I before and during the Puritan Revolution she described events "as far as possible in the order in which they happened" for that age of the "great rebellion," "deliberately avoiding analysis and seeking rather to give an impression of its vigorous and vivid confusion."[120] Meanings there perhaps were, but they were to be determined not by a sovereign author or by a self-proclaimed critic but by an educated, or at least educable, public. But this attitude was in its own way also a "philosophy of history": as Carl Becker put it in 1931, "Everyman his own historian."[121]

Where does Marxism belong on this map of the modern philosophy of history? In fact the reason for Marxism's success was its status not as a science but as a religion, as Joseph Schumpeter argued, and indeed authors like Georg Lukács and Antonio Gramsci struggled to preserve the orthodoxy of the doctrine against revisionist and counter-revolutionary critics. For historians in the West, however, it was more for the questions it asked about the human condition than for the doctrinal answers or cures it offered.[122] After the First World War Marxism, though centered in political activism and later attached to the Communist Party and the Soviet sphere of power, infiltrated not only the social sciences, where it stirred up or exacerbated a variety of theoretical debates, but also academic history. Although it acted more often as an incitement to research than as a doctrinal commitment, nevertheless, Marxist, or quasi-Marxist, or Revisionist influence helped to shape historical interpretation through a number of key concepts, that is, terms, of orthodox Marxist theory, including historical materialism, capitalism, class conflict, social revolution, bourgeois revolution, dialectic, hegemony. Authors like Lukács and Gramsci wrote to adapt Marx's ideas and methods to modern conditions, and their views, however irrelevant to historical inquiry, reinforce the place of Marxism in the tradition of philosophy — whether seen as a doctrine of decline, through its critique of capitalism and (via Leninist extension) imperialism, or progressivist, through its revolutionary eschatology, though this has proved detachable in revisionist perspective. Yet Marxism lives, either as absorbed into social thought or in renewed forms that have not lost the belief in the predictive or therapeutic power of conjectural history and its allies among the human sciences. At the very least its ghost haunts the more materialist forms of cultural history, at least for those whose memories extend back before the "end of history," which some have hyperbolically and pseudo-apocalyptically dated to 1989, which has replaced 1984 as the pivotal (if not terminal) date for metahistorians.[123]

After the Great War

Each torpid turn of the world has such disinherited ones, to whom neither the past belongs, nor yet what has nearly arrived.

— *Rainer Maria Rilke*

Germany after the Catastrophe

The Great War taught humanity to revise its vision of the past. In his fascination with the patterns and cycles of time, T. S. Eliot drew attention to

The backward look behind the assurance
Of recorded history, the backward half-look
Over the shoulder, toward the primitive terror.[1]

The dream of Enlightenment was tempered by the "nightmare of history." So Freud turned from the pleasure principle to the death instinct, with *eros* being joined by *thanatos* in a fuller conception of culture in the continuum of time — and "in the shadow of tomorrow."

After 1914 was it still possible, beyond such poetic and intellectualist gestures, to learn from history? Some philosophers thought so. As Karl Jaspers admitted in 1932, "what is really happening eludes us," and yet he held out hope for "what mankind can become." José Ortega y Gasset had forebodings about "all these multitudes which nowadays fill to overflowing the stage of history," and yet he did not altogether give up on the process of history, with certain provisions. "There is no hope for Europe," he wrote, "unless its destiny is placed in the hands of men really 'contemporaneous,' men who feel palpitating beneath them the whole subsoil of history, who realize the present level of existence, and abhor every archaic and primitive attitude. We have need of history in its entirety, not to fall back into it, but to see if we can escape from it."[2] Finishing his philosophical studies and military service, the young Martin Heidegger turned from his Catholic faith to phenomenology, a nonpolitical acceptance of postwar existence, and whatever the future held for his generation.[3]

But what was historical perspective on the postwar period? How to account for what was (at least from the standpoint of the generation of 1914) the greatest tragedy in European memory? The short answer was given in 1919 by the victors in the Treaty of Versailles—signed 23 June 1919, "the day of Germany's deepest humiliation," said Hans Delbrück—which was to look for human agency and therefore responsibility and guilt, the culprits being the Central Powers and Germany and its allies.[4] Such had been the judgment of propagandists during the war, such the judgment of the politicians and lawyers who drafted the treaty, and such the starting point of later historians, who continued at first mainly to seek archival evidence to prove or to disprove these charges. French, English, and American historians carried on the same sort of debates with the Germans as they had done during the war—at least until the "revisionists" turned the arguments around, on the basis not so much of new evidence in the "secret documents" as of different political and in effect pacifist values. Increasingly, too, economic, social, and financial (if not cultural) factors were admitted into the analysis. Thus in 1924 Erich Brandenburg published his history of German foreign policy from 1870 to 1914, writing "often with anguish of heart" but denying "the warlike aims of German foreign policy"; and in 1927 Pierre Renouvin, "professor of the history of the Great War" at the University of Paris, published his study of the immediate origins of the war, claiming to set aside "all preconceived ideas," deploring the "spirit of war" among scholars and the equally extreme propaganda of revisionists like Harry Elmer Barnes and yet asserting that "Germany has steadily rebelled against the world."[5] The war-guilt debate (*Kriegschuldfrage*) has continued voluminously for three generations, whether or not tinged with national prejudice, and it merged later with the connected question of the origins of the second—and, though derivative, even "greater"—world war, which in retrospect added up to a "Thirty-One Years War."

The Great War marked a break in the lives and professional careers of German historians, but even more remarkable in a general way were the continuities from the old to the new Reich — and indeed from the period of the Wars of Liberation, with Heyne, Wolf, Heeren, Schlözer, Luden, Schlosser, Wachler, and their students. Wolfgang Weber has traced the genealogies of dozens of academic descendants of Ranke, Droysen, Treitschke, Mommsen, and other scholars over several generations.[6] In Ranke's case there were five generations of students (*Enkelschüler*), beginning with Waitz, Sybel, Schäfer, Oncken (Delbrück, Lamprecht, Brandenburg, and Goetz), G. Ritter (Brackmann, Grundmann, Stadelmann, and Tellenbach), and Nürnberger, down to the late Thomas Nipperdey, who was likewise a master interpreter of modern German history, while for Droysen it was (among others) Hintze, Conze, and Wolfgang Mommsen. In the 1930s some opponents of the regime fled into exile or were replaced, though others remained in place or advanced, according to their service, and in 1945 supporters of Nazism also lost their positions, at least temporarily; but even so the patterns of historical research and interpretation, despite revolutionary turns of events and efforts of criticism, innovation and "revision," followed the paths charted by the founding fathers of German *Historik, Geschichtswissenschaft,* and *Geschichtsphilosophie.*

In many ways the patterns of historiography, though marked by intramural quarrels, mirrored national politics, policies, and imperial expansion; and the writing of national history continued along familiar lines. In November 1918 the jurist and constitutional historian Fritz Hartung, even before being demobilized from service in eastern France, began writing his history, beginning with the founding of the German Empire and ending with the historically and diplomatically "unheard-of" peace conditions, which rendered Germany helpless and represented a "Celtic peace, whose slogan was 'Vae victus.'"[7] The mood of German historians in 1919 was generally bitter, and they found targets for their frustration besides the punitive Treaty of Versailles, including the continued imperialism of their former enemies, the Bolshevik threat in the East, the radical revolution in German cities, and, for some, the unwelcome imposition of an unnatural parliamentary democracy. Yet they also held out the hope of a rejuvenated German *Volk,* a restored empire, and a continued, though peaceful, expansion.

The war left the judgment of historians impaired in many ways, even as they maintained the old fiction that it was not the historian's business to pass judgments. The one thing in common among historians of all national persuasions was the insistence on privileging political, diplomatic, and military policies, decisions, and events in explaining the "causes" of the war and of historical processes more generally. This fascination with questions of power politics can be seen in the articles of Willy Andreas on Venetian diplomacy in the Renaissance, which for him, following Ranke, marked the beginning of the modern world (and not Renaissance culture, as Burckhardt suggested, or the Reformation, as Troeltsch argued), and in Meinecke's study of reason of state, which arose in this same period, as Andreas also believed.[8] In this context, too, arose that concept, or pose of "objectivity," which inspired Ranke as he was working on this very material. The concern with unrestrained power can be seen also in the many surveys of the German Reich which continued to be produced during and after the war, including those of Brandenburg (1916), Brandi (1919), Hartung (1920), Haller (1922), and Marcks (1936, begun in 1920), who also published a series of articles on England's power politics (*Machtpolitik*), starting in 1903 and collected in a publication edited by Andreas in 1940. In these and other writings by professional historians holding university chairs and working on and publishing archival sources Ranke's spirit prevailed and his words were often invoked.

There was little opposition to this archaic and inertial trend, the more so because the cultural history associated with Lamprecht (who died in 1916) was largely discredited, although some *Kulturhistoriker* continued to ply their trade, especially in the form of *Volksgeschichte*.[9] One exception was the brilliant young historian Eckhart Kehr, whom Gordon Craig has called the "father of German revisionism." In 1926 Kehr, under the influence of Marx, Weber, and Charles Beard (for his economic interpretation of the American constitution), submitted a startling thesis on "battleship building and party politics 1884–1901" and a number of articles published later under the rubric of "the primacy of inner *politics*" — in contrast to the focus on "outer" (*äuser*) politics — which attended to economic interests, the financiers, bureaucrats, and the military establishment.[10] Kehr also criticized traditional German historiography, including not only Treitschke and Ranke but also Delbrück, Lenz, Marcks, and even Hintze, for unreflective devotion to the unholy alliance of the bourgeoisie and the officer corps. Graduate students of his generation, Kehr complained, were still writing their theses on foreign rather than domestic affairs — and as Thomas Mann remarked, " 'Intellect and power,' this is nothing more than '*domestic policy and foreign affairs*.' "[11] Lamprecht had been one exception to this convention, as was Gustav Schmoller, though too conservative for Kehr's tastes, and Meinecke, though too old-fashioned in his vacillation between ideas and power. Kehr saw himself, according to his friend Felix Gilbert, "as the leader of a new historical school"; but his subversive but unfortunately timed work was ignored during the Nazi period and only revived after the Second World War.[12]

It should be noted that an alternative to political history was offered by the sub-discipline of economic history, whose roots (setting aside the Marxist tradition) can be traced back to the "old" and "young" historical schools of political economy of the nineteenth century. For historians the works of Schmoller (1917), leader of the *Verein für Sozialpolitik*, and Werner Sombart (1941), which reflected an economic sort of "historicism" opposed to the liberal school, were of particular importance. Besides monographic research they sought larger syntheses of Western history based on economic factors, illustrated especially by Sombart's *Modern Capitalism* (1915), which Schumpeter called "*histoire raisonné*, with the accent on the reasoning."[13] As Max Weber had associated the capitalist spirit with Protestantism, so, much less successfully, did Sombart with the Jews. Although Weber criticized the theoretical excesses and methodological inadequacies of Schmoller, he also indulged in his own conjectural economic history.[14] In his *General Economic History*, which originated as lectures given in Berlin in 1919–20, Weber sketched a very derivative conjectural history of the Western economy from primitive origins, including the idea of primitive communism suggested in the previous century by Maurer and Hanssen, through feudal society and the development of private property to modern industrial, commercial, and financial capitalism, now detached from its religious roots, and the role of the secular state — and of course of modern war.

From 1918 on German historiography was agonized or even apologetic, yet reluctant to surrender old assumptions about national unity — the coherent *Volk* under a powerful sovereign *Staat*. Within this tradition differences still existed between *grossdeutsch* and *kleindeutsch* ideals, which had long divided historians, including medieval historians of the Catholic Empire, going back to the debates between Sybel and Ficker.[15] In 1924 Karl Brandi celebrated the new direction being taken by a *grossdeutsch* ideal, but the old Austrian conception remained in play.[16] Debates continued over the expansionist policies of the medieval emperors to the east but especially to the south, where the Italian dream, according to some nationalist critics, distracted the Hohenstaufens from their German mission. Others disagreed: "Austria-Hungary Awake!" was a cry that went up during the war in pamphlets and papers promoting a new design for Europe including domination of Mitteleuropa, and in the 1930s Srbik, in his four-volume study of "German unity," proposed a similar plan, judged by many critics to be utopian, based on a Catholic Austro-German empire. Because of such issues, nostalgia for Bismarck's Empire and the earlier "thousand-year Reich," medieval history continued to be a vital and controversial field of study, especially because of the problematic Franco-German roots of the first — the "holy Roman" — Empire of the German nation, as it was retrospectively called from the fifteenth century and not only projected back to Charles/Carlos I/Karl V but carried forward constitutionally through the Habsburgs until its dissolution by Napoleon in 1806. The "battle of the Middle Ages" and the search for a viable national past was intensified in the wake of the war, when German decline provoked dreams of the old Reich and a possible successor, as expressed in many books published in that trans-war generation.[17] From the eleventh grade, according to E. R. Curtius, many hours of European medieval history, including the "inner life and intellectual development of Germany," were imposed on students in the Weimar period.[18] Among scholars one center of controversy was the sensational biography of the Emperor Frederick II , by Ernst Kantorowicz, who studied with Emil Gothein, Karl Hampe, and Alfred Weber and who took a doctorate but did not pursue a professional career until much later. Kantorowicz's more direct inspiration came from the Stefan George circle — more like a spider's web — of which he was a member, and perhaps from Friedrich Gundolf's biography of Caesar (1924).[19] By the 1920s George, the "Master" (and *Führer*) to his disciples, had become the towering intellectual figure in Germany not only as poet but also as priest and prophet; and while he was contemptuous of the academic establishment in general, a number of scholars fell under his sway, including the cultural historians Gothein and Breysig as well as Kantorowicz and Gundolf, great admirer of the salvational power of war. George's ideal of a sacred or "secret Germany" permeated the spiritual atmosphere in which the search for a general pattern in Germany history was pursued, though it should be added that George was an enthusiastic anti-Prussianist and leaned toward the Austrian-imperial (*grossdeutsch*) view of the German past, along with its pessimistic view of German destiny. A less tangible aspect of George's extraordinary influence (with its ostensible but ambiguous Nazi ties) was his poetic and Nietzschean idea that it was the will of the artist — and by analogy the historian — that created, shaped, and ruled the world.[20]

In contributing to George's megalomaniacal mission Kantorowicz turned away from the Rankean view of history to myth and contemporary involvement — not only literary artistry but also a political and prophetic vision of a "secret Germany," or "secret Reich" — and offered a highly interpretive and stylized portrait of the ruler called "wonder of the world" (*Stupor Mundi*), which not only conjured up a heroic past but also, somehow, suggested solutions to problems of that day. The Emperor Frederick II seemed to fulfill the prophecies of Joachim of Flora as well as Vergil, and for Kantorowicz he "had his fulfillment, in the greatest vassal of the Empire, the aged Bismarck."[21] Kantorowicz displayed romantic indulgences which drew criticism even from conservative historians like Albert Brackmann (in the *Historische Zeitschrift*, which he coedited with Meinecke), Herbert Grundmann, and Karl Hampe (who had himself published a work on the image and afterlife of Frederick II);

and a later volume of texts, ostentatious scholarly annotations, and *Anmer-kungswissenschaft* hardly deflected such criticisms. Brackmann himself traced the beginnings of the modern state to medieval Germany and the Norman monarchies, concluding that by the end of the twelfth century, with the theocratic world empire falling into disarray and the first *Kulturkampf* being decided in favor of the secular powers, "the future lay with the princes and the national states."[22] As Theodore Mayer wrote in 1935 in a study of the dukes of Zähringen, with a bow to Below's pioneering work on the socioeconomic foundations of the German state, "As at the beginning, so at the end of fifteen centuries of political development, state and folk are one."[23] Kantorowicz pursued the theme of sacred kingship in a more scholarly and theoretical way in his last masterpiece, *The King's Two Bodies,* which, in another echo from the Weimar period, he subtitled "a study in medieval political theology."[24] The political theology of Kantorowicz was not that of Carl Schmitt back in 1922, focusing as it did on corporate mysticism, institutional continuity, and immortality ("the king never dies," nor do corporations), but it did share mystical premises concerning the spiritual roots of society and the historical sanctity of the *patria* and the State.

The depth of the involvement of historians in recreating a new national past — including Andreas, Brackmann, Brandi, Haller, Hampe, Hartung, Hölzle, Marcks, Mayer, Meinecke, Oncken, Ritter, Rörig, Srbik, and Stadelmann — may be seen not only in the academic *histoires à clef* which drew support and analogies for current issues but also in the vast outpouring of popular and polemical articles which were published in support, direct or indirect, critical or unreflective, of the policies and goals of the Nazi regime, if not all that often of the *Führer* himself. In all of this, moreover, scholars continued, or resurrected, conventional themes of German history that had been debated for centuries — political versus cultural, German versus Roman (and French and British and Polish and Russian), Protestant versus Catholic, national versus universal, and other invidious polarities that enhanced the position of the German *Volk,* nation, and state and intensified the "crisis of historicism." Some historians even tried to place the new Germany in a larger context of European *völkisch* history in the twentieth century, with invocations of parallels with American racism and the Ku Klux Klan.[25]

The study of the history of history continued to be popular, as evident in the surveys of Moritz Ritter (who died too soon to update his 1919 book), Brandenburg (1920), Wilhelm Bauer (1921), Karl Brandi (1922), and Below (1924, revised from the 1916 edition) — as well as the classic handbook of the Swiss scholar Eduard Fueter, published first in 1911 (also 1925 and 1936) in a series edited by Meinecke and Below, and translated into French, Italian, and

Spanish but not English.[26] In this book — the first full survey since that of Wachler a century before — Fueter treated only "path-breakers" and not "epigones" according to literary types and the historical categories of humanism, Enlightenment, and Romanticism. Although he himself wrote a Rankean textbook on the European state system in the early sixteenth century (1919), Fueter (who died by suicide in 1928) favored the turn from political to cultural history and sociology, as he admitted to Croce, and his historiographical work was criticized on these grounds by his brother-in-law Below and others. By contrast the position of Below was unmistakably conservative: "We oppose the cosmopolitanism of the Enlightenment to political [*staatliche*] and national consciousness, the free-market dogmatism of the Manchester school to the economic autonomy of the national state, state control over economic relations, with the mobility of systems as they evolve historically."[27] Germany would keep to its own path, rejecting pacifist "errors," cosmopolitanism, and internationalism, and move in the old channels cut by Ranke and his followers, though with a deeper appreciation of the culture, political organization, and ethos of the *Volk*.

All the traditional themes of national historiography were invoked by Johann Haller's popular sketch of the "epochs of German history," published in 1922. Haller's own early optimism had changed fundamentally in the past fifteen years. In the perspective of the Great War, Haller admitted, the German past could appear as "a succession of fruitless endeavors, doomed everlastingly to end in failure"; but things were looking up. Haller surveyed the major "critical moments," which included the breakup of the Carolingian Empire, the intrusions of the Church, the "dreams of World Empire," the career of that first "great personality," Frederick I, the German colonization of the East ("the greatest achievement of the German people in all the centuries of its existence, a place among the pioneers of civilization"), the calamitous accession of the Spanish Burgundian Charles V to the imperial throne, the rise of particularism, the effects of the "imperial compulsion" of Louis XIV, the "triumph and eclipse of Prussia," the Enlightened "War of Liberation of the spirit" led by Lessing, and the final unification under Bismarck. A mixed heritage, and Haller admitted that the hopes of his generation had been dashed; but he believed that the next generation might "find what their fathers had lost"; and so he turned, as so many of his contemporaries were doing, to prophecy: "If we Germans do our duty, we are justified in looking to the future with faith in our hearts. He who listens to the voice of history will hear the words of promise echoing down the centuries: We bid you hope!"[28] Or in the words of his Greek epitaph: "The day will come!"

Before the "day" came German historians frequently gave evidence of a rising imperialist mood. This began with the old critique of British and French aggression, which long predated the charge against Bismarckian Germany. In a series of articles beginning in 1903 Erich Marcks carried on an analysis of Britain's traditional "power politics" (*Machtpolitik*), from Elizabeth I to Pitt. reaching a climax with the capitalist expansionist before the war; and these essays illustrating the "tragic interaction between England and Germany over the centuries," become timely again in the Second World War, were republished by Marcks's disciple Andreas in 1940.[29] After the "drive against England," Andreas noted, came that against France; and this conflict, too, had a long history, which was traced by Haller in his study of the "thousand-year German-French relationship," beginning with Carolingian fraternalism and ending with a final German victory in 1870, followed by German national consciousness (*Selbstgefühl*) and the French policy of "Revanche" — a book published in 1930, 1936, 1939, and again in 1941.[30] It was a "fable," Haller argued, that France had always desired peace in the face of German militarism; even in 1919 the war had not ended, and Haller cited the French expert on Germany, Ernest Lavisse, to show that France did not want reconciliation. Yet France might well live to regret a weak Germany, and unfortunately it was "too late," politically at least, to remedy this situation through diplomacy.

Another aspect of suppressed German imperialism was the age-old "drive to the East," involving especially East Prussia and Poland. "Eastern Studies" (*Ostforschung*) was given an institutional base in 1902 at the University of Berlin in the Seminar for East European History and Regional Customs, headed by Theodor Schieman and Otto Hoetsch (student of Lamprecht) and which became involved in political controversies, especially during the war, and in the East Europe Institute founded in 1918.[31] In the 1920s this new field was exploited by scholars who wanted to project the eastern connections both back into the middle ages and forward into a new imperial destiny. In 1920 the medievalist Karl Hampe published his study of this "great colonial achievement of the German people in the middle ages" (*die kolonisatorisch Grosstat des deutschen Volkes im Mittelalter*), which might again, when directed against the Bolsheviks, contribute to a brighter future.[32] Nor did Hampe have sympathies for the peoples without a legitimate claim on nationality, such as Belgium and its "false politics," without a proper cultural base.[33]

The *Drang nach Osten* was promoted by other historians, especially Brackmann, who succeeded to Dietrich Schäfer's Berlin chair and who lent his prestige and the control of scholarly resources attendant on his offices as coeditor (with Meinecke) of the *Historische Zeitschrift* and director both of the *MGH* and of the Prussian Archives, which was "the archival embodiment of German claims to lost territories." Joining and yet preserving the values of both Rankean objectivity and national service, the premise of the archival staff was that "this scholarship can supply the politicians with the material from which they can draw their conclusions." The well-funded scholarly pre-campaign reached a high point at the Seventh International Historical Congress meeting in Warsaw in August 1933 (of which Harold Temperley was president), for which German participants — including Brandi, Schramm, Aubin, and Kehr — were provided with guidebooks to explain the issues correctly. Directly connected with this was the collection of scholarly essays on "Germany and Poland" published by Brackmann in 1933.[34] Written with the usual invocation of Rankean truth and against contemporary errors of the French and others about "injustice" and Polish "liberty," these papers, which were written by Oncken, Ritter, Hartung, Aubin, and others, celebrated and documented the geographical, cultural, and legal ties between Germany and Poland from prehistorical and medieval times down to the time of the "German Romantic," Adam Mickiewicz (whose statue, however, would later be torn down). This well-funded and officially sanctioned collection was translated into French and English, and forty-nine copies were sent to German government officials. So as Michael Burleigh has shown, scholarship prepared the way for political and military action, so that by 1936, according to the North-East German Research Community, "the times are gone when everyone can do what he likes."

The generation of historians surviving the war period were all waiting for the dawn of a new Germany, but they were deeply divided and ranged from enthusiastic or reluctant and anti-democratic republicans to conservatives and reactionaries who wanted to see the Reich revived and who celebrated the accession of Hitler as the revolutionary moment opening up just this backward-looking future.[35] Historians like Marcks, Stadelmann, Hölzle, Kienast, Haller, Hartung, Rörig, and Srbik were swept up by, or at least favorably inclined to the new regime, while Goetz, Schnabel, Erdmann, Kern, Ritter, Alfred von Martin, and Meinecke distanced themselves, if they could not actively oppose, Nazi rule and policies. Others fled or were forced into exile, including Veit Valentin, Hajo Holborn, Felix Gilbert, Hans Baron, Arthur Rosenberg, Hans Rosenberg, Ernst Kantorowicz, Theodor Mommsen, Gerhard Masur, Dietrich Gerhard, and the young Peter Gay. The Nazi revolution also brought significant changes in the leadership of the historical profession, including changes in the *Historische Zeitschrift* and the Monumenta Germanica Historica, the replacement in 1935 of the Imperial Historical Commission (*Historische Reichskommission*), which was established in 1928 under the direction of Meinecke and Oncken, by the Imperial Institute for the History of the New Germany (*Reichs-*

institut für Geschichte des neuen Deutschlands) headed by Walter Frank. By then Meinecke had been dismissed from both the commission and the national journal which he had served faithfully for over forty years, a number of the aforementioned exiles having been his students and carrying his teachings to the new world.

In the Weimar period some historians sought a more critical view of Germany's past, such as the cultural historian Walter Goetz, though he was opposed by conservatives in the Rankean mold, like Below, and in 1933 he lost his professorship on political grounds (the only historian in a list of almost two hundred scholars purged in a civil service law).[36] Other left-leaning critics were Veit Valentin, a student of Marcks who took an anti-Prussian line about German history following the revolution of 1848, of which he published a massive study in 1930, and who was likewise dismissed; Hans Rosenberg, whom Hans-Ulrich Wehler called the father of social history in Germany; Arthur Rosenberg, who wrote studies of the Weimar Republic from a democratic point of view and one of sympathies for the working classes; Hans Rothfels, a leading revisionist student of Bismarck who also went into exile in America, who later wrote a book on the resistance to Hitler, and who was the only Jewish leftist historian who returned to Germany after the war; and Hajo Holborn (about whom Felix Gilbert recalls Eckhart Kehr saying, "Oh, he is one of us").[37] But many of "them" were already seeking refuge abroad, where the best traditions of historiography would be pursued in new and often alien environments.

In 1931 Karl Jaspers surveyed the critical condition of "the present situation of mankind" in the light of history and the Western premises of rationalism and self-hood, which he contrasted to the "unworldliness" of the East. Space had been conquered, he wrote, and so what of time? Historical experience had brought Europeans to the "crisis" of the present and to an awareness of the impossibility of escaping the limits of one's "epoch." Always unpredictable, the future was a horizon that suggested both immense dangers (Fascism, Bolshevism, another war) and immense possibilities, and for Jaspers a "new world" could arise only out of human "will," with a "genuine leader" operating in a time of mass culture and "technical sovereignty," yet without severing ties with the past.[38] History has taught the brevity's of human undertakings and the possibility that the destiny of humanity is to perish. Jaspers refused to follow Marx and Spengler in the vain practice of the "contemplative forecast," and contented himself with an "active forecast" of the present "battlefield" and the "possibility" of freely chosen destiny. The vision of Jaspers, informed by historical and self awareness, still rested, however, on the old premise of a unified process within the framework of universal history, and he did not try to "contemplate" in any specific way the fundamental fragmentation of humanity and the existential possibilities which this threatened.

Post-Imperial Britain

For historians of Britain, unlike those of Germany, its was mostly business as usual after the trauma of the Great War, except for the problem of assigning guilt for this disaster, and on this question neither side could avoid preoccupation with diplomatic and political history. Despite bitter memories of the useless carnage, English historians preserved a confidence in their national destiny, though accompanied by some anxieties about loss of empire or guilt about social questions, while German scholars had, temporarily at least, lost their sense of a triumphal and communal march into an imperial future. They were deeply disillusioned by the outcome of their still-young national tradition, and yet, while drawn to prophecy, prognosis, and uncertain hope for a turn of fate, they for the most part clung, too, to old-fashioned national-statist ideals. Another interest which historians of both Germany and Britain shared, though in very different ways, was a growing interest in social history — with *Volksgeschichte* prevailing in Germany and a left-leaning social, or socialist, history emerging in England. As for major fields of study beyond contemporary history, or *Zeitgeschichte,* British, German, and other European historians restored, or continued, the cooperative practices which had appeared in the nineteenth century and found institutional expression in quadrennial international congresses established in 1900, broken off during the war, and resumed, with some political anxieties, in the 1920s.[39]

In general British historiography, aside from capitalist and socialist apologetics, was pursued after the war along conventional lines and under a cloud produced by depression, decline of empire, and threats of another war still greater than the Great War. Political and ecclesiastical history remained dominant, as evident in the Cambridge and Oxford series, but they were rendered in more detail, and they were supplemented by discussions of economic, social, and cultural matters in the disjointed manner of "meanwhile, back among the people . . . ." The Puritan Revolution became the object of special inquiry and veneration, G. P. Gooch (no social historian) characteristically associating it not only with "English democratic ideas" but also with modern socialism. Gooch referred to Robert Owen, who, however, was not aware that his doctrine "was directly descended from the thinkers of the Interregnum."[40] A turn to social history was apparent not only among the socialists but also, less tendentiously but more picturesquely, in the collaborative volumes of

H. D. Traill and J. S. Mann and the old-fashioned books of G. M. Trevelyan and G. M. Young. Traditions of constitutional and legal history were continued in textbooks and monographs, though with criticisms of the foundational work of Stubbs, as in the snottily revisionist studies of Richardson and Sayles. The analysis of Parliament was continued along tracks both old, as in the work of Pollard and J. E. Neale on the Elizabethan period, and new, especially in the eighteenth century, which was revolutionized by the prosopographic labors begun even before the first war by Lewis Namier, who scorned ideologies left and right.

In the early twentieth century British historians were concerned with collecting scholarly capital accumulated in the previous three or so generations by professional and occasionally "amateur" historians, with codifying the results of the researches of European scholars over the past century, and with forming and adding to what amounted to a master narrative, which was designed both to regularize history on the university level and to define the frontier for further exploration. This can be seen in the series of volumes on national history pioneered by German scholars, but more especially in the fast-growing series of historical series published by the Cambridge University Press, beginning with the model planned by Lord Acton. The Cambridge Modern History (beginning in 1902) was succeeded by the Cambridge Medieval History (1911), the Cambridge Ancient History (1921, but planned before the war), and then many more specialized collections, including Cambridge Histories of British Foreign Policy (1922), of the British Empire (1929), of India (1963), and dozens of more specialized (and later illustrated) surveys of every area of the globe and of particular fields of study, including national literatures, philosophy, and political thought. Specialization was a major theme of historiography between the wars, as evident also in the establishment of historical organizations, new journals, dissertations, and reference works, such as the Dictionary of National Biography (1885–1900) and its ten-year supplements, with counterparts in all the European states, and now the new and controversial replacement.

The intensive postwar investigation of diplomatic history can be seen in the work of G. P. Gooch, who, as a disciple of Acton and his near equal in erudition, was a member in effect of the Cambridge school. Gooch studied also on the continent and came into contact with Treitschke, Harnack, Gierke, Lavisse, and Sorel, but unlike Acton he never held an academic chair.[41] He was active in social work, journalism, Parliament (briefly), and government service; and after the war he became active not only in the peace process but also in the publication and interpretation of diplomatic documents. With Harold Temperley he began publishing a collection of archival sources (from 1922), rivaling *Die Grosse Politik,* which the Germans began to publish at that same time, with rival protests concerning suppression; and in 1926 he and A. W. Ward began editing the Cambridge history of British foreign policy. But Gooch was also involved in more conventional historical scholarship, most notably his *History and Historians in the Nineteenth Century* (1913), which might be seen as a huge expansion of Acton's famous essay, published in the first issue of the *English Historical Review,* on "German Schools of History." Gooch's book received admiring praise from Eduard Meyer, Fisher, Pollard, and others, despite some criticism that he was a bit narrow—for example, ignoring the smaller national traditions (which was not entirely the case)— even though he considered ancient and medieval, American, Byzantine, Near Eastern, Jewish, Catholic, and "history of civilization." Gooch especially deplored the antagonism between political history and *Kulturgeschichte,* which he attributed to the fact that both had been defined too narrowly.

Although working largely outside the profession, Gooch himself contributed to this narrowness to the extent that he helped reinforce diplomatic history as a separate field. In fact this was only one example of the drift toward specialization. One shift already begun before the war was that from constitutional to administrative history, led by T. F. Tout and the Manchester school of historiography. Tout's *Chapters in Administrative History* (1920–33) were directed in part against the grand Whig narrative which had found classic expression in the work of his teacher, Stubbs, and been continued by scholars like A. F. Pollard, but in part also by an empirical (and perhaps ideological) turn to the permanent apparatus of government that underlay and survived the partisan rhetoric and political ups and downs of Parliament. In concentrating on this aspect of state-building Tout drew inspiration from French institutional historians of an earlier generation such as Achille Luchaire and Paul Viollet; but it may be that his work was also partly the product of disillusionment with party politics and the parliamentary tradition—if not as severe as that of contemporary German historians. For Tout the real power rested in the hands not of elected officials (or perhaps even the monarch) but of the faceless bureaucrats who staffed the governments in offices such as the wardrobe, the chamber, and the privy seal continuously and over a large span of time; and it was evidence of their unpublicized activities and the mechanics of administration that Tout wanted to extract from the archives.[42] His work focused on internal, not external history, but otherwise it was quite in the spirit of Ranke; for here rather than in chronicles or histories it was possible again to find the signs of historical agency. There were other, largely unconnected, special fields appearing in the twentieth century. In England as well as in France the Industrial Revolution, with attendant social questions, led historians to economic and social (and colonial) history. The former, which was publicized by Edwin Seligman in 1902 as a way "to search *below the surface,*" may be illustrated by William Cunningham's pioneering survey of English industry and commerce published in 1882 and again in 1915–21, William Ashley's study of English economic history and theory (1888–93; fifth ed. 1901), Thorold Rogers's collection on agriculture and prices (1866–1902), and Arnold Toynbee's classic work on the Industrial Revolution (1884; 1908), which recommended the field as more scientific (being based on statistics) than the political history which served the purposes of party-men.[43] Economic history was for Cunningham a discipline separate from political economy. Yet sections of this field had been cultivated for generations, especially in histories of particular crafts and trades. In the half-century after Cunningham's book, volumes appeared, for examples, on the wine trade (1906, 3 vols.), on transport and communication (1912), on the grain trade (1913), on the woolen and worsted industries (1921), on the stanneries (1924), on the corn market (1926), brass and copper (1926), tobacco (1926), and coal (1932). Four of these appeared in the Harvard Series in Economic History written as dissertations before the war, three of them under the direction of Edwin Gay; and in England even earlier there was a series of monographs edited by Henry Higgs on "National Industries," including banking, building, shipping, the linen trade, etc. All these and others, written at least tacitly in the perspective of economic progress, provided materials for more general and interpretive works on English economic expansion and accompanying social and political problems of what R. H. Tawney called the "acquisitive society."

These books and their successors, written in a Whiggish spirit and according to an empirical or positivist method, were—like English economic theory in general—opposed to continental ideas, such as the abstract "historicism" developed by the younger German historical school led by Schmoller.[44] English historians wrote on continental economic history, too, most notably J. H. Clapham's survey of the economic development of France and Germany from 1815 to 1914 (1921), which was founded on detailed statistical studies of agrarian, industrial, and labor conditions, transport, and banking but which, in the spirit of specialization, displayed neither the broad cultural horizons and social concerns of the earlier works nor even an effort to connect the subject with the world war which had ended just three years before. Clapham's crypto-utilitarian conclusion was merely that, negative elements aside, the French and German peoples were materially better off and perhaps happier in 1914 than a century before.[45] Clapham stopped with the war, but he had no insights to offer about it or its connections with economic or social forces.

In early twentieth-century Britain women scholars—that is, professional scholars, for as "amateurs" women had been making important scholarly contributions since the eighteenth century—were becoming increasingly prominent; and it is perhaps not surprising that many of them turned away from political to economic and social history and what male professors regarded as "women's topics," meaning usually the study of prominent women in history, or at least domestic life. One extraordinary example, was Eileen Power, who studied at Cambridge (Girton College) and who finished her professional training in France, where she worked with Langlois and met, among others, Elie Halévy.[46] After doing a thesis on Queen Isabella, wife of Edward II, she turned to the neglected topic of English nunneries, not only expanding the field of monastic history by her study but also giving a social dimension to the question of "the condition of women," which had been taken up by German but not English scholars. Her work was published in 1922 in a Cambridge series on medieval life and thought, in which its editor G. G. Coulton proposed, invoking Mabillon, to rival modern science in its earnest search for certainties. Power herself followed the training of the contentious Coulton and A. H. Thompson in her rich, erudite, and heavily documented work, which surveyed the world of the 138 listed nunneries—social context, domestic life, government and finance, moral and sexual behavior, education, attempts at reform, and reflection in literature. In general Power avoided the bias and "tainted" sources of Henry VIII's dissolution of the monasteries but did not hesitate to comment on the general moral decline before that period and (against a critic in the *Manchester Guardian*) to defend the textual base, especially in Chaucer and Langland, for her charges of ecclesiastical "antifeminism."[47]

The breadth of Power's vision was more apparent in the little book she published two years later, *Medieval People*, in which she heeded Carlyle's call for not merely the praises of famous men but also for notice to be paid to ordinary people. In this enormously popular work Power tried to rescue social history from lifeless abstraction by presenting a pre-Reformation gallery of case studies of the *vie quotidienne* of individuals who usually escaped the attention of historians; viz., a typical peasant ("Bodo"), a Venetian traveler (Marco Polo), "Chaucer's Prioress in real life," a Parisian housewife, a merchant of the wool trade, and a fifteenth-century clothier, using a wide variety of sources, published and unpublished, literary and historical, public and private. So Power introduced readers to the invisible persons of past times, for, as she argued, "History is largely made up of Bodos." And not just Bodos, but also female counterparts like the fourteenth-century ménagier's wife, who provided an entry into the "kitchens of history."[48]

For Power, who succeeded Lilian Knowles in the chair of economic history in the London School of Economics, this field was "the newest of all branches of history," but in fact there was a substantial tradition going back to the Victorian period. In 1926 J. H. Clapham — who fifteen years later would edit with Power the Cambridge Economic History — began publishing his economic history of modern Britain, dedicated to Alfred Marshall, who in 1901 had urged him to write such a survey, and to William Cunningham, whose *Growth of English Industry and Commerce* (1882) was a sort of economic parallel to Stubbs's constitutional history, and he noted also the recent economic study of the British Empire by Lilian Knowles. But Clapham claimed to supersede this "semi-legendary" older tradition and, through the critical use of statistics, "to make the story more nearly quantitative than it has yet been made."[49] Clapham was a devout believer in progress — progress not only in historiography, through improved censuses and statistics and monographic works in German and French as well as English, but also in economic history itself, including here implicitly opposing the line taken by socialist writers, which was the idea that the condition of the working man had declined continuously with economic growth.

English economic history showed two faces in the early twentieth century: one was the chronicling and even celebrating of industrial and commercial progress, and the other was investigating the contributions, sacrifices, and social predicament of the working classes in relation to this process. Labor history was more partisan than the scholarship associated with the major parties — Tory, Whig, and Liberal — for it was committed indeed to the improvement of the workers in the face of an exploitative capitalist system. Socialist historiography in England in the early twentieth century was dominated by a sort of network of three remarkable husband-and-wife teams — the Webbs, the Hammonds, and the Coles — and R. H. Tawney. These activist scholars, all touched by Christian socialism, wanted both to write economic history and to promote social reform and justice on a political level; and this they succeeded in doing to the extent that in the 1920s the workers' movement indeed found a political base in the Labour Party, which then acquired its own triumphalist history.[50]

Sidney and Beatrice Webb were married in 1892, published their history of trade unionism in 1894, and founded the London School of Economics in 1895. In this work they recognized a few forerunners, but it was a pioneering effort in terms of the wide range of sources employed, including manuscripts as well as newspapers, pamphlets, and parliamentary reports. For them modern unions were not connected with medieval guilds and other associations but dated from the eighteenth century and were mainly a response to the

"Industrial Revolution," as the elder Arnold Toynbee had recently called it. Trade unions had passed through a "struggle for resistance" in the early nineteenth century, then a revolutionary interlude in the age of the Chartists, and finally, despite persecutions, had achieved institutional status in thousands of local organizations on the path to a "new social order." Much work remained, and a quarter of a century later, as the Webbs published a new edition of their work (1920), Sidney wrote an introduction to the English translation of the older work of W. Hasbach on the agricultural laborer — and the "history of freedom" — while lamenting that it took a foreign scholar to fill in this important gap. "Will no such man provide the endowment," he asked; "will no student devote his or her energy; will no head of a history school suggest the subjects for serious historical investigation of this kind?"[51]

J. L. and Barbara Hammond were married in 1901 and, though they were not socialists, were likewise enlisted in the cause of social reform reinforced by historical scholarship. From then until the end of the war they dedicated themselves not only to journalism and politics but also to their great trilogy on the village laborer (1911), town laborer (1917), and skilled laborer (1919), which chronicled the misdeeds of "conscienceless capitalists" in the "bleak age" of the nineteenth century and the social misery their practices brought about.[52] They opposed the conservative and academic views of Clapham and his "complex" inclination to celebrate the positive side of the Industrial Revolution and to ignore the social problems which it had generated. Their argument emphasized illegitimacy of the aristocratic and capitalist classes and the hard condition of the workers, and while they defended their facts and interpretations from their critics, they made no apologies for their partisan and present-minded stance. In their *Rise of Modern Industry* (1925) they paid credit to their comrades in books, including Harold Laski, Cole, Tawney, the younger Toynbee, and Trevelyan. In the first of these books the Hammonds denied the justice of the proprietary elite in their claims to property and in effect to lordship; in the second they described the "revolutionary" character of the class conflicts, including the violent actions of the Chartists and the Luddites, and in the third the "civil war" that resulted.

Another "marriage in history" (in Stewart Weaver's phrase), G. D. H. and Margaret Cole were younger associates of both these scholarly partnerships, and they traveled much the same paths as their elder colleagues, crossing and recrossing the terrain of working-class and socialist history. Cole, who took over J. L. Hammond's project for a life of Cobbett, extended the work of the Webbs in his own study of the British working-class movement (1925), which paid tribute not only to Marx, the Webbs (of whom Margaret Cole published a biographical account in 1949), the Hammonds, Tawney, and Dobbs but also to

Cunningham and Clapham (ideological differences overridden by a common allegiance to economic history). Cole's often reprinted work drew on the books written by socialist friends and predecessors, including Robert Owen, the Webbs, the Hammonds, Tawney, Dobbs, G. B. Shaw, Raymond Postgate (his brother-in-law and collaborator), and his own and his wife's publications as well as classic works in economic history by Toynbee, Cunningham, Clapham, and Sombart.[53] For Cole, despite the radicalism of the post-revolutionary period, the working-class movement and in its wake socialism really began after 1815, and it took many forms, both violent and cooperative, before the institutional devices of trade unionism in the later nineteenth century and the Labour Party in the twentieth. Cole ends with a warning about the disastrous effects that would follow from a "copartnership" between trade unionists and capitalists.[54] Yet, despite such worries and the influence of Marx, British social-ism always inclined to milder evolutionary ways. Converging with the conser-vatives on practical matters, they believed that the working classes could im-prove their condition only by contributing further to the production of wealth and peaceful trade with the rest of the world.

Their friend R. H. Tawney was a journalist and public servant rather than a regular academic scholar, although he did teach at LSE from 1923 to 1931 and was a founding editor of the *English Economic Review,* and he was even more the model of the committed socialist intellectual who turned to economic history (and away from economic doctrine) for ammunition. He was a social critic and preacher rather than a revolutionary, although he had enough class identification to refuse a peerage toward the end of his life. In 1920 his study of the "acquisitive society" presented not only an indictment of the obsession with the pursuit of wealth, focusing in particular on private property and its expansion under capitalism, but also a vision of a "new social order" based on function rather than individual rights and the incentives of a purposeless and soulless economism.[55] His masterpiece, written in the wake of the works of Weber, Troeltsch, and Sombart, was *Religion and the Rise of Capitalism* (1926), which joined his religious sympathies with social concerns and which sought to analyze the paradoxical union of Protestant morality and economic competition and, through a socialist teleology not unlike the rival "Whig" view of history, to connect the medieval condemnation of avarice and usury with modern social critiques, such as that of Marx — whom he called "the last of the Schoolmen" — as well as his own. "History is a stage where forces which are within human control contend and cooperate with forces which are not," concluded Tawney, who hoped to form his own agenda in the light of one such confrontation at the threshold of modern times.[56]

In a more orthodox vein British Marxist scholars studied and quarreled over the question of a "bourgeois revolution" manifested in the civil war of the mid-seventeenth century, in which the Puritans took the leading role.[57] For Christopher Hill (author also of a life of Stalin) economic and social questions were essential in understanding the "Puritan Revolution," but even before leaving the Communist Party in 1956 he did not believe that the class lines between aristocracy and bourgeoisie were clear, nor was the "transition from feudalism and capitalism"; and indeed the debates over this issue focused on the complexities rather than the twofold division of English society in this age. Increasingly, Hill turned away from the material base of history and the sociology of religion to intellectual and ideological questions of a "world turned upside-down," as reflected in printed pamphlets and propaganda, in the Stuart age and illustrating a long tradition of English radicalism going back at least to the Lollards. Here Hill raised criticisms for his focus on disparate "radical ideas" selected, often decontextualized, from his reading in pamphlets and polemics, and the "teeming freedom" that always pointed in a crypto-Whiggish way toward the "age of reason."[58] His radical bias made him the target of criticism by J. H. Hexter, Perez Zagorin, and other conservative scholars.

E. P. Thompson took up a later stage of this English radical tradition — though he also regarded it as the lower part of the English "constitution" — which was that rejuvenated by the social problems caused by the rise of industrial society.[59] By the 1960s the study of the Industrial Revolution, which had been marked out first by Marx, Toynbee, the Webbs and the Hammonds, resembled a "battlefield," remarked Thompson, with the lines drawn between the "catastrophic" school of critics and the "anti-catastrophic" school of economic historians like Clapham and Aston.[60] Like Hill, Thompson built his story around the vast literature of protest generated, in this case, with the help of Jacobin ideology, in the age of the French Revolution in England; and through the multiplication of testimonies and anecdotes, he found a sense of "catastrophe" and growing class consciousness — among various groups of workers. England did not go through the same sort of revolutionary experience, but this "heroic culture" did persist, if only as an "incoherent presence," finding expression in a syndicalist movement even before Marx and eventually being in some ways incorporated into English constitutional tradition.

Another influential Marxist (in a revisionist and "humanist" way) was Raymond Williams, who followed the later stages of British social history and the "long revolution" defined more by future hopes than by past accomplishment. Williams, operating on the edges of professional historiography and writing with one eye on a socialist future, tried to bring together cultural, social, and economic conditions (a more elegant version of superstructure and material base) in a literary and linguistic solvent, straying from orthodox Marxism but never forgetting its power and authority. For Williams "culture" was the key term, at the very center of the "human sciences," of which he recognized Vico as a "startling pioneer," anticipating the goal of social and cultural self-creation; and it was intended to encompass the whole life of society in the style of the French study of "mentalities," though remaining within the intellectual (if not revolutionary) tradition of Marx and attendant fields such as the sociology of culture.[61] For Williams modernism ended with a surrender to bourgeois values, though he sought answers not in "postmodernism" but in an alternative but still socialist tradition. Through his personality and "commitment" as much as leftist journalistic and literary writings, Williams was a founding figure of "cultural materialism," which paralleled the American school of "new historicism" and preserved its own sort of leftist Whiggery and pretensions to analyze society through literary texts and artistic productions.

France after Versailles

After the war, the "four years of criminal folly," as Lucien Febvre looked back on it, French historiography was still emerging from a positivist mode and struggling for survival in an increasingly complex and competitive interdisciplinary matrix. Shaken and driven off course by the war, that generation of historians were soon back not only on track of national history but also seeking international cooperation and global perspectives, beginning with a reorganizational meeting at the international congress in Brussels in 1923, the establishment two years later of an International Committee of Historical Sciences, with the Marxist Halvdan Koht as president and Pirenne and Alfons Dopsch as vice-presidents, and the financial support of American foundations. Henri Berr's *Revue de Synthèse*, broken off in 1914, resumed publication in 1920, and his even grander project, the hundred-volume collection, *L'Evolution de l'Humanité*, was also revived in the 1920s. The comparative history enterprises encouraged in Berr and Pirenne, already evident at the beginning of the century in the second congress (Paris, 1900), found top priority in the congress in 1928 held in Oslo, where Berr sought further support for his "synthetic history" and where Marc Bloch gave his famous manifesto on "histoire comparée." German scholars were brought back into the international community, and their own revived ambitions became painfully evident at the Warsaw congress of 1933, which for them was connected intellectually with their eastward expansion. The Zurich historical congress of 1938 was the last until another revival in Paris in 1950 in a new world.

National historiographies were deeply affected — and divided — by the ideologies of the interwar period. In contrast to German scholarship, which tended to link "culture" with politics, as in the national ideal of the *Kultur-staat,* French scholars marginalized the state and conceived of "civilization" as having material and spiritual dimensions and a promise of a "solidarity" that had a social rather than a political base. One result was that historians of the French Revolution like Labrousse, Albert Soboul, and Georges Lefebvre sought explanations not in the structure of political life but rather in fiscal problems, which for Labrousse constituted in themselves a "revolution," and class conflict. The question of race was central to both French and German historians, and in fact they shared views about medieval and "barbarian" aspects of their national pasts, the difference being that the French, with their mixed cultural heritage, grew critical of racialist theory and distanced themselves from the ideas of Thierry a century before, while in Germany racism in a crude and exaggerated form was reinforced by Nazi ideology.

In France Marxist ideology persisted, especially in the great national industry of French revolutionary studies, from which, indeed, Marx — under the influence of Sieyès and Guizot, among others — had drawn much of his line of argument about class struggle, if not national reintegration. Jean Jaurès, Alfonse Aulard, Albert Mathiez, Lefebvre, Soboul, and others carried on the Marxist line and did change emphases and details and made qualifications that expanded horizons beyond vulgar economic determinism, ideas of a "bourgeois revolution," and an end to (bourgeois) history — Lefebvre, for example, emphasizing the aristocratic prelude to this highly publicized phenomenon and the psychological dimensions of pre-revolutionary turmoil, especially in the "great fear" on the eve of revolution.[62] Yet no doubt was cast on the view that, despite unfortunate "excesses," what occurred after the agitation of the nobility and radicalization of the countryside leading to the abolition of "feudalism," was a "national revolution," a necessary step in the march toward constitutional liberty and democracy, and a central, if not entirely unprecedented, category in collective human experience. Since then, of course, various revisionisms have shifted emphases both back from social to political history, as in the case of François Furet, and up to levels of "political culture," which depart further from the orthodox Marxian paradigm. Yet down to the end of the twentieth century Europe and much of the rest of the world lived under the shadow of "the Revolution," real and imagined (and some still do).

But for twentieth-century historians as for Michelet, the Revolution was only the most dramatic episode in a vast national epic composed of many ages and levels of experience; and moving behind the nineteenth-century classics, they promoted a newer "new history," which grew and expanded beyond its socioeconomic orientation under the efforts of scholars such as Henri Berr (1863–1954), Lucien Febvre (1874–1956), Georges Lefebvre (1874–59), Ernest Labrousse (1895–1988), Georges Dumezil (1898–1988), Marc Bloch (1886–1944), and Henri Maspero (1883–1945). Before the second war the move to economic and social history had already been made, especially under the influence of the sociology of Durkheim and Simiand and the geohistory of Vidal de la Blache, and it was prominent in the early volumes of Berr's "Evolution of Humanity" series (which was truly worldwide in its compass) and in the later work of Fernand Braudel and his students. Yet this series, as well as the work of Berr, Febvre, and Bloch, also showed an inclination toward the history of "civilization," including art, religion, and literature.

In this interwar period French historical methods and publications set the style, and indeed continued to do so for two generations, through another war and its aftermath. The roots of the interdisciplinary "new history" in France are to be found in Berr's ambitious project and its extension by his protégés Lucien Febvre and Bloch, members of the "generation of 1905," in their own journal, the *Annales d'histoire économique et sociale*. Febvre, who had made contact with Berr as early as 1905, started a lifelong correspondence in 1911, just as he was publishing his doctoral thesis on Philip II and Franche-Comté; and indeed he accepted the assignment of writing the first volume, *La Terre et l'évolution humaine* (1922), translated as *A Geographical Introduction to History* (1924), after the death of Berr's first choice, who was Febvre's former teacher, Vidal de La Blache.

In this book, to which he returned after his war service, Febvre tried to distance himself from the implied determinism (*fatalité géographique*) of Friedrich Ratzel and Huntington as well as the sociology of Durkheim and Simiand, and Huntington, preferring the complexities of life, of "human geography" and "geohistory" (a term derived from Bodin), over abstract and systematized sociology. Febvre was less interested in geographic "influence" (originally an astrological term, he reminded readers) than in specific factors such as borders, frontiers, climate, and race. Man (*l'homme*) was an abstraction, and such disciplinary fictions as *homo politicus*, *homo geographicus*, or *homo economicus* were barriers to historical understanding. As a follower of the Durkheimian comparative philologist Antoine Meillet, Febvre was also making his own sort of linguistic turn with the aim of assembling a "historical vocabulary," which would include such terms as "frontier," "generation," "anachronism," "crisis," "milieu," "capitalism," "Renaissance," and "civilization," especially in rivalry with (German) "culture."

Throughout his career Febvre struggled to gain a place in the international network of scholars as well as a position in Paris, hoping first to succeed his nemesis Seignobos at the Sorbonne in 1926 and in 1933 succeeding finally in getting a new chair of the history of modern civilization at the Collège de

France, where he was followed in 1936 by Bloch, who, after a number of unsuccessful efforts to find a place for his "comparative history" with the support of Febvre but against the opposition of older scholars, finally succeeded Henri Hauser in a new chair of economic and social history. Fernand Braudel was already emerging as a favored disciple of the younger generation.

Meanwhile Febvre worked furiously between the extremes of the particular and the universal, between micro- and macrohistory, accompanied in his effort by his comrade — first in 1920 at Strasbourg (called by a colleague "waiting room for the Sorbonne") and then in Paris — Marc Bloch, son of a prominent Roman historian who had been a disciple of Fustel de Coulanges. The main lines of the story of French historiography for the next three generations may be followed in his correspondence with Berr and Bloch (designed to be published eventually), filled with judgments on and gossip about contemporary scholars.[63] For the *Revue de Synthèse* and later the *Annales* he wrote scores of reviews and articles on particular problems — solving which was the scientific mission of history — while at the same time carrying on "combats" for his view of history and against the voices of the past, such as the antiquated diplomatic histories appearing after the first war, and working on encyclopedic schemes to organize "universal history" along the lines of Berr's great series, to which indeed he (as well as Bloch) continued to contribute.

The micro-impulse was apparent in the vast array of articles and reviews he published on questions of geohistory, economic, social, cultural, scientific, linguistic, literary, psychological, intellectual, and art history, gathered later in a volume advertised as "combats" and "an entirely different sort of history."[64] The macro-impulse, which also underlay the project for a new French Encyclopedia to rival that of Diderot, was at all points tied to a rejection of theoretical systems and to a promotion of the autonomy of history in the mode of his vision of "histoire-problème" (recalling Acton's "Study problems, not periods"), signaled by Febvre's own interrogatory style. Even his biography of Luther, published in 1928, was devoted to a problem, that of the relation between individual and society, as was his study of Rabelais and the "problem of unbelief"(which was a long-delayed response to Abel Lefranc's biography representing Rabelais as an atheist); and the same could be said of Bloch's anthropological analysis of the "royal touch." The historical vision shared by Febvre and Bloch finally received institutional form in 1929 in the founding, after long discussions and negotiations, of their own journal (Pirenne having turned down the editorship), the *Annales d'histoire économique et social;* and the "Annales paradigm," with its large chronological, international, and interdisciplinary sweep, soon moved into the center of European historical studies, where in varying forms it has remained for the rest of the century.[65]

Throughout the 1930s Febvre and Bloch, casting about from their professorial centers of command for contributions from European scholars ranging from Scandinavia to Hungary and Romania, sought to extend their influence, to build in effect a scholarly empire in the new, postwar Republic of
Letters, and to impose their vision of a "new history" that was super- as well
as interdisciplinary. Although it was not a "system," history had its own
"method" and did not need other sciences, such as sociology or Marxist theory,
to provide guidance — to reduce life to one single set of principles. as Lamprecht
had claimed to do.[66] For historians the "capital crime" was philosophizing, the
original sin anachronism, "projecting the present, that is, our present, into the
past," which was exactly what psychological or sociological history — or philosophy of history — was often guilty of doing. It was an anachronism, for
example, to call Rabelais an "atheist" or to seek national or institutional origins
for the Reformation, which was a European-wide social and cultural transformation. Returning to the goal established by seventeenth-century scholars,
Febvre aimed not at certainty but only at "historical and psychological proba-
bility."[67] It was for this reason that the "new history" proposed a return to the
study of language and biography and to empirical research in general (though
not to the antiquated empiricism of Langlois and Seignobos), the aim being not
to give definitive answers to problems but to open up further lines of research
and to fill in gaps in the understanding of history, which was to say human life in
a long perspective.

The "Annales paradigm" (as Traian Stoianovich has called it) grew out of the
effort of professional history to gain parity with the social sciences, which set
themselves apart from the art of history through devotion to quantitative and
especially statistical methods and the search for regular laws. From Thucydides' employment of Ionian medicine to Bloch's borrowing from Durkheim, as
Paul Veyne wrote, historical inquiry had sought theoretical justification.[68]
Though "idiographic" in origin and method, historical interpretation aspired
to the heights of a nomothetic discipline and what Henri Berr called historical
"synthesis," an ideal which he spent a long lifetime promoting. In this he was
following the lead authors like Louis Bourdeau and Paul Lacombe as well as
Emile Durkheim and François Simiand, who both issued challenges to historians at the turn of the century. Berr, Febvre, and Bloch were among the first to
face this challenge, although they wanted to meet it without undermining the
autonomy and authority of history; and the upshot was the "new history"
accompanying the imperialist efforts of Febvre, Bloch, Braudel, & Co.

During the past century this new history went through several phases, but
these are less well understood as chronological stages than as aspects of a
historical movement, which included four interdisciplinary thrusts: geohis-

tory, which can be traced back in French historiography through Vidal de la Blache and Febvre to Michelet, Montesquieu, and Bodin (who spoke of *geo-historici* like Strabo); economic and serial history, which employed quantitative and statistical methods (scholars like Ernest Labrousse, following the lead of Simiand); anthropological history, especially the study of "mentalities" taken up by Febvre, Bloch, Philippe Ariès, and many others; and finally, a composite "total history" — a restoration, as it were, of the providential view of theologians and philosophers of history (and perhaps the *historia perfecta* of Renaissance theorists) — which employed the services of all the human sciences available at the time and which sought both global range and several levels of time from human reckoning of events to environmental *longue durée*.

These patterns can be seen in the transformations of the *Annales* itself, which was founded in 1929 after long discussions and which in the wake of the Oslo conference sought contacts with authors not only in the major Western states but also in Scandinavia and Eastern Europe. This journal has passed through three significant terminological changes reflecting not only various public pressures but also the widening horizons of *Annaliste* discourse — while not entirely rejecting the at least implicit Marxoid pseudo-scientific devices of material base and superstructure. First, the journal was devoted to "economic and social history," suggesting the conspicuous importance that economics held in a time of Marxist fashion and financial depression; then in 1939, the title was changed simply to "Annales de l'Histoire Sociale," to avoid suggestions of economic reductionism and determinism and the emphasize that, as Braudel later argued, capitalism is not an economic system but a social order almost on a level with the state; and finally, in 1946, it became "Annals: Economies, Societies, Civilizations," to accommodate the whole hierarchy of historical experience and disciplines needed for an appreciation of "total history." Febvre's own work, expressed in books and in many "combats" for the new history, prefaces, and reviews, ranged up and down this whole scale, from geohistory to "mentalities," with exhortations to open one's eyes to the entire "great drama that unfolds before us." In his lifelong quest for "an entirely different sort of history" (*une histoire à part entière*), Febvre remained abreast of and wrote critically on the mounting literature on geographic, economic, social, cultural, intellectual, art, and technological history within the context of the "synthetic" vision which he inherited from Henri Berr and, in deeper retrospect, the great project undertaken by Michelet, who indeed became in style, range, and aspiration, if not the model, then at least the tutelary saint of the Annales school.[69]

"Mentality," which was a key concept of the Annales paradigm, was a term borrowed from Lucien Lévy-Bruhl's anthropological investigations of the "primitive mentality" before the First World War, referring especially to mystic and mythical — pre- or extra-rational — forces, which historians like Febvre and Bloch transported into later stages of Western society and cultural contexts. Thus Febvre could not accept Lefranc's anachronistic charges of Rabelais's "atheism" without inquiring into "some habits of mind, some ways of living, believing, and thinking that were peculiar to the odd little world" of early sixteenth-century French religion and literature — an evident analogy with the complexities of geographical environment.[70] In particular Febvre rejected Lefranc's prime document, which was a volume of poetry published by Visagier, attacking a modern "ape of Lucian" — whom Febvre, however, preferred to identify not with Rabelais but with Etienne Dolet, that "Martyr of the Renaissance" beloved of modern freethinkers (though he was no atheist, either). Beyond pointing out this misused documentary evidence Febvre moved further out into the semantic field, first by examining the ambiguous and flexible meanings at that time of the term "atheist," of which even Erasmus had been the target, and then by exploring the larger areas of religion, philosophy, science, and the occult, none of which gave support to the notion that the sixteenth century (that age of ferocious religious wars!) was turning away from faith. Men of learning wanted to restore the unity of thought, the harmony between the facts of nature and history and the ideals of religion and philosophy — a harmony which needed to be underwritten by a caring God. This was the goal of reformers like Erasmus and Luther — and, Febvre surmised, Rabelais. Febvre's emphasis on the "deep religiosity" of the sixteenth century and "unthinkability" of true atheism was overdrawn, but his portrayal of the mentality of that age set historical inquiry on a solider methodological foundation.[71]

Marc Bloch was Febvre's comrade and partner for a quarter of a century, though he followed his own medievalist path on the other side of modernity; and he was mostly in agreement on questions of methodology.[72] Like Febvre he began his work with a study of the economic and social history of one of the "regions of France" (title of one of the section's of Berr's *Revue de Synthèse*), the Ile-de France, first published in Berr's journal between 1903 and 1913, when he also began turning to less familiar areas of cultural history, pursued especially in his anthropological study of ceremonial and "thaumaturgic kings" — *The Royal Touch*, begun before the war but published in 1923. Like Febvre, too, he believed in historical autonomy, if not "objectivity," and rejected the practice of imposing theory on historical facts, though he did invoke Durkheimian "collective consciousness" — and regard belief in the royal miracle, which lasted into modern times, as a "collective error."[73] After the war at the University of Strasbourg Bloch, under the influence of Durkheim, Pirenne, and the linguist Meillet, and perhaps of the Franco-German (Alsatian) environment, began his turn to a comparative method, though he was suspicious of the old conjectural practice, common in the eighteenth century, of extending this beyond the common ground of European civilization—i.e., French, German, and English—and preferred, following perhaps the assumptions of historicism, to limit comparisons to "parallel study of societies that are at once neighboring and contemporary, exercising a constant mutual influence, exposed throughout their development to the action of the same broad causes . . . and owing their existence in part at least to a common origin."[74] This was especially apparent in agrarian history (like Febvre's "human geography"), and a major product of his researches in provincial archives was his study of French rural history, published in 1931 both in Oslo (where he gave his manifesto of comparative history) and in Paris.

Comparativism did not open the doors of the Collège de France for Bloch (where he came, belatedly and in an atmosphere of antisemitism, as an economic historian), but it did lead him to expand his horizons from the area around Paris to wider exploration of the French countryside and finally to a large interdisciplinary synthesis of "feudal society" in Europe and perhaps beyond, published in 1939 as the thirty-fourth volume (following those of those of Louis Halphen on the Carolingian period) in Berr's great series, with a preface by Berr. Bloch noted that "feudalism" (*la féodalité*) was a construction of the revolutionaries of 1789, but he kept it as a residual sort of Durkheimian social "type."

Bloch's *Feudal Society,* opening with a survey of the edges of Europe, especially the Arabs, Magyars, and Normans, departs from the old-fashioned emphasis on legal and constitutional history and the origins of the fief or benefice —and the question, Germanic or Roman?—to take up questions of social structure, material conditions, the role of the family, and commercial relations in the style of Maitland or Pirenne rather than Fustel or Waitz, but brought together in an original literary synthesis with more general heuristic considerations of language, custom, culture, "collective memory," and "mentality." In trying to join the particulars of feudal society to larger historiographical problems, Bloch did not neglect issues of "class" and "government," but these he treated, too, in interdisciplinary—and comparative (or as with Japan, contrasting)—rather than legalistic or doctrinaire terms.[75] What survived the feudal regime in the long run especially were the principles of aristocracy and of contract, which made possible modern practice of limited and parliamentary government through the Estates of the various European states—the old Anglophile argument championed by Guizot a century earlier.

Despite his fascination with comparative history, Bloch also turned to the history of *la patrie,* shown especially in his deep involvement in the countryside of the French provinces, where he found, talking to peasants, that surviving customs were often more enlightening than the written legal sources for revealing the surviving patterns of life. In the middle ages life was ruled by tradition, but "group custom" and the perpetuation of juristic "long usage" justified the *Annaliste* focus on matters of *longue durée* (whether or not carried over from Marx, who also sought changes unperceived by contemporaries): "So the past continues to dominate the present."[76] After 1789 the "lines of continuity" were too obscure to be traced accurately, but Bloch did not doubt that the past persisted in many forms, as suggested vividly by the aerial photographs that revealed the outlines of ancient field systems. What Bloch hypostasized (or sociologized) as "society" — and "feudalism as a social type" — had to be analyzed not through written sources produced by lawyers and functionaries but by underlying human relations and "solidarities" (flag word of the time of Bloch's youth) which left all sorts of unofficial traces; and moreover the progress of society was measured not by legislation but by "the curve of technical improvement." Yet like Febvre, if more cautiously, Bloch tried to reach beyond material conditions and social structures to matters of individual psychology, thought, language, and sentiment. As for what remained in the medieval heritage, Bloch pointed not only to the habits and chivalric values of the nobility but also to the urban-inspired "idea of contract" which still lay at the basis of Western civilization.[77]

American Exceptionalism

The American historical profession, while drawing on and imitating its continental European counterparts, had to establish its own direction, sense of nationality, and original "covenant," and as John Franklin Jameson, one of the founders, told Henry Adams, to pursue the "proper development of historical work in America."[78] As early as 1883 American scholars had published a handbook of historical method, which was a late descendant of the old *ars historica* and comparable to, though more elementary than, those of Bernheim and of Langlois and Seignobos and which included such founders of the profession as A. D. White, A. B. Hart, Ephraim Emerton, H. B. Adams, C. K. Adams, and the Englishman J. R. Seeley.[79] But Jameson was the leading figure in this development. In the United States "scientific" history was rooted either in philology or in biology, the crude model of Buckle being superseded by Darwinism, and it was reinforced by the rise of professional organization. In a career spanning three universities (Johns Hopkins, Chicago, and Brown), the Carnegie Institute, and the Library of Congress, Jameson was concerned above all with the collection and publication of archival documentation of America's unique history. Avoiding the usual emphasis on constitutional history, he turned to religious history, which for him was to be illustrated from sources on prominent Americans analogous to the medieval *Acta Sanctorum* and yet liberated "from the traditions and conventions of European historiography."[80] At the same time he insisted on the need for cooperative and organized research—and associated funding—to advance historical knowledge; and he was a supporter of the renewed international congresses after World War I, omitting all Germans but suggesting Trevelyan, Lavisse, Fredericq, Pirenne, Blok, Altamira, and Pais, as a historiographical parallel to the League of Nations.[81] While at Johns Hopkins University in 1887 he may also have been the first to teach a graduate course on historiography.[82]

But Jameson was a man of the old school, passed by for the most part by the new history, which rose and fell during his lifetime (he died in 1937). He also resisted the idea of James Westfall Thompson for a journal devoted to European history, which the *American Historical Review* had largely neglected.[83] This was in 1916, and such a plan was not realized until the founding of the *Journal of Modern History* at the University of Chicago in 1929. Mainstream history has always depended on fixed dates, and for the "New History" in the United States the chosen moment has usually been the appearance of James Harvey Robinson's book of that title published in 1912, although the term had been around for more than a decade—and indeed, in other contexts, for centuries. There were larger connections in space as well as time; in this case the association was with the "new histories" of Karl Lamprecht and Henri Berr and other currents of novelty brought into the study of history in American universities in the previous generation, not mention the westward and exceptionalist turn introduced by F. J. Turner in 1893 under the influence of the Italian economist Achille Loria.[84] For Robinson the task of the scholar and teacher was directed not to "past politics" (in Freeman's phrase) but to total and meaningful history (similar to Berr's "historical synthesis"), based on sources ranging from material artefacts to works of high literature and placed in the service of a society "engaged in an unprecedented effort to better itself in manifold ways." In this effort Robinson attached special importance to the history of history, especially the tradition of the cultural, conjectural, and "philosophical" histories written by Voltaire, Herder, and their more national-minded followers, who were also open to "the new allies of history," notably anthropology and archeology, and who championed the idea of unlimited progress. Nor did the experience of World War I, despite the resurgence of diplomatic history and questions of the causes of war, undermine the faith of Robinson and his disciples in this vision of progressive history.

American New History was in large part (like most of its descendants) a self-constituted community that ignored its own history *avant la lettre*. Even before Robinson, for example, the New History in the United States had found a practitioner in the pioneer of domestic history Lucy Maynard Salmon, who found "history in the backyard," in the kitchen, on Main Street, and in the newspapers as well as other neglected sites of social and cultural interest. Salmon had studied at Bryn Mawr under Woodrow Wilson before beginning her teaching career in 1887 at Vassar, where she taught generations of women methods of and new paths in historical research, relying especially on Robinson's famous textbook of 1903, and carried on a campaign of educational reform in which history occupied a central place. Among other things she praised the historical museum, hoping that the open-air museum of Scandinavia would be introduced into the new world, and she also anticipated the "linguistic turn," that is, words as a special field of study. Above all, following the lead of the old cultural history, she championed the cause of "research for women," especially in areas of "everyday life."[85]

Among the most enthusiastic champions of the New History was that maverick scholar Harry Elmer Barnes, who associated the movement with the cause of revisionism, lamenting the fact that there were practically no pro-Germans, not even his old teachers Burgess and Shotwell, at the peace negotiations.[86] In 1925 Barnes sought not only to enhance the pedigree of the New History by making connections with earlier efforts of historical interpretation but also to push its frontiers further in an interdisciplinary direction—complaining to Jameson about the refusal of the *American Historical Review* to review the work of the sociologist Albion Small, which drew on the German Historical School.[87] Barnes pointed to advances in geography, psychology (including social and "folk-psychology" [*Völkerpsychologie*]), anthropology, economics, political science, and ethics—gathering them all into the deep perspective of Robinson's ambitious agenda. Like Barnes, James T. Shotwell also, though belatedly (1939), wrote a volume on the history of history in the light of his Columbia colleague Robinson's program and the "historical renaissance in American education," carrying the story from mythical "prehistory" down to the "new era" opened up by Augustine's *City of God*. In 1937 Barnes published a broader survey of historiography down to the aftermath of the war and offering the "revisionist" argument against the assignment of war guilt exclusively to Germany, citing Shotwell's multivolume edition on the social and economic history of the war, which he called "the most gigantic example of successful cooperative work in the history of historical writing" and which (like his own book) was dedicated to guiltless peace.[88] Echoes of the agenda of the new history were heard a generation later in a volume sponsored by the American Historical Association, though with notice neither of Lamp-recht nor even of Robinson in introducing a presumably novel interdisciplin-ary miscellany which included techniques of cultural analysis, social groups, nationality, institutions, ideas, and sources for cultural history.[89]

In American historiography novelty was torn between the European inno-vations represented by Lamprecht and Berr (and the still alien disciplines of sociology and anthropology) and the presentism and exceptionalism that de-manded turning away from influences from the old world, whether to Turner's frontier or to homegrown democratic and progressivist ideals. Robinson's and Becker's colleague Charles Beard, who served his apprenticeship in the study of English history, made his contribution with his economic interpretation of the U. S. constitution (1913), which like Namier's studies of Parliament (rather than Marxist doctrine) focused on material interests rather than pro-fessed or inferred ideology. Beard went on to collaborate with Robinson on a textbook of European history in the style of the New History (1907–8) and, twenty years later, another with his wife, Mary Ritter Beard, on a broad and colorful survey of American civilization. Economic history and the Industrial Revolution were still novelties in America, and social history even more so, and James Shotwell, a Columbia medievalist who was very sympathetic to the New History (to the extent indeed that his departmental chairman suggested that he shift to sociology!) claimed that in 1905 he was the first to teach a course on that subject at Columbia, "pioneering on farther frontiers of history than the economist had ever thought to explore."[90]

Yet conventional national historiography continued to prevail, both before and after the war, especially in the multivolume efforts of James Ford Rhodes on the United States from 1850 (1893–1906), John Bach McMaster from the Revolution (1883–1913), and Edward Channing from the beginnings to the Civil War (1905–25). Coming from a business background, Rhodes was a conservative and, according to his northern lights, impartial historian, though he was an unapologetic nationalist, and he did little to hide his prejudices against Negroes, Jews, and even Europeans.[91] As an amateur in the tradition of Bancroft, Rhodes was not a subtle thinker, his biographer concluded, "but simply the uncritical child of his time, region and class." His narrative, de-tailed and colorful but limited mainly to diplomacy, politics, and war, cele-brated the Anglo-Saxon heritage of America and, aside from the immoral burden of slavery, benefits of material progress, though later experiences, es-pecially that of the war, dimmed his optimistic vision. The book, which drew especially on newspaper sources, was criticized by scholars like his friend Woodrow Wilson and John Burgess for neglecting the west and for its dogma-tic overemphasis on abolition; but it was praised by many others, including

Theodore Roosevelt, and it gained enough influence and popularity to encourage Rhodes to move from Cleveland to Boston and make him into a public figure.

The work — an "overnight success" — of another amateur, McMaster, which Rhodes reviewed favorably, reflected the shift from political history in a derivative style reminiscent of Macaulay and especially J. R. Green's famous history of the English people. Taking a much wider view of American historical experience, it achieved even greater popularity, and Rhodes's friend Roosevelt came to regard McMaster as the leading national historian. In an unabashedly Whiggish fashion McMaster aimed "to describe the dress, the occupations, the amusements, the literary canons of the times; to note the changes in manners and morals; to trace the growth of that humane spirit which abolished punishment for debt, which reformed the discipline of prisons and of jails, and which, in our time, destroyed slavery and lessened the miseries of dumb brutes" — as well as to celebrate the "prosperity unparalleled in the annals of human affairs."[92] The first volume of the book brought McMaster to a chair of history at the University of Pennsylvania, where he became a publicist for imperialism and where he continued to turn out the successive volumes of his history as well as many successful graduate students, including E. P. Cheyney, W. R. Shepard, and H. E. Bolton. In 1897 he also published a pioneering textbook which reinforced the trend from political to social and progressive-democratic history, later carried on, and still more successfully, by the textbook of Robinson and Beard.

The last old-fashioned grand narrative of national history in the national evolutionist style of Bancroft, though transferred to an academic context, was that of Edward Channing, who had been a student of Henry Adams and who recreated the past from the perspective of his Harvard chair. His investigation of sources went beyond the efforts of Rhodes and McMaster, but Channing followed them as well as Bancroft in casting his story as an epic narrative of heroic Englishmen (preceded marginally by Scandinavians and Spanish) carrying civilization to remote parts of the globe. By 1660 the "nation" had been assembled by the English, whose character remained constant, in the north and in the south; and only the experience of the frontier brought out the deeper Germanic elements which made the colonists into autonomous Americans — so the Germanist theme of Bancroft, Adams, and other contemporaries was joined to the exceptionalist argument popularized by Turner and the New Historians. Increasingly, too, Channing turned to the new areas of economic and social history, though without resorting to the trivia contained in newspaper sources which Salmon prized.

The trend to social history — as well as to national historiography in general

— was represented contemporaneously not only in works like Jameson's monograph on the American Revolution considered as a social movement but also in
such series as that on "The American Nation" edited by A. B. Hart of Harvard
and the Chronicles of America (1918–21), which also reflected the New History. Although social history had a distinguished pedigree in Europe in the
work of Macaulay, Michelet, Lamprecht, and others, exceptionalists like
Turner seemed to claim it for their own. "Whatever be the truth regarding
European history," wrote Turner, "American history is chiefly concerned with
social forces." Progressivist social history, was also emphasized in the series
edited by Schlesinger and Fox and in the popular work of the Beards, which
both appeared in 1927. The Beards set the epic story of America and "the sweep
of economic and social forces" — and the role of women — within the framework of universal history and against the background of other "far-reaching
empires," from Babylon and Egypt to the Mongols, Turks, and English, and of
cosmological speculations from Anaximander to Hegel and (not Marx but)
Sombart as well as Adams and Spengler. Despite heavy borrowing from Europe, America emerged as a model of modern democracy for critics and prophets as well as historians. For Beard the promise of future progress, set between
"ideology and utopia" (implicit invocation of Karl Mannheim), was signaled
by writings on the left, such as John Dos Passos, Matthew Josephson, Edmund
Wilson, and Malcolm Cowley, who combined "biting portraiture of American
miseries [with] the quenchless optimism of Moscow."[93]

Arthur Schlesinger had written his doctoral dissertation on the colonial
merchants in the revolutionary period (1918); and though he did not think
that the current "new history" had reached Americanists except for Beard, in
1922 he published a summary of "new viewpoints" in American history,"
invoking J. R. Green as well as Turner and Beard and commenting on many
aspects of social history, including geographic and economic aspects, the rise
of industry and democracy, and immigration — which led him to a Wilsonian
attack on isolationism. Schlesinger was an enthusiast for the frontier thesis of
Turner (now transported to Harvard), though he believed that technology
would reduce the influence of environment.[94] He also defended the economic
interpretations of Turner, Wilson, and especially Beard, and even the sugges-
tive, if "untrustworthy," insights of unnamed Marxist scholars; and he celebrated the "educative" impact of women's suffrage in the betterment of humanity. This book was in effect a bid for a leading role in the "new school,"
and indeed Schlesinger, deserting the now closed frontier, soon followed Turner to Harvard to carry the revisionist word to the American historiographical
establishment.

The "new school" referred to by Schlesinger projected its opinions, too, into the public sphere. In 1932 Beard edited a volume of essays by prominent figures devoted to the idea and reality of progress in a wide range of areas — from "invention as a social manifestation," industry (a collaborative essay by Henry Ford), agriculture, labor, and finance to medicine, education, science, the arts, the position of women, and government and law (covered by Beard himself).[95] Extraordinary advances in transportation alone justified "that glorious name — a Century of Progress," the motto of the World's Fair of 1933. Another contributor recognized a "revolution in the forms and concept of property," and concluded that this circumstance, together with mass production, made "planning and organization necessary to cover all areas." That an invidious sort of exceptionalism still existed was evident in the survey of modern literature by John Erskine, who admitted censorship but added that "We were unappreciative of Poe, but we didn't try to put him in jail as the French tried to put Baudelaire." He defended "vulgarity" as a vital part of the daily life of American society and as inseparable, fortunately, from artistic expression. For Beard the idea of progress was universal and transcendent in ways that contemporary ideologies could never be, and it opened a vision of world unity that was "in harmony with mankind's noblest dreams." A critic of the "noble dream" of objectivity, Beard had his own "noble dream," which led him further down the revisionist path to isolationist opposition to and criticism of Roosevelt's machinations which (he argued) drew the United States into war.

The New History, with its pedagogical and popularizing orientation, was not for everyone. Samuel Eliot Morison, for example, flirted with this fashion, but for the most part he turned back to the Harvard tradition of Romantic grand narrative, at least in part in reaction to the pacifist and isolationist tendencies of new historians like Beard and Barnes.[96] Son of a wealthy Boston family and the historian of Harvard (author of the three-volume tricentennial history) as well as a graduate and later a professor, Morison wrote on the maritime history of Massachusetts and on Puritanism, which, in agreement with Kenneth Murdoch, Perry Miller, and (in a theoretical way) Max Weber, he interpreted more favorably than did many historians like V. L. Parrington, who were critical of the supposedly intolerant and repressive character of Puritans.[97] In any case Morison's major work was a Parkmanesque survey of the European voyages of discovery, especially that of Columbus, whose story he retold, as a sort of tour guide, in a narrative which combined color, drama, high scholarship, and personal judgments and which he extended to other maritime heroes, English and French as well as Portuguese and Spanish. Morison even sought to join their legendary ranks by retracing the voyages of Columbus in a sailing sloop, with the help of a Harvard crew, and later he continued his maritime interests by gaining an appointment in 1942 as historian of the war in the Pacific, necessarily following (as Beard lamented) the official line.

Medieval history was an area much cultivated by American scholars, beginning with Charles Gross, Henry Osborn Taylor (not a professional historian, though he was a president of the AHA), George Burton Adams, Charles Homer Haskins, and Charles Howard McIlwain, who worked mainly in the tradition of Stubbs and Maitland. Haskins, however, who published his classic study of Norman institutions in 1918, pioneered other areas of scholarship, especially the history of medieval science and culture. His best-known book was an interdisciplinary and international survey of the "twelfth century renaissance," or "medieval renaissance," which, appropriating the term made famous by Burckhardt, sought to rehabilitate the persisting reputation of the "dark ages" by pointing out the foundational achievements in education, learning, language, literature, jurisprudence, philosophy, science, and historical writing. In particular, Haskins concluded, "By 1200 vernacular history had come to stay" — thus beginning the sort of popularization of history which Haskins himself promoted.[98] But the significance of this movement was broader and deeper. Before there was a Latin renaissance in fourteenth- and fifteenth-century Italy there had been an even more subversive Greek (and Arabic) revival culminating in the "greatest of centuries," the thirteenth, according to a Catholic scholar — which introduced Aristotelian philosophy and its associated "scholastic" and empirical methods, which laid the foundations of the medieval "university" (*studium generale*), and which transformed European culture as a whole in the twelfth century.

Before his early death in 1937 Haskins was also active in public life both as a member of the American delegation to the Paris peace conference in 1919 and as graduate dean at Harvard, and indeed between the wars he was the center of what might be termed the Harvard School of European history. Other members of this school included McIlwain, whose dissertation on "the high court of Parliament," by emphasizing the judicial function, brought a revisionist perspective to English constitutional history and to the future of modern democracy, whose roots go back to the English civil war; Roger B. Merriman, who, having published a biography of Thomas Cromwell in 1902, took up, in his history of the rise of the Spanish Empire (1918–26), the project of William H. Prescott and indeed, having used Prescott's own annotated books in the Harvard Library, dedicated the book to his memory; Sidney B. Fay, who in 1928 published what was long regarded as the standard study of the origins of the First World War; William L. Langer, who the next year began publishing his own investigations of the deeper diplomatic background of the First World

War; Donald MacKay, historian of modern France; and Crane Brinton, who ranged widely over European intellectual history. On the American side there were Morison, Schlesinger (Sr. and Jr.), Perry Miller, Kenneth Murdoch, Turner's replacement, Frederick Merk, and Oscar Handlin, who all worked to turn out an impressive number of doctoral disciples in their efforts to bring American historiography up to European standards.

As Peter Novick has argued in his comprehensive study, objectivity was "the founding myth of the historical profession"; and it divided academic historians for generations, especially after the experience of the First World War, when many scholars were drawn into government (as well as military) service and propaganda.[99] After the war many of these historians were ashamed of their violations of professional ideals and turned back to professional impartiality, illustrated by efforts to review the immediate past in the spirit of Ranke, whose injunction to seek only what "really happened" stamped him for Americans, in their hostility to philosophy, as a pure empiricist — mistakenly, since philosophy informed Ranke's work despite his hostility to Hegelian idealism. Thus Sidney Fay, in his influential book on the origins of the war, proposed neither to defend the Versailles Treaty nor to demand its revision but rather to follow the rules of "the great master" (like Ranke, also unnamed) Tacitus in refusing to take sides. Historical objectivity was a way of reinforcing the claims of history to autonomy, perhaps also of defending against intrusions by other disciplines and theories; and yet it could also present an obstacle to political and social utility, a problem with which continental historians had long struggled. The pressures of political and military crisis and foreign threats (if only ideological) forced historians to the latter side, as more indirectly did the demands of public education and national unity. Yet the debate between pure history (history for the sake of history) and applied history continued in many forms throughout the ideologically charged decades before, during, and after the next war.

After the first war American historians felt the invasion of ideas of relativism and "point of view" in the wake of the works of Mannheim, Croce, Vaihinger, Korbzybski, and others, for which they generally had to wait for English translations in order to take part in the European philosophical and historiographical conversations.[100] Such ideas, reinforced by some varieties of Pragmatism, helped to accommodate the periodic revisionisms, especially of such standard issues as the Civil War, the frontier, and involvement in international politics, and they permitted more insightful study of sensitive questions, for example, slavery as a system with cultural as well as economic dimensions. Among the results of this change of tone in historiographical discourse were not only backlashes against defenders of the absolute (if no longer religious) values of truth and democracy (and narrative) but also acceptance of complexity and attitudes of irony that were difficult to reconcile with the science of history and conventional and foundational conceptions of hard "fact" and indeed anticipations of later notions of cultural construction.

American historiography had a literary side that intensified these attitudes, expressed most prominently in the work of Vernon L. Parrington, who followed the trail of Moses Coit Tyler in his studies of literature of colonial times (1878) and the American Revolution. Reacting to his brief Harvard experience, the "gentile tradition," and professional orthodoxy, Parrington took a critical and democratic line, drawing on literary sources but set in a social and cultural context. In this turn toward intellectual history he was followed in more scholarly terms by Merle Curti, Ralph Gabriel, Richard Hofstadter, Henry Steele Commager, and Arthur Schlesinger, Jr., who all sought positive interpretations of the American political heritage, and with emphasis on what Curti called the "exterior" as well as the "interior" of ideas. From a different angle came Allan Nevins, who had established his reputation as a journalist, biographer, and business historian and, though without a doctorate, became president of the American Historical Association, to whom he preached the cause of historical writing as a literary art and source of public influence.[101] So indeed did other historians with even fewer claims to professional status, such as Van Wyck Brooks, who produced a comprehensive and colorful but undervalued five-volume survey of "the writer in America" from 1800 down to the "generation of 1915," in the spirit not only of the traditionalism of T. S. Eliot's criticism but also of the progressivism of James Breasted's "dawn of conscience," which brought America, despite its special experiences and self-absorption, back within the horizons of world history.

Beyond the Horizon

Mainstream European historiography in the Herodoto-Thucydido-Polybio-Livio-Eusebian tradition was situated not only in national but also in universal and world contexts, with ethnocentric historians looking out on mysterious edges, from Herodotus's "Scythians" to the "barbarians" and "pagans" invidiously and self-servingly labeled by classical and Christian cultures. The impulses to explore the more remote reaches of global history in both space and time were intensified by the great discoveries of the Renaissance, the rise of science, and the Enlightenments of the eighteenth century, as in the work of authors like Vico, Herder, Voltaire, and Gibbon; and the result was the expansion of historical horizons in the form of the history of civilization, of *Weltgeschichte, Kulturgeschichte,* and the genre defined oxymoronically as the "philosophy of history." Yet beyond this neo-Polybian imperial thrust were alien traditions of written memory which had different centers and visions and which were in the course of time incorporated into the Western mainstream, whether or not with adequate "historical" understanding. In modern times these included, on the most visible edges of Europe, the "mini-nationalisms," which followed the lead of the major states, even as they were being intimidated or dominated by them.[102] The old theory of the "Four Mon-archies" was replaced in modern times by the imperial dynastic states of Spain, Britain, France, and, less successfully but more destructively, Germany. In a long perspective Eastern Europe emerged under the conflicting rules of four empires—the Roman (Byzantine), the Habsburg, the Ottoman, and the Rus-sian, all of which had disappeared in the wake of the European conflicts culminating in the Great War of 1914–18 and were replaced by the new states of the Baltic and the Balkans.

In all of these nationalist and mini-nationalist traditions historiography played a central role in the process of state-building and especially what has recently been designated nation "inventing." The Livian model of confecting a national tradition out of myth as well as official records was continued, or revived, by Renaissance scholars, who were hired to produce elegant Latin histories of the various European states (France, England, Spain, etc.), or would-be states (Italy, Germany, Hungary, etc.), and by their more critical vernacular successors and imitators, who nevertheless preserved their pro-pagandistic function. The genre was expanded, too, to include histories of cities, institutions, families, and notable individuals (although the debate as to whether biography was really a form of historiography continued), which were all normally apologetic and designed to serve particular interests and to reject external criticism. Other sorts of expansion opened historical narrative not only to parts of society not part of the ruling elite—middle and laboring classes, women, colonial possessions, slaves, and others—but also to private occupations and activities connected (in the terms adopted by German histo-rians) not to the actions of the *Machtstaat* but to the life of the *Kulturstaat*.

According to Ranke, the major units of universal history were the powerful national states, that is, the "great powers"—Rome being the reigning para-digm and Livy the historiographical model—with smaller polities operating, if at all, in their shadows and spheres of influence. The writing of history was carried on largely in these terms, and the little states, or mini-nationalities, imitated their dominating associates in the "European state-system" by seek-ing to tell the stories of their own origins, growth, and emergence into moder-nity, even if this meant imagining or inventing a national past. As "France," "Spain," "England," "Italy," and "Germany" had projected their political structures and cultural identities into a deep medieval or even ancient past, so the states, or would-be states of Scandinavia, the Baltic, and the Balkans (not to mention minorities within sovereign states) sought to define their own traditions and heritages as cultural foundations or supplements for political autonomy, independence, sovereignty, and perhaps further expansion. From the Romantic period (or even earlier) Belgians, Poles, Estonians, Latvians, Lithuanians, Czechs (Bohemians), Hungarians, Finns, Romanians, Bulgarians, Yugoslavians (and various mini-nationalities assigned to this rubric),[103] Basques, Catalans, Bretons, Irish, Swiss, and many others sought their national roots, pedigrees, languages, heroes, monuments, and "places of memory" in the light of a hopeful or defiant vision of national identity and destiny. And the pattern was recapitulated in the wake of the collapse of the Soviet Union and emergence of a dozen nationalities (besides the Baltics) as independent states, not to speak of (among others) those of the Mid-East, Africa, Latin America, and Quebec.

One case in point is that of Belgium, which established its independence in the revolution of 1830 but which could claim a cultural, quasi-political tradition going back to the Burgundian state of the fifteenth century. Though divided *between* French- and Dutch-speaking populations, "Belgium" (a coinage of Renaissance humanists from the tribe mentioned by Caesar) had a cultural and spiritual heritage that made possible the rich and full-scale national story told by Henri Pirenne in the early twentieth century comparable to the grand narratives assembled by eighteenth- and nineteenth-century French, English, Spanish, German, and Italian historians. Within a standard geographical and linguistic framework and on the basis of archeological remains, coins, art objects, and written records, Pirenne — devotee of "scientific" as well as nationalist and royalist history — fabricated a continuous story of an imagined, if divided, "people" and their various conquerors and rulers from the state-building projects of the first Burgundian dukes down to the nineteenth-century political incarnation. Of course Pirenne, despite his European horizons and sympathies, did not escape criticism from French and Dutch scholars, including that of his friend Pieter Geyl, but the main lines of his narrative have remained intact. Even Geyl, while rejecting Pirenne's "Belgian soul" (*âme belgique*), introduced his own mythical concept of racial stock (*stam*).[104]

One of the factors that blurs this outline even further is the fact that the small nationalities cannot really join the master narrative of Western history except through the intermediary of translation (especially in the imperial languages of English, French, German, Italian, and Spanish) and interpretation of sources by Eurocentric scholars who have come late to the study of alien, colonized, and decolonized peoples. Even the classic compendia such as those of Geijer (Sweden), Keyser (Norway), Friis et al. (Denmark), and Szilágy (Hungary) have never been translated into the major European languages, and of course this is the case also with more remote national traditions of the Far East. Postmodernism is said to have undermined grand narratives, but such failures of scholarly exchange have contributed to this more concretely. Under these conditions "global history" can hardly aspire to a simple story line, and like current views of evolution and human nature, human history can only appear in fragmentary form, with many conflicting story lines and no particular goal beyond the remnants of ancient ideals. Yet the requirements of the genre of Western historiography depend on particular points of view and coherent narrative, and so, like the nation-builders and inventors of old, we are forced to imagine and even to invent story lines and meanings which make sense from our current centrally located perspectives.

A special case among the "great powers" was the Austro-Hungarian Empire, multi-national descendant of the old Holy Roman Empire dissolved by Napoleon in 1806. Austrian historical scholarship, centered in Vienna, followed the German pattern, especially after the defeat of 1866, although in the twentieth century new directions were taken by scholars like Ludo Hartmann (d. 1924), whose history of medieval Italy (1897–1923) adopted a materialist and evolutionary interpretation, and Alfons Dopsch (d. 1953), whose *Economic and Social Foundations of European Civilization* (1937) emphasized the continuity of Western society from Roman times through German invasions and settlements.[105] The central problem of modern Austrian history, the conflict with Prussia and the *kleindeutsch* view of German unification, was addressed most famously by Heinrich Friedjung (d. 1941) in his study of the Dual Monarchy and his *Age of Imperialism*, (1920–23), praised by A. J. P. Taylor, and Josef Redlich (d. 1936) in his study of the political problems of Austria up to 1687 (1920–26) and of Austrian war government (1924). The *grossdeutsch* line was continued by Metternich's biographer Heinrich Ritter von Srbik, both before and after the *Anschluss*, and was in effect absorbed by the new form of imperialism and the view of the future of *Mitteleuropa* created by Prussianist National Socialism, defending the West from Asianist "barbarism."

After independence Hungary had a rich production of historical research and writing, which continued along two rival lines. One was the history of ideas (*Geistesgeschichte*) under the influence of Dilthey and the "Minerva School" of Theodor Thienemann and also Gyula Szeckfű, who shifted emphasis from political to cultural history and the "spiritual life of Hungary" expressed in its Magyar heritage. This approach was highlighted by the volumes edited by him and Bálint Hóman (7 vols.; 1927–34) and by Sándor Domanovszky (5 vols.; 1923) and the manifesto on "new paths of Hungarian

Historiography" edited in 1931 by Hóman, who also contributed a chapter to the Cambridge Medieval History the following year. The "Hungarian Review Society," led by Szeckfű, also sponsored a Universal History (1935–37) according to the *geistesgeschichtlich* methods. The other line of interpretation was a radical, materialist historiography in the Marxist mode, which continued under Soviet domination and rejected the "bourgeois" and "counter-revolutionary" views of the national cultural historians. Other schools included those of economic and sociological history and of ethnohistory.[106] One of the great Hungarian historians, torn between political activism and scholarship, was Oskár Jászi, who wrote classic books on the dissolution of the Austro-Hungarian Empire and the Hungarian revolution, and spent the last two decades of his life at Oberlin College until his death in 1957.[107]

Most prominent among the second-level European powers were Poland, Czechoslovakia (itself a "dual" nation," the Slovakian part coming late to national consciousness),[108] Hungary, and Romania, which all had rich national traditions that asserted claims to deep antiquity but which were all swept up by the destructive forces of Nazi and Soviet ideology. Polish history was divided by the pessimism of the Cracow school and the optimism of the Warsaw school, which struggled to control the interpretation of national history, although they moved to a sort of synthesis after the war and in the period of independence, when there was a flowering of historical scholarship up to the German invasion in 1939.[109] Polish historians were concerned above all with the old question of origins and with the impact of the partition of their state by the great powers, but in following the ups and downs of their national traditions they also considered political, military, and ecclesiastical history and relations with the Baltic, Scandinavian, and other foreign states. The Polish Historical Society represented the nation in the third of the postwar international congresses. After the outbreak of the Second World War Polish scholars continued work in exile. One of the most prominent of these was Oskar Halecki, who taught and published especially in the medieval field at both Cracow and Warsaw universities until 1939, when he moved first to the Sorbonne and then to American universities (Vassar and Fordham). In 1952 Halecki published a classic revisionist book in English on the "borderlands" of Europe, which—following political events—looked to the further horizons and edges of world history.

In the twentieth century Czech historiography took a "critical" turn under Jaroslav Goll (d. 1929) and his followers, including Josef Šusta and Josef Pekař, who, though they were favorable to the Austrian background of their national history, rejected the legends of the Romantic school, led by Palacký and continued by Thomas Masaryk, professor at Charles University, who wrote on the philosophy of history from a moral, or religious, and anti-Marxist standpoint. An admirer of the tradition stemming from the Czech Reformation and the heroic figure of Jan Hus, Masaryk was nevertheless a critic of polemical history, as indicated by his part in the "battle of the manuscripts" over the use of falsified documents in the national cause.[110] He was also a dedicated defender of liberal democracy, and he became the first president of the newly created Czechoslovakian Republic. Masaryk was joined in his critical efforts by Goll (d. 1929), whose aim was to restore the Czech-Bohemian story to a larger European context. As reflected in university courses, the seminar method introduced by Goll, periodicals, and monographs, Czech historical scholarship enjoyed a significant revival between the wars, though unfortunately this was cut short by the Nazi invasion, followed by the Communist coup.

Scandinavia, an integral part of Europe, though marginalized by most historians since the eighteenth century, followed European patterns in the explorations of its pasts—Danish, Swedish, and Norwegian—with corresponding institutions, museums, journals, source collections, monograph and textbook series, and teaching practices. Scandinavian scholars agreed on the Germanic roots of their early settlements, but not on the more remote ties with Indo-European culture, being divided about the northern or southeastern origins and, like their European colleagues, being dependent on mythical traditions as well as the relatively rich archeological remains. In the nineteenth and twentieth centuries they adopted the methods of German and later French professional historians, that is, the seminar as a teaching device and ideas such as "mentality" to interpret the materials assembled to define and to defend their national traditions. Among the major published but untranslated works were the histories of Denmark (1896–1907) and of Norway edited by Alexander Bugge et al. (6 vols.; 1907–17); Edvard Bull's history of medieval Christianity in Norway (1912), emphasizing the institutional rather than the religious aspects of this subject; Halvdan Koht's revisionist studies of Norwegian history; Johann Steenstrup's five volumes on the Normans (1876–1925); and many specialized publications on particular periods and problems. Norway not only developed its own "historical school" but took part in conversations about Marxism and historicism.[111] In Sweden the leading historian was Harald Hjärne (d. 1922), who was professor at the University of Uppsala, whose (untranslated) work focused on the seventeenth and eighteenth centuries, and who left a number of disciples. No less rich and even more isolated linguistically is the historiography of Finland, including not only national topics but also a collaborative six-volume universal history (1912–21).

In general outline the story of national historiography was much the same for the Baltic countries, which also enjoyed nineteenth-century "awakenings," the professionalization of history, with institutes, journals, and a large volume of scholarly publications, especially in political history, and a brief period of interwar independence before Nazi and Soviet set-backs. Some of the classic works were published in German, such as Theodor Schiemann's study of Russian, Polish, and Lithuanian history down to the seventeenth century (1886–87). The leading twentieth-century historian of Lithuania was Zenonas Ivinskis (d. 1971), though there were contributions as well by German, Polish, and, later, Russian historians. For Estonia it was Hans Kruus (d. 1976), whose survey was translated into German and French, while the major history of Latvia was published by exile scholars during the Soviet period in Sweden. The Latvian Historical Institute, founded in 1936 with a journal starting in 1937, supported the study of world as well as national history, though this expanding scholarship was also cut off by German and Russian occupation.

Of all the East European nationalities Romania claimed the closest ties with the West and with classical antiquity, its historians defending the idea of a Roman pedigree by way of the Dacians, modern identity after the union of Moldavia and Wallachia in 1859, and independent status in 1877. Romanian historiography entered the European mainstream with the work, philosophical as well as historiographical, of Alexandru Xenopol and Nicolae Iorga, and with its own "critical school" and concomitant publication of documents, establishment of institutes of historical research, and development of auxiliary sciences.[112] Iorga, a political leader as well as Romania's premier historian, worked voluminously in ancient, Byzantine, Ottoman, and Hungarian as well as national history, in French, English, and German and Romanian versions, toward larger visions not only of Southeast Europe but of "humanity" in general. In the 1930s Iorga became prime minister and minister of education; and despite his conservative, xenophobic, and antisemitic nationalism he was assassinated in 1940 by Romanian fascists of the Red Guard, as Romania fell under the domination first of Germany and then of the Soviet Union until 1989. Older traditions continue, and recently Lucian Boia has sought deeper historical truths extractable from myth.[113]

Another precarious multi-national state was Yugoslavia, though its complex nationalism was fueled by the separate national traditions of Serbia, Croatia, and other minorities, including Montenegro, Slovenia, and Dalmatia. The Serbian revolution of 1805 was described by Ranke himself (using the account of a friend), although he regarded Serbia generally as outside the European sphere of activity. Serbia developed its own national tradition beginning with research into chronicles and folksongs and continuing through derivative scientific and Marxist phases of historical writing. This was paralleled by Croatian historiography, which moved from national enthusiasm to critical scholarship, including the review of the Croatian people by Ferdo Šišič, which appeared in 1917, and also by the newer divergent traditions of Bosnia, Herzegovina, Dalmatia, and Slovenia, especially in reaction to Austrian domination. Under Tito such mini-traditions were united, at least temporarily, behind a unified, Marxist state, but they diverged again after the death of Tito with new waves of national awakening and movements of "national" independence. Bulgarian historical writing, which began in the eighteenth century, displayed similar patterns, seeking medieval origins, struggles for emancipation, and modern identity before its submergence by Marxist ideology, yet remaining convinced of the political value of historical scholarship, as did so many nationalists and internationalists in the wake of the Great War. Nor would they lose this conviction after the experience of an even greater war a generation later.

The national awakenings of the generations before the war hoped for fulfillment in Wilson's plan for redrawing the European map along national and ethnic lines—a program which in 1918 Maurice Francis Egan, former ambassador to Denmark, referred to as "the great reckoning which the world awaits to-day."[114] After the war Seignobos suggested a meeting in Paris of a "syndicate of the small discontented nations," but nothing could be done in the shadow of the League of the major powers.[115] For the rest of the century there was a rough road ahead—or no road at all—for the mini-nationalities in the face first of German and then of Soviet imperialism and international agreement; but the national historical traditions beyond the European sphere and outside the areas of modernization continued to gain force, and world history remained fragmented by cultural "points of view," including gender differences as well as the multicultural and multi-ideological confusion which still confronts us (and "them").[116]

These scholars all participated in the international community of historians working to pile up the unimaginable and unmanageable mass of scholarship that defined the historiographical canon in its largest expanse, and justice cannot truly be done to this literature except through endless bibliographical listing. This is the case even of the major national traditions, whose representatives are practically beyond such a quixotic bibliographical or prosopographical listing. Yet the history of history in the twentieth century cannot be separated from the efforts of the thousands of professional scholars who, whether they admitted it or not, worked on behalf of the common goal of historical understanding.

As far as mainstream historical writing was concerned, intellectual continuities are apparent in the long careers and memories of a significant number of master historians who lived through much of the past century and had a place in the international community, the globalized form of the Republic of Letters. Examples of these, right, left, and center, include, in Italy, Gaetano Salvemini (1873–1957), Luigi Salvatorelli (1886–1974), Federico Chabod (1901–60), Delio Cantimori (1904–66), and Arnaldo Momigliano (1908–87); in the Netherlands Johan Huizinga (1872–1945), Jan Romein (1893–1962), and Pieter Geyl (1887–1966); in Spain Rafael Altamira (1866–1951), Ramón Menéndez Pidal (1869–1968), Américo Castro (1885–1972), Claudio Sánchez Albornoz (1893–1972), and Jaime Vincens Vives (1910–60); and in America, among others, Carl Becker (1873–1945), Charles Beard (1874–1948), Mary Beard (1876–1958), Lynn Thorndike (1882–1965), C. H. McIllwain (1871–1968), S. E. Morison (1887–1976), George Sarton (1884–1956), R. H. Bainton (1894–1984), Wallace Ferguson (1902–83), Garrett Mattingly (1900–1962), and J. H. Hexter (1910–96). Yet if such scholars, prominent citizens of a professional province in the international community, collectively brought coherence to the historiographical project, they also, as individuals, illustrated the fragmentary nature of the historical calling in a war- and ideology-torn century; and collectively this is even more apparent in their successors in the twentieth-first century. To do real justice to the work of this aspect of the modern Republic of Letters would turn this scattered story into an immense bibliography beyond powers of even computer-assisted synthesis. Henri Berr's dream remains unrealized.

4

Modern Times

History must always be rewritten.
— *Johann Wolfgang von Goethe*

History à la Mode

Disillusionment with history was a common attitude among intellectuals of the generation of 1914, but the upshot was not so much rejection as skepticism. As T. S. Eliot put it in 1920,

> History has many cunning passages, contrived corridors
> And issues, deceives with whispering ambitions,
> Guides us by vanities. . . .[1]

Like Kafka, Eliot exaggerated his own age and, despite his reliance on Western tradition, regarded the Europe of his day as a "decayed house" — "heartbreak house," Bernard Shaw called it. "And what are poets for in a destitute time?" asked Heidegger, repeating the question posed by Hölderlin well over a century before.[2] The same might be asked about historians, especially those who had been trumpeting the values of culture, progress, nationalism, and world order. So what was left after turning once again against the Old?

"Make it new," said Ezra Pound, and in the past century historians as well as poets have often taken this advice.[3] In America and continental Europe the original (though not entirely unprecedented) "new history," conceived along national lines, continued into the 1930s and beyond, but it was increasingly supplanted by still newer so-called "new histories," which took many directions — up and down, in and out, right and left, etc.[4] In other words it turned to new philosophies of history, new ways of seeing history from below, especially economic and social, psychohistory, global history, and ideological interpretations in the service of state, party, or method. From the eighteenth century a shift continued to include overlooked layers of society, from rulers and aristocracy to the middle, lower, and "dangerous classes," to women, servants, the disabled, the destitute, the mad, colonial and post- colonial populations, and domestic animals. The old fascination with statistics as a basis for scientific history continued in the forms of quantitative and serial history, and the recent "new" economic and social histories continued the often reductionist quest for underlying causes. The newer "new cultural history," however, has turned away from such residual positivism to a larger, more inclusive, and more indiscriminate interest in "everyday life" and activities marginal to questions of power, politics, and war — except perhaps as indirect or symbolic reflections or correlates of these. Cultural history, high, low, and in between, micro and macro: human behavior around the clock, from cradle to grave, across the world in time and space, and so what next? But perhaps the greatest transformation is the shift, "postmodern" some would say, from efforts to construct grand narratives either of Western or global history to particular, often microhistorical stories or problems leaving the great questions about the human condition unanswered. Yet in a longer historical perspective such efforts should usually be classified under the rubric not of "new" but rather of "renew."

The careers of many French historians were of course broken by military service, but this hardly gave them second thoughts about their national traditions, and indeed some reverted to older patterns of chauvinism, as with Febvre's lectures on "honor and fatherland" delivered in 1946–47.[5] In some cases the lives of historians came to enhance national tradition, as with Bloch and Maspero, both sons of eminent scholars, Bloch's father a historian of Rome and Maspero's father a leading Egyptologist. Bloch was executed in the resistance in 1944, his tragic story, legend, and manuscript remains being tended by Lucien Febvre, while Maspero died in a concentration camp the following year. And how many lesser lights and lights to be were also extinguished?

Historical scholarship was swept up even more forcibly in the Second than in the First World War. Febvre and Bloch both served in the First, but only Bloch volunteered for the Second, being fifty-four and eight years younger than his senior partner in the *Annales,* even as he was working on a large synthesis of French history (which he intended to dedicate to Pirenne, who had died in 1935). Bloch was executed by the Vichy government in 1944 as a member of the resistance, leaving his account of the war years in his *Strange Defeat.* Until his own death ten years later Febvre continued his work (with the help of Braudel and other disciples) as editor of the *Annales,* academic patron, critic, and leader of the cult of Bloch (despite his dispute over the control of the *Annales*).[6] He was also instrumental in founding the famous "Sixth Section" of the Ecole Normal des Hautes Etudes Practiques in 1947, which carried on the Annales paradigm. Staying in his imperial position in French academe, Febvre published his *Combats for History* in three volumes, and saw to the publication of Bloch's works, including his *Historian's Craft,* which was written during the war and dedicated to Febvre. Bloch's achievement Febvre did not hesitate to compare with those of Pirenne and Fernand Braudel, who likewise had carried on their scholarly work in German prisons.

Bloch's unfinished, posthumous book, at once an exercise in the Renaissance genre of *ars historica* (or *laus historiae*), an introduction to the historical methodology of the Annales school, and his own historiographical testament, was designed more specifically to answer the question asked by his young son but in fact posed many years earlier in the old handbook of Langlois and Seignobos: "What is the use of history?" For Bloch history was still the old Herodotean project of unlimited inquiry—that is, citing Leibniz, "the thrill of learning singular things"[7]—but it had come to transcend the simple narration of deeds; for now, Bloch argued, "it struggles to penetrate beneath the mere surface of actions, rejecting not only the temptations of legend and rhetoric, but the still more dangerous poisons of routine learning and empiricism parading as common sense."[8] In this argument Bloch still felt the pull of Marx as well as Durkheim (and indeed Febvre had criticized his overdependence on sociological categories in his volumes on feudal society), but like Pirenne, Febvre, Braudel, and their colleagues (as well as all the proponents of *Lebensphilosophie* of that generation) Bloch celebrated not theory but "life," and this he found in abundance in the middle ages—whose "dark" legend has been exposed and chronicled by Febvre's former friend and largely unacknowledged collaborator, the medievalist Lucie Varga, who had been a student of Alfons Dopsch and who, after breaking off relations with Febvre, returned to Austria after 1934.[9]

At the same time Bloch continued to defend the critical and technical tools of the historian's craft, which were a measure of the profession of history since Mabillon, since Voltaire, since Guizot, since Fustel, since Langlois and Seignobos, and again since Febvre. History, like prehistory, needs intelligent questions, though not judgments or artificial categories like "centuries" or even the "middle ages" in its projects, and (according to Fustel) needs "linkages" as well as facts. Moreover — here invoking Maitland rather than hermeneutical theory — history had to be read backwards, though not as far back as the conjectural level of "origins." Most important, the historian had to be equipped to explore alien terrain, especially that of unfamiliar languages, although again, with reference for example, to the serf (or the Russian *krepostnoi* or the Romanian and Hungarian counterparts), underlying linkages were more important than particular names — although on the other hand one should remember that the so-called "feudalisms" from China to Greece should not be lumped together under one rubric. At all times the concern of the historian was the search for causes, and — as Bloch remarked in the concluding, broken-off sentence of the book, which might be taken as the motto of the Annales school, "the causes cannot be assumed," as philosophical determinists tended to do: "They are to be looked for."[10] So the Herodotean quest was continued by distant and more sophisticated offspring.

The Second World War, like the First and no less traumatically, shattered many lives, and yet in methodological terms it had limited impact on the theory and practice of history, at least among the victors. The idea of progress was no longer a dogma for most intellectuals, but it was still an issue to be debated between the emotional poles of optimism and pessimism, and it was still an unreflective premise in popular historical writing, at least in the form of "modernization." In 1950 Toynbee could feel more confident about "Western Civilization's future" than he had in 1929, and the debates around his continuing *Study of History* showed that he was not alone in his tempered optimism.[11] As with the first war there were many careers which, however disrupted, displayed continuity from the 1930s — and some indeed from before 1914 — to the 1950s, with historical scholarship in general remaining in many of the old institutional and methodological channels, with émigré scholars, especially from Germany, reinforcing these continuities. The *Annales* school continued its old — but always rhetorically innovationist — ways, and so in many ways did American "new history." If history was a "seamless cloak," in Maitland's complacent words, so despite the rhetoric of rupture and revolution was European historiography, although the connecting strands were apparent more in the national traditions than in the new global genre that was continuing and extending the old Christian universal history.

Nevertheless, professional historians, whatever their differences, did maintain an international intellectual community extending over a large span of time, and indeed the careers of some scholars carried over two wars and three generations. Continuity, if not consistency, can be seen in all the national traditions, despite ideological, institutional, and military disruptions. In Germany Friedrich Meinecke (1862–1954), Percy Ernst Schramm (1894–1970), and Gerhard Ritter (1889–1967), and in Austria Heinrich Ritter von Srbik (1878–1951), Alfons Dopsch (1868–1953), and Otto Brunner (1898–1982) carried on their scholarly projects within violently shifting perspectives on the role of Germany in European and world history; and so did such exiles as Ernst Kantorowicz (1895–1963), Hans Baron (1900–1988), Felix Gilbert (1905–91), and Walter Ullmann (1910–83). In many ways they still worked in the shadow of Ranke, whose association with power politics and the state made him controversial, although to some his orientation seemed more relevant than ever because of its relevance to the questions about the origins of two major wars and because of his importance in "the shaping of the historical discipline."[12] In the wake of the war, however, the Rankean hegemony was challenged, for example by Friedrich Meinecke and his student Felix Gilbert, who turned rather to the critical views of Burckhardt and the cultural focus encouraged by his work.[13] German historians also resumed the social and economic history which had been studied under the impulse of social science and materialism if not doctrinaire Marxism, but which had been largely discredited during the Weimar and Nazi periods.[14]

In Italy Gaetano Salvemini, activist and exile as well as historian, brought Marxist theory to bear in his major study of Florentine social struggles in the late thirteenth century (1899), but later he turned to modern themes, including the French Revolution, Mazzini, Fascism, and historical method, especially in his lectures on "history and science" given at the University of Chicago (1939).[15] The "new historiography" of the younger generation was represented by scholars like Federico Chabod (1901–60) and Delio Cantimori (1904–66).[16] Nevertheless, both worked under German influence and in the tradition of Italian liberal and nonconformist thought deriving from Renaissance humanism. Chabod wrote variously on Machiavelli, unification, diplomatic history, Fascism, and more generally the opposition between freedom and power in Italian national history, while Cantimori's subject was the sixteenth-century Italian heretics whose contributions were in the area of religious toleration and liberty. Both also wrote on questions of historical method in conventional professional terms, Chabod in particular, though an admirer of Croce's own historical work, rejecting the abstractions of his overarching *Storicismo*.[17]

In France, under the leadership of Febvre and Bloch, then Febvre alone, and later Braudel and other epigones, the *Annales* school was the intellectual, academic, and professional center of activity both before and after the war and continued to be so for the rest of the century, though with several generational changes. In Britain, though the old political and constitutional fields of research continued to be pursued with ever more specificity, the Whig-Tory ideological dominance was challenged by socialist, usually Marxist, scholars, who operated on the margins of the profession, especially in economic, social, and labor history and later by anti-ideological revisionists, who preferred the trees to the putative forest. German and to some extent Italian historians were plunged into a frenzy of anxious reviewing and guilty revising of their national history, seeking the roots, causes, responsibilities, and exculpations of the ostentatious turn taken in 1933, and a new story to be told about their tragedies. Nevertheless, the study of history was also, through increasing interdisciplinary contacts, expanding into a wide range of specialties, which were received into the academy and which produced sub-disciplines, with attendant courses, monographs, textbooks, conferences, and journals devoted not only to the histories of mini-national traditions but also to the history of science, literature, art, religion, women, children, psychohistory, and "the history of everything" (*l'histoire de tout*).

This latter formula was one of the ambitious dreams of Fernand Braudel, who in the 1950s succeeded Febvre as leader of what he did not hesitate to call the "French historical school." Following the drift of Durkheimian sociology (and perhaps Tainean history) by way of Berr and Febvre—who suggested that Braudel reverse the order of his plan for a book on Phillip II and the Mediterranean—Braudel did indeed give priority to the latter (and dedicate the book to Febvre). In it he focused not on men and events, not on the "surface agitation," which Simiand, after Lacombe, denigrated as "l'histoire événementielle," but on geohistory and socioeconomic patterns (if not "laws") and so on synchronic rather than diachronic analysis, or rather on both together by means of a view of an "almost immobile history"—"history that stands still," in the words of Le Roy Ladurie[18]—"that relates individuals to their milieu."[19] Nor, as was apparent in a debate with Lévi-Strauss, did Braudel want to surrender to doctrinaire structuralism, useful as it was in matters of *longue durée;* but he deplored old-fashioned fascination with discrete historical "events" and the intellectual "prison" of "short duration"; and like Berr and Febvre he opposed the pernicious influence of the handbook of Langlois and Seignobos. He wanted to revive a "grand history" that touches all dimensions of life, believing that history was multi-rhythmic, distributed into geographic and social as well as individual and psychological time, and open to a wide and interdisciplinary range of methods. This was the "new history" which he invoked again in his inaugural lecture at the Collège de France in 1950 and which he saw reaching out beyond the Mediterranean world to the rest of the globe, including the Far East.[20]

Braudel's agenda included the conscription of virtually all the human sciences into the service of a history that was conceived not only as "grand" but even, potentially, as "total," and in this effort his focus was not periodization but rather hierarchy, though temporal elements were incorporated into his version of Berr's historical synthesis. His work on the Mediterranean in the early modern period, conceived during the war and written during various intervals in the times of catastrophes, was published in 1949. In his second masterwork on capitalism and civilization Braudel moved from the Mediterranean to the global arena, although the marketplace and long-distance commerce still provided the field of historical synthesis. For Braudel history was a sort of three-tiered system, beginning with geohistory, the environment, overlaid by economics, the market and capitalism, and rising to the level of civilization. In this system, as in that of the sociologists and Marxism, events were downplayed, but, unlike in Marxism, reductionist factors were denied an explanatory role. Instead Braudel developed, or rather accepted and elaborated on, rhetoric of total history that accommodated all levels of activity as well as his own personal descriptive and conjectural style, which placed him again just in the tradition not of Fustel (as Bloch noted in his review of Febvre's first book) but of Michelet, whom he called "a seductive master but occasionally a dangerous one."[21] This was even more obvious in his last, unfinished work, which was a reverentially rich quest for the "identity of France," reviewed, as he said, "from the perspective of every single social science."[22]

Yet if the new history turned inward for its vision and outward into *tours d'horizons*, temporal and spatial, the systematic thrust of social science left its imprint, so that chronology was subordinated to ordered levels of collective and individual life. For Braudel historical presentation took the form of a cabinet of curiosities arranged according to the steps between material and spiritual existence and the three time-scales which he drew from his interdisciplinary sources — or perhaps a multi-course meal, and (as he confessed privately to Jack Hexter) his eyes always tended to be bigger than his stomach.[23] In any case Braudel's cabinet was replicated on the cultural level by the "essay on historical psychology" by Robert Mandrou, who took and completed an old project of Febvre within the categories of mental "structures and conjunctures" and mental "climates."[24] To Braudelian history (as to Terentian poetry) nothing human was alien. As a "science" history was drawn to the general and the collective, and so to statistical, quantitative, and serial history, but as a human science it could not ignore the human self and its preoccupations — religion, art, science, philosophy, and other facets of "civilization." Moreover, the old correlation between material base and superstructure, although its ghost may be perceived in the Braudelian hierarchies, was inadequate, and conventional chronology often inadequate, for an appreciation of "total history," which continued to be a "noble dream" for French scholars even if restricted mainly to the small French hexagon, which no longer dominated the lower part of the Eurasian peninsula, except perhaps in cultural memory.

Britain in Decline

In Britain before and after the Second World War there was no "new history," but there were some movements which, within a framework of British empiricism, altered the course of earlier trends. Among the most prominent historians in the postwar period were A. F. Pollard (1869–1948), G. M. Trevelyan (1876–1962), R. H. Tawney (1880–1962); Lewis Namier (1888–1960), Eileen Power (1889–1940), J. E. Neale (1890–1975), E. H. Carr (1892–1982), David Knowles (1896–1984), A. J. P. Taylor (1906–90), Christopher Hill (1912–93), and Hugh Trevor-Roper (1914–), carrying on the old projects of national history, with others, such as E. H. Carr (1892–1982), Maurice Dobb (1900–1967), Joseph Needham (1900–1995), Alfred Cobban (1901–68), Geoffrey Barraclough (1908–84), and Isaiah Berlin (1909–97), working beyond insular concerns, and Arnold Toynbee (1889–1975), wandering still further afield to extend the British historiographical empire with the help of the universities and presses of Oxbridge. Among other contemporaries were Marxist historians, who carried on in a materialist mode without the unwieldy apparatus of a philosophy of history; those who adopted the methods retrospectively known as "Namierization," a more rigorous sort of economic and prosopographic examination of Parliament than Charles Beard's study of the economic background of the American founding fathers; and still another kind of "revisionists" (this time proudly self-styled and not of pejorative Marxist usage) — to which academic divisions were added the usual tendency of one generation to contradict another. Nor did a shift of emphasis from political to social history change old positivist habits, except to transfer attention to different sorts of evidence, especially with a view to improve methods of headcounting. The ideological overlays, or underpinnings, of Tory, Whig, and Marxist interpretations acted less to transform these old methodological habits than to incite argument, narrow the focus, and carry on the search for more, though often less relevant or enlightening evidence. Beyond some kinds of ideological correctness, British empiricism and the underlying advice of Mr. Gradgrind remained in force — stick to the facts.

Most of these writers were working in heavily cultivated fields, for in general the British did not seek novelty in their researches, except (following the French precedent of a century earlier) to give still greater weight to the laboring classes, extending the socialist concerns of the Victorian period. Most scholars visited the familiar old places, trying to see new sights according to varying ideological and academic fashions. So went the Puritan Revolution, passing from the hands of Gardiner & Co. to the Marxists to the "revisionists" and "post-revisionists." Maitland and the "Cambridge school" were revised, cautiously, as was Stubbs, more ferociously, as the grand narratives of British history were undermined, if not dissolved, in contentious, anti-Whig microhistory. But such projects — even in the hands of so adept a practitioner of prosopography as Namier — were the product less of postmodern sophistication than of modern British empiricism, which prefers head-counts to intangible cultural patterns, behavior to "ideas," anecdotes to theories, trees to the forest — and of course British to continental ways of understanding history.

One of the premier investigators of early modern English history was J. E. Neale, Pollard's successor to the chair at the University of London, who devoted himself to the study of the Parliament, or anyway the House of Commons, under Elizabeth I, of whom he also wrote a standard and laudatory biography. Neale went far beyond Pollard in researching the sources, manuscript and published, official and unofficial; and indeed because of their extent he limited himself to the dramatic story of the conflicts with the crown, which for him formed the prelude to the civil wars of the next century, despite the "old illusion," soon to be revived, "that early-Stuart Parliaments had few roots in the sixteenth century."[25] Although Neale avoided other business that came before this body, he was interested in the life of the membership and in the speeches, the queen's in particular, which reminded him of those of Churchill in his own time. In general Neale took the old Whiggish line of Stubbs and Pollard — and indeed English authors of the Elizabethan period — that in this period England succeeded in resisting the common tendency of representative assemblies to fall into decay and moreover created other benefits of modern government, such as freedom of speech and conscience, however inflammatory these might be in an age still torn by religious division. Though England passed through its own civil wars, the "strange, underlying harmony" underlying "the repeated collisions between Crown and Parliament" suggested — to Neale as well as his authors — something providential in the pattern of English history.

This was one conspicuous example of the Whig view which was already coming under assault by scholars perhaps even more devoted to the study of the sources, if less receptive to the assumptions and values of the Puritan and parliamentary agents and observers of a bygone age. The outstanding example of this sort of revisionism was Lewis Namier, a Polish Jew exiled by the Russian Revolution, who ascended to the heights of the British academic intelligentsia and became a recognized expert in eighteenth-century parliamentary history as well as twentieth-century diplomacy, though he never received a major university appointment (except for Manchester, where he retired in 1953). He rejected German methods and ideas on the level not only of scholarship but also of politics, in which his sympathies inclined to Zionism. As a diplomatic historian Namier was a relentless critic of nationalism, especially in its German forms, and he attacked the unenlightened revolutions of 1848, which marked not only the collapse of the Metternichean system but also the coming state rivalries leading to at least two major wars, largely through German aspirations and designs.[26] Starting before 1914 Namier had always hoped to write a history of Europe from 1812 to 1918, but other projects prevented this, including keeping up on the period between the wars, on which he wrote many journalistic and scholarly studies. His attention became especially focused on this after the so-called "German revolution" in 1933 — about which he commented in the *Manchester Guardian* that "History supplies no analogy for that lifeless but horrible counterfeit of revolutions"; and he continued his analysis through successive studies of the official "coloured books" and the Nuremberg papers.[27]

Namier's major impact, however, came in his revisionist studies of eighteenth-century British history. His background, conservative politics, and long immersion in diplomatic history led him to a sort of historical nominalism, which made him distrustful of ideas and ideology (and the rhetoric which conveyed these) and the Whig view in general. In his controversial prosopographical and "structural" analysis of the Parliament in the age of the American Revolution he studied the House of Commons empirically and behavioristically — and, as E. P. Thompson said, "lovingly" — as an "ant-heap," asking the question why, party politics aside, members came in the first place. The "Imperial Problem," Namier argued, had to be understood not in the study of public opinion, "not so much in the conscious opinions and professed views bearing directly on it, as in the very structure and life of the Empire."[28] He was concerned more with short-term behavior and turned rather — as Charles Beard had done for the American Congress and Ronald Syme for the Roman republic — to private interests to explain this structure with emphasis on the influence not of individuals but of the great patriarchal families in the House of Commons before the rise of the party. "Namierization" was in effect the first version of the "revisionist" attempts to atomize, localize, and de-historicize the interpretation of British constitutional history by treating individuals, local areas, and ruling elites. This was not theory but, as Syme said of his own prosopographical target, "something real and tangible."[29]

Namier's scorn for professed ideals drew criticism from scholars such as Herbert Butterfield, a champion of the alliance between Christianity and history, who attacked the interpretation of Parliament in the reign of George III by "the Namier School" and its method of alternating microscopic and telescopic scrutiny — the "occupational disease" of overimmersion in details.[30] Butterfield was himself famous for an assault on the "Whig interpretation of history," but he did not mean to include intellectual history in his indictment, and indeed he made important contributions to the history of modern science within the framework, in effect, of the "Whig fallacy," which plotted scientific discoveries and ideas along a triumphalist narrative that, avoiding false and irrelevant paths, kept to the highroad of contemporary scientific philosophy. For Butterfield the Whig view was a natural survival of the religion of Victorian gentlemen, who identified British progress with human welfare and, if only unconsciously, with God's will, and he regretted excessive criticism of the Whig view. His underlying assumption, the cornerstone of intellectual history, is that the past is not quite a "foreign country," that we can to some degree enter into the minds of persons of bygone ages, and so the present can connect with the past. In an institution like the Parliament the inference for English historians is a political, constitutional, and perhaps philosophical "We" that transcends particular ages and contexts, that shares ideals and goals, or at least language and presumptions, and that has the right and duty to reflect on and even judge the process which we observe and in which we participate.[31]

These are some of the premises that led Butterfield, like his target and model, Lord Acton, to deeper explorations into the history of history, first for English tradition (during the second war), then to Western historiography more generally and in a longer perspective.[32] For him, as for Burke, history "is a living thing, and it resembles poetry rather than geometry," as illustrated by the continuity of English history in its Whiggish and Liberal form.[33] As for historical scholarship Butterfield followed Acton (through his study of the rich Acton MSS in the Cambridge University Library) and others in celebrating its German origins, though he pioneered the revisionist view that this meant not so much Ranke as his eighteenth-century precursors in Göttingen; and moreover Butterfield looked more deeply into the European historiographical past, helping to resurrect the forgotten *Histoire des histoires* of La Popelinière, published in 1599.[34] Butterfield's *Man on His Past* was, among other things, a manifesto for this enduring genre, which, he wrote, "involves an enquiry into the manner in which men have changed their sentiment for the past, their feeling about time and their awareness that they are part of the long, unceasing stream of history."[35] In his last work Butterfield traced the roots of this sort of historicism back to its Judeo-Christian origins in the Old Testament and the ancient Near East, especially to the record-keeping predecessors of Ranke and Acton, who likewise professed to "love life and hate death."[36]

Talk about the "Whig view" and Butterfield's criticism of it are still with us, and the only work which rivaled his book of 1931 in popularity was the even more "memorable" *1066 and All That,* appearing a year earlier. "History is not what you thought," the authors of this spoof of the Whig view declared. "*It is what you can remember.*"[37] The book was dedicated not only to students but also "to the Great British People, without whose self-sacrificing determination to become top Nation there would have been no (memorable) history." This was the last word on the subject, since history came to an end when — "a Bad Thing" — America replaced Britain as "top Nation." Like Queen Victoria, Ranke would probably not have been amused.

Namier's main rival as a popular-professional author in the area of diplomatic history, was A. J. P. Taylor, who likewise taught at Manchester and failed to gain a "major" university post. Taylor criticized Namier for "tak[ing] the mind out of history," though he was even more suspicious of generalizations like the idea of a European "state system," invoking (like Namier) the effects of contingency above official policy and (unlike Namier) the power of public opinion. Yet Taylor, for whom "all sources were suspect," also spoke of "the perpetual quadrille of the Balance of Power," which he traced in detail in his survey of diplomatic history from 1848 to the end of the first war, when "Europe ceased to be the centre of the world" and a new pattern would emerge out of Germany's legacy, which was Bolshevism and American intervention.[38] Taylor cultivated an even more personal style than Namier, relying on irony and paradox and even flippancy. He was also concerned with the German (and Austrian) problem in European history, to the extent indeed that he resisted the Nuremberg-inspired tendency to employ Hitler as a symbol of evil transcending the political patterns of Germany and accounting alone for the Second World War. Yet he had no doubt that for the great powers in 1939 the central issue remained that of the Versailles settlement and the start of the real war began with Germany's attack on Russia.

Taylor also undertook a major work on modern Britain, accepting an assignment for a textbook survey of the early twentieth century, which he carried out with his usual opinionated thoroughness, his irreverent sense of humor, and his own brand of wry patriotism, not to mention heavy scholarly apparatus. For Taylor it was a piece of the epic story of the British people, who, though they were the only ones to go through both wars from beginning to end and were on their way to imperial decline, "remained a peaceful and civilized people, tolerant, patient, and generous."[39] Yet he was puzzled by interwar writers, all of whom saw the barbarians breaking in ("The decline and fall of the Roman Empire were being repeated"), and Taylor himself preferred the mass media, where he was a star. Like his nemesis Trevor-Roper, he exemplified Trevelyan's notion of history as an art, but under conditions of modern technology.

Although the old-fashioned tendency to remain within national channels was widely preserved, not all leading historians in Britain were committed to their national history, as is apparent in the works of Geoffrey Barraclough, Alfred Cobban, and E. H. Carr, who devoted their lives to the histories, respectively, of Germany, France, and Russia. Barraclough was deeply immersed in German scholarship and was not deterred by involvement in Nazi politics, including for example the work of Albert Brachmann on the origins of the national state in his collection of papers by German medievalists.[40] Barraclough's own scholarly survey of "the origins of modern Germany" was extraordinarily foreshortened from a contemporary perspective, as a result no doubt of his own exposure to twentieth-century German fascination with medieval and feudal phases of their "national development"; and he allowed only a very brief overview of the modern phase (1806–1939), in which—still in the spirit of the old tradition of German scholarship—he expressed the hope that a united Germany could regain the path of progress to democracy lost in the wake of the first war and join the European community.[41] Alfred Cobban showed a much more original and indeed "revisionist" view in his survey of French history and especially in his study of the French Revolution, in which he opposed the vulgar (and already "exploded" as a theory) Marxist interpretation of a "bourgeois revolution" and prelude to emergent capitalism, opening the way to a more empirical study of the Revolution and its context.[42] For Cobban the notion of class struggle was an oversimplification, if not a fiction, and the Revolution was a political revolution, a struggle for power opposing and not promoting capitalism. Carr was a diplomat and journalist as well as historian and, though not a Communist, sympathetic to Marxism, especially its "empirical" side, and this carried him through the volumes of his history of the Bolshevik revolution and the Soviet state, which he began in 1944 and completed in 1978. Trevor-Roper, a combative expert on early modern British history (whose prominence arose from popular essays on many aspects of early modern European history and scholarly rebuttals of Tawney and Stone regarding the putative "rise of the gentry"), was distracted by the war to contemporary German history as well, as shown especially by his book on the last days of Hitler. The one conviction that united these scholars, especially those who contributed to the national narratives, was that theory was largely extraneous and that immersion in the sources was the royal road to understanding.

"What are historians for?" Virtually all established British historians have had their say about the nature and use of history, working (whether they knew it or not) in the tradition of the *ars historica,* casting judgments on their predecessors; and few of them rose very far above the level of the old platitudes which fill this professionalized genre. Unlike their French and German colleagues they tended to resist the inroads of the social sciences, with the aim of preserving the autonomy of professional history and perhaps extending its imperial domain, as Britain itself tried to preserve its position in the world (though with little hope of improving on it). In the cases of J. H. Plumb, A. L. Rowse, and Richard Pares the lessons offered were little more than a conventional profession of faith through an increasingly thorough study of the past, although Plumb framed his quasi-Whiggish argument within a simplistic view of the past as outmoded tradition or oppression, which Western historians (unlike their Chinese counterparts) were escaping through impartial and critical history.

British historians of the interwar generation were on the whole suspicious about claims to novelty in history, although E. H. Carr (who himself alluded to the Gradgrind syndrome) was receptive to some dissenting views that the historical profession would find suspect and inconvenient in the drive to master the sources and to find suitable levels of exploration to do justice to the growing mass of documentary detail. How to manage this avalanche of facts, especially after the abandonment of Marxism or a similar doctrinal support, asked Carr, invoking the words of Sombart, that in this situation "we feel like drowning in the ocean of facts until we find a new foothold or learn to swim."[43] "Facts speak," Carr remarked, but only through the historian, not for themselves; there was no invisible hand behind historical inquiry, no Whig teleology that would pre-arrange the results of research. The historian himself ("or herself" was not yet part of historiographical etiquette) was a product of history, which is perhaps why Namier chose to ignore all the revolutions except the — failed and scorned — "revolution of the intellectuals" of 1848, and why Butterfield seemed to reverse himself when he shifted from rejecting the Whig view in 1931 to embracing it in 1942 during the Second World War to include British imperialism which "the shock of 1940" made men remember that this institution "had become an organization for the purpose of liberty."[44] Namier preferred to say that Parliament was not just an "institution" but a way of life that had shaped the nation.

An exception to this conservatism, in terms of field of inquiry if not methodology, was Geoffrey Barraclough, who was appointed in 1956 to succeed Toynbee as director of the Institute of International Affairs. Having spent many years reviewing German medieval history in the old institutional vein before being appointed Toynbee's successor, Barraclough did issue a call to abandon such antiquarian subjects and to pay attention to contemporary history (which the Germans called *Zeitgeschichte*), especially the fast-changing state system taking shape during the Cold War, and he turned his eyes to more urgent questions about "the new world coming to life" after 1945. He exchanged the medieval not only for the modern but also for the "postmodern," which for him, however (as for Toynbee), was merely a provisional label, to which he hopes to begin to give some substance, in the wake of "the dwarfing of Europe."[45] As Barraclough remarked, World War I marked the end of European hegemony and the rise of "new nationalisms," the "new diplomacy" (American style), and a new global system, enhanced by new forms of communication, whose outlines or political axis were not clear, though the political and cultural contours, he was persuaded, would surely take shape within a "world civilization." Barraclough's admonitions, however, seem closer to journalism than the sort of (national) history he began by practicing. British scholars did of course stray from their usual Anglo- and Eurocentric fields of operations, but this occurred for the most part along the lines of narrow—and still national— specialties, with the Oxbridge presses extending the British historiographical empire and spheres of influence with volumes on Poland, China, Japan, Africa, India, Latin America, Islam, and other peripheral areas that played a role in the European game of power politics.

Finally, Britain too benefited from the prewar crisis through the immigration of continental scholars, and especially from the transfer of the Warburg Institute and its magnificent library from Hamburg to London.[46] Like Lord Acton but more aesthetically inclined, Aby Warburg was a scholar-collector who turned away from national restrictions and, like Jacob Burckhardt, Ernst Cassirer, Karl Vossler, Erich Auerbach, Felix Gilbert, Hans Baron, Paul Kristeller, Ernst Panofsky, Nicolai Rubinstein, and others, to the life and culture of the Italian Renaissance and the legacy of antiquity on which it drew. Warburg followed the ideas of Lamprecht in studying cultural transmission and change, with an emphasis also on iconography, the semantics of art history, and questions of patronage. Warburg's great library was the product not only of indefatigable and ingenious collecting but also of an original (and to many scholars puzzling) scheme of knowledge that was concerned less with philosophical categorization than with cultural and serendipitous affiliations, juxtapositions, eccentricities, comparisons, and serendipities. In 1933, after his death, Warburg's library, along with a growing stream of individual exiles, left Germany and took up residence in London, where ever since it has been a powerful and illuminating influence, turning Ernst Cassirer, for example, from neo-Kantian philosophy to cultural history and his own anthropology-inspired "philosophy of symbolic forms."

Germany on the March

After the emergence of Hitler, Robert Musil posed a question relevant to historians of his own generation, that of 1905: "You must believe in the future of National Socialism or in the decline of Germany. In any case, then, in the end of the tradition in which I know myself to be embedded. How can one work under these circumstances?"[47] In 1933 the lines were being drawn again between historians like Meinecke and Oncken, who clung to Rankean ideals of history as an objective science, and supporters of the new regime like Walter Frank, who saw historical scholarship as a political force in the manner of Treitschke. National conservatives and liberals alike continued to criticize the new proclivities toward racialism and official "myth," as in the case of Kantorowicz, but they seldom pressed their criticism to matters of policy. In any case not even conservative historians presented a united front, for the old opposition remained, or was revived, between *kleindeutsch* champions of Prussian dominance and nostalgia and utopian supporters of a *grossdeutsch* and pan-German empire, such as Schnabel and Srbik, who naturally favored the *Anschluss* with Austria. A division continued to exist, too, between old-style political history, which largely prevailed, and cultural history, which survived in Lamprecht's Institute in Leipzig, in which Hans Freyer succeeded Goetz in 1933. In the form of *Volksgeschichte* cultural and social history could be cultivated not only by Marxist or socialist radicals but also by sympathizers and enthusiasts for National Socialism, for whom not only the party but also the whole nation was awake and on the march. In retrospect, divisions remained, too, separating Meinecke and Ritter (and Ludwig Dehio), who both pointed out the "demonic" nature of power, from others who wanted to do business as usual despite calls for some sort of "revisionism."

After 1933 German historical scholarship experienced significant changes in personnel, leadership, and organization, as serious critics, many of them Jewish, suffered forced retirement or went into exile, especially to the United States. In 1935 Meinecke was replaced by K. A. von Müller as editor of the *Historische Zeitschrift,* while Walter Frank, a student of Müller, became head of the new Imperial Historical Commission, likewise calling for an activist and apologetic historical science to serve the new revolution. Conservatives and Nazi sympathizers continued scholarly debates, and historians like Oncken and Meinecke resisted the resurgence of vulgar nationalist and racist myths cultivated by the regime. But Oncken's mild protest and critical independence was countered vigorously by Walter Frank, and the "Oncken case" showed the limits of criticism and interpretation under the new regime and its propagandist designs; henceforth debates concerned matters of emphasis rather than serious revisionism. The "battle of the middle ages" continued, revolving still around the old poles of Prussian and Austrian policies; but after the *Anschluss* of 1938 even these divisions were blurred, as scholars like Percy Ernst Schramm, who was the author of a study of the theme of a religious and political renaissance of the Roman imperial tradition and who was swept along by the neo-medievalist vision of a "new Rome," supported the annexations of Czechoslovakia and Poland as well as Austria.[48] After 1935 the emphasis in circles of scholarship as well as propaganda was turning to *Reich, Volk,* the "Jewish Question," the "Christian West" (against the "barbarian" and Bolshevik East), and a "New Order" that would encompass not only Germany and Europe but—a residue of Austrian universalism—the whole civilized world. Yet except for the retrospective taint of Nazism, none of these themes were totally alien to the Western historiographical tradition.

Conventional historiography still lived, for instance in Franz Schnabel's four-volume history of Germany in the nineteenth century (1929–37), which was the first survey of the period since that of Treitschke, whom he called "herald of the *kleindeutsch* Reich," and which sought to see the subject "with new eyes."[49] German historians had become too specialized, Schnabel thought, collecting bricks while foreign scholars build the house; and in reaction to this he turned away from the archives to the libraries and from politics to the "inner life of people." Rejecting the nationalist and backward-looking policies of Bismarck, he celebrated the "new humanism" of Herder and Goethe and deplored the fact that this classical "German spirit" diverged from the Prussian state—and, on another level, from the "technical culture" of the later nineteenth century. In the third volume (1934) Schnabel surveyed both the empirical and the human sciences, especially the *Geschichtswissenschaften,* including philology, literature, the arts, archeology, and theology as well as the historical writing of Niebuhr and Ranke and the academic organization of the disciplines. The last volume was devoted to religion—Catholic and Protestant religion, that is, for *Judentum* was marginal to the "inner life" of the people. In the third edition, published after "the catastrophe" (1947), Schnabel was happy to report the testimony of the English economic historian J. H. Clapham concerning the value of the work and especially its freedom from the "myths" propagated by Treitschke and the Third Reich.

Another revisionist, *grossdeutsch* surveyor of German history—also Catholic but Austrian as well—was Heinrich Ritter von Srbik, whose biography of Metternich appeared in 1925 and whose study of "German unity" appeared between 1935 and 1942.[50] Like Schnabel and to some extent Meinecke, he celebrated the cosmopolitan and universalist traditions of German culture and its civilizing mission into Mitteleuropa. Srbik favored a pan-German agenda, supported the *Anschluss,* was a member of Frank's commission, and even served in the Nazi-controlled Reichstag. His book, focusing in great detail on the years 1859–66 and employing newly published materials, was written under the twofold impetus of love and sorrow—love for the German people inside and outside of the Reich and sorrow for the conflicts between Prussia and Austria that undermined this cultural and racial unity. The German Volk was both one and many (as illustrated by the old Empire and the Confederation), and Srbik's goal was a true union. Because of associations with the Nazi regime, Srbik's last years were isolated, but in 1950 he did publish, and dedicate to Meinecke, his great survey of German historiography from the Renaissance down to the time of cultural and folk history in the wake of Lamprecht and in the context of Nazi racial "science," beginning with the remark by Goethe, cited by both Ranke and Meinecke, that every age had to rewrite history — and indeed the history of historiography, as Srbik sought to improve on the surveys of (to mention the most important) Wachler, Wegele, Lorenz, Fueter, Moriz Ritter, and Below. It is significant that Srbik, while disillusioned about his Austrian-universal vision, opened his account not only to political history but also to the history of culture, literature, the arts, economics, law, and religion.

In various ways historians were encouraged to legitimize and collaborate with the policies and events succeeding the accession of Hitler, which (whatever their judgment on the man and the regime) they celebrated as a national revolution that promised to fulfill the hopes and prophecies of the older generation and the ambitions of the younger generation, grafting onto the new regime the glories of a partially invented German past dominated by the figures of Luther, Frederick the Great, and Bismarck. Sometimes the enthusiasm was unpolitical, as with Richard Benz, who invoked the intellectual and spiritual grounds for a new Reich and the "Third Volk," which would triumph peacefully; but this hardly mattered for the endorsement of the new regime.[51] Explicitly or implicitly, most members of the historical profession, among them Hampe, Haller, Oncken, Brandi, Brandenburg, Heimpel, and Andreas, supported the new, "third," thousand-year Reich that seemed to bring Germany back to her true historical path and imperial destiny.

As in the Wars of Liberation, this path was seen not only as political but also cultural and national, and historiographical style was enlarged to encompass the entire nation through the practice and theory of *Volksgeschichte*, with direct or indirect racialist (as well as "spiritual") implications that applied to a "new order" not only for Germany in the most extended sense but also for "white" Europe as a whole. Such was the argument of Brandenburg's book of 1937, *Europe and the World*, which distinguished Western from "west-Asian" and "East-Asian" "cultural circles," which defended the "blood and culture" that defined the superiority of European and Indogermanic society, and which aimed not at an isolated existence for Germany but at "the solidarity of the white race over the whole world."[52] Brandenburg ended his German history published in 1939 in virtually the same words as he had used in 1916, celebrating German unity, most recently that accomplished by Hitler "in an incredibly short time," and future hopes "even if our neighbors [1939: "the old enemies"] should again seek to throw us back into our former condition of powerless-ness" (*Ohnmacht* [1939: "powerlessness and disunion," *Ohnmacht und Zerissenheit*].[53] The old German paranoia — as well as the old dream of na-tional unity and imperialist expansion — still lived on in historiographical tra-dition, though not without some looming anxieties.

An extraordinary testimony to the pernicious conditions of scholarship dur-ing the Nazi regime is that of Victor Klemperer, a romance philologist who found it impossible to be a teacher in the sensitive area of modern language and could "only lecture on the history of ideas," though he did collect material for a critical study of Nazi linguistic innovations and perversions which he published after the war.[54] This was a time when "intellect, scholarship were the enemies," when Hitler's ranting (compared by Klemperer to Cola di Rienzo and by his wife to Jan of Leiden) symbolized the corruption of the language of Lessing and Goethe, and when Klemperer himself, a marked Jew, was forbidden the use of public libraries and his typewriter was confiscated. Also: "The fear that my scribbling could get me put into a concentration camp"; yet: "The feeling that it is my duty to write, that it is my life's task, my calling."[55] Klemperer's major project was a history of the French Enlighten-ment, which he saw as the obverse of Germany in the 1930s, although the French Revolution bore many resemblances to the German Revolution of 1933, especially in Jacobin efforts to turn the tide of history and rename everything in the expectation of a new world. Other colleagues and rivals, such as E. R. Curtius, Leo Spitzer, and Erich Auerbach, suffered the same constrictions, but unlike Klemperer they somehow managed to carry on their work on the history of world literature in exile.

Professional German historians who lived through the Nazi regime, whether surviving at home or in exile, preserved some continuities through and after the war, though not without casualties, physical and moral; but the alliance be-tween "pure science" and national destiny had obviously collapsed.[56] After the war, emphasis on the *Volk* was replaced by emphasis on "structure," as in the work of Brunner and Conze (and the early stages of *Begriffsgeschichte* and Gerhard Oestreich's writings on the military and neo-Stoicism in the process of state-building.[57]

Walter Frank, who like Müller continued to support a Nazi-oriented histo-riography, ended up committing suicide just before Germany's surrender in 1945. From this time the energies of German historians were directed toward criticizing and perhaps lamenting the grand traditions of historical scholarship and national fulfillment, though somehow also to salvaging them.[58] In his extreme old age Friedrich Meinecke emerged from the war convinced that "spiritual factors are of primary importance in history" — Goethe's, not Bismarck's Germany — and, like Gerhard Ritter and Ludwig Dehio, that there was something "demonic" about power and reason of state.[59] The "degeneration of the German people" was seen in the un-German "pan-Germanism," which Hans Delbrück had denounced long before. Not that Meinecke ever achieved very deep insight into the social roots of Nazism, and as for Hitler, Meinecke saw his rise as the result of a chain of "chance" circumstances and saw the man himself as an alien who, as Hintze had remarked, "really does not belong to our race at all," being a member of "an otherwise extinct race that is completely amoral in nature."

These were some of the views expressed in 1946 by Meinecke, in his *German Catastrophe,* which argued from the same dualism and imbalance of power and culture that informed German history. After 1933 Meinecke still tried to see something positive in Nazi innovations, and although his own professional position went into decline, he remained in contact with historians, young as well as old, including students like Hajo Holborn, who went into exile; and he labored over his great study of "historicism," whose contemporary "crisis" touched not only religious and philosophical values but also the same questions of power and culture that brought Germany to another tragic development. As usual Meinecke placed more emphasis on "spiritual factors," lamenting the breakdown of the "synthesis of intellect and state," which had been expressed by Herder and had been achieved after the Wars of Liberation, and the rise of "mass Machiavellianism," which Burckhardt had criticized and which Meinecke himself had begun to analyze in his wideranging study of "reason of state" (1924). He differed in particular with his friend Srbik (who was publishing his grand survey of German unity in the 1930s) over the Rankean principle of the central place of politics, especially the "primacy of foreign affairs," in German history.

One major historian of prewar Germany was Karl Brandi, expert on the Reformation and professor at the University of Göttingen, who, though not a Nazi, was a conservative nationalist and a prominent figure at the international historical congresses in the 1930s.[60] In 1939 he published his biography of the Emperor Charles V (soon translated by C. V. Wedgwood), who came into possession of the greatest of all empires, though it had a dynastic foundation and came to grief as a result of the first great rising of the German people under Luther. "Tragic and fateful moment in the history of the nation!" Brandi exclaimed in connection with the Diet of Worms and the condition of the German people at that turning point — "their feverish excitement was the outcome of a mighty desire, still but remotely conceived." But Charles, though a "great man," was not the long-hoped-for leader, and the German nation called into being by Luther fell, not for the first or last time, into disunity. Two years later Brandi could be seen supporting a new imperial expansion, under the German-Italian axis, which itself recalled the medieval empire, against both eastern "barbarism" and the revival of Europe on behalf of a "new world order."[61]

Perhaps most typical of the old guard of German historians who kept the Rankean faith was Gerhard Ritter, a student of Oncken, who held a professorship at the University of Freiburg from 1925 to 1956. Ritter was critical not only of the cultural history of Lamprecht but also of the idealism, historicism, and "literary" proclivities of Meinecke; and he continued to support the ideals of national unity before and after the Second World War, as apparent in the biography of Luther he published during the 1920s and of Frederick II in the 1930s, distinguishing both from the distorted Prussianism of the Nazis. Though no democrat, he tried to keep the liberal faith against the Nazi tide, and he defended Oncken against the assault by Frank. In 1940, forbidden to leave Germany, he published a book on *The Corrupting Influence of Power* (*Machtstaat und Utopie*), opposing that (not necessarily evil) "reason of state" associated with Machiavelli to the utopian view of Thomas More, that is, the continental to the insular position.[62] This argument he continued after the war in his great work on the "problem of militarism," *Statecraft and the Art of War*, which he finished in the last year of the war, though he did not publish it for another ten years. As with other historians hoping to combine *Geist* with *Realpolitik,* Ritter prescribed a fusion of state and culture, the body and spirit of national tradition, while admitting that an imbalance between the two had occurred in the past generation. Ritter was also associated with the resistance to Hitler and was imprisoned in the last months of the war, four years later becoming president of the Association of the Historians of Germany (*Verband der Historiker Deutschlands*).

In 1948 Ritter published his reflections on "the German problem," opposing the "revisionists," who rejected the idea of national unity but also seeking to transcend the terrible dualism which had informed German history, torn as it had been between the spiritual ideals of Luther and Pietism and the Realpolitik of Prussianism as represented by Frederick the Great and Bismarck.[63] Ritter had been "tragically disappointed" in the hopes he entertained for German recovery after the first war, and in another prophetic moment almost a quarter of a century later, in the wake of a second catastrophic war, he recognized the possibility of even a third international conflict. The demonic element of power emerged after Bismarck in the context of European imperialism, the misguided movement of pan-Germanism, the descent of "Protestant-socialism" into

"National-socialism"; and the "dangerous germs" nourished by the First World War infected even historians like Max Lenz and Dietrich Gerhard as well as intellectuals like Thomas Mann, Max Scheler, and Werner Sombart. However, despite the destructive effects of the radical and racialist policies and efforts of Nazism, Ritter did not lose all hope in the ideal of a fusion of power and culture in a revived nation-state. As so many times before, Germany had to "earn a new place in history" — although this time, some scholars, including even ex-Nazi sympathizers like Richard Stadelmann, agreed — by going back to the Western traditions lost in the wake of two wars.[64]

In this spirit and too old for novelties, Meinecke took comfort in the alternative myth of a "good Germany," which rather fatuously he hoped would be restored by "Goethe Communities" and a shift of focus in the historical profession. Rereading Dilthey and especially Burckhardt, Meinecke concluded in 1948, "Today we begin to ask ourselves, will not Burckhardt finally become more important than Ranke to us and to other historians?"; and so, like Srbik, he turned to cultural questions and the cosmopolitan path that Prussia had abandoned. About the future Meinecke was more optimistic than Ritter, returning to the old values of cosmopolitanism, which he had surveyed in his first major work almost forty years before and which he hoped would be fulfilled in some sort of world federation.

A younger Prussian contemporary of Meinecke and indeed, in 1948, a successor as editor of the *Historische Zeitschrift*, was Ludwig Dehio, who wrote a number of articles in the early 1950s reviewing the German question. He repeated the old geohistorical arguments about German "encirclement," regarded "war guilt" as a distraction from the main question, and Versailles as itself a "catastrophe"; but he did not deny that Germany had embarked on the wars (in an earlier terminology "just wars") to gain hegemony and parity with the "great powers" — nor that Hitler was "a nihilistic demon," who, if he had led others and himself "into the abyss," acted like a "sleepwalker" and was not an integral part of the political process. Dehio's aim was to historicize the German experience by placing it in a long perspective of European national rivalries going back three centuries. In a survey of Ranke's influence, which paralleled the rise and decline of liberal imperialism in Bismarckian Germany, Dehio, without excusing himself entirely, concluded that the work of the "lesser gods," especially Lenz, Delbrück, Oncken, and Marcks, was in retrospect a failure, though he praised Meinecke's "clarity," and agreed with him that after 1919 "Jakob Burckhardt's star was in the ascendant."[65] Like Delbrück, Dehio did not regard economic interests as prior to politics; for in his view the real problem was the collapse of the "European state system," which continued to be the intelligible field of Rankean historiography.[66]

After 1945 Ranke, despite some revised estimates, remained the great fore-bear of German historiography, and Bismarck the founder of the modern German political tradition, though disassociated from Hitler; and there was little immediate break with old habits and assumptions in the sense that national traditions — while divorced from alien Nazi racism — were looked to for ways of restoring unity and securing a place in European society. This was the view even of the Jewish scholar Hans Rothfels, conservative historian of Bismarck and his social policy, who had been a supporter of German expansion to the East in the 1930s but who in 1958 published an apologetic book on the German resistance to Hitler.[67] Nor did the founding of the Association of German Historians mark a deviation from old conventions — with Ritter, as president, attacking his Marxist colleagues — before the formation in 1951 of the Institute for Contemporary History, which took as its task the postwar problems left in the wake of the Third Reich.[68] There was a sharp break with East Germany, which officially adopted the doctrines of Marxism, yet with little change in the method of old-fashioned historical "science." This was painfully apparent in the pedantic *Introduction to the Study of History*, published in Berlin in 1978, which restored all the apparatus, auxiliary sciences, and documentation of Rankean historiography, set them in discussions of and footnotes to Marxist-Leninist materialist doctrines, and joined them to the policies and needs of the GDR.[69] But this is a world mainly forgotten. Over half a century a huge outpouring of historiography came from East German scholars, some of it of value, especially in areas of economic and social history, but now largely lost to public and academic view; and it will take a major effort of disinterested scholarship to restore this dimension of modern historiography.

The American Century?

What was left of the "new" history after the Second World War? In Britain, with the decline of the socialist left, the only serious movement was promoted by "cultural materialism," which was formed by a literary dilution of revisionist Marxism, and a more self-advertising sort of "revisionist" narrowing of political and social focus (and significance?). In France the *Annales* paradigm was transformed by a turn (or return) to anthropology, the emergence of Foucault, and other sorts of modern, or postmodern conjectural history. In Germany the Marxist line was playing out in the DDR, and there was a delayed turn to social history as well as a continuing debate over "the problem of Germany," especially through the debates provoked by Fritz Fischer. American historiography was marked by the emergence of "new" economic and social histories and a mania for quantification leading to a short-lived school of "cliometrics," paralleled by the reception of continental scholarship and ideas, an Americanized literary turn, and the renewal of efforts at a genuine "world history." What was apparent in all areas was fragmentation of research, breakdown of "grand narratives" (given belated justification in "postmodernist" discourse), and resurrection of personal "points of view" to organize the long-standing and fast-growing information overload generated by the printed book and intensified by electronic technology. Yet interpretations continued to pile up, traditional topics were revised, if not cast aside; and professional careers were made, and unmade, on the basis of the originality as well as soundness of epigonic contributions and their reception into "the literature," including textbooks and reference works. World history loomed larger than ever, but the quest for national identity continued to occupy the center of historiographical attention in all the Western countries, and post-colonial ethnocentricity remained in force despite rhetorical efforts to evade or to deny it. After the second war American historians struggled to escape the grip of Turner's and Beard's visions of the national past, creating interpretations ranging from David Potter's *People of Plenty* (1954) to Michael Kammen's *People of Paradox* (1972), and Oscar Handlin's *The Uprooted* (1951).[70] In general terms the portrayal, diverging from relativism and progressivism, inclined to what John Higham called "consensus history," exemplified by the work of Louis Hartz and Daniel Boorstin, which emphasized continuity and conservatism but which also had doubts about liberalism, recognized the irony and tragic elements of the American experience, and added soul-searching to the inventory of historiographical discourse.[71] For Richard Hofstadter American historians—"interpretive historians"—had prized the dimension of space at the expense of time, using the myth of the frontier to turn their backs on the European inheritance and falling frequently into the fallacy of "presentism"—as indeed he himself tended to do, as in his projection of McCarthyism and anti-intellectualism into earlier periods of American history. His critical study of the classics of American progressive historiography—Turner, Beard, and Parrington—was intended to set the stage for a new complexity and appreciation of failure in understanding the national past. As Turner had oversimplified with his geographical obsessions, so Charles Beard did in his own way through arguments about the inferred connections between ideas and economic interests (at least before his discovery of Europeanist relativism), and Parrington with intellectualist "counters" such as "idealism" and "democracy," which made him the very model of "Whig" historical thought.[72] According to Hofstadter these progressives represented a "conflict model" of history (though not Marxist), against which not only the "consensus model" of interpretive historians like Boorstin and Hartz but also a "monographic uprising" of "revisionists" operating on a more empirical level were reacting. Yet for Hofstadter something was lost in strict adherence to either model, especially for the historian *engagé,* which — still hoping to "change the world" — was his own self-conceived function.

Resistance to the consensus model came from the left, especially the "interpretive historians" William Appleman Williams and Reinhold Niebuhr, whose keys to the Cold War predicament of the United States were, respectively, the "tragedy" and the "irony" of American history. For Williams the "tragedy" arose from capitalist and imperialist policies adopted in the wake of a generalized "frontier" mentality, while Niebuhr, moving "beyond tragedy" (and beyond liberalism as well), took a less dramatic stand in his criticism of the misguided American self-image, urging a shift from the values of innocent virtue to a pragmatic and pluralist recognition of the threats of universal destruction which was central to Cold War rhetoric both on the left and on the right — meaning recognition, too, of the European and capitalist background of life in the "American century." This return to the cave of error, confusion, and conflict was also illustrated, if more remotely, in Perry Miller's magisterial study of the Puritan mind. In his first volume (1939) Miller portrayed Puritanism as a hierarchical system, arranged in encyclopedic fashion — and, as he admitted, in an artificially "topical" way, influenced by the rhetorical views of Peter Ramus, whom he rehabilitated — from conceptions of nature to rhetoric, anthropology, and sociology and aimed not only at thinking but also at coping humanly with a hostile world. This project was broken off by Miller's war service. His second volume (1953), which shifted its mode from scholasticism to jeremiad, treated the "declension" of the Puritan mind into intellectual chaos and conflict and the "splintering of society," arising from the secularization of ideals, as the "errand into the wilderness" was being transformed into a manifest imperial destiny.

American historiography has usually been turned in upon itself, from Crevecoeur's "What is the American, this New Man?" to Turner's Frontier and the turning away from the European background; but such time-honored exceptionalism has survived twentieth-century experiences only — exceptionally. Expanding and enhancing the national tradition of American historiography was the extraordinary influx of émigré scholars between the wars, especially exiles from Nazi Germany, who helped to revitalize medieval and early modern European studies as well as the study of national traditions. Among the most prominent of these were Veit Valentin, Arthur Rosenberg, Gustav Mayer, Hans Rothfels, Felix Gilbert, Hans Baron, Hajo Holborn, Hans Rosenberg, Eckhart Kehr, Ernst Kantorowicz, Dietrich Gerhard, Guido Kisch, Theodor Mommsen, Carl Landauer, Adolf Berger, and (from a younger generation) Peter Gay and Fritz Stern and Austrians like Gerhard Ladner and Friedrich Engel-Janosi.[73] From Germany Meinecke's students were among the most prominent, beginning with Hajo Holborn, who (as Meinecke wrote in relief) found a "safe harbor" at Yale, where he established himself as the leading American authority on German history. Felix Gilbert and Hans Baron, carrying their academic rivalry across the Atlantic, came to occupy the center of Italian Renaissance studies, and were joined by the great historian of philosophy (and student of Heidegger) Paul Oskar Kristeller, exiled first from Germany and then Italy before settling into a distinguished career at Columbia.[74]

Many of Meinecke's and Troeltsch's students were drawn to historical thought and writing, Baron with a study of the "awakening" of historical consciousness in the Italian Florentine Renaissance and Gilbert with a dissertation on Droysen and a collection of Hintze's translated writings as well as a comparative study of Machiavelli and Guicciardini; and this field continued to be cultivated by a generation and more of their American colleagues and students. Gerhard Masur's interests were in intellectual history; and later, under the influence of Troeltsch, he published a rich and searching survey of the culture of Europe before World War I (1961)—although, in examining the "prophets of yesterday" (running from Goethe, Kierkegaard, and Nietzsche to Freud, Van Gogh, and Unamuno), despite opening his book with the symbol of the doomed Titanic, believing that "the days of [Europe's] supremacy were numbered," and accepting the historicist idea that "all forms and structures built by the human mind are destined to be superseded," he disassociated himself from the apocalyptic pessimism of Spengler.[75]

During the war the European connection was reinforced by the recruitment of historians by William Langer for the Office of Strategic Services, and among other scholars attending this "second graduate school," as Carl Schorske called it, were Gilbert, Holborn, Schorske, H. Stuart Hughes, Franklin Ford, and Walter Dorn.[76] In 1952 Stuart Hughes began reviewing the seminal period of the crisis of historicism with a study of Spengler's sensational and largely discredited work, whose relevance he hoped to restore in another age of "cultural exhaustion"—of a "new barbarism" (Vico's term) threatened still by technology and a loss of confidence in reason. Yet, while continuing to insist on Spengler's prophetic value, Hughes came also to a more positive view; Spengler was a "crude" speculator, and other thinkers and imaginative writers had probed deeper into the human condition. Even before Masur, Hughes (invoking the names of Gilbert, Holborn, and Berlin, among others and emphasizing his own cosmopolitan background) surveyed the seminal period of the generations of 1890 and 1905 as "the reconstruction of European social thought" (1890–1930), which, like Masur's work, included literature and the arts as well as philosophy and the human sciences, though historical writing only marginally. When the war broke out Europe, according to Hughes, was dominated by conflicting tendencies of proto-fascism and a renaissance of culture, and his book followed this drama of contrasting and interacting destinies down finally to his own time (the generation of 1930?).[77] After the second war Hughes, like Arthur Schlesinger, Jr., his colleague at Harvard, also became involved as a public intellectual in politics at the national level. To this extent at least history retained its old "pragmatic" pretensions.

But — through invasions from the modernizing human sciences and European intellectual fashions as well as fall-outs of the aging New History — interdisciplinary studies continued to shape academic scholarship. One novelty that attracted enthusiasts was psychohistory, referring not to the general "psychology" of Dilthey or Lamprecht but to Freudian psychoanalysis, which, like the rival doctrine of Marxism, also produced a variety of revisionisms and anti-doctrines as well as efforts of synthesis, such as Herbert Marcuse's *Eros and Civilization* (1962). The impulse to a psychological sort of history was intensified after the second war by the personal experiences of scholars like William Langer and Peter Gay with psychoanalysis, and of course it was applied especially to biography, which was the locus of sexual drives, neuroses, hidden motives, and the "family romance" — conspicuous examples being Erikson on Luther and Gandhi, Binion on Hitler, Mazlish on the Mills (father and son), and Gay on Freud himself. As in the Enlightenment, however, the analogy between individual and society led to larger extrapolations. The premise was that in order to be intelligible history could not be the narrative of the way things were, that is, "historicism," but rather had to be something deeper, something bound to the subconscious and infantile residues that not only created and betimes subverted the will and intellect but also that helped to shape larger patterns of history, such as generational conflict, slavery, racism, and the rise of Nazism. There was of course nothing new in emphasizing the irrational (Gay gave the example of E. R. Dodds on the ancient Greeks — and why not Nietzsche?) and denying that the simple confrontation between reason and reality exhausted the story of human behavior, individual or collective; but what Freudianism brought to the problems of historical experience was an elaborate doctrine. Peter Gay admitted that he had "taken contemporary practices rather than past realities for my principal materials," though not in a "reductionist" way, and diagnosis rather than commemoration as his goal; and he defended his choice specifically "against the historicists."[78] This conviction was a way of guaranteeing, if not predetermining, meaning.

In contrast Peter Loewenberg insisted that psychohistory was "truly *historical*" on the grounds that it was dynamic and developmental, but of course this is a conjectural sort of history because the historical meanings are determined by a theory based on the interpretation of individual behavior — in this case Freudian ego psychology as it stood in the 1970s.[79] The fact is that like psychoanalysis, psychohistory itself (as one could say of Marxism and Marxist history) had a history, though perhaps of a shorter life span, and indeed it might almost be seen as a generational phenomenon. Doctrinaire psychohistory is preserved only by the dwindling faithful, yet its teachings have resonated through the historical profession, as usual not only through unthinking protest but also through reflective criticism, revision, partial selection and absorption and even synthesis, as in Marcuse's attempted synthesis of Freud and Marx, a vision shared as well by Gay.[80] But the fashion seems largely to have passed, psychohistory as such surviving only as a small adjunct to new forms of cultural history, especially in the forms of problems of sexuality, selfhood, and identity.[81] Like Marx, it seems, Freud has become "history" — has been, however reluctantly, "historicized" (though surviving followers of both may disagree).

It may be that the backlash against psychohistory, or at least its marginalization and dilution, was encouraged by the rise of the "new" economic and social history, which, extending the statistical enthusiasm of the previous century, sought to avoid the perils of subjectivity, complexity, and ambiguity by applying quantitative methods not to hard "facts" but to computable factors. The headquarters of what Jacques Barzun called "quantohistory" was as usual economics and its concern not only to identify the measurables of prices, wages, production, consumption, business cycles, and the like but also to raise them to the level of historical explanation. This was the highest ambition of what was called "cliometrics." After Beard's "economic interpretation of the Constitution" the flood gates seemed to open for economic history, including studies of industry, business, commerce, labor, taxation, and finance, though at first in a specialized way without much incorporation into general histories, except to the extent that key questions such as the causes of the Revolution, industrialization, the frontier, slavery, and the origins of the wars were analyzed in economic terms. There were parallel developments in England and France, where the Revolution came, under Marxist influence, to be subjected to economic interpretation. Even (or especially) in its "new" form economic history has been open to the sort of criticism brought by David Landes in his ambivalent epic, *Unbound Prometheus* (1969), pointing out that this field has classically been "interested in one half of the problem — the determinants of economic change — rather than its non-economic effects," and "holding non-economic variables constant."[82] So economic history has remained a special field, on the edges of visions of "total history."

The thrust of the "new social history," though necessarily more flexible and open, was also in the direction of quantification, simplification, and reductionism — and moreover, echoing efforts made over a number of generations to escape from elitist concentration on the ruling classes to study history democratically and "from the bottom up." Ignoring social-science models and methods would, argued one promoter, condemn historians "to technological obsolescence."[83] Lawrence Stone endorsed this view, and in France — responding to "the American challenge" — the call was taken up by Le Roy Ladurie in still more up-to-date terms: "Tomorrow's historian will have to programme a computer to survive."[84] As François Furet put it, sources either had to be "structurally numerical" or had to be given "a univocal significance in relation to the question [the historian] is asking."[85] Nor for Furet was this novelty merely mechanical, for "it is a revolution in the historiographical consciousness." As Peter Stearns admitted, social history was an international field, or approach, and its novelty consisted not in methodology but in opening up new areas of research focusing not on social structures but on the problem and not always quantifiable category of "experience," caught inescapably within the framework of demographic growth and technological "modernization" (vulgarization, too, it might be added, recalling the "bottom-up" T-shirts advertised in an early issue of the *Journal of Social History*). Among these fields are the history of women, the family, blacks, disease, crime, childhood, old age, death, and animals, all of which open out into cultural history — which itself, of course, had to be made new.

In 1977 fourteen prominent American historians gathered at a Wingspread conference to comment on "new directions in American intellectual history," but a quarter of a century later their conversation sounds almost quaint. Setting the tone, the introduction to the resulting volume noted a shift away from literary criticism and psychology, lamented confusing talk about "myths" and "holistic statements" about American thought and the "pretentiously grandiose" writing in American studies in the 1950s, deplored premature generalizations, and called for perhaps a generation of "toned down" empirical research before continuing such projects. Another paper considered ideas as "causes" within a framework set by the social sciences and concluded that they should instead be treated functionally and that historians should employ a sort of "zoom lens" to shift from the micro-world of the individual to the world of collective mentality and "collective cultural system." One writer asked whether religion may be obsolete except as a cover for "conservative patriotism" and concluded that religious history still deserves study, if only to illuminate elusive phenomena such as social reform; and another, invoking Kuhn and Collingwood, took up the old questions of determinism and voluntarism. These historians had moved away from consensus history but without giving up the idea of an integrated narrative of *the* history of American culture based on a balanced study of ideas and institutions (or economic base) and (in the words of another scholar) efforts "to see ideas in things." As the "Afterword" concluded, emphasizing continuities as well as novelties, contemporary historians had lost both the enthusiasms and the illusions of youth, and so they were "thus more cautious, more careful, and at times more defensive than their predecessors," resulting in "a more narrowed focus but improved quality." Only a few years later these reflections and prescriptions would sound more like the old history which was emerging after the linguistic, literary, and culturalist turns already then under way.

Well under way, too, were the inquiries inspired by women's and gender history, although again the novelty of such forays has as usual been obscured by failure of professional memory and urges to claim pioneering status on a frontier already crossed by earlier scholars.[86] The importance of gender for historiography has been shown by Bonnie Smith, who pointed out the contributions of women not only in the amateur sphere but also in areas of professional history as barriers slowly were breached, Lucy Maynard Salmon of Vassar being a remarkable example. Smith also analyzed the role of early experience in the lives of male historians, in historical epistemology and "objectivity," and the male-bonding promoted by the practices of "value-free" scientific history, including the "fetishism of the archives," obsessions with political and military history, and institutions like the archives and the seminar.[87] Long before the rise of women's history to prominence women writers had been crucial in encouraging the shift not only from political to cultural history but also from the public to the private sphere. As a result the whole landscape of national and world history has been changed by the end of the millennium, and more new histories are appearing on the horizon.

A Wider World

World history (or universal history) itself has a deep history going back to antiquity, as in Polybius (*historia katholike*) and Dionysius of Halicarnassus (*koina historia*) as well as Eusebius (*preparatio Evangelium*), the medieval world chronicles, and Ibn Khaldūn, but it took a modern form in the wake of Renaissance scholarship. Voltaire and Herder, among others, admitted the orientals and the barbarians into the realm of "humanity," and even Gibbon made note of China on his horizon, if only in a footnote. In the later eighteenth and nineteenth centuries world history was included in textbooks and especially large-scale (and illustrated) treatments of the history of culture, with self-congratulatory promotion of growing cosmopolitanism. Thus in his *Cultural History in Its Natural Development* (1874) the social Darwinist Friedrich Hellwald included annotated accounts of the "Empire of the Middle," that is, the "origin and antiquity of Chinese civilization," and of the "Island Empire," Japan, as well as Islam and the Near East, though he did not follow these cultures down to modern times. At the same time, of course, the time scale of human development was vastly expanded as geology replaced Genesis as the standard of calibration, as human evolution was joined to conventional periodization and the "four-stage" scheme that still weighed on Marx, and as the new discipline of prehistory expanded temporal horizons. In 1873 Victor Duruy published a general history of the world (English translation 1898), relied on by later writers, including Florence Deeks, whose unpublished history was allegedly plagiarized by H. G. Wells for his *Outline of History*.[88] Such textbook coverage was continued and expanded immeasurably in the twentieth century, although it was the philosophers of history — modern descendants of Enlightenment conjectural historians — who reflected more widely on the world beyond the small end of the Eurasian peninsula, known since Herodotus's time as "Europe," including Spengler, Toynbee, Wells, Sorokin, Teilhard de Chardin, Dawson, Mumford, and McNeill.[89]

How can historians manage to encompass the whole world in their narrative scope? A good beginning is through spatial expansion, an approach which has its roots in ancient, biology, geography, and climatology and which has found a place in national and universal history ever since the Renaissance, with geography indeed taking its place among the primary "auxiliary sciences" of history. Nature, too, has a history, and participates in historical processes. "Geohistory" brings topography and environment into the picture, which involved artificial cartographical constructs such as boundaries and continents, discriminations between peoples of the river valleys, the deserts, and the mountains, the formation or recognition of frontiers, and the rise of cities — and all this in terms not only of natural endowment or Toynbean "challenge" but also of cultural constructs. In European history historical geography was for a long time associated with political geography and imperialism, not only for German historians but also for American exceptionalist scholars writing in the wake of Turner's frontier hypothesis and ideas of sectionalism. In recent years ecological and environmental history has achieved new emphasis, especially in connection with social, demographic, and technological problems, which again rise to global status with larger threats to the biosphere, though here we begin to move from history to futurology.[90]

World history has been a meeting place for interdisciplinary research and speculation, with economics in particular offering a way to conceive a global field of exchange and interaction through long-distance trade, world markets, exploitation of labor, colonialism, and war. "World systems" theory was located first in the early seventeenth century — favorite period for Marxist explanations of the "transition from feudalism to capitalism" and arguments about the "crisis of early modern Europe." There have been other "crises," of course, and other "world systems," too, have been pluralized and located in other parts of the world and in earlier periods of economic activity.[91] World system analysis was originally formulated in terms of Marxist sociology, although it was adapted by some historians, including Braudel, who moved from the Mediterranean to the "perspective of the world." Braudel had always been attracted to a global perspective, publishing the first aerial map of this sea assembled from satellite photographs, and he extended his own historical horizons through comparative analysis of Asian and African parallels. Every economy, according to Braudel, following Immanuel Wallerstein, has a core and a middle area and a large periphery; and historical — political, economic, social, and indeed cultural — change takes place within this flexible capitalist framework, though slowly and not in terms of discrete "events."[92] The core is the locus of high culture and cities; the middle "holds no mysteries"; the periphery is where the foreign and exploited are to be found, usually with a large state exerting political influence and control; and the world economy is the set that includes these sub-sets. So geography, economics, social science, and mathematics, or at least the rhetorics of these disciplines, are employed to give structure to human history on multiple levels of space and time. And of course Braudel's derivative framework has been adopted by others, including Traian Stoianovich in his studies of the Balkans within a world economy and K. N. Chaudhuri, who transfers Braudel's vision of the Mediterranean and the world system to the Indian Ocean and surrounding Asian territories.[93]

World history is interdisciplinary at its core (as indeed national history had become), but the various alliances established with disciplines changed the orientation of history, whether seen as art or as science, and it may be useful at this point to suggest some of the deflections from traditional historical narrative brought about by interdisciplinary histories in a global perspective, many of which may be regarded as modern forms of what in the eighteenth century was called "reasoned" or "conjectural" history. Each dependent discipline represents, perhaps in a synecdochic way, one or more aspects of history to carry the weight of narrative, interpretation, analysis, or explanation. Political science, including the state, institutions, diplomacy, and the military, has not disappeared, but since Foucault interests have shifted to more hidden sources of power, except for contemporary problems and policy. The same may be said of economics, at least the classical doctrine which is tied to psychology and motivation on the one hand and statistics and market behavior on the other, though it is still featured in long-term trajectories and in background conditions of historical change. Sociology depends on abstract categories and assumptions transcending national and cultural boundaries and relying on even more conjectural views of historical change. Anthropology blurs all these explanatory traditions by privileging "local knowledge" and cultural differences, while also undermining the old historiographical goal of explanation in favor of interpretation. Recourse to the literary dimension reinforces the goal of interpretation and moreover the notion that instead of a single grand narrative to be told about a unified historical process, there are multiple stories to be told about the manifold human hordes on a globe inhabited by friends, enemies, neutrals, and drop-outs alike.

Since the eighteenth century the relationship between anthropology and history has been especially fruitful but also periodically troubled. According to Jack Goody, anthropology in the early twentieth century turned against history because of its associations with the conjectural systems of Darwinisn and Marxism and sought more empirical ways to study human nature.[94] The result was that anthropologists of this disposition had to find other frames of reference than temporal or causal succession for their interpretations and found them especially in naturalism (geography rather than biology), or structuralism, and in that connection comparativism. Another implication was that national or ethnic traditions lost their conceptual jurisdiction over cultural phenomena and patterns. Anthropologists found that traditional, or traditionalist, historians had exaggerated local, national, and Western differences at the expense of human parallels and similarities, for example, in areas like family structure. Anthropologists on the other hand, often with anxieties about appearances of residual colonialism, emphasize the common life and heritage of humanity across artificial divisions such as that between Occident and Orient — "us and them."

But the "Other" is a Western creation, too, which has been sought by poets as well as historians. "And what are poets for in a destitute time?" asked Heidegger. In 1967 Paul Celan provided one answer: "But the poem speaks. It is mindful of dates, but it speaks. True, it speaks only on its own, its very own behalf. But . . . the poem has always hoped , for this very reason, to speak also on behalf of the *strange* — no, I can no longer use this word here — *on behalf of the other*, who knows, perhaps, of an *altogether other*." Historians have also aspired to visions of alterity, but they have usually tried to reduce the foreign to their own measure. In world history, in other words, the West opens up to the East, and the rest, but without leaving behind Western categories such as modernity, modernization, civilization, traditional concepts of social science, politics, nationalism, liberty, kinship, family, property, labor, capital, gender, mentality, and of course "Asia" itself. This is the case even, or especially, with such anthropologically informed works as Eric Wolf's *Europe and the People without History* (1982), which restores and refurbishes the Marxist exploitation mode, as, more subtly, does Jack Goody. "Comparative history," too, requires metahistorical categories or standards which must usually be drawn from Western intellectual traditions even as they employ the rhetorical devices of first encounter, cultural shock, and incommensurability. Nor do such complications disappear when historians get down, like anthropologists, to cases "in the field." The most appropriate interpretive model is perhaps that of language and translation, but here again, according to the old adage, something must be lost. As K. N. Chakrabarty suggests, another discourse, an alternative logic, is needed to "provincialize Europe," to give some symmetry to mutual exchange and understanding (if these are not contradictions in terms), to accommodate "subaltern studies," and so to tell the whole story of modernity.⁹⁵ And so are we back to "total history," this time with all the races and classes?

In the latter part of the twentieth century world history, behind a burgeoning bibliography, has shown three faces which connect it with mainstream Western history even as it seeks separate status.⁹⁶ One is the ambitious attempt to change the "shape of history," but except for adjustments to conventional geography (a belated critique of the Mercator projection, which is another by-product of print culture), there does not seem to be much difference from the old "Western civilization" model, except for anxieties about Eurocentrism, the addition of a rhetoric of globalism, a greater emphasis on cultural encounters and exchanges, and a certain lack of perspective on the whole enterprise — for example, attributing the new orientation on "civilization" to Toynbee, without reference to the Enlightenment background, including the "four-stage" theory, which likewise saw a progression from hunters-gatherers to agriculture to trade to industry. Moreover the new shape retains old assumptions about "modernization" based on this same conjectural projection toward industrialization and what Heidegger called "the question of technology" — which was essential (via Lewis Henry Morgan) even to the late Marx and Engels as well as Weber and other critics of modernism. The second face is the pursuit of international themes such as migration, technology, food, disease, borders, ecology, and diasporas, not to forget capitalism, war, and state-building; but illuminating as investigating such subjects may be, they are marginal to the question of history's shape. The third face is "comparative history," but here emphasis is less on historical inquiry than on application of such metahistorical disciplines as geography, economics, political and social science, and anthropology to preexisting historical knowledge and to social and cultural forecasting, once left to philosophers and futurologists. Indeed the thrust of contemporary "world history" has been toward pedagogical manifestos, textbooks, and the teaching of introductory courses with more extensive topography if less intensive cultivation, than the Euro- (not to mention Americo-) centric surveys of recent vintage.

World history has not yet found its grand narrative, although "globalization," bidding to succeed "modernization," has been seeking "models" from various disciplinary sources. It is true that globalism touches universal values through world markets, international transportation, migrations, medicine, law, standards of measurement, communication networks, and other means of connecting local communities and promoting "global culture" and even an Enlightenment-style utopian global future — to the accompaniment of course of localist protests. Yet it seems clear that like postmodernism, globalism is designed not to designate commonality but to accommodate diversity and chaos, and it resists historical interpretation as well as prediction. That is, the discussion of globalism has been monopolized by social and political scientists who are torn as usual between normative and scientific models with history marginalized in the drive not merely for historical understanding but also for political and social policy. As usual, history must come later, when the owl of wisdom, or speculation, has finished its flight — though where or if it lands no one can know.

5

After the Good War

The past that will not pass.
　　　— Ernst Nolte

New German Paradigm

Historians have always, though not always ostensibly, sought a "usable past"; and reviewing historiographical practice around the world and back over two and a half millennia, one cannot be surprised that ideas of objectivity, a single "big story," and other "noble dreams" have given way to even older notions of history as the product of social creation or authorial imagination. "Representation" has become a watchword of contemporary historical writing; and the upshot, Foucauldian warnings about the tyranny of the subject notwithstanding, is to restore the "point of view" as sovereign, whether or not the historical viewer is in full command of the language of representation and fully aware of his/her audience and readership. Again historical interpretation turns away from the model of science to that of art — "the will to power as art," in Heidegger's adaptation of Nietzsche — and here again is the triumph of representation over reality — and perhaps the grounds for another new history. Of course every European nation has its historiographical performers, and the international chorus we have heard in the last part of the twentieth century has been maddeningly cacophonous. Nor have the soothing efforts of global history brought resolution to the chaotic and conflicting patterns of national traditions.

Of all the European nations in the past century Germany had been least attracted to notions of a "new history." Lamprecht's variety, combining material and psychological aspects, was discredited in the 1920s by its apparent left-leaning and unprofessional stance and was continued only in popular and conservative forms; and Ranke was still up-to-date enough for most academic historians. Yet a potentially subversive turn to social history was promoted by younger scholars from the 1920s under the influence of Weber if not (overtly) Marx, as attention was directed to economic and social history, especially the dislocations caused by Germany's rapid industrialization and imperialist ambitions — anticipated by Thorstein Veblen's book on imperial Germany (and England) and the Industrial Revolution (1915). Meinecke's student Hans Rosenberg was, along with the short-lived Eckhart Kehr, a pioneer in the investigation of this field, though his study of "bureaucracy, aristocracy, and autarchy" did not appear until 1958 (and in German translation much later) and Hans-Ulrich Wehler's book on "Bismarck and imperialism" not until 1969.[1] The former Marxist Arthur Rosenberg and G. W. F. Hallgarten also began looking into the social and economic aspects of Germany's predicament in the face of professional disapproval. The impulse for this was most directly a critical interest in exploring the social basis of Prussian society and the rise of National Socialism, but there were implications for the whole range of European history, as suggested by Otto Brunner's book on "land and lordship," published in 1939, which showed a similar shift of emphasis from political to social history.[2] The *Behemoth* of the émigré scholar Franz Neumann had linked Nazism with economic and social factors, but though it appeared in English in 1942, it was not translated into German until 1977.[3]

However, such subversive novelties were not followed up systematically until after the Second World War, when Wehler, Werner Conze, and Jürgen Kocka, made a clear and unopposed turn — "paradigm change" (in the Kuhnian term that became popular in Germany) — to social history (*Gesellschaftsgeschichte*). This was accomplished, however, not to back up the demands of their Marxist colleagues for just such a social-democratic stance (shades of Weimar!), but rather to follow the "structuralist" style of Braudel and the *Annales* school, which, according to Friedrich Jaeger and Jörn Rüsen, served as an alternative to a restored historicism.[4] This movement toward a "structural history" (*Strukturgeschichte*) was the purpose of Conze's Working Group for Social and Economic History in Heidelberg in 1957, the interdisciplinary center of Wehler and Jürgen Kocka at the new University of Bielefeld founded in

1971, and *Geschichte und Gesellschaft*, a new periodical established in 1975 and edited by Rothfels, Wehler, Kocka, Wolfgang Mommsen, Heinrich-August Winckler, and others. What Wehler promoted was a "historical social science" that, following the methods of the Frankfurt School, brought sociology, economics, and psychology back into play in order to analyze processes of modernization, which Germany had not followed normally.[5] On the less theoretical side was an interest in the history of everyday life (*Alltagsgeschichte*), reverting to old practices of cultural history going back to the eighteenth century and supported as well by East German historians, who of course had their own class- (and corporatist-) based theories about Germany's disastrous path to modernity and the two anti-democratic and "imperialist" wars.[6] Such was the "Eastern problem" and *Ostforschung* in the wake of World War II. The premise of the historical profession in the GDR remained the sovereign validity of Marxist dialectical materialism and the continuing contradictions of capitalism. What is the standing of the huge scholarly output in the retrospect of the new century and millennium? Is the historiography of the GDR, as one historian concluded, a "dead dog"?[7]

The "paradigm change" indicated by the work of these scholars altered German historiography in formal as well as substantial terms and affected the line of questioning. In his study of social classes during the First World War, for example, Kocka, addressing that war and answering the call for "more theory," emphasized his departure from the two conventional issues, which were that of war guilt (reignited by Fritz Fischer in 1961) and that of the constitution and parliamentary democracy. By contrast Kocka in 1973, employing models (not Marxist or Bismarckian but Weberian and *idealtypisch*) rather than a historical description and admitting a concern for *longue durée* (*lange Strecken*), inquired into "organized capitalism," the structure of society as a whole, and the divisions and changes which it suffered before the revolution succeeding the war and which deflected Germany from the Western path to modernity.[8] In this same year Wehler published a survey of German history from Bismarck to the end of the first war, concluding not with the traditional list of complaints and grievances about the situation in 1918, but with another sort of list: "in the reversion to authoritarian politics, the antagonism to democracy in educational and party contexts, the influence of pre-industrial elites, norms, and aspirations, the tenacity of German statism, the myth of bureaucracy, the intersection between the decline of estates and the conflict of classes"—here begins a long catalog of "historical burdens" which, he concluded, are essential to understand the history of the next fifty years.[9] The synthetic work published by Thomas Nipperdey in 1990, even as it reproduces the old political narrative of the rising *Machtstaat*, gives priority to the new paradigm of historical social science.[10]

Another product of the new paradigm was the work of Reinhart Koselleck, who moved from Heidelberg to Bielefeld in 1973 and who in 1967 had published his book on Prussia "between reform and revolution" in the series brought out by Conze's Working Group. Koselleck's book, following the old path of Ranke's Prussian history and the new departure of Hans Rosenberg on Prussian bureaucracy and society, took the Prussian Code of 1791 as a vehicle for a political-legal-social analysis of the transformation of Prussia before 1848 as it moved from the old system of estates to an industrializing economy, which was encouraged by legal reform and post-revolutionary liberal policies.[11] Yet though beginning as a social historian, Koselleck took a "linguistic turn" leading to an emphasis on texts, language, discourse, and the semantic field in the *Sattelzeit* between Enlightenment and industrial society and so to a "social history of concepts" (*Begriffsgeschichte*); and this in turn brought him into association with Conze's project of a comprehensive dictionary of "basic concepts" (*Geschichtliche Grundbegriffe*) which he joined Brunner and Conze in editing. This monumental reference work, with a related series on French concepts and with important ties to the hermeneutics of Gadamer and the parallel series, *Historisches Wörterbuch für Philosophie,* was begun in 1972 and completed in 1993.[12]

More recently Koselleck has broadened his intellectual interests to include other aspects of historical thought, the Enlightenment, revolution, the international order, varieties of "crisis," representation, topoi, structure, hermeneutics, the "parthogenesis of modern society," the "space of experience," the "horizon of expectation," and other themes of conjectural history and the philosophy of history, all set within the new discipline of *Begriffsgeschichte.* For Koselleck the meaning of actions cannot be read directly from social analysis but must be carried through levels of language from the discourse of actors to the interpretations of historians in a different semantic field in a different time.[13] By going back to concepts of point of view, perspective, and "positional commitment" formed in the eighteenth century by Chladenius in particular Koselleck reframes ideas of historical truth and objectivity.[14] The movement of concepts is from synchronic analysis of past experience to diachronic interpretation of transformations, balancing persistence and change, examples being that of "legitimacy," which arose in jurisprudence and was appropriated by many political causes, and that of "history," which from about 1789 could be conceived as something that can be made and disposed of. In the *GG* such semantic analyses, often including the ancient and medieval background, are gathered into a massive dictionary in which words, mainly social and political terms, have become the protagonists and in which their histories are offered as the full representation of the corresponding concepts changing over time.

But the reconceptualization of history could not impede the pursuit of more urgent questions, which as always meant the spoiled glories and inherited sins of the German state, and here it was Fritz Fischer who reignited the question of war guilt for the first but by implication also the second war in his sensational book of 1961 on the ideas of 1914 — Germany's "reach for world power" — which to be sure was not entirely original, having been anticipated in many ways by Luigi Albertini's discussion of the origins of the war of 1914 published in 1942.[15] Fischer assigned the main responsibility — indeed premeditation — for the outbreak of the first war to the imperial government and to supporting German elites. His views were criticized by members of the professional establishment such as Ritter, Schulze, and Erwin Hözle (scholarly celebrator of "ancient German liberty" — and ex-Nazi), and even Rothfels, supporting the cause of "official nationalism"; but in the course of the controversy they were accepted not only by younger historians but by a major sector of the public. It was in this connection, too, that the new work in social and economic history came to endorse Fischer's critical line of argument, while also, through structural social analysis, supplanting the old-fashioned sort of document-based diplomatic historiography in the style of Fay and Langer which the book represented.

An even more sensitive episode in Germany's dark past — "the past that will not pass," in the words of Ernst Nolte — was the "final solution" of the Jewish problem, and this provoked an even more sensational controversy in the 1980s (*Historikerstreit*) not only among historians but also among other intellectuals, journalists, and a wider public, and led to an even more drastic revisionism. The contestants included Jürgen Habermas as well as historians like Kocka, the Mommsen brothers, Nipperdey, Nolte, and Winckler; and the positions ranged from unconditional repudiation, including the notion that the Holocaust was unique — unhistoricizable — and that the state murder of millions of Jews went beyond the abilities of historians to investigate, to accommodation, at least to the extent that historicization of antisemitism on this level amounted to a kind of legitimization. Among the questions posed were how the *Judenvernichtung* was related to the continuity of German history: was it another and even sharper "break" with the good humanist German past, or was it the product of deep flaws that were vastly magnified by racism and modern technology? These were not questions that could be answered easily, and certainly not by historians, who could only search further into the details in which, as Kocka suggested (reversing Warburg's aphorism), "the Devil resides."[16]

At the start of the third millennium the big question has to do with the new unity and how to fit it into the revisionist efforts to understand the course of

Germany since its first unification.[17] These days there is no Bismarck, nor indeed any national figure who can, at least for historians, stand for the national past as any one from Luther to Hitler — and certainly none that can span the traditions which have produced the process that created the dual political identities, especially the tensions and conflicts between west and east, of the past half century and more, which now continue in economic, social, and cultural forms, behind the cover of political unification. The debates go on, but the task remains to retell the story of the German people, the east and west still in tension but within a single uncertain political framework, as of the new millennium, and this is a chapter of historiography yet to be written, especially in economic, social, and cultural terms and perhaps on the basis of "re-nationalization."[18]

There is one theme in German historiography which has not failed throughout all the ideological ups and downs, that is, historical thought and writing — *Historiographiegeschichte* — and, over the past century, "historicism." The periodic reviews of perennial themes and the canonical authors of the self-reflective national tradition are illustrated not only by hundreds of articles and books but more prominently by the nine-volume reference series *Deutsche Historiker,* covering the period from the Göttingen school of the eighteenth century down to the twentieth century, published by Wehler between 1971 and 1981 (and, just to highlight the continuity, in Göttingen). During the past century, in this drive to professional self-reflection, there were few prominent German historians who did not have their say about the practice and theory — and the history — of history as well as the implications of their particular work for the "German problem," and there is hardly any way to do justice to this gigantic conversation without relapsing into bibliography. One synthetic work is that of Winfried Schulze, which surveys German historical studies after "ground zero" (*Nullpunkt*) 1945, beginning with the residues of Nazism and the search for a new beginning — or a new way of establishing continuity, that unavoidable premise of historical understanding — within the expanding apparatus of the historical profession, whose agenda of inquiry apparently remains unchanged even after so many catastrophes.[19] A much broader, more conservative, and philosophical portrayal is Ernst Nolte's survey of European historical thought in the twentieth century published in 1991, which, despite the Marxist/anti-Marxist division, finds an "inner unity" in a long, modernizing retrospect, at least among the intellectual elite, of the judgment that Nazism and Bolshevism were both "totalitarian" aberrations.[20] Needless to say such historicizing complacency has not been shared by his critics.

Perhaps the most comprehensive attempt to legitimize and to define the function of historiography in a "post-national" age has been that of Horst

Blanke, who has fulfilled the prediction made by Harry Elmer Barnes in 1937 that "it will not be long before someone would be writing 'a history of the history of history.' "[21] For Blanke the history of history is a paradigm defining historical method in general, and a central purpose of historiography is the criticism of tradition, which was so obviously lacking in much of German experience and historical writing, tied as it usually was to old-fashioned historicism and suspicious of extraneous theory, foreign ideas, and the other human sciences.[22] What was needed is another "paradigm change," though one which draws extensively, but subtly, on the ambiguous career of the grand and still honored canon of German historical scholarship. But the impression left from Blanke's work, as from that of Georg Iggers, is in effect that of another, more intellectualized "Ranke-renaissance," this time chastened by the experience of atrocities.

As for historicism—which also has its history and transformations—it has for some scholars come to subsume all the various topics and dimensions of historical inquiry, except for those who regard it as discredited by its past ideological associations. It is not a method or a discipline but a transdisciplinary but professional "paradigm" (Blanke) or a "disciplinary matrix" (Rüsen), but in fact it has so outgrown or overflowed older meanings, such as that of a combination of individuality and development (Meinecke), the human philosophical condition in general (Croce), or merely interpretation in temporal terms, that it has become a flag, a tattered flag, whether red, black, white, or multicolored, to be waved by intellectuals of many nationalities, commitments, and causes, producing equally questionable "old" and "new" historicisms which have little value either for theory or for scholarship. Yet, older than "postmodernism," which in effect denies its relevance, "historicism" promises to last as long as the newer and even more elastic term—if only because both are subject to further historical inquiry, which is to say, historicization.[23]

Civil Wars in England

British historiography after mid-century followed traditional channels, but the waters were troubled, as divisions not only ideological but also "revisionist" provoked professional historians to disputes ever narrower in extent and significance, recapitulating the patterns of other fields, especially literary criticism, of which Pope wrote,

> Critics I saw that other names deface,
> And fix their own, with labour, in their place:
> Their own, like others, soon their place resign'd,
> Or disappear'd, and left the first behind.[24]

It was only historical perspective — the history of literary criticism, of which Pope was a practitioner — that could make these revisionist patterns clear.

British revisionism, unlike the French or American (or Marxist varieties), did not entail a qualitative shift. Like their German colleagues most British historians retained a commitment to old-fashioned political and institutional history even as others, especially of a leftist if not specifically Marxist disposition, tried to shift attention to social history and, implicitly or explicitly, to social issues. The Whig pattern of triumphalism was preserved no matter who the protagonists were, but it was at the same time countered by critics of British government, society, and especially Empire who followed the lives of other protagonists, and the result was a symbolic posthumous conflict between the makers and shakers and the made and the shaken. This was especially the case with the bloody ground of the Puritan Revolution, which was seen variously as the planting ground of modern English liberty and the launching ground for an oppressive class riding the crest of the Industrial Revolution and nascent capitalism, but carrying over into the trajectories of both ruling and laboring classes. Add to this the cautions of revisionists who aspired to rise above — or sink below? — the recognition of large historical patterns altogether. Christopher Haigh and his colleagues reacted to the old story of a gradual reformation by emphasizing the vitality of English Catholicism as well as the demands of local and empirical research.[25] Yet British history has seemed to thrive on such controversies, old and new, though the new has not deviated far from traditions of old-fashioned state-building.[26]

One extraordinary career fashioned in this climate but according to deep traditions of English historical scholarship was Geoffrey Elton, who endorsed the theories (or anti-theories) as well as the practices of earlier generations, especially their fixation on the sources.[27] Like Namier, Elton, who was the son of the distinguished historian of ancient Greece, Victor Ehrenberg, began as a European outsider and even more enthusiastically and uncritically embraced the older, though not Whiggish, traditions of British political and administrative history, though unlike Namier, he ended up regius professor at Cambridge. His *Tudor Revolution in Government* (as his thesis was retitled in its published form) continued the work of T. F. Tout and S. B. Chrimes but with a dramatic modernist twist, assigning the flowering of English administration to Thomas Cromwell and provoking a long controversy, carried on in *Past and Present,* a journal that normally favored social and economic history. These exchanges highlighted his reputation as a polemicist; and his brand of revisionism likewise brought him notoriety and controversy but also his regius professorship. Like Namier, Elton distrusted Whiggish ideas of the progress of representation, and he studied the later sixteenth-century Parliament as an arm of government, led by the monarch (as in the case of Henry VIII) or ignored by the monarch (as in the case of Elizabeth).[28] For him Parliament was a place for either the monarch or men of influence to do business, and "the rest was pretense." As a result he rejected the earnest accounts of Neale and other efforts to connect parliamentary rhetoric, which was divorced from power, with the turmoil and finally the civil war under the Stuarts. The Whig story of the deep roots of parliamentary government was myth, even if contemporaries accepted it and their decisive roles as historical fact — nor for Elton was the myth itself, enshrined in political theory, worthy of historical consideration.[29]

   Elton was obsessed with the sources and techniques of history. Immersed in his Tudor documents and committed to positivist methods, he rejected not only the philosophy of history and psychohistory but also the "arrogance" of champions of sociology and of the "new ways" celebrated by Keith Thomas and others; and he insisted on the autonomy and isolation of the discipline of history. He disputed E. H. Carr's complaint that Mommsen's "greatness" should be associated not with his massive work in Roman epigraphy but with his youthful *History of Rome* (which later gained him a Nobel Prize) because this showed his "philistinism" and deviation from his former accomplishment. For Elton, whose father was an associate of Eduard Meyer, exhaustive research and detailed narrative were both necessary forms of professional historical study. From this combination truth and facts could indeed be extracted from the sources — that is, all the available sources, and Elton permitted himself to criticize his predecessor Pollard for relying on published calendars instead of the originals. Elton praised Lawrence Stone's industry in his researches into the English aristocracy, but doubted his leap into conjectures about structure and long-term change; and in rejecting the possibility of a linear universal narrative Elton was also casting doubt on the practice of comparative history. He was even more incensed with the relativist implications of E. H. Carr's acknowledgment of the role of interpretation in establishing historical "facts," for the historian "must become the servant of his evidence."[30] This denigration of the role of the observer carried over into the sources, for as Elton declared (shades of Ranke!), "The large corpus of work produced by Christopher Hill on puritanism and the civil wars in seventeenth-century England rests in effect on overlooking the difference between the evidence for what happened and evidence for, celebrations for, and lamentations about, whatever people said was happening."[31] That, for Elton, history did not have to be rewritten every generation was shown by Namier's "bomb" — and "triumph of conservatism" — of 1929 on "the structure of politics at the accession of George III." In these and other defenses of historical convention Elton, preaching a "return to essentials," seems to assume the posture of

Doctor Johnson in kicking the stone of common sense in the face of new-fangled skepticism and the pernicious influence of the Annales school.[32] Like Thompson and Namier, Elton and Hill are both dead, but their legacies remain in the work of English and American disciples who hope to ward off new revisionisms and postmodernisms. It was ironic that the appointment of Quentin Skinner as regius professor at Cambridge came at the high tide of English revisionism, since his philosophical background placed him as far as could be imagined from that dominant, if anachronistic attitude of head-counting.

Philosophers of history and reflective historians have tended to reject the attitudes of scholars like Elton as naive realism, and while there may be something to this charge, the practical basis for their position is not so much epistemological naivete as heuristic conviction; that is, their belief in the primacy of source materials over interpretive virtuosity and an basically unreflective and sometimes doctrinaire "normal science" of history (Kuhn's term for a reigning professional paradigm). The problem is that dedicated and anti-interdisciplinary scholars like Elton, Taylor, and Namier were neither equipped to provide nor interested in providing a philosophical justification for their activities beyond their professional habits and procedures; and their critics, remaining on the elevated and often empty level of theoretical argument, were placed in a similar relationship of incompetence to the scholarly practices and local knowledge of their targets. So there has not been a meeting of mind or even words, to the detriment of all parties; and as in other connections historians and philosophers of history live and work in different worlds even as they occasionally meet in the same world of discourse.

In England as in Germany, and for an even longer time, some scholars turned from the political surface to the social depths of the historical process, and for them the period of the Reformation and its aftermath, including the civil wars of the mid-seventeenth century—the "transition from feudalism to capitalism" as Marxist would have it, toned down to the "general crisis of the seventeenth century"—was the center of attention. The main controversy was set off in 1941 by Tawney's arguments concerning the "rise of the gentry," which sparked a long series of studies by Lawrence Stone, Trevor-Roper, J. H. Hexter, Perez Zagorin, Eric Hobsbawm, and others, who in the fading enthusiasm for Marxism, shifted emphasis from "revolution" to "crisis." The culmination was Stone's *Crisis of the Aristocracy, 1558–1641* (1965), which, setting the polemic aside, reviewed the whole question and broadened it to include ideological, social, and cultural as well as economic factors. There was also a parallel controversy carried on, producing as much heat as light, notably by Christopher Hill, with similar avoidance of political action and institutions, about the nature and even existence of "Puritanism" (the major "ideological factor" referred to by Stone), which represented (in antiquated Marxist terms) the superstructural aspect of the problem as distinguished from the material base of the rising and falling social classes. Of course all of this massive research and the often virulent discussions of large-scale social and intellectual transformation were aimed ultimately at explaining what older historians regarded as a discrete "event," namely, the Puritan Revolution, and its proximate and long-term "causes," of which Stone offered a synthetic interpretation in a later book, though he finally returned to his main interest, which was the life and fortunes of English aristocratic families.

Another stage of the struggles with the Marxoid, or post-Marxist, theme of transition from feudalism to capitalism which did not quite depend on the doctrine of a bourgeois revolution was the theory of a crisis, later promoted to "general crisis" in the early seventeenth century, which was propounded by Eric Hobsbawm and Trevor-Roper. This thesis, inseparable from the social problems created by the Thirty Years War, attracted economic arguments concerning dislocation of markets and social upheavals, especially what R. B. Merriman designated as the "six contemporaneous revolutions," generalized with the help of the vision of a global market and expanded both in space and in time—in space through the comparative study of economic and social distress which, as in Braudel's later work, brought the Far East and the new world into the picture, and in time though the idea of a "world system" which pitched the conditions of the crisis back to the thirteenth century—and later to antiquity and a plurality of world systems. Here is another product of the encounters between history, economics, and social science, though recent historians have not kept faith with theories of transition, general crisis, or world system, except perhaps as pedagogical devices, which often seem to remain a legacy of the more remote past.

For some critics, including Elton, not surprisingly, all of these issues and speculations, as far as England was concerned, distracted from the proper business of the historian, which was to work ever more intensively on the political records of the realm. Elton complained the social and intellectual interpretations represented a return to the old-fashioned Whig (if not Marxist) view behind new-fangled theoretical apparatus and aimed at ungrounded long-term conjecture (usually within the framework of modernization); and yet his own response was to return to an even older-fashioned institutional history read myopically in denial of larger patterns, especially underlying connections with the English Revolution—no "high road to the civil war"— which suggested anachronism and a neglect of the riches of contingency. This attitude, shared by many younger historians, was honored with the over-used label "revisionism," but the revising was, if technically critical, largely negative, localist, and conventionally insular in its drift. It also (in a sort of unconscious parody of Hume's critique of causation) cast doubt on social and intellectual connections as, for example, the historical links (argued by A. G. Dickens) between Protestantism and late medieval heresy and, more generally, denied grounds for a "contextualized" history of political thought, including the time-honored values of "liberty" with a life extending back to Milton or the Tudor Parliament (as chronicled by the cooperative series inaugurated by J. H. Hexter). For Elton the Elizabethan Parliament, despite medievalizing lapses in discourse seized on by Whiggish historians, was fundamentally (irrelevant talk and contingencies aside) an instrument of royal government and contained no significant seeds of resistance or revolt. Its members were men brought to do business and not political theory (for the benefit of later historians), and this focus on business (rather than what Elton called "pretense") has dominated revisionist views of parliamentary history down to contemporary "post-revisionist" qualifications.

Despite the strictures of the revisionists and Peter Laslett's defection (and pronouncing of the obituary of political philosophy in 1956),[33] the history of political thought indeed enjoyed a revival beginning in the 1960s, especially with the work of J. G. A. Pocock and Quentin Skinner, who were early converts to the linguistic (and rhetorical) turn, in which political and social discourse was again set at the center of efforts to recover the "world we have lost." Elton's privileged "sources," even the most legalistic ones, were not transparent windows into the thought, policies, and action of the early modern period; for the terms of discourse and negotiation have their history and fortunes which (as the proponents of *Begriffsgeschichte* also believe) must be understood before they give entry into that "foreign country" which is the past. The historian is a sort of archeologist, as Pocock has written, and it is his/her first charge to explore bygone semantic fields and to disinter lost meanings before imposing retrospective interpretations.[34] These are the premises underlying his own analysis of the "ancient constitution" in English political tradition, more generally, and his tracing of the "Machiavellian moment" and the associated mindset of "civic humanism," derived from the Florentine experience and carried over into continental and British contexts, and underlying also Skinner's survey of the foundations of modern political thought before the overly discussed constitutional conflicts of the Stuart period—historical concerns drawing him back from an original interest in the mid-seventeenth century to medieval and early modern precedents and underpinnings.

British historiography has in many ways declined along with the Empire and the national confidence which being one of the "great powers" brought to

England as to some of the other European states in the last century, and it is at least arguable that revisionism, with its emphasis on the local and the contingent, its suspicions of theory and large generalizations, is a reflection of this. In quantitative terms British historiography has expanded mightily, though focusing narrowly in special fields of legal, economic, social, and cultural matters and directed more and more to details in which neither God nor the Devil could be found; and interest has grown in areas such as women's history, gender, globalization, and cultural studies (often with a residual leftist orientation), and in interdisciplinary explorations, such as Eric Hobsbawm's extra-insular ventures into social history and Keith Thomas's study of religion and magic in the early modern period, which did not figure in the older accounts of the past, the heritage, and the destiny of the English people. Yet the readership, or at least the writership, of British history seems to have changed little at the start of the third millennium, despite the loss of the old supporting ideologies.

In general British history treated by American historians remained in narrow, if less insular, channels, taking pride in the unrevolutionary development of liberties and other benefits of the parliamentary and common law traditions. J. H. Hexter began as an expert in the Puritan Revolution, but he had no use for the Marxist interpretation of this pivotal event as class struggle and bourgeois revolution, and he rejected the work of Hill and others who promoted these ideas, and the topic along with them. Not that he accepted the hyper-empiricist and microhistorical criticisms of so-called Revisionists, who turned increasingly to local history; for he insisted in a Whiggish way on the leading role of the Parliament in the development of liberty in the West. It is perhaps not surprising that British historians turned to historiography to illustrate the enduring quality of British political, legal, and institutional tradition, which was territory explored by Herbert Butterfield, who sought "the whole historical side of our mentality," as history was subjected to a critical self-examination.[35] Another example of this position is that of Pocock in emphasizing the "ancient constitution" and the "common-law mind" as major themes in the development of British political thought and discourse. In a curious way, with old linguistic continuities restored, this may be seen as a posthumous victory of Coke, Selden, and Burke as well as of Stubbs, Pollard, McIlwain, and Hexter, albeit in the realm of intellectual rather than institutional history.

The Annales *Paradigm and After*

The later generations of Annalists preserved their fondness for the classic historians of French tradition, and for Febvre, Bloch, and their colleagues in the continuing *Annales* establishment. Jules Michelet remained the founding father of the new history — not of course for his critical acumen but for his national vision, for his promotion of archival research, and not less for his egocentric style. This proclivity was most conspicuous in the autobiographical reflections and manifestos of Febvre, Bloch, and their colleagues, for instance, in much of Braudel's work on the Mediterranean and (as Michel de Certeau had pointed out) in Le Roy Ladurie's preface to his *Peasants of Languedoc;* and it assumed first-person-plural form in Braudel's comradely rhetoric invoking "nous des Annales," in Richard Cobb's rendering — that ornamented the heavily annotated discourse which displayed his vast erudition.[36] "I have passionately loved the Mediterranean," Braudel exclaimed ("J'aime l'histoire," confessed Febvre in 1941) at the outset of the great work begun before the Second World War, his own "adventure of a 'total history'"; and Le Roy Ladurie did not hesitate to confess that he, too, "loved the Mediterranean countryside."[37] The strategy was apparent also and most systematically in the well-titled collection of "ego-histoires" published by Pierre Nora, which was a sort of prosopo-autobiographical gallery of some celebrities of the contemporary Annales school. One reason for the use of the first person was Bloch's concern to open the door of his laboratory a bit for the benefit of readers and to interest them in his work. Another reason, explained Bloch's disciple Georges Duby, was to emphasize that his discourse was not unadulterated truth but only what was probable and, opposing the old dogma of Fustel ("Gentlemen, it is not I but history who speaks") the product of imagination — of *his* creation.[38] A third reason, I might add, is that it is impossible for scholars to use a modest passive voice in pursuing the aggressive publicity and condescending "combats" initiated by Lucien Febvre — in the tradition, perhaps, of the "new history" of Thierry.

Braudel was followed in his time-mastering impulse by a number of more or less wayward disciples in what one disciple has called "the crisis of paradigms."[39] Another effort to transcend chronology — and another excursion into neo-trinitarian speculation — is Georges Duby's imaginative study of the "three orders" of medieval civilization (*oratores, bellatores, laboratores*), which invokes not only the stereotypical categories of priest, noble, and peasant (and anticipates the classic "three estates"), with a wealth of illustration, especially from literary sources — "The division of every hierarchy is ternary," he quotes from Dionysius the pseudo-Areopagite — but also the controversial structural tri-functional theory of Georges Dumézil concerning Indo-European history and prehistory.[40] This theory was commonplace from the tenth century, was given classic expression by the seventeenth-century lawyer Charles Loyseau in his "treatise on orders," and lasted for a millennium, surviving the threat of heresy and class divisions, especially in the work of Roland Mousnier. Jacques Le Goff, who also made imaginative expeditions into the hidden recesses and representations of cultural history, rejected the old ancient-medieval-modern chronological trinity and followed Duby in concluding that the middle ages — that is, the "extended middle ages," for he had little use for a separate "Renaissance" — is "the period in which Georges Dumézil's tri-functional schema appeared (or reappeared) in the West," an example of the "evolution of deep structures" that lasted until they were outdated by the modernizing globalizing forces of the Industrial Revolution and railway communication.[41]

Still deeper and more impenetrable was the world of private life — *Alltagsgeschichte, la vie quotidienne* — which takes place, as Duby put it, "behind closed doors and under lock and key."[42] This topic was as old as the distinction between public and private, rose and fell with the state itself, and had been studied by cultural historians for two centuries and more, as well as by French historians in the old series on *l'histoire quotidienne* of various national traditions two generations before; and yet characteristically, Duby celebrated the novelty of the richly illustrated series *A History of Private Life*, initiated by Ariès, in terms of new sources, new insights, emphasis on *longue durée,* sensitivity to the individuality (in contrast to the insensitivity of quantitative methods), and — with a self-conscious bow to the example of archeology — the modest (and scientific-sounding) aim of offering "a program of research rather than a finished survey." In this experiment in modern conjectural history the first volume, including contributions by Paul Veyne, Peter Brown, and others, traces the transition, on the basis of an "old abolished empire" from "civic man" (Roman, not Greek) to "inner man" (in Veyne's masculinist phrase); the second volume examines the "revelations of the medieval world," with Duby's usual conjectural explorations into the semantic fields, primarily literary and artistic sources and documents, treated in the same way; the third volume, edited by Roger Chartier, takes up the "passions of the Renaissance," following the rise of "civility," intimacy, and expansion of domestic space and family life; volume four carries the analyses of emergent individualism and the "triumphant family" from the Revolution to the First World War, when the "primacy of the public" again asserted itself; and the last volume treats "riddles of identity," cultural diversity, and national models and myths of families in modern times.

The search for an understanding of ordinary life is perhaps best pursued in local and "microhistorical" terms, as Le Roy Ladurie showed in his virtuoso study of a village in southern France that was a last hold-out of the Catharist heresy. Montaillou was a small community whose bishop, Jacques Fournier, in his official inquisitorial proceedings, happened to have left a precious record of the lives of less than three hundred persons, their work, their family life and sexual practices, and their *mentalité* more generally. In the twentieth century social historians always sought to shed light on the silent and oppressed groups, and Le Roy Ladurie was especially pleased with the Fournier register because "it is largely concerned with downward social mobility, whereas most documents of the *ancien régime* treat chiefly of upward mobility." Another explorer of small worlds in this style is Carlo Ginzburg, who also passed from Marxism to microhistory, especially in religious and occultist contexts. In general microhistory prides itself on its freedom from doctrinal debates, its closeness to social reality, and its status as an unattached "interpretative practice"; but here we can see that interpretive practice and methodology itself can be turned against the intimidating doctrine of Progress.[43]

French historical thought was the product in part of a profoundly anti-Cartesian impulse apparent in the works of Saint-Simon, Chateaubriand, Michelet, Proust, and others who exchanged the decontextualized *Cogito* for a nostalgic *Re-Cogito,* in which memory replaced reason — and the "search for lost time" replaced logical reflection — as the mode of construction. This move, systematized within the framework of Durkheimian sociology, was also reinforced by literary influences, although these tended to emphasize the representational character of memory. For Proust "intellectual memory" presented only "pictures" and "nothing of the past itself"; for "the past is hidden somewhere outside of the realm, beyond the reach of the intellect, in some material object."[44] Nor has Vico's identification of memory with imagination been lost, and indeed it has also served to reinforce the aesthetic drift of historical interpretation over the past century. This identification has been received into popular culture to the extent that the cartoon character Dennis the Menace could remark to his smaller friend, "Imagination is like a memory of stuff that *never* happened." Or alternatively, according to Wallace Stevens, "Only the imagination is real."

Memory is indeed a topic which recent French historians have taken up with energy and ingenuity, following the model of "collective memory" established by Maurice Halbwachs (who had been Febvre's and Bloch's colleague in Strasbourg) and the idea of "mentality."[45] Le Goff has touched on the underlying but highly speculative subject of time itself, not in the artificial Braudelian tripartite levels but rather concrete human contexts — psychological, linguistic, primitive thought, historical consciousness, philosophies of history (and the future), and what Bernard Guenée has called "historical culture" — as well as the various mnemonic institutions that support and organize memory, including museums, monuments, photographs, libraries (from manuscript to printing to computer), cemeteries, commemorative events, and geographical "places of memory"—analogous perhaps to Proust's "place names" (*aides mémoire* in the project of research into "lost time")—as presented in the work of Pierre Nora and his disciples.[46] Of course the question of memory and its ambivalent relation to history has been followed up in many other connections, from antiquity to modernity to postmodernity, by other English and European scholars, one of the most relevant to historical scholarship being Patrick Hutton's virtuoso survey of history as a modern example of the "art of memory" (*ars memoriae*), with reference to Vico and Freud as well as Halbwachs, Ariès, Foucault, Michelet, Aulard, Lefebvre, Nora, Gadamer, Ricoeur, and others.[47] Another offspring, as Nora suggests, is the recent interest in the history of history.[48]

The problem of memory is central, too, to recent French explorations of the antiquity, and especially the *mentalité* of the Greeks in their passage from myth to reason (*mythos* to *logos*) and from oral to written culture. How is it possible to recover what Paul Ricoeur called "our Greek memory"? An original text does not exist, so Marcel Detienne cites Marcel Mauss, and so one must seek to plumb "social memory," or what Thucydides dismissed as "archeology," through a retrospective sort of ethnography.[49] "Did the Greeks believe in their myths?" asked Paul Veyne, situating his project in the "uninhabited regions" which located for Lucien Febvre the frontiers of historiography.[50] For Veyne the question is badly posed, since the Greeks' myth was beyond human truth or falsity, and belief was a function of the "constitutive imagination." For the ancient Greeks so-called Truth (*aletheia*) could not be separated from religion and the muses, and it was kept in the custody of those whom Detienne calls the "masters of truth," who appeared first in "magicoreligious" and then, with the process of secularization, in philosophical form, inheriting and squabbling over their cultural heritage.[51] This transformation also involves a shift from a logic of ambiguity, which accommodates falsehood, and a logic of contradiction, which produces modern rational thought, whether or not closer to "truth." It is to the mythical model, then, that Steven Shapin seems to revert in surveying the "social history of truth."[52]

There is a specter of Marxist theory behind the efforts to place ideas, including scientific ideas, into a social context; and indeed many of the innovations and pseudo-innovations of the twentieth century, including those of the *Annales* school, have come in the wake of, and often as a replacement for, older notions of superstructure and material base. Marxist theory, which has become ideologically, or terminologically, taboo has continued to inform historical inquiry in terms not of macrohistorical speculation and prophecy but of human questions and values. Many ex-Marxists have moved to cultural history as a potentially "leftist" site even after the political spectrum derived from the French Revolution has become an anachronism in all but emotional or moral terms. This is evident in British cultural materialism, the sociology of Pierre Bourdieu, and Jürgen Habermas's version of Critical Theory, which is post-Marxist but still devoted to what Paul Ricoeur has called the "hermeneutics of suspicion." So the new cultural history continues, under the aegis of Foucault, to focus on "power" and its implementation, though in a broader sense than the "demonic" political power studied by Ritter and Meinecke.

But power needs a vehicle, and here the primary medium was the printing press. One of Lucien Febvre's projects was the history of printing, and indeed he was assigned this volume in Berr's series in 1930, published with the help of Henri-Jean Martin after the war.[53] The problem of the printed book and its "world" linked the middle ages and the Renaissance, and here again Febvre and his collaborators were concerned to open up new avenues of research; for in fact the history of the book was a locus of many particular questions, among them those of paper, technology, distribution, institutional organization, geography, and intellectual, religious, political, and cultural impact through the various national languages. This line of research has been one of the most fruitful in the later Annales paradigm, as typography and the information revolution have become central areas of inquiry at the turn of the twenty-first century, as illustrated by the work of Martin, and of younger scholars like Robert Mandrou, Michel Vovelle, Roger Chartier, and Americans such as Elizabeth Eisenstein, Robert Darnton, and Anthony Grafton, who have studied the finer details and case studies of the history of mentalities. In his recent book Martin has placed Febvre's "problem" in the longest perspective, that of writing in general, that is, speech rendered as graphic sign, and its "power" — though without mention of Foucault or Derrida, as if such theories were a kind of anachronism irrelevant to proper professional historical inquiry.[54]

Roger Chartier has carried the *Annales* tradition, in its culturalist phase, around the literary and textualist turns, seeking in post-Marxist terms to find the social world in discourse, especially as preserved in the printed and illustrated books of the Old Regime. Focusing on "culture" and "civility," with reference to the works of Norbert Elias, he examined the representation and appropriation of high culture and in effect how to be "bourgeois" before the Revolution. He collected case studies of popular culture, relying often on literary sources but, like his French predecessors at the start of the century, asserted the autonomy of history and its separation from literature, taking exception to Hayden White for his avoidance of original and archival sources.[55] For Chartier as for Foucault, language was a condition not only of culture but also of historical writing, and not exclusively open to authorial choice. In this spirit, too, Chartier shifted from old-fashioned intellectual history to the study of "mentalities"—for him history was still a "social science" in a Durkheimian mode—by considering reading practices, book distribution, literacy, and cultural reception. Like the practitioners of *Begriffsgeschichte*, Chartier wanted in effect to do intellectual history and at the same time follow the contours of society and its transformations.

In this post-*Annales* generation French methods became eclectic and, in a consolidating mood, as Chartier says, concerned with directions and research agendas instead of theories, and moving in the territory of "culture," which brings together the "ideas" of old-fashioned intellectual history with the collective and anthropological views of non-essentialized "mentality" in the style of Febvre, yet accepting "the retreat of the great explicative models." Yet in Chartier there are still echoes of Marx, especially in the emphasis on "practice" (pseudo-Greek *praxis* which Marx opposed to Hegel's spirit), which revealed the patterns of culture, although this is the world behind the linguistic turn, in which "symbols" and "representation" became the currency of interpretation. For Chartier the trajectory in the twentieth century has been from the reality of positivism, grounded in politics or economics, to the history of ideas (in the decontextualized style attributed to Lovejoy or of *Geistesgeschichte*), to the mediated world of culture accessible through anthropology, though still by way of mainly literary sources and "traces and signs."

In general many disciplines, including psychology, anthropology, archeology, literature, and the arts, had to be called upon to fill out the historian's account of the human condition in time. The implicit hierarchy—a sort of great chain of total history—still seems quite obvious in the work of the third generation of *Annalistes*: viz., geohistory and climate, agrarian history and population, kinship and classes, production and trade, national and international markets, money and capitalism, internal and external imperialism, science and technology, arts and literature, everyday life and death, food and sex, crime and disease, institutions and the state, politics and war, and then . . . what, total history? But it is always humanity acting between nature and culture, and even the interjection of memory studies (via the *lieux de mémoire*), with the distracting debate over the connection with "history" proper, does little more than shift the ground of historical research to a more presentist perspective, except for uncovering another level of sources. In this encyclopedic pandemonium of "historical" inquiries other shifts are often apparent; but overall there have been (I think) no long-term changes or cycles within the Annales paradigm; interest in "mentalities" was apparent from the first; quantitative history, with its reductionist assumptions and devices, has risen and fallen (and risen again in the age of computers); and the dream of "total history" has never quite been forgotten. The wheel must always be reinvented, the fire restarted, the book rewritten; "new Columbuses," as Pareto put it, periodically appear; and novelties are announced so frequently that one is tempted to take innovationism — the "fetish of the new" — as a permanent condition of the life of professional historians.

America and the World

The political and ideological confusion of 1960s produced more new histories and "turns" both left and right, social and linguistic as well as massive demographic expansion of the historical profession in the context of the Vietnam War, with attendant repercussions, student movements, and radicalisms which sought not only to view history "from the bottom up" but also to shift it into a "new left" activist mode, though increasingly in the interests not of an imagined international proletariat but of women, blacks, neglected ethnic groups, and others seeking identity through a history of their own. The upshot was that the historical profession was fragmented, or if not fragmented, set in a pluralistic and multicultural framework which inverted the goal of consensus historians and the "old left" alike. Ideological divergences were also reinforced by the influx of "postmodernism" ("post-" entering the rhetoric of novelty that has been employed to set off generations and movements), which rejected the viability of "grand narratives," including that of a triumphant and modernizing Western civilization — although globalization and a revived world history seem to be competing these days for the place of a new grand narrative.

After the war American disciples of German scholars — and indeed many of their disciples — continued to work within while at the same time broadening and deepening the Eurocentric paradigm and probing its origins. In 1957 Leonard Krieger, student of Hajo Holborn, contributed a wide-ranging study of the German concept of freedom from its early modern philosophical, constitutional, and social roots down to the period of unification, showing its deep ambivalence and interplay with the theory and practice of absolute sovereignty before its destruction by the Nazis.[56] Fritz Stern looked more directly at the ideological antecedents of Nazism and other aspects of the never-ending "German Question." Peter Gay, emigrating from Berlin at the age of thirteen (and bringing with him his own "German Question") celebrated various aspects of Weimar culture, including Freudianism, nineteenth-century psychohistory, and especially the deeper Enlightenment background, which — in conscious opposition to Carl Becker's thesis about the "heavenly city of the eighteenth-century philosophers" — he characterized in terms of its paganism, rationalism, and search for modern freedom.[57] Peter Paret continued the study of military history, still essential to this question, but from an interdisciplinary angle, including art history.[58] From the 1960s Carl Schorske, who began as a political and social historian, turned in an encyclopedic way, anticipating recent attitudes toward cultural history, back to late nineteenth-century Vienna to examine the roots of several aspects of modernist culture — not only political but also psychological, literary, artistic, musical, and architectural, though not including historiographical.[59] H. Stuart Hughes devoted himself to a reevaluation of European intellectual history from the fin-de-siècle to the Cold War, with attention to the "sea change" that enlivened American scholarship with the experiences and teaching of European immigrants.[60] Martin Jay, whose career has built productively on his early study of the Frankfurt School, has also diverged further from social into cultural history, and especially the problem of and the attacks on the visual in modern culture.[61] All of these scholars, faithful in their ways to the values of historicism, accumulated an extensive academic following which has preserved Europeanist traditions.[62]

Meanwhile "American studies," which had an interdisciplinary but also ethnocentric orientation, keeps alive the smoldering flame of consensus history. This was, is, a field which had roots in the rich field of the history of American literature, which emerged from the shadow of Moses Coit Tylor in the twentieth century, beginning with the impassioned survey of Parrington and continuing along two lines — academic scholars like Kenneth Murdock, Perry Miller, F. O. Matthiessen, and Howard Mumford Jones of Harvard and maverick intellectuals like Bernard De Voto (who never succeeded in getting a Harvard post), Granville Hicks, Lewis Mumford, Alfred Kazin, and Van Wyck Brooks, whose grand but sentimental survey was assaulted by F. O. Matthiessen. The popular surveys produced by such authors were divided along American-European-leaning preferences and disciplinary alliances in their efforts to construct, to control, and to disseminate the canon of American literature (and in its train, American society) — the "great tradition," in Hicks's phrase. Parallel to such virtuoso works came the accumulation of scholarship, reference works, new journals, and scholarly debates which marked the emergence of an autonomous discipline, capped by the cooperative project that codified the field and subfields of American literature, that is, the *Literary History of the United States* edited by Robert Spiller and published in 1948.[63] Yet ties with history proper were maintained, as illustrated by Harvard's renowned History and Literature department, as literary patterns paralleled and reflected the social movements and turbulence of the postwar period and as historians increasingly drew on literary (no longer in a pejorative sense) sources and methods.

American literary historians have devoted themselves in particular to groups and movements that suggested new directions in literary and perhaps general culture, beginning especially with the Puritans, whose reputation, after generations of denigration, was not only salvaged but also elevated by the studies of Kenneth Murdock, Perry Miller, S. E. Morison, and their students, while the New England transcendentalists were celebrated in the influential book on the "American Renaissance" by F. O. Matthiessen. Even more attractive in the past half-century has been the noisy and careerist field of the "New York intellectuals," who were mainly "literary journalists" (as Edmund Wilson called them — and himself) and cultural critics but who also included a few historians like Richard Hofstadter, Arthur Schlesinger, Jr., and J. P. Diggins.[64] The New York intellectuals were concerned primarily with postwar international politics and how to remain on the left and socialist — and intellectual, if not scholarly and academic — without giving in to Stalinism, and of course there were revisionist implications of the polemical studies of the Cold War, its champions, its victims, and its confusing aftermath, which suggested (in Daniel Bell's famous phrase) "the end of ideology," if not the end of utopia. Now in their fourth or fifth generation the New York intellectuals have turned from ideological and aesthetic bickering to repetitious recollection and celebration of their own legacy, image, and continuing (self-) importance as cultural and political critics.

In the generation after the Second World War we have seen the appearance, viewed Eurocentrically at least, of another celebrated turning point — 1968 — where, as in 1848, history failed to turn. More than at the beginning of the century historical studies were internationalized through conferences, fellowship programs, faculty and student exchanges, journals, reviews, and translations. Throughout the Western world national traditions preserved their dominance, as did established specialties like diplomatic, military, and economic history, and American historians continued to pay filial respect to the older generation.[65] Increasingly, however, political history was undermined and expanded through inroads into, alliances with, and appropriations from the social — or, more flexibly, the "human" — sciences. Yet with the decline of Marxism economic and social history were challenged by (an also "new") anthropology and a self-conscious "cultural turn" which emphasized aspects of human behavior that formerly were marginalized because of their historical irrelevance, inaccessibility, and lack of explanatory power. This suggests some of the background of still another new history — a self-designated "new cultural history," which emerged in the 1970s and '80s and which, though aging or dissipating a bit, is still with us.

The "new cultural history," proclaimed by Lynn Hunt in 1989, aspired to succeed and to overshadow the fading fashions of Marxist history and the

Annales paradigm as the dominant mode of historical interpretation of the last quarter of the twentieth century.[66] The key was in the concept of representation which was intended to combine or to transcend the old polarity of mentality and social reality, although the upshot was necessarily to privilege literature, art, symbols, and the expert (or not) interpreters of these cultural expressions and to rely on anthropological interpretation rather than scientific explanation (a language model rather than a natural science model) for historical under-standing — the leading influences being Clifford Geertz and Hans-Georg Gada-mer. Yet the aim of the new cultural historians — and their British counterparts, the "cultural materialists — was still for the most part what Paul Ricoeur calls the "hermeneutics of suspicion," a hermeneutics which does not give up hope of explanation and disclosure of a reality "behind the back of language" (in Gadamer's disapproving phrase), in the sense that, in the spirit of Foucault and Bakhtin, they sought traces of power and protest and the voices of the under-classes in representations of high culture and "political" culture, often founded in anecdote. The scientistic rhetoric of causal analysis and the metaphoric (and Marxoid) recourse to "reflections" were replaced by linguistic and textualist analysis within the framework of "historically contingent discursive forma-tions." So literary critics, or at least the apparatus of literary theory, took command of historical inquiry and interpretation.

"Should intellectual history take a linguistic turn?" asked Martin Jay twenty years ago, when in fact historians of all sorts were making just this move, whether inspired by philosophy or literary theory or a critical impulse derived from their own discipline.[67] The phrase "linguistic turn" was itself coined by Gustav Bergman in 1964 and made famous by the collection published by Richard Rorty under that title in 1967. Discounting anticipations by Valla, Vico, Herder, and others in the humanist tradition, Jay gave primary credit to twentieth-century theoretical writers like Wittgenstein, Saussure, Foucault, and Gadamer, although Linda Orr might associate it rather with the "revenge of literature," which has so often risen up against the pretensions of scientific history; Hayden White draws more particularly on the ancient and modern tradition of rhetoric, which had always privileged discourse above pure ideas and logical disputation, Dominick LaCapra accepts it as a signal to restore literature to its primacy over history and Frank Ankersmit to raise literary theory above both, and (though without the same surrender to literary theory) Lawrence Stone takes it simply as the restoration of old-fashioned narrative.[68] In any case from the 1970s historians became more aware of the linguistic character of most of their sources and the hermeneutical problems arising from this condition. For Rorty the linguistic turn suggested "the thesis that philosophical questions are questions of language"; for historians the implication was that historical research and interpretation likewise had to be carried on within the cultural limits of language, which was never a transparent medium but rather inseparable from the "reality," which was otherwise inaccessible and inexpressible. What the linguistic turn defines, in short, is what I call the hermeneutical predicament, which no scientific methodology can escape if it hopes to achieve human meaning.

Another by-product of the linguistic turn is the self-styled movement called the "new historicism" (announced in another form by Croce as early as 1942), which likewise seeks to wrest control of historical interpretation from old-fashioned "old historicist" scholars, though with a greater respect for the primary sources underlying the historian's narrative. Here the dominant concept is "representation," which designates the problem that historical narrative cannot be just of "what really happened" (*res gestae* in the classical formula) but mimetic or critical representations thereof (*narratio rerum gestarum*), according to Chladenius's view of textual exegesis and Nietzsche's view of interpretation, which is an endless, a bottomless, and a foundationless process, carried out in a linguistic medium with all of its prejudices and forestructures. To read history out of a text or to read history as a text, either way we have to adopt a language-model rather than a science-model, which has the virtue of combining the local and the global — *la parole* with *la langue*, in Saussure's terms — according to which history is not a process to be explained but a putative field of bygone activity which can be represented only by interpreting traces, mainly linguistic. History is a matter not of demonstration but, in Huizinga's phrase, "a rendering account to oneself."[69] Not propositional but narrative, not apodictic but heuristic, not purely rational but commemorative and imaginative; and there is no Archimedean point from which to view, still less to move, humanity in its passage. We can pose questions but not link cause and effect in any rigorous way. We tell many stories, true as well as probable, about the past; but we cannot tell *the* story, the whole truth, the metanarrative, as scientific, philosophical, and theological historians used to do, and indeed sometimes still do. Despite philosophical baggage and technological apparatus, inquiry into the varieties of humanities and the vagaries of the human condition remains the primary task of the modern historian as it had been that of Herodotus and his epigones.

And then, in the scramble for labels of novelty, we have the "new philosophy of history," which is the motto of a number of recent literary scholars, including Ankersmit, Allan Megill, and Robert Berkhofer, who have made the literary turn and have embraced rhetoric as the primary condition of historical understanding.[70] One feature of the NPH is the emphasis on irony — by which is meant, however, the restoration of the subject, the "'I' foregrounded,'" in the words of Philippe Carrard, referring to the ego- (or *nous-*) centered rhetoric of the *Annales* school.[71] The NPH rejects what Robert Berkhofer calls "hegemonic viewpoints" and denies that there can any longer be a "great story" that overlooks the losers or victims of Western history.[72] The solution to the relativism implied by such criticism lies somehow, Berkhofer thinks, in representing polyvocality, that is, dialogism and multiple viewpoints—a *Rashomon* or Joycean model of historical narrative—to satisfy the postmodern pressures of multiculturalism and voices clamoring to be heard above the din of official history. Yet as one contributor, who happens to be a medievalist, asks, "Is there anything new here?"[73] For Nancy Partner the much touted "linguistic turn" is rather a re-turn, to judge from the practices of Herodotus, Thucydides, and Gregory of Tours, so that the idea of a realistic historiography purged entirely of fictional elements may actually be an aberration in Western history. The writing of history must be an imaginative (and at the same time innovative) as well as a conventional and traditional operation.

The first volume of the present work began with the conceit of the two faces of the two foundational master historians, Herodotus and Thucydides, and approaching the end we may return to this symbolic distinction, this time to represent the difference between early and contemporary history—and also between global and local (national or ethnic) history. In his bibliographical appendix to his *Method of History* on the descending order of reading histories Jean Bodin had distinguished between universal historians and "universal geographistorians" and historians of particular religions (or superstitions) and nations, eastern as well as western, followed by biographies; and it seems to me that these categories, received into historical pedagogy in the eighteenth century, are still in place, as is the logical descent from the general to the individual. Formerly, "universal history" (a coinage of Polybius) was conceived as the sum of national or special histories, or more recently civilizations, and beyond the miscellany humanity has been conceived within different formal or informal organizational arrangements from empire (Rome and its emulators) to oecumene to modern "world systems"; but in an age of globalism, "metageography," and ecological history concerns, scholars have tried to give it a more distinctive shape, as usual with the help of other disciplines and comparative methods and with attention to super-national phenomena such as migration, trade, disease, and cultural exchange.

Just as historians in the nineteenth and early twentieth centuries called for a shift from ruling (and fighting) elites to the making and consuming middle and lower classes, so historians in the later twentieth century have turned increasingly from national and Eurocentric history to world and "global" history, downplaying the economic and cultural leadership of the West. With a sort of inverted chauvinism scholars point to African origins, Chinese civilization, and innumerable borrowings in the realm of high as well as material culture to reduce the claims of European states and the classical and Judeo-Christian roots of Western civilization and seek other points of view and other narratives that do justice to the life of humanity since prehistorical times. There are of course interconnections and global themes — agriculture, disease, slavery, migration — which expand the old genre of universal history; but it must be said that much of the novelty of modern (and postmodern) practices is on the level of textbook writing and "rethinking" in terms of old-fashioned social science interpretations and the "intelligible fields of study" — civilizations — along the lines of Toynbee's model. Like the old New History, the new Global History has been more talked about and summarized in a derivative fashion than investigated, except in "area studies," which display the same parochial and amnesiac limitations as the national-international horizons of mainstream European historiography in the long wake of Gibbon, Voltaire, Niebuhr, Ranke, Guizot, Michelet, et al. One of the first motives of historical study was the honoring and the memorializing of ancestors and their predicaments, and in professional terms it is essential at least not to forget the two and a half millennia tradition on which our practice still rests. No doubt the Moderns and Postmoderns know incomparably more than their predecessors, including the giants of our profession, but no matter how loudly they declaim, no matter how widely they are read, their works are no less transient; and in any case, as Voltaire put it, *gloria primis.*

Newer Histories

By the end (if not the beginning) of the twentieth century the "new history" had become a tired cliché, enlivened mainly by debates around the various self-advertised, quasi-novel practices which were gathered under this catchall promotional label and by a counter-fashion of a self-serving and sensationalist (but not new) notion of "the end of history."[74] The innovations, renewals, or changes of emphasis involved less the discovery of new insights or sources of information than shifts of point of view, disciplinary connections, theoretical models, and ideological commitments, and proliferating and career-enhancing controversies over what is new and what is old — "what is living and what is dead," in Croce's formula — in current practices. Many of the apparent novelties, aside from technical and methodological advances, were the products of the rhetoric of particular schools, which indeed often proceeded to examine their own histories, celebrate their own heroes, and construct their own canons; so that in the process many of the conventions and themes of the old history were recycled and displayed in updated terms, showing that the "new history" could neither escape its past nor even, very often, justify it own newness.

For centuries history has been defined through two categories, one the singular (event, person, fact, institution, etc.) and the other the chronological (change in time). For classical historicism this was reduced by Meinecke to the principles of individuality and development, and the former was given pejorative form in François Simiand's famous coinage *l'histoire événementielle.* In his positivist, neo-Baconian, Durkheimian campaign for the methodological hegemony of social science Simiand identified and challenged three historiographical "idols," viz., politics, the individual, and chronology, with the implication that they should be replaced by collectivities, rational and static fields (such as Braudel's *longue durée* and Le Roy Ladurie's *histoire immobile*), and a broad and non-linear view of the human condition. Thus the general would replace the particular, synchrony replace diachrony, and science replace outmoded history, or at least render it philosophical. For social scientists history was restored to its proper subordinate role; for historians on the other hand these altered categories led to a larger, global, and even "total" vision of their discipline, with the social sciences rendered subordinate. Yet this shift of point of view also produced historiographical specialization or fragmentation, which was difficult to reconcile with the old ideal of an integral, comprehensive, even "total," and philosophical history of humanity.

Historiography has always proceeded on several levels — political, economic, social, cultural, psychological, etc. — but in the twentieth century its projects overflowed the maps of historical knowledge envisioned by scholars; and the range may best be suggested by a correlate of the eighteenth-century notion of a human "point of view," which the decentering effects of the Copernican theory could not dislodge. The "point of view" (*Sehe-Punkt*) implies a horizon-structure of knowledge, or a multi-sphere historical universe turning on a psycho-center and extending concentrically through human space-time toward a transcendent and (within today's cosmology) fast-retreating periphery hardly less conjectural and subject to prophecy than in Dante's time, associated as it is with modern myths of creation, genesis, and origins. All these must of course be expressed in a linguistic medium which conveys structures, connections, and meanings from a subjective point of view, which governs the act of history-writing if not modern epistemology, skeptical as it has been of the god-emulating thinking, creating, writing, and debating subject.

In the most rudimentary sense the historian is like Joyce's "artist as a young man":

Stephen Dedalus
Class of Elements
Clongowes College
Sallins
County of Kildare
Ireland
Europe
The World
The Universe.[75]

Based on consciousness of identity and an egocentric point of view, the order is determined by education, more formal learning, faith in modern science, and imaginative projection; and so it is with reflective historians but sub-lunar, who can only imagine their way up the scale of nature.

So let us imagine a ten-sphere universe, a sort of historicized new encyclopedia, or tableau of human thought and action, individual and collective, drawing on ancient and even prehistorical structures, which, moving as it were from the inside out, give form and meaning to the range of human experience, action, and expectations in space-time, and offer a rough way of classifying the histories, old and new, of past centuries.

1. Psyche: the level of human consciousness and unconscious, psychohistory, questions of mind-body, gender, sexuality, health, birth, aging, debility, and deviance, embedded in the larger system.
2. Kinship: the family, immediate and extended, marriage, parental and sibling relations, patriarchy, matriarchy, and other emotional and cultural dimensions of the domestic sphere.
3. Community: extra-familial social groupings, including neighborhoods, guilds, classes, schools, workplaces, playgrounds, unions, cooperatives, teams, gangs, armies, and civil society.
4. Culture: human creativity, production, and destruction in areas of social interaction, love, language, work, play, the arts, sciences, technology, commerce, crime, violence, and war.
5. Institutions: formal organizations in the public sphere, including the church, schools, universities, professions, law, medicine, corporations, administration, and bureaucracy.
6. State: political, legal, economic, and military structures, government, councils, courts, police, social planning, control of institutions, and diplomacy.
7. Empire: the extension of state power over native and foreign populations, establishment of colonial territories, international affairs, and analogous "imperialisms."

8. The Other: discovery, confrontation, and interaction with foreign and exotic cultural, ethnic, and linguistic groups, and questions of understanding, coexistence, and control.

9. Globe: prehistory, the biosphere, natural environment, geography, oceanography, natural history, geological and astronomic background — "world history."

10. Cosmos: the "view from a distant star," furthest reaches of the universe, larger questions of the origins, nature, and destiny of the human species within a "total history."

(But keep in mind that it is language — Heidegger's "house of being" — that draws together these imaginary concentric, intersecting, and interacting spheres into a field of meaning in space-time, which is at the same time open to further historical inquiry, interpretation, and, as ever, "revision.")

The first sphere, the psychic realm, has been made the avenue of new fashions in historical research and interpretation, which in a way represent the posthumous revenge of the subject, whose demise has been proclaimed so often in the wake of Nietzsche (not to mention Hume).

Psychohistory, with psychoanalysis, has declined in popularity over the past generation, at least among historians, though psychobiography, in less doctrinaire forms, continues its conjectural ways. But despite the collapse (or absorption) of theory, history cannot escape the psychological dimension, however imagined. Religious history is particular rich in revealing the neurotic side of human experience, as Huizinga had shown long before and as appeared more systematically, and indeed in the spirit of Durkheim's "collective conscious" (or unconscious) in Jean Delumeau's discussion of "sin and fear" in early modern Europe.[76] However, contemporary psychohistory is not the abstract and disembodied reflection of Cartesians or Kantians or the psychodrama of Freudians; rather it is the exploration, in cultural terms, of the human body — its functions and changes, its pleasures, disorders, and torments. The new introspection has shifted from inner reflection to the carnal base, parallel to Merleau-Ponty's shift within phenomenological tradition; but in practice this means a return to material and tactile culture, this time closer to home, and the physiological and medical dimensions of experience, to the extent that these are accessible to historical inquiry. The dualism of flesh and spirit — like that of letter and spirit — runs through Western history; and Christian tradition has subordinated the carnal aspect of humanity in deference to man's higher nature. So did modern philosophy, which rested on the usually inarticulate assumption that, in the words of Poullain de la Barre (1673), "the mind has no sex."[77]

In the wake of cultural history and theory, however, post-Freudian psycho-history, while it takes a universal, biological point of departure, opens windows on the private world, including both the social structure and culture of the family and the private feelings of individuals defined in terms of gender, age, sexual activity, mental and bodily condition as well as class and locale. This eclectic range of topics invited not only new sources but also personal impressions, since historians took part in the experiences of the private sphere. Along with this focus on the body as the basic unit of the human condition and the ground of the acting, reacting, and perceiving subject has come a growing list of attributes and states of bodily existence, including childhood and old age, health, sexuality, abstinence, and disability, each of which participates in the subject of history. The recent works of Peter Brown and Carolyn Bynum have also reminded us of sexual attitudes and practices often overlooked in this secularist age, including sexual renunciation and notions of the resurrection of the body.[78] The study of the varieties of sexuality has also been broadened by ethnographic explorations. In the eighteenth century Christoph Meiners already noted the cultural significance of male homosexuality (*Männerliebe*) among the Greeks, but the modern "ethnographic imagination" has vastly expanded the territories of "perversion."[79]

"The hour of our death" was the first of the "four last things," the others being final judgment, hell, and heaven; and Huizinga's evocation of the poetic and pictorial renditions of the image and the "art of dying" was again pursued more systematically, and with more ingenious use of historical sources, by historians of "mentality" like Philippe Ariès and Michel Vovelle.[80] To Huizinga's poetic and artistic sources Ariès added liturgical, testamentary, epigraphic, and iconographic testimonies to death scenes, with particular attention to the question of the understanding of self and the types of death experience, or perception. For Ariès death was not only private but also a public matter (and of course a natural one, too), sometimes dramatized and in any case tied to conventional burial ceremonial and ultimately made familiar and secular—though not, like so many other emotional sites, modernized, except perhaps in funereal practices. In any case death can never be fully historicized, only its images and its cultural and literary trappings. It is one of the few human phenomena which is fully amenable (whether or not fully intelligible) to comparative study within a global framework.

A no less challenging aspect of the psychic sphere is the mysterious phenomenon of human memory, which for the ancients was even identified, though unreflectively, with history itself, though its first conveyors were oral tradition and poetry. Again the modern connection was the *Annales* connection, and again Ariès was the central figure, not only through his work on childhood and death, the ends of the temporal life-cycle, but also through his early book *The Time of History,* which set the medieval "existential sense of the past" as the ground of the written tradition of French historical scholarship leading from Gregory of Tours to the official historiographers of the sixteenth century and to Bossuet. A key figure in the twentieth century (though no historian) was Maurice Halbwachs, a colleague of Febvre and Bloch at Strasbourg and later appointed to the editorial board of the *Annales,* who as a Durkheimian sociologist and a critic of Freud promoted memory to a collective phenomenon. This was the conception which Pierre Nora appropriated, in politicized form, for modern French historiography as "places of memory," which were concrete sites of collective memory, tradition, commemoration, and museology and which became a generalized category for the revision of national history. Patrick Hutton reviewed memory studies as a longer conceptual tradition, leading from the ancient "art of memory" through Vico, romantic poetry, autobiography, Michelet and other historians of the French Revolution, Freud, Halbwachs, Ariès, and Gadamer, who restored the thread of meaning to history by shifting from a crude historicism to hermeneutics. As a field which has produced a special journal on memory and history as well as a vast amount of literature, the joint field of memory and history has been attached, especially and controversially, to the study and commemoration of the Holocaust.[81]

Family history is a very old genre in the sense of celebrations of great dynasties and noble houses (Bodin called the family a "little republic," *res privata* corresponding to *res publica*); but as a site of history it is more recent, including forays into questions of kinship, patriarchal power, marital strategies, inheritance, domestic architecture, furniture, shopping, food, leisure, issues of "privacy," romantic love, contraception, child-bearing, childhood, nursing, birth order, adoption, adolescence, sickness, hygiene, education, the "civilizing process," old age, and at the end the customs surrounding death. As Lawrence Stone wrote, there are at least six approaches to the topic — political, sociological, biological, economic, psychological, and sexual — and singling out one dimension leads to "sterility or myopia."[82] Yet an eclectic mixture of all of these, and attendant sources, invites conjecture and appeal, implicit or explicit, to personal experience or stereotypes drawn from nineteenth-century conventions. Nevertheless, the family itself is a determinable locus, the most fundamental focus, where the individual and society intersect in the most concrete (and ostensibly "familiar") fashion, and as such it has attracted attention from many angles and disciplines which historians have to consider. Attempts at synthesis range from Stone's own tracing of the fortunes of elite families and marital ties in early modern England to Edward Shorter's even bolder and more impressionistic study of the "modern family," especially that of the lower orders, as it emerged from a "traditional" form, based on private opinion as well as ostentatious use of quantitative materials. Neither has escaped criticism (especially for their neglect of aspects relating to women), but as yet no consensus has been reached about the institution itself, except perhaps that it must be explored in even more specific and empirical terms.

Leaving the domestic circle means entry into a different world, in which blood ties are of secondary importance and may indeed generate hostility, to the extent that the old custom of feuding remains embedded in "mentalities." In any case here it is that the distinction between "private" and "public," a residue from ancient Roman law and its vernacular offshoots, comes into play, beginning with the definition of the person (in law) and including the institution of private property and inheritance through private "will." A prejudice against politics, to which Ariès admitted directly, was a premise of the *Annales* school over several generations, whatever other differences might occur, a premise that also underlies the notion of a "civil society" detached from political structures and controls; and this corresponds to the third sphere of historical experience. The history of private life, which overlaps with the family and larger areas of civil society, has a considerable history going back to the illustrated antiquarian collection of Alfred Franklin, Paul La Croix, and others on French life "autrefois," and indeed seminal eighteenth-century discussions of "material culture"; but it was the "new history" of the twentieth century that laid disciplinary claim to this field of inquiry. The most impressive assault was undertaken from the headquarters of the *Annales*, especially with the publication, beginning in 1986, of the five-volume *History of Private Life* initiated by Ariès and edited by him and Duby, with commitment to the principle of *longue durée* and much ado about the problem of sources not yet revealed and the originality of the quest, compared to the labors of archeologists plumbing unknown territory and forced to interpret unprecedented finds within an indeterminate framework. In this work private life is given ancient (Roman, not Greek) roots, it grows in medieval households (especially of the aristocracy), and it flourishes in the Renaissance, with the development of intimacy, new perceptions of the body, and forms of sociability and civility, including the salons and clubs inspired by printing and reading. The pioneering character of these voluminous but also miscellaneous discussions is recalled again at the end of these 1,200-plus pages by Roger Chartier, who remarks, characteristically, that the collection represents merely "the first fragments of a new kind of history."[83]

Here we find ourselves in the presence of an allegedly "new cultural history," which confronts this world of intimacy, sexuality, and mental disorder through techniques not of measurement but rather of imagination, to which both literary sources and literary theory are central. In such terms we have historical studies of, for example, the culture of desire, the culture of love, the culture of pleasure, the culture of pain, the culture of narcissism, the culture of unbelief, the culture of sensibility, the culture of redemption, the culture of complaint, the culture of contentment, and on and on — representing new (or not-so-new) targets of historiographical reach if not grasp that again bring together the local and the global. Like humanism of old, the new history of the past century, especially in its French incarnation, regarded nothing human as alien, but with different aspirations it tried to reduced the vagaries of the human condition to science, especially through quantitative analysis, or expand the agenda to accommodate some sort of "total history" — but the latter could only be achieved, or approximated, by the intrusion of the subject, that is, the creative and critical historian who, like Hegel and in a derivative way Michelet, Febvre, and Braudel, loved and hoped to assimilate historical experience through a rhetoric that was at once richly traditional and eccentrically personal.

They hoped to assimilate, too, the history of high culture, as suggested to begin with by the "synthetic" history" of Berr and his successors, and Febvre in particular reviewed books in the history of art, science, literature, philosophy, psychology, and linguistics as well as the standard branches of history, especially economic and social — all in pursuit of a "wholly different sort of history." The post-Marxist, but still Marxoid, idea of joining a world view or mentality (superstructure) to a material base was pursued with the help of anthropology, as in the work of Aaron Gurevich and, in a more literary manner, of Mikhail Bakhtin, who hoped to plumb the depths of the social world in its most inarticulate corners. Gurevich paid respects to his French colleagues, remarking of Le Roy Ladurie that in his *Montaillou,* "He was able to hear the living voices of peasant men and peasant women."[84] So indeed Bakhtin had hoped to do by reading between the sometimes outrageous lines of *Gargantua* and *Pantagruel* for echoes of folk culture.[85] For Gurevich, Bakhtin's "insights made earlier views on medieval culture at once outmoded," although the sharp break he made between popular and official culture was exaggerated, in contrast especially to the work of E. R. Curtius; and Gurevich hoped to reconstruct a more integrated "world view," perhaps along the lines of the collection edited by Jacques Le Goff surveying "medieval callings," including not only peasants, nobles, monks, and merchants (the latter by Gurevich) but also city-dwellers, women, marginal men, saints, artists, and "intellectuals," that is, clerics and men of letters. The elitist literary approach to the history of culture is even more pronounced in the self-advertised "new medievalism" of American scholars, who claim no innovating methodology but only a privileged place in the avant garde of Romance studies and literary theory.[86]

In Germany the "history of concepts" (*Begriffsgeschichte*) had a similarly encyclopedic and totalizing goal, though dissolved in a quasi-philosophical solution and more political and ideological in orientation. What Reinhard Koselleck proposed, in effect, was an approach to social history through a large semantic field of public discourse across several centuries — social history from the bottom down.[87] The procedure, which projects a contemporary "we" into a bygone field of meaning, follows that of hermeneutics, which likewise regards meaning as something to be determined by a present observer rather than a vain and Romantic attempt at retrospective mind-reading. Unlike *Annaliste* historians, Koselleck rejects neither the event nor chronology, but tries to comprehend the notion of time and experience in a present-oriented discipline that joins the private and the public, the mental and the social through the enduring medium of discourse, the transcendental subject being demoted to the hermeneutical level of "positional commitment" — and Koselleck does not hesitate to credit Chladenius with the insight that past positions could not be represented in retrospect.[88] Although not as immersed as Febvre in questions of language, Koselleck has made his own sort of "linguistic turn," though without entirely separating it from the idealist (and "subjective") tradition of concepts. Nor does he quite claim "total history" as the aim of *Begriffsgeschichte*, "for, as we know, the future remains unknown."

The fifth level of my historiographical cosmos is the public sphere in its most tangible form, that is, the institutions that give legal form to collective activities and organization within civil society but below the level of politics. This is illustrated by efforts to avoid political narrative by seizing on other mechanisms, especially economic and social, that show and perhaps even measure, historical change in the short or long term. The most elementary choice for historians has been material interest, economics, and of course this is most easily demonstrated and calibrated through the statistical analysis of such accessible factors as population, prices, wages, production, consumption, etc.; and the temptation is to tie such figures to general explanations, so that (for instance) the sixteenth century could in one textbook, building on the classic researches of Earl Hamilton, be reduced to "the price revolution and counter-Reformation." Social historians, too, have tried bypass conventional political and legal sources and to determine collective behavior by direct statistical inquiry — another way to find "what really happened." Ironically, the "new economic history" and "new social history," following another wave of quantitative fetishism, diverged sharply from the culturalist thrust of the "new history" *tout court*, and in the process doomed themselves to an early demise, or depreciation, even in this age of computerization. In any case and as always, of course, the problem of interpretation still remains, especially if historians abandon the old professional habit of privileging source materials over analysis — or indeed, on the contrary, if they insist on asking questions without the possibility of finding any relevant materials to examine.

Meanwhile, traditional histories in particular fields — parliaments, councils, police, church, universities, commerce, diplomacy, the military, etc. — have been continued, often with cultural associations that may justify claims of novelty. Nation-"inventing" (pace Benedict Anderson) has tended to replace the old theme of "state-building" as the political narrative — as becomes clear by juxtaposing the study of the "myth of nations" by Patrick Geary to that of "the medieval origins of the modern state" by his former teacher Joseph Strayer — but is itself subordinated to recent efforts to conceptualize global history, if not actually to formulate it beyond the level of textbooks, series, and collections of articles celebrating the "new world history."[89] The problem of "point of view" remains, and a multi-traditional approach multiplies perspectives but does not globalize the human past, except (as before) for a largely conjectural prehistorical past set in a controversial and fast-changing evolutionary story of the human species. Crypto-Marxist "world-systems analysis" seems to do this, but only by reinstalling a world market defined by long-distance trade and narrowly economic measures, enhanced marginally by evidence of cultural influence and exchange, including disease as well as technology and symbols. For the history of particular political, legal, and administrative institutions it has been for the most part business as usual, except for comparativist effort, usually limited to related national traditions separated by language, at least in the modern period.

The question of "empire," real and metaphorical, and the horizons it opens up goes beyond the inflammatory issue of competing imperialisms that divided nations before the first war and furnished a target for economic analysis and Marxist criticism of capitalism. Imperialism in the twentieth century was tied not only to political and economic expansion but also to exploration and the gathering of information about natural environment, racial and religious differences, and legal problems, especially the question of slavery. Ancient Rome and modern Spain and Britain provided the familiar models for imperial structures and ideologies, but current historical interest has shifted from political to cultural topics, especially those connected with cartography, technology, disease, gender, and sexuality. Fantasy as well as knowledge underlies the structures of global power that claim imperial status, and of course this links empire with the exotic and confrontation with cultural and linguistic alterity, which has acted further to open the horizons of global history which arose in the Enlightenment. To speak of the "globe," however, is to expand the historian's view still further, to what Teilhard de Chardin called the "biosphere," corresponding to the most ambitious geohistorical implications of the Annales school as well as the philosophy of history according to Toynbee and others. Would this correspond to the ancient and modern conception of "total history"?

The last sphere — the historian's Empyraean, as it were — is what may on good Western precedent be called the Cosmos, which in a Dantean way suggests metahistorical questions of the origins, nature, and destiny of the human species — that is, a return to religion and to the philosophy of history. From the 1960s this meant especially the "analytical philosophy of history" in the style of F. H. Bradley, Maurice Mandelbaum, and Morton White. Such analytical philosophy, which found a home in the periodical *History and Theory*, was based on a unitary and propositional, not to say algebraic, conception of truth, and deference to Hempel and the Covering Lawyers; and it seems to have run its course, or at least outlived its usefulness for historians, and indeed its "decline and fall" has been traced by its former sympathizers.[90] It was in any case a philosophy for readers of history who wanted to raise their reading to a higher rational, or logical, plane, and perhaps to escape "historians' fallacies" (of which David Hackett Fisher identified over a hundred varieties), and it was largely unconcerned with history as a project of human inquiry and self-understanding.[91] There may be no bottom to historical interpretation, but it should probe beneath the surface of received and processed popular knowledge, however revised and reconceptualized, whether or not it can illuminate (in Huizinga's words) "the shadow of tomorrow."

Circumspect and Prospect

A way a lone a last a loved a long the riverrun . . .
                                    — James Joyce

My Times

The story told eccentrically in these volumes has finally come down to "my times," so that history becomes for me more overtly autobiographical, and like *Finnegans Wake,* my ending connects with my starting point in that this volume covers the period of my own learning, teaching, and writing from the beginning. According to my juvenile records, my serious reading of history (after the Oz books, popular science, and many classic novels) started with Ferdinand Schevill's *History of Modern Europe,* H. G. Wells's *Outline of History,* R. H. Tawney's *Religion and the Rise of Capitalism,* Toynbee's *Study of History* (abridged), and a *History of the World* (author forgotten). When setting off from Elgin, Illinois, to Harvard, I recall saving to read on the train Thomas Wolfe's *Of Time and the River* for its account of Eugene Gant's train trip to Cambridge and then his frantic reaction to the stacks of Widener Library, tearing omnivorously through thousands of volumes, and to the anecdote about Ben Jonson — "Other men read books, he read libraries" — though this had "nothing to do with scholarship, nothing to do with academic honors, nothing to do with formal learning."[1] Reading Proust, Joyce, Mann, and Kafka (in the same course which Norman Mailer had taken a few years before) may have improved my tastes, but even so I remained under the spell of Wolfe's "orgy of the books," though more academically focused, as I gave up my ambitions to follow the leads of these two reckless literary adventurers.

Serious reading aside, my primary education in European history was carried on in college through the twenty-volume "Langer Series," which set the American canon formed before, during, and after World War II. My memories of Harvard go back to the last years of the triumvirate who retired simultaneously: Frederick Merk, disciple of Frederick Jackson Turner and teacher of the famous course on "Cowboys and Indians" ("The Westward Movement"); Arthur Schlesinger, Sr., still carrying on his innovative work in social history; Samuel Eliot Morison, who still wore his uniform to class, had the door locked before his lectures began, and walked across Mass. Ave. to give separate lectures to the Radcliffe "girls"; and also Arthur Schlesinger, Jr., and Oscar Handlin, whose daughter was later a friend and colleague of mine. In ancient history there were Sterling Dow and Mason Hammond; in Russian history Michael Karpovich (who once performed a mock session of the Communist International in the style of the Byzantine service, emphasizing factors of continuity in the face of violent secular revolution), and Martin Malia (who interjected a mini-course on Kremlinology the week after Stalin's death); and in literature Perry Miller, Howard Mumford Jones, Douglas Bush, Harry Levin, Walter Jackson Bate, and Albert Guerard. However, I was drawn rather to European history, or rather "History and Lit.," and had the good fortune to hear, among others, William Langer, Sidney Fay (come out of retirement to finish the course when Langer returned to Washington) on the nineteenth century, H. Stuart Hughes, and Carl Schorske; also Helen Cam and Bryce Lyon on the middle ages (the latter offering insights on medieval historiography, especially that surrounding Pirenne, who was the mentor of his mentor, Carl Stephenson); Crane Brinton on the Enlightenment (among other things), Donald McKay on modern France, David Owen on modern English history; and especially Myron Gilmore, who attracted me eventually, as he did so many others, into Renaissance history and historiography.

Historiographically, then, I came of age in the 1950s, when two large orthodoxies seemed to prevail, one the mainstream practice of academic history, with political, institutional, and diplomatic emphasis, and the other Marxist history, which focused on the material base of society, if not on revolutionary promise. After college I was pressed into military service in Germany, following James Conant, who left the presidency of Harvard to become U.S. High

Commissioner in 1953. Moving in 1955 from MP duties (and guarding the first atomic installation in Europe) to graduate studies at Columbia, I did not fully embrace either of these lines of practice, though I was drawn to archival research and to post-Marxist social theory and philosophy of history. I did follow professional convention to the extent that I turned to legal history as a way of joining social thought and social reality, though my own sort of linguistic turn gave this an unorthodox twist. The radical option seemed an impediment rather than an aid to historical understanding; nor did my New York and later my Rochester Marxist friends dispel my misgivings. Was it my post-military depression or continuing commitment to literature and criticism that kept me off the intellectual barricades? Even less than to the agenda of the new left was I attracted to the "new" economic and social histories, or the ventures of psychohistory (despite a juvenile fascination with Freud and vicarious psychoanalysis through the experience of friends), though my eyes were later opened to women's history by colleagues, including Renate Bridenthal and especially my later wife, Bonnie Smith.

As a Fulbright scholar in Paris in the late 1950s I attended the seminar of Fernand Braudel, but his focus at that time on economics and Mediterranean trade did not strike me as any closer to a "new history" than the work of Roland Mousnier (whose lectures I also attended) or the work on Spanish prices by Earl Hamilton (later a colleague at SUNY Binghamton).[2] By then I was already committed to the study of historiography, as were two of my colleagues in France: Orest Ranum, who was then working with Mousnier, later shifting to the terrain of Braudel, and who later still wrote a fine book on seventeenth-century French historical writing; and especially Samuel Kinser, who was then finishing his thesis on the sixteenth-century historian Jacques-Auguste de Thou and who joined me in fantasizing about a large historiographical undertaking to replace the great survey of Fueter, which is one remote root of my current project. About this aspiration I was in touch with others, including Eric Cochrane and Max Fisch, but the bibliography needed for such an enterprise seemed preventive even in that pre-electronic age of 4 × 6 cards.

From the 1960s the "new" economic, social, and military history appeared on the scene and attracted many followers among my colleagues and students, as did ideological movements, especially on the near and far left and among women, blacks, minorities, and associated "advocacy" groups, which acted to expand, to popularize, to democratize, to globalize, and to polarize historical scholarship in many ways, though my own interest was still in estimating the significance of these areas for the project(s) of historiography; for these phenomena, too, had their precedents and models in earlier kinds of advocacies, especially those in ages of racial, religious, and national rivalries. History "from the bottom up" was a ghost of more pointed efforts to uncover structures of power and their often malignant agents, and microhistory seemed to me a still more remote and toothless remnant of radical history. As for the non-Eurocentric (and non-Americocentric) worlds, close friendship with a Chinese historian, Roxane Wittke, and marriage, in the late '70s, to a French historian who become a leading scholar in women's and world history opened my eyes to some of these regions, though my perspective, point of view, and commitment to local knowledges kept them on the edges of my intellectual map. With an irredeemably working-class background and plenty of factory time behind me, I was never attracted to working-class history; sent early to a fundamentalist church, I had been very early disillusioned by dogmatic causes, right, left, center, and beyond; and I had a general suspicion of Dickensian Jellybism — "telescopic philanthropy" — especially attempted from the groves of academe. Nor was I ever attracted to the reductionisms of political, economic, and social history, and while the "new" cultural history led away from these antiquated projects, this self-advertising movement seemed all too often an unfocused way of filling the intellectual vacuum left in the wake of Marxism, changing the words but retaining the ideological music and the hope of activism, or at least some academic or rhetorical surrogate, which would allow historians to be not only critics of but also participants in power. Even then, I suppose, I was inclined to reverse the advice of Marx's pivotal eleventh thesis on Feuerbach, to interpret the world rather than to change it — hard enough to get even the first right, which few members of my generation did, as evident from the perspective of the 1990s.

My field of interest to begin with was "Ren.-Ref.," in the days of the scholastic debate over the nature (*quid sit?*) or even existence (*an sit?*) of the Renaissance, my own preference being to explore continuities with the middle ages. My points of departure were defined by two of my mentors who then dominated the field: Paul Kristeller's strictly academic and value-free view derived Renaissance humanism from the faculty of arts (*studia humanitatis*), while Hans Baron's focus was on "civic humanism" (*Bürgerhumanismus*) as a product of the "crisis" of the early Italian Renaissance, with later incarnations traced by John Pocock and others. My own notion was to combine or to reconcile these rival visions (Ranke vs. Burckhardt, in the formula of Meinecke and Gilbert) and to pursue them into areas of historical scholarship, broadly conceived. From Baron I differed by emphasizing the importance of the legal tradition — what I called "civil humanism" — while I deviated from Kristeller by exploring civil law as a humanistic discipline and in its relations to grammar, rhetoric, and especially history, and also by trying to uncover the conceptual riches concealed by these liberal arts. At Columbia I also learned from J. H. Randall, Walter Dorn, Shepard Clough, Allan Nevins, Marjorie Nicholson, John Mundy, Norman Cantor, and Herbert Dean; and later on I joined Jack Hexter and Dick Popkin on projects of common interest.

In the 1970s I was deflected into "real history" (in the ironic phrase of my mentor Garrett Mattingly, archival historian par excellence), and indeed my biography of the jurist and Huguenot ideologue and agent François Hotman was in a way inspired by Mattingly's own life of Catherine of Aragon, based on his Supplement to the Letters and Papers of Henry VIII. His attitude toward hard history was softened, however, by his literary artistry, reinforced by a long collaboration with Bernard De Voto.[3] My own way was illuminated by similar collaboration with three older scholars—Ralph Giesey, Julian Franklin, and the late John Salmon—whom I fancied as the three (other) musketeers accompanying my seizièmist adventures, which were continued in a study of the French Reformation, pursued across multiple levels—social, institutional, and intellectual.[4] I followed ideological questions into the later modern period, especially through the law of property, which was central to the French Revolution and its aftermath and more particularly to the writings of Savigny, Marx, and Proudhon.[5] My major project in this connection, however, was surveying the Western legal tradition as a continuum of thought and judgment about social structures, values, and change;[6] and here I have profited by several periods of scholarly refuge at the Institute for Advanced Study, with the support of, among others, Felix Gilbert, John Elliott, and Peter Paret, and stimulating contacts with scholars such as Marshall Claggett, Tom Kuhn, Clifford Geertz, Morton White, Irving Lavin, Jonathan Israel, Sebastian de Grazia, Robert Palmer, Lawrence Stone, Jerrold Seigel, Theodore Rabb, Robert Darnton, and Quentin Skinner.[7]

My teaching apprenticeship was served mainly at SUNY Binghamton, where Norman Cantor was history department chair for a time before his ambition led him elsewhere, and the University of Rochester, where the history department was under the controversial leadership of Eugene Genovese, who had an even more colorful career. At both institutions I made close friends, especially Charles Freedeman and Sanford Elwitt, but my real intellectual community was scattered about the world, which was another motive, besides research, for European travel.

In the 1980s I was drawn back into intellectual history when (besides excursions into the wilderness of Vichian studies) I was elected editor of the *Journal of the History of Ideas* (in which I had published my first article) and transferred shortly thereafter to Rutgers.[8] Since the time of Arthur Lovejoy this has been an interdisciplinary field, though increasingly supplemented by more specialized periodicals in the history of philosophy, literature, art, music, the natural and human sciences, and historiography. I continued to pursue inter-disciplinary interests in other ways, most notably in a seminar I gave at the Folger Library in the 1990s on a old topic introduced to me many years before by Paul Kristeller, viz., the classification of knowledge — one consequence of which, besides a published volume, was the formation of the International Society for Intellectual History headed by Constance Blackwell.[9] In recent years intellectual history has been reoriented by literary and linguistic theory and constructivism, as well as deconstruction, poststructuralism, and espe-cially hermeneutics. As editor I am skeptical of recurrent claims to novelty, and indeed I have tried to recall the deeper roots of the history of thought and its contexts in a recent study of the "descent of ideas."[10] Lovejoy probably would not have cared for this (some might say anti-philosophical) revaluation, though I think the expansion and international colonization of his field would have pleased him.

I try, at least as a professional requirement, to move with the times, but at the start of the third millennium (still following the Christian chronology of Bede programmed into the computers of the world) I continue to be suspicious about claims to novelty, although interdisciplinary exchanges are more intense than ever and the applications of technological innovations have changed procedures of inquiry. The contrast between micro- and macrohistory is not one of principle and in fact does little more than to give recognition to long-standing practices of universal and particular, or local, history. Nor, in princi-ple, has the proliferation of cultural studies, or of "everyday life" (*Alltagsge-schichte, histoire quotidienne*) expanded the range of high and low (spiritual and material) culture. "Global history" has made world history more of a presence, but its celebrations have almost always neglected the grand tradition embedded in Western thought going back to the Old Regime and indeed to Christian and pagan antiquity. Moreover, the options for a global perspective remain much the same: the updated and secularized grand narrative of a putatively unified humanity; a biological, or evolutionary framework, in which experiences such as birth, death, disease, and food production represent lowest common denominators; and artificial frameworks, especially those based on economics (Marxism, modernization, or world-systems theory). World history may likewise accommodate microhistorical projects, such as recent global studies of cod, coffee, tea, salt, beer, coal, nutmeg, and perfume, but these are also artificial for purposes of historical narrative, not unlike the old serendipitous cabinets of curiosity. However, such global perspectives, while (like the history of universal "ideas") they may allow conjectural and comparative study, all transcend local knowledge and to this extend the discipline of strictly historical inquiry.

But the history of history itself has always been my major preoccupation. My introduction to the subject came, as with most Harvard undergraduates, through Collingwood's *Idea of History* (1946), though few had any sense of the traditions of learning underlying this venturesome book (from myth, Herodotus, Thucydides, and Polybius, to medieval and Renaissance historians to historicism, including Vico, Herder, Windelband, Rickert, Simmel, Dilthey, Meyer, Spengler, Bergson, and especially Croce) and were content to accept the naive epistemology that rested on the old — romantic — hermeneutical principle of the "re-enactment of past experience," the paradigm of Hercule Poirot as historical investigator, and the goal of human self-knowledge. Through Collingwood and Meinecke I also encountered the debates over "historicism," old and new; and indeed the search for the roots, or fragments, of historicism became a major aim in my studies of European historiography in the Renaissance. These interests were reinforced by fruitful contacts with scholars around the world, including Hans-Georg Gadamer, Arnaldo Momigliano, Reinhard Koselleck, Paolo Grossi, Jörn Rüsen, Hans Troje, Paolo Grossi, Georg Iggers, Richard Popkin, Charles Schmitt, Isaiah Berlin, Giorgio Tagliacozzo, Robert Kingdon, Nancy Roelker, Donald Verene, Peter Munz, Quentin Skinner, Anthony Pagden, Peter Burke, Ulrich Schneider, Martin Mulsow, Jonathan Israel, and especially J. G. A. Pocock, whose trail I have followed, often inadvertently and serendipitously.

The study of historiography itself, associated still with historical method, was long established as a field when I began graduate school in 1955, and it was increasingly drawn to theoretical concerns, always including philosophy but also the social sciences and then literary criticism. It also retained its ties with heavy erudition, as in, among others, John Pocock's study of the "ancient constitution," Eric Cochrane on early modern Italian history, Antonia Gransden on English historical writing, Joseph Levine on the Ancients and Moderns, Georg Iggers and Horst Blanke on the history of German historiography, and Joachim Knape on the term "Historie" and its semantic fields, not to mention the old standards by Fueter, Harry Elmer Barnes, and James Westfall Thompson. In France there has been a shift to a quantitative approach to professional history, as in the works of Charles Carbonell and Pim den Boer — responding to the avalanche of historical literature in recent years, reflected too in editions of the works and correspondence of major scholars, international conferences, specialized periodicals such as *History and Theory,* the quadrilingual *Storia della storiographia,* and E-journals, volumes of collected articles, bibliographies, and more recently, more globally, and more miscellaneously, large reference books on history and historians. My first academic enthusiasm, which initially seemed to be a pioneering product, now is more like a snowflake in a bibliographical and theoretical blizzard—the trajectory being from Herodotus to Herder to Huizinga to the Joycean HCE ("Here Comes Everybody").

My first thought was to shift focus from *historia* as the classical description of past actions (*narratio rerum gestarum; geschehene Begebenheiten; l'histoire événementielle*) to more enduring products of human cultural activity; and so I turned to the residues of history preserved in language and the law, becoming aware only later that I was following a trail already blazed by Vico on his way to an even more ambitious project, and being enticed further into this field by Giorgio Tagliacozzo. If the subject of my grand narrative ("history") was polyvalent to an extreme, the plot was simple enough—that is, the Western tradition of history proper, as it developed, under the coinage of Herodotus, from art to genre to discipline to profession to "science"—and then back to art? In my previous two books on the "faces" and "fortunes" of history I have taken the story up almost to my own time—up at least to the time of my mentors who served in the Second World War.[11] I say "the story," although of course I realize that whatever coherence the history of history possesses derives from the sense of tradition—or of consciously breaking from tradition— and my choice of authors has largely been made on the basis of this self-selecting process underlying the canon of Western historiography as interpretive surveys from the time of Bodin to Fueter have progressively shaped it. In fact (to invoke a cliché of postmodernism) there is no "grand narrative," for there have been many stories, with many plots and protagonists, and the accumulation of books, articles, and reviews have multiplied the "faces" of history, have complicated its "fortunes," have opened frontiers, and, at least from perspective of the new millennium, have produced the present state of fragmentation.

I was an early (indeed *ante literam*) devotee of the "linguistic turn" and student of literary criticism and theory, though drawn less to the derivative sources of French fashions than to German originals. Reading Nietzsche, I was already on the trail of "interpretation" and its discontents and the point of view of modern, post-Romantic hermeneutics, as formulated later by Heidegger and Gadamer. My starting point became the phenomenological horizon-structure of experience, though not forgetting Nietzsche's warning that "beyond this horizon there remain men, passions, doctrines and purposes."[12] Yet attention must continue to be paid to the authorial point of view, with historical inquiry carried on at the cultural frontier, defined by encounters with unfamiliar cultures and languages. This may seem counter to the thrust of world history that has tried to reject centricisms—ego-, ethno-, Americo-, and

Eurocentrism — but though I have never wanted to be a national historian, I never believed that the historian can be an omniscient observer, that is, can, under pretense of avoiding bias or prejudice and finally achieving "objectivity," escape his or her cultural situation and take the view from a distant star, except perhaps philosophically, metaphorically, conjecturally, or for pedagogical purposes; and for the history of historical *inquiry* I prefer to avoid this fallacy. As with Joycean narrative and the implications of hermeneutics, historical "objectivity" can be approached only by multiplying particular "points of view."

But even with disciplinary help how can interpretation be undertaken from the center of a particular cultural circle? For me hermeneutics means not the Romantic and Collingwoodian idea of empathy, or retrospective mind-reading, but the awareness of what Nietzsche called "the interpretive character of all that happens."[13] The "introduction of meaning," Nietzsche added, is not a matter of rational, ahistorical explanation but rather "in most cases a new interpretation over an old interpretation that has become incomprehensible, that is itself only a sign."[14] As Paul Ricoeur has remarked, "To make one's own what was previously foreign remains the ultimate aim of hermeneutics"; or as Gadamer wrote (and as I have quoted before), apparently still making room for a grand narrative, "History is, as it were, the great dark book, the collected work of the human spirit, written in the languages of the past, the text of which we have to try to understand"; and no interdisciplinary effort will permit historians to avoid this challenge. This message, expanded by Heidegger and Gadamer from a historical formula into philosophical hermeneutics, has found a postmodern audience, especially among literary theorists and intellectual historians. Nor do I believe that the siren songs of quantification or postmodern technology, which promise a different kind of knowledge, can release us from this charge.

In conclusion, and to complete my ego-historical circle — my "ego-histoire," in the phrase of Pierre Nora — history is still a form of human inquiry that seeks meaning, but this meaning, as Gadamer has argued, cannot be simply that of a bygone age, of the "foreign country" that is the past, but only a constructed meaning at a present cultural moment and in a local cultural context. Hermeneutics is a new kind of skepticism — "the most important form of skepticism today," claims Odo Marquardt — and there is no evading its implications for the interpretive predicament of modern historians.[15] We have learned from our professional forebears, from the experience of historiographical tradition, to speak of revival (humanists), of resurrection (Michelet), of restoration (modern antiquarians), or of reenactment (Collingwood), and of course of "revision" (almost every young historian at some point); but these are metaphors for a less conjectural operation which employ a rhetoric of alterity that establishes a relationship between us — author and readership — and an "other" whose behavior we can never bring back to life and whose ideas we can never quite "rethink" within our cultural and linguistic horizons. Despite postmodernist maneuvering and evading we remain part of a tradition of interpretation, of a search for self-knowledge, which leads, through inherited linguistic usage, back to Herodotus and his poetic predecessors.[16]

The Linguistic Turn

What is perhaps most remarkable about historical studies (and the human sciences more generally) in the last quarter of the twentieth century is the linguistic, or literary, turn taken by many scholars engaged in historical inquiry. In the most elementary form this meant a return to narrative in the sense of Macaulay's and Trevelyan's conception (and Lawrence Stone's rediscovery) of history as an art and the call made by Allan Nevins (who himself had journalistic training and no degree in history), repeated many times since, for an effort by professional historians to reach for a popular readership.[17] This attitude was displayed in a more sophisticated way by Peter Gay, who commented on a few nineteenth-century historians in terms of style, turning Buffon's famous phrase (*le style est l'homme même*) into the hypothesis that "style is the historian" and anticipating the later emphasis on rhetoric and "representation," as also did J. H. Hexter.[18] Gibbon was able to balance the deep study of sources with a large, almost global vision, the writing of virtuoso prose, but what Linda Orr has called "the revenge of literature" has for many resulted in the journalistic emphasis on the production of extensive narrative and, marginally at least, the temptation to imitation and plagiarism, which forms the second part of the old joke attributed to conventional historiographical practice ("history repeats itself, and historians repeat one another").

A still more remarkable consequence of this literary — and linguistic — turn has been the invasion of literary theory, marked by the emigration from history of historians such as Hayden White, Dominick LaCapra, and Hans Kellner and the immigration into history of literary scholars such as Jonathan Culler, Frank Ankersmit, and (under the banner of the "new historicism") Steven Greenblatt. These authors all write about "history," but the world they inhabit is that of representation, printed texts, and underlying intertextual traditions derivative of the "new rhetoric" and charted by pioneers like Kenneth Burke, who, among other things on his mind, dissolved history, "without origin or telos," into literary forms and criticism.[19] This rhetorical stance situates both historians and their causal and moral arguments in a prose medium constituting "reality" and connecting them as a professional community with intended and unintended readerships. Whence rhetoricians and literary critics command the field that historians had always believed was their territory — and the same goes for philosophy, at least in its written forms, as once again "Scripture" and scriptural critics take command of the field of meaning. One bold effort to reduce history to its narrative incarnations is Ankersmit's study of narrative logic, which is wholly divorced from historical inquiry, which has to do with research and the "facts."[20] From such a point of view the conceptual framework of "historicism" itself was the product not of heuristic insight but of the choice and manipulation of terminology, topoi, tense, and copulae.

The most celebrated example of the literary turn (and, for historians, expressions of the linguistic turn) is Hayden White's *Metahistory*, a now-classic interpretation of nineteenth-century historiography based on the formation of a literary canon (not unlike F. R. Leavis's *Great Tradition*) judged according to a far more elaborate and "formalist" conception of "style" than that of Gay. White's book seeks meaning through literary categories taken, via Croce and Northrup Frye, from classical literary criticism and rhetoric, and applied to the literary structure of works by Michelet, Ranke, Burckhardt, Marx, and others. What concerns White is historical knowledge, especially through the intuited, metahistorical "deep structure" of historiographical representation as embodied in well-publicized works — the preexisting "content" of "forms."[21] He moves beyond the classical and Crocean distinction between chronicle and history to deeper meanings found in modes of "emplotment," "argument," and "ideological implication," inherent in the literary language employed by these authors in treating otherwise unproblematized "events" (the disputes of professional scholars being irrelevant to these higher meanings). For White "formist" historians like Herder, Niebuhr, and Mommsen apply their arguments to the vivid description of events; "organicist" historians like Treitschke, Stubbs, and Maitland, to the coherence and laws of history as a process; "mechanist" historians such as Tocqueville, Buckle, Marx, and Taine to extra-historical agencies; and "contextualist" historians like Herodotus, Burckhardt, and Huizinga to a combinatory view of phenomena related at the particular historical moment. According to White's neo-scholastic scheme, these modes, which may appear in combination in any particular author, are also associated with four ideological inclinations (anarchist, conservative, radical, and liberal), four modes of emplotment (romantic, tragic, comic, and satirical), and four basic tropes (metaphor, metonymy, synecdoche, and irony), which — the first three anyway — introduce figurative language into the rendering of historical reality. Following Barthes, Hayden White argues that the result of imaginative historical writing within these categories is not secondary "representation" but primary "constitution" of a historical field.

This is the formalist framework within which White richly illuminates nineteenth-century historiography, and it has had an extraordinary international fortune over the past generation and more.[22] The problem which White deliberately avoids, or evades, is that foundational element of historicism, which is the (by no means neutral) source material to which historians are bound. For White, for example, Michelet is a "realist" writing in a metaphorical mode, taking the contemporary view of social (and national) progress as reality and trying to express it through an emotional process of identification and revitalization. What Michelet sought was not autopsy but the literal "resurrection" of history. I would not quarrel with White's interpretation nor venture into the crowded playground of Michelet scholarship, where textualist and psychoanalytical enthusiasts frolic together; but I would merely remind readers of the heuristic dimension of Michelet's creations. Of course he wanted to be a celebrated author, a worthy successor of Descartes, Voltaire, Rousseau, et al., and the conscience of his Nation, among other things; but he also wrote from an extraordinary familiarity with the archival sources of French history — though it is true that they themselves can be seen as a species of imaginative literature, especially for the revolutionary period. In 1830, just after the *Trois Glorieuses* that for him marked the beginning of a new age, Michelet was appointed head archivist of the Archives Nationales; and for twenty years he worked in those sacred "catacombs of manuscripts" almost every day. Here was the dead corpse of History into which Michelet wanted to breath life, here the voices of the heroes and victims of the French past: *le bon Dieu est dans le détail.* Michelet took the substance of his narrative from national remains and relics, though he was too much the Man of Letters to give in to fashions of *Anmerkungswissenschaft* (footnotes, historiographical criticism, etc.). What did he make of the sources which he was one of the first to use systematically? We have biographical, psychobiographical, and literary studies of Michelet, but none I know of, including White's "metahistorical" analysis, that examines his heuristic practice.

Similar remarks are even more appropriate in the case of Ranke, whose great (no doubt exaggerated) claim to fame was based on his pioneering employment of archival materials, especially those of Venice. Ranke's notorious comment about describing history "as it really was" (*wie es eigentlich gewesen*) is hardly ever appreciated; for aside from being a tired old rhetorical topos from classical tradition (Lucian: "stating the facts," etc.), the phrase, understood in context, is not intended to be merely an epistemological principle, as the subsequent words make clear: "But whence the sources for such an investigation? The basis of the present work [*History of the Latin and Teutonic Nations*], the sources of its material, are memoirs, diaries, letters, diplomatic reports, and original narratives of eyewitnesses . . ." — another echo of Lucian (and Thucydides) and the Renaissance "arts of history." Ranke meant that such sources, intended for private information rather than public consumption, were of another order than the uncritically followed accounts of historians like Guicciardini and Sleidan, whom Ranke severely criticized. For him the way things really were was the way that men of power and influence judged them to be; and to this extent he was the prisoner of his sources as well as of language and religious and philosophical heritage. Once again, however, this reality was particular rather than (as for Ranke's nemesis, Hegel) general: *der liebe Gott wohnt in der Einzelheit* — God (if not the Devil) is in the details. At the very least we should be able to get this first-order reality straight — though of course Ranke's Lutheran background led him to a belief that he could discern larger patterns as well.

Burckhardt is a different story, but again heuristic questions occupy a central position. It was in more or less conscious reaction to Rankean history that Burckhardt turned to the fine arts and aesthetic lines of inquiry and to a different level of historical reality — *Kulturgeschichte*. No doubt Burckhardt's metahistorical achievement, like those of Michelet and Ranke, can be expressed in literary terms, but his implied philosophy of history was based more consciously and methodologically on his choice of sources, which was tied in turn to notions of what mattered in historical inquiry. As White notes, Burckhardt wanted to escape the resounding "isms" of the contemporary world, and this distaste as well as nostalgia led him away from the excretions of industrial society back to the relics of "the old culture of Europe" — and to larger questions of how to give historical meaning to these sources. The contrast between Ranke and Burckhardt has often been set in political and philosophical — and by White in literary — terms; but their heuristic attitudes also suggest a major difference. For Ranke every age might be equal in the sight of God (*unmittelbar zum Gott,* as the German states had been *unmittelbar zum Reich*), but for him, too, each of these ages was, in principle, describable; and they did all add up to a determinable universal history. About such questions Burckhardt was not only a pessimist and an elitist but also a relativist (which I find hard to reconcile with White's "realist" classification). "To each eye, perhaps," Burckhardt begins his most famous book, "the outlines of a given civilization present a different picture." It all depended on what one looked for, and what sources were chosen — and only secondarily, it seems to me, on the literary mode of expression. Paraphrasing Burckhardt, in fact, I might suggest that "to each eye" the outlines of a given historical narrative, too, present a different picture; it is just that the picture depends irreversibly on heuristics.

Dominick LaCapra has been hardly less influential than White in recent discussions of historical theory, which he has taken even further from conventional questions of historiography. In some ways he is still fighting the old battle against naive, objectivist, "scientific" history, though to be sure he has done so with new tools derived from continental (primarily French) philosophy as well as literary theory.[23] LaCapra's strategy has been to insist first on the dialogical character of historical inquiry and the legitimate place of "interpretations of the historian" in our dialogues with the dead and second on his — that is Heidegger's — distinction between "documentary" and "work-like" aspects of texts, the latter designating literalist readings in search of Mr. Gradgrind's and Prof. Ranke's (at least as seen through the eyes of Anglophone scholars) "facts" and the former suggesting a Heideggerian dimension of Art and its metahistorical origins. These arguments are quite consistent with a critical view of history after the surrender of ancient ideals of objectivity, "total history," and vulgar-Rankean *Wissenschaft*. From the standpoint of the historian's craft, however, LaCapra's formulations leave something to be desired — and in some ways seem to encourage us to leave the historians' hunt and to cast our lot with literary (and "cultural") critics, as LaCapra himself has largely done.

Following LaCapra (where I'm not sure LaCapra really went), Kellner seems to deny narrative status to "archives or monuments of the past" — though it is precisely in the archives where Natalie Davis found a rich lode of "fiction" and where there is already, in my experience, a "deep structure" of history writing.[24] To assume, as Kellner does, that narrative "is the product of complex cultural forms and deep-seated linguistic conventions that have traditionally been called narrative" should not imply that it is the exclusive preserve of literary artists or highly trained academics — this would be truly Vico's "conceit of the learned" and a most disabling principle for the understanding of "sources," and therefore history in any meaningful sense. The "return to literature" has reminded historians of the essential role of imagination in historical reconstruction and metahistorical meaning, but ultimately there can be no "imagined history" (though this is a useful oxymoron), at least not without footnotes and bibliography, any more than there can be a "reasoned history" or a "remembered history." There can be only narratives or arguments or less formal assemblages of information derived from the reading of sources — words, ultimately, about words. Yet while historical judgment may well draw on imagination, common sense, and experience — including not only unreflective life experience but what Gadamer has called the "experience of tradition" which historical training is supposed to provide — it is always constrained by the sources which are accessible and readable, even though they can not promise access to the bottom of reality. Nevertheless, it is this reliance on and deference to sources that preserves a connection between historiography and the old problem of historical knowing of that "foreign country" which is the past.

It seem curious that (philosophers of history aside) the theory of history in former times was engaged in, if not controlled, by practicing historians (most notably Droysen, Lamprecht, Meinecke, Burckhardt, Huizinga, Febvre, Bloch, Braudel, Duby, and Le Goff), whereas the current and past generation have so often skipped, or repudiated, this practical apprenticeship; and while this produces fresh views on historical understanding, it essentially evades the first step in grasping a remote past, which is engagement in the sources, traces, and relics of human behavior in an otherwise forgotten time. This criticism might be dismissed as conformity to an outmoded professional convention based on *Quellenforschung* and *Quellenkritik, documents pour servir à . . . ,* etc.; but this level of research introduces epistemological questions that do not survive the transmission to the printed pages of historiography. The radical textualization of history is reflected in Ankersmit's early book on "narrative logic," which remains on the surface of "representation," reifies the "historian's language," and eliminates research except as the "philosophy of research." "*This book is about historical sources,*" proclaimed Kellner in the introduction to a book subtitled provocatively "Getting the Story Crooked," but he uses the term in a literary sense associated with "origins" and "originality," and specifically not the generic "archives," which are part of the "documentary" material for which LaCapra wanted to substitute the literary "work" — and so the literary critic. In Kellner's book there is in fact no trace of the sort of heuristic problematic that I am referring to here, but only a report on the author's reading and, with the assistance of post-White rhetorical ideas, a search for unintended and unnoticed "meanings" in "secondary" sources. Like Ankersmit, Kellner has made the linguistic turn without ever looking back, and so begs the question of "reality," or at least its first accessible traces. Through hermeneutics and phenomenology Heidegger also made a linguistic turn, but he did not omit to turn back to "being," housed but not replaced by language.

It would be pleasant, perhaps, to think that the historical works of Michelet and Ranke could be read in the same way and in the same terms as the literary works of Balzac and Thomas Mann, and indeed both the former authors have been read along both lines of interpretation. However, Michelet's (and Ranke's even more impartial) writings were surely governed and inspired much more by the "experience of tradition" which they pursued obsessively, perhaps naively, and with contempt for "literary" sources. For twenty years Michelet spent much of his time in the national archives in the company of those he called

"Messieurs les morts," whose testimonies were essential in his project of "resurrection" and of "biographizing history." Mid-way through his *History of France* Michelet's political involvements and hubris lost him both his chair at the university and his access to the archives, which was another form of death: "Suspension," he wrote tersely, "Interment."[25] But his hubris did not desert him, and of course he kept on writing, from the sources whenever possible.

It is unfortunate that debates over heuristics should be polarized and pitched at such a low and invidious level—on the one hand the stone-kicking truth-tellers such as Elton, Himmelfarb, Handlin, and the Hunt-Jacobs-Appleby team, and on the other hand the condescending literary critics Ankersmit, LaCapra, and Kellner. This career-promoting debate has also opposed a stereotypical "old historicism" to a clubbish "new historicism" that covers a variety of literary practices and miscellaneous insights set in a rhetoric of innovation that denies, on ideological as well as epistemological grounds, the possibility of a single "unitary story" and turns instead to a new sort of anecdotalism.[26] This "counterhistory," as Catherine Gallagher and Stephen Greenblatt call it, justifies "practice" without theory, "representation" without a heuristic base, and incoherence in the name of rich diversity and expanding historical curiosity as "a social rebellion in the study of culture"; drawing on philosophical and anthropological as well as literary, historical, and art-historical arguments and admitting debts in particular to E. P. Thompson, Raymond Williams, and Clifford Geertz, not to forget Michel Foucault, it is essentially a fishing license for microhistorical interpretive experiments. The Big Stories are, in effect, the fictions of the winners, while new historicist anecdotes, like the old "new social history," try to catch "the real bodies and living voices" (Ranke updated and democratized) of the lost, the forgotten, the oppressed, the feminine, the gay, the people of color, and other sorts of alterity, aspects of a cultural proletariat obliterated in the narrative of mainstream history. History is seen not only from the bottom up but also from the outside in, though usually through an intervening interpretive or anecdotalist grid.

At the end of the last millennium the philosophy of history also took a "linguistic turn" in the direction of literary theory and in association with topics often relegated to the chaotic rubric of the "postmodern." A recent collection advertised as a "new philosophy of history," assembling six literary scholars, four historians (intellectual historians, that is, who have never, perhaps, descended into the dark confusion of an archive), and one lone philosopher, considers a number of themes strange to the old tradition of philosophy of history, especially "representation," "irony," and what Robert Berkhofer calls "the great story."[27]

The first of these topics, the notion of representation, has been inherent in the literary tradition of the "art of history" from ancient times. Scholars coming late to the theory of history seem continually to be rediscovering the obvious, such as the view that there is no observation without an observer, no story without a story-teller, no view without a viewpoint, and so no history without a historian. "Constructivism" is the current term which collects these notions and raises them to a theoretical level which privileges Representation above Reality and which, for literary scholars, gives literature and imagination creative as well as critical roles in historical study. This had also been the implication of what Ann Rigney calls "the Romantic project," that is, the "nouvelle histoire" of Thierry and Michelet; and the result has been to undermine the congruence between narrative and the world it describes and so reinforce the shift from political history, which relies on chronology and unreflective recording of events, to cultural history, which takes an imaginative, synthetic, and literary, or painterly, attitude toward historical evidence.[28] Rhetoric — where the linguistic and textualist turns intersect — is in many ways the key to the NPH; and here Kellner invokes not only Vico, Nietzsche, and White but also the ancient Sophists, whom he calls "the first cultural relativists, the first *historicists* in their way." This rhetoric rejects not only high-minded Platonism but also the vulgar realism of Rankean history, and seizes instead on the field of discourse and interpretation rather than on abstract argument, "further research," and the quest for final meaning. In classical tradition history was virtually identified with rhetoric, which there preserved its ties with truth and yet could never accommodate the notion of absolute truth in the sense of a single necessary story about the past. Long ago, Vann recalls, J. H. Hexter recast Ranke's notorious formula, *wie es eigentlich gewesen,* into "the most likely story that can be sustained by the relevant extrinsic evidence." The NPH extends this cautious statement by questioning notions not only of relevance but also of extrinsic evidence, and it goes on to suggest that these elements, too, are within the domain of the creative historical imagination.

Irony, which is also a Romantic concept (with classical antecedents), is a trope which is awakened, or reawakened, when Hegel's owl begins its ascent. Irony brings self-consciousness and a distancing between present and past — between self and the other — especially in the act of writing; and as such it is almost a form of historical consciousness, though without the temporal assumptions of time lost and found. For several of these authors the major manifestation of irony is the restoration of the subject, the " 'I' foregrounded," in the words of Carrard, discussing the ego- (or nous-) centered rhetoric of the *Annales* school.[29] Under *Annaliste* influence (itself influenced by Michelet's ways of writing) the "I" of historians no longer has to hide behind the passive voice to display a spurious objectivity but can enter into the process of historical inquiry and interpretation. This is equivalent to the practice of historians like Herodotus or Livy, who not only spoke of events happening but also of his belief in and judgment about their happening. No longer, in other words, does meaning arise out of an authoritative but colorless and emotionless record; rather it is represented to us by an authorial voice, much in the way, perhaps, that Trollope and Tolstoy tell the readers the meaning of their creations, or that the puppeteer Thackeray steps out from behind his curtain to show the audience the apparatus of his little show. If this is irony, it may be a bit heavy, but at least it is not duplicitous in the way that narratives told in a passive voice, *sub specie aeternitatis* — or *unmittelbar zum Gott*, in Ranke's words — may be.

Robert Berkhofer, in his recent book as well as in his essay for *A New Philosophy of History*, discusses these questions in the literary terms of "voice" and "viewpoint." Who can speak from the standpoint of, on behalf of, or in the name of a race, class, or gender — not to mention of History itself? History has been dominated by "hegemonic viewpoints," Berkhofer remarks (not to speak of deafening voices), and it is one of the aims of the NPH (as well as, once again, the "new history" of the Romantic period) to make visible the hidden viewpoints, the suppressed voices, of actors and victims outside of the "Great Story" which generations of historians have sought, at least until the "end" of such history, as announced by Francis Fukuyama. The solution to the relativism implied by such criticism lies somehow, Berkhofer thinks, in representing polyvocality — that is, dialogism and multiple viewpoints (a *Rashomon* or Joycean model of historical narrative?) to satisfy the postmodern pressures of multiculturalism and the rising voices clamoring to be heard about the official lines of linear history.

Like Berkhofer, Allan Megill also opposes grand narratives as represented on the surface of *l'histoire événémentielle*.[30] Megill pursues Lyotard's postmodernist argument and indeed follows it to the end, denying even the possibility of a unified and universalist narrative along the simple lines of conservative, liberal, radical, or any other ideological standpoint: it is impossible and even undesirable, Megill believes, "to homogenize or to synthesize the diversity," the Derridean *différance*, which the late twentieth century has revealed to us. On the basis of this critique of the modernist project, Megill sets down some rather universal-sounding rules about how to avoid the fallacies of History as Single Story: viz., reject any notion of a single authorized method or subject matter, operate in interdisciplinary terms, acknowledge the fictional aspects of historical writing, and finally, and paradoxically (paraphrasing Fredric Jameson's — now superseded or perhaps discredited — "always historicize!"), "Always theorize!" But — perennial question — how to turn this theory into historiographical practice? How about (short of Marx's eleventh thesis on Feuerbach), "Always inquire!"? For some story, from some stand-point, is always just beginning.

Ventures in Time and Space

Habits and continuities aside, the study of history has become some-thing rather different from the small and comfortable field it appeared to be at mid-century, and this especially because of demographic and generational change, although these are of course tied to larger cultural, social, and political currents of the aftermath of what has been called the "Thirty-One Years War." The Chicago-, Americo- and Eurocentric horizons (and whatever lay beyond) which I hoped to cross a half-century ago have receded faster than my or any person's knowledge could hope to match or even to appreciate except in long imaginative retrospect. Looking around is more difficult than looking back, but it seems fitting to end this inquiry with a brief circumspect of the current state of the field — viewed as before Eurocentrically and via the major Western languages and categories within which "history" has been defined.

A primary task of historical scholarship has always been making soundings in the deep past — that "archeology" about which Thucydides, in contrast to Herodotus, was so skeptical. My own first introduction to earliest history in grade school still began with the land between the Tigris and Euphrates, though supposedly detached from the old Bible story which still held the faith of the fundamentalist part of my family and indeed which I learned mnemonically in Bible school (though Herder had transcended this parochialism a century and a half before). By the end of the past century, despite flat-earth and creationist resistance, the picture had been changed radically through archeological and paleontological finds, techniques of DNA research added to radio-carbon dat-ing (replacing the old dendrochronology), and a growing consensus locating human origins in Africa — exacerbated by the controversies surrounding the provocative publications of Martin Bernal and his critics.[31]

The chief consequence of this has been a new (neo-Herderian) form of conjectural history that plays down the "miracle of Greece" and, by the exam-ination of material remains, seeks to trace the wanderings of humanity from southern Africa to Asia and Austrolasia, Europe, and America over tens of thousands of years through a debatable mixture of peaceful settlement and military conquest. A secondary result is a vast expansion of global history, with large-scale mappings and small-gauge soundings in cross-cultural con-tacts, gender, race, technology, ecology, questions of frontiers, and often ten-dentious colonial and post-colonial studies, which as so often before look to other disciplines for assistance in historical understanding. That there is still no "grand narrative" is due less to the insights of "postmodernism" than to expanding horizons and the fragmentation of interdisciplinary research and competing theories.

Since Cicero and before, history has been associated and even identified with memory, but it has been identified with imagination, too; and the introduction of ego-psychology and "psychologism" into historical inquiry invites confusion. This is one of the legacies of the pioneering work of Halbwachs on collective memory, in the wake of Durkheim's brand of sociological reasoning. This effort has been given a more specific material base in the movement headed by Pierre Nora on "places of memory," which has spread from French to other national traditions. Attempts to read back from written sources to oral culture continue with increasing boldness and ingenuity, as, for arbitrary examples, Jan Assmann's tracing of the traces of Egyptian civilization in the West, Gordon Shrimpton's work on ancient historiography as a form of public and transmitted commemoration (and judgments of "truth"), Janet Coleman's philosophical examination of ancient and medieval memory, M. T. Clanchy's journey "from memory to written record," Patrick Geary's study of medieval names and other signs of remembrance reflected in records and histories, Mary Carruthers's work on the medieval arts of memory and reading habits, Rosamond McKitterick's explorations into medieval literacy and written communication, and Elisabeth van Houts's emphasis on the cultural context of medieval historiography.[32] Memory studies have also made their way into recent political, diplomatic, and military history, not to mention the Holocaust, revisionist views of Nazism and Communism, and the changing idea of Europe.[33] Yet collective memory, which is at most an analogue of individual psychology (and depth psychology), remains a form of conjectural history, more valuable for synthesis than for analysis.

The old specialties, including political, institutional, ecclesiastical, and social history, continue in the channels dug centuries before, though the landscape changes from time to time, while cultural history spreads out in all directions to accommodate modern (and postmodern) life. One trend in historical inquiry, though available to thinking scholars for two centuries and more, seems to have become a premise of historical writing, and this is (to adopt a contemporary formula) the replacement of reality by "representation" and the admission of the historian into the field of action and creation. "Something happened," (in the phrase of Panofsky), but it does not exist in a human sense until it has been recorded and interpreted, if not explained.[34] Hence the "objectivity question," long dismissed as irrelevant or badly framed by European scholars, still has enough presence in American academic circles to warrant a recent historical survey and critique and to be taken seriously by some leaders of the historical profession.[35] Like physicists, economists have long understood that the act of observing and formulating (and communicating) disturbs the field being observed, so that the observer is a — nonobjective — part of the process. Historians may not have moved this far, but they have, many of them, shifted their attention from the bare and perhaps inaccessible facts of political action to the second removes of an essentialized political expression and "political culture." And from here it is but a short step from text to context, from cultural creation to cultural construction, which can supply conditions and even explanations for, say, works of art and scientific discovery as well as political action. It is true that scholars have often tried to keep a foot on social ground by focusing on "practices" (ghost of Marxian "praxis") — "historians do not make literature" — but the screen of interpretation and critical judgment remains in place.[36]

Yet this shift of dimension is largely a matter of rhetoric and subject matter, and research continues to focus on social phenomena — that is, representations of social phenomena — from nationality to public spectacles to everyday life. The distance between world and local — macro- and microhistory — is greater than ever, with few ways way I see of closing the gap; and the gain in geographic and cultural range has in many ways been offset by a shrinking of perspective, so that neither world historians nor cultural historians can manage a deep perspective on their own resources and practices. As for historiography, the tendency has been to focus on contemporary fashions and opinions by a few sanctioned critics and theoreticians, with other historical craftsmen and women being resigned at best to bibliography, which these days means the dustbin of historiography.

In intellectual history there has been a pronounced shift from doctrines and schools to reception, interpretation (and translation), and transmission, from authors to readers, and so recourse to the modern fields of rhetoric and hermeneutics.[37] Along with this awareness of the gap between the message conceived and sent and the message received has come renewed interest in the question of truth and its various guises — or rather, "what passes for truth" in particular contexts.[38] Another way of avoiding claims of objectivity or direct access to a particular phenomenon is to designate the inquiry as the "culture of (whatever)," and examples of this practice are beyond counting (or at least they keep piling up on the Web every day). "Culture is one of the two or three most complicated words in the English language," Raymond Williams once wrote, and of course this is true of other languages as well. Indeed "culture" is a semantic monstrosity — by turns laudatory and offensive, idealistic and materialistic, high and low, microscopic and global, exclusive and expansive; and in the past century "culture" has become so amorphous that it defies definition, except as an often superfluous — though for many unavoidable — way of indicating random and undetermined human context and connections with other phenomena. One of the side benefits has been to vouchsafe "culture" to otherwise deprived or persecuted minorities such as workers, slaves, or the victims of Soviet rule and moreover to make it, as Williams did, a species of modern revolution.[39]

Under the continuing impulse of anthropology (following the leads of Vico, Heyne, Herder, and critics of Kantian rationalism) historians probe the cultural patterns underlying the civilizations reflected in philosophical, literary, and artistic sources and carried over as educational models, with an emphasis on difference and "alterity" — the Other, whether remote in space or in time, philosophically anticipated by Hegel's *Andersein*.[40] The interest in the alien, or barbarian, is as old as the Western art of history itself, as evident in Herodotus's views on the Scythians. For François Hartog the Scythian logos of Herodotus could not reveal the "real" tribes reflected in external archeological evidence but only the "imaginary nomads" that satisfied the cultural needs of Athenians, and he has pursued this question in earlier poetic contexts.[41] Modern representations of alterity, as in early American explorations, have likewise been seen as projections of a settled cultural "us" trying to make ethnographic sense of an alien "them." The search for cultural Others is a popular pastime of early modernists, though again the primacy of representation over direct encounter is apparent in the recognition of a conventional rhetoric of alterity designed to celebrate the marvelous and madcap and the unprecedented. Lorraine Daston and Katherine Park have provided a survey of the "wonders" of nature — marvels, miracles, monsters, prodigies, curiosities, relics, errors, and jokes of nature — which challenge "normal science" but also expand the horizons of the imaginative and terrifying aspects of knowledge.[42]

If history must rely on conjecture and imagination to plumb the past, so it must also to conceptualize the spaces of human activity, which, more than time, offer an invitation to apply to the other, more static human sciences for assistance.[43] One controversial area of historical space is the "public sphere," which, in the wake of Jürgen Habermas's brilliant *Habilitationsschrift* of 1962, has been extensively discussed not only by social and political theorists but also by historians, especially *dix-huitiémistes*.[44] That Habermas's classic analysis is a now rather dated product of the Frankfurt School, a revisionist form of Marxism, and designed as part of a dated offshoot of the "transition from feudalism to capitalism" has not been ignored by dissenting critics and admiring scholars. For Habermas "public opinion" (*öffentliche Meinung, opinion publique*) is a creation of the new "public sphere" accompanying the "new social order" of capitalism, in which "news" became a commodity and "publicity" a force not only for Enlightenment but also for revolutionary ideology and political action. It is a commonplace of Hegelian and Marxist theory that "civil society" was a by-product of a market economy; but while this is reasonable for an early modern context, it is a rather crude and myopic identification in the long perspective of political discourse and action, especially of what has been called "civic" — and "civil" — humanism.[45] "Civic humanism" is Hans Baron's English rendering of *Bürgerhumanismus,* a term which might originally have been translated as "bourgeois humanism," except that Baron wanted to emphasize the republican and long-term classical aspects of this concept.[46]

In his analysis Habermas recognizes a wide range of social vehicles of public opinion in civil society, including societies, salons, coffee houses, art exhibits, theater, and especially journalism; and he acknowledges the early appearance of some of these phenomena.[47] Yet for him they are always tied to the phenomenon of "emergent" capitalism, and his focus remains on the pre-revolutionary period, when public opinion seemed to rise to a political level. In fact, however, though the phrase "public opinion" first appeared in the eighteenth century, the phenomenon, *ante litteram,* has a much deeper background, going back indeed to antiquity in the form of "public" opposed to "private" law and recurrent throughout European history. Most fundamentally, public vs. private law (*ius publicum* and *ius privatum*), the republic vs. private property (*res publica* and *res privata*), sovereignty and paternal power are polarities embedded in the tradition of Roman civil law and its modern offspring.

Habermas's foreshortened and politicized view neglects the fact that the historical origins of "public opinion" and the "public sphere" are premodern (and indeed premedieval) and a function of elite culture, as illustrated by Erich Auerbach's study of literary language and its public (*Publikum*) in late antiquity and the middle ages, which for him was a precondition of "a common social and cultural life on our planet."[48] Rosamond McKitterick shows the underestimated extent of literacy and written culture in Carolingian times, emphasizing its role in "cross-cultural interchange," although without drawing conclusions on the theoretical level of Habermas's work.[49] Other medieval signs of a public sphere, in the making, have recently been surveyed by Sophia Menache, who writes of an "opinion making process," the role of rumor, sermons, scribal and oral vehicles of what amounted to "news," the significance of journeys and pilgrimages, ecclesiastical, imperial, and royal channels of intelligence and propaganda, and (even more striking) the transmission of heresies in the later medieval period.[50] Central to the formation of modern public opinion are the communication networks produced by both church and state, including the competing legal systems based on the sources and procedures of Roman law, civil and canon, and the polemical literature of the "publicists" (*Publizistik*) produced by the Investiture struggle and the conflict between Boniface VIII and Philip IV.[51] Essential, too, was the legal profession, an international community of professionals constituting a "republic of the jurists" (*respublica jurisconsultorum*) and contributing to what Menache calls a "culture of officials."[52] It should also be recalled that lawyers, who contributed so extensively to the humanist movement in Italy and to secular learning throughout Europe, also formed a significant part of the Republic of Letters, which was reinforced as well by the late medieval university and the humanist movement.[53]

Another factor of importance for the emergence of public opinion and a public sphere was the ancient and especially Ciceronian tradition of forensic rhetoric, which—in particular contrast to philosophy—emphasized and celebrated the virtues of "civil science" and the persuasive force of public oratory.[54] This represents the rhetorical dimension of "civic humanism," born in the boisterous politics of the Italian city states but extending also to other parts of the European public sphere. According to Melanchthon, "It is by eloquence [*oratio*] that [rights, religions, legitimate marriages, and the other bonds of human society] are maintained in commonwealths."[55] But if rhetoric contributed to social solidarity and public forms of virtue, it could also, when divorced from truth, produce public disorder and revolution. "Rhetoric is a tool invented to manipulate a mob and disorderly commoners . . in sick states . . as in Athens, Rhodes, and Rome . . . , where things were in their worst state and when the storms of civil wars agitated them."[56] This was the dark side of the public sphere, which has also attracted modern historians.

What put the Republic of Letters on the map, beyond scholarly correspondence and academic *itinera,* was the extraordinary increase of printed books and periodicals in the sixteenth and seventeenth centuries. To understand the historical foundations of the public sphere it is useful to recall the over-argued but still often underappreciated thesis of Elizabeth Eisenstein on the printing press as an agent of change.[57] In the sixteenth century printing had become a commercial network as well as the art of an intellectual elite. The typographical art was a source at once of enlightenment and of subversion, of humanist learning and of popular protest; and it was at once promoted and repressed by learning and of popular protest; and it was at once promoted and repressed by the state. Ever since the humanists of the Renaissance, reinforced by the vision of Bacon, the coming of the printed book has fascinated historians, and this phenomenon has been magnified by the work of Lucien Febvre, Henri Jean Martin, and Elizabeth Eisenstein, followed by a new generation of historical bibliophiles, including Roger Chartier, Robert Darnton, Carlo Ginzburg, Anthony Grafton, Ann Blair, Jacob Soll, and Adrien Johns. Born in bibliography and library science, the history of the book passes into intellectual and cultural history to become a discipline in its own right, concerned with literacy, reading practices, authorship, publication, and reception. The warning of Chartier, writing in the shadow of Foucault, is that the study of texts should not be confused with the study of the thoughts and actions underlying these texts, but it is also the result of the historical experience and culture on which the book in its many printed and cyber forms touches. Yet it remains true that the history of the book and its spin-offs in journals remain tied to major, headline events, including the Reformation, the New Science, the French Revolution, and disputes of a doctrinal or public character — though not, of course, as specifically "causal" factors as suggested by the arguments of Eisenstein.[58]

The printed book is only one aspect of the larger field which has come to be called the media, of which the most conspicuous part is journalism, popular as well as learned, which is almost as old as the printed book and which has also produced a new discipline, or sub-discipline, that of journalism history, which arguably may be traced back into medieval times.[59] Years ago I examined a later phase of journalism in the context of the propaganda of the French civil wars, and more recently there has been extensive exploration of the journalism of the eighteenth century, especially by Robert Darnton, Jeremy Popkin, Jack Censer, and Nina Gelbart.[60] The same can be said for the study of learned journalism, a neglected area recently exploited by François Waquet as a cornerstone of the Republic of Letters and political culture.[61] Originating as political intelligence, popular entertainment, and "news," journalism became not only an easy source of information for historians but also a crucial dimension of cultural history, especially as a defining factor in the emergence of public opinion, in the formation of social identities, class conflict, political manipulation, and war-mongering, and in the process of nation-building and nation-inventing. From the beginning the invention of print seemed an ambivalent gift — alternately miracle and curse — and it may be that the overflowing of news in the seventeenth century contributed not only to piecemeal knowledge but to suspicion and skepticism.[62] In various ways the two faces of journalism, positive and negative, have persisted down to the present.

The history of the book is an expanding field at the start of this millennium, despite the dire predictions and extrapolations by experts in library science about its disappearance in the excesses of electronic technology. As the book was celebrated in the first age of information explosion, so it is, in a different key, in a time of "information overload," which marks both the long-term result of the typographical revolution and the predicament of modern communication.[63] While refraining from prophecy, Marshall McLuhan over a generation ago invoked the spectacle of a "new electric age."[64] This age is now upon us and offers, according to one commentator, two nightmares, one in which everything is lost and the second in which everything is saved — everything, that is, except for the wisdom that historical perspective brings. As typography produced a sense of history in the West (a common hyperbole among historians of the book and media), so the new information technology may create an environment in which history becomes impossible, irrelevant, or unusable, as it disappears in the universal solvent of computer language.

The other side of public space is the private sphere, the domestic world, and the site of the self and the subject, where social patterns are formed by family relations, home life, age, intimacy, sexuality, child-rearing, sickness, death, and mourning. In traditional history this was the realm of women, and so of women's history, although with the ubiquity of gender in recent cultural studies this invidious view has been changed. In any case the upshot has been to reinforce the orientation of history both as life and as inquiry — as field of experience and as field of interpretation and representation. From the time of Herder and later of Ranke historians have opposed the idealist conventions of philosophers, and in the twentieth century this problem appears in the opposition to the spiritualist stance of phenomenology as apparent in Husserl's intentionality and Heidegger's Dasein, especially in Merleau-Ponty's shift of attention from the mind (the soul) to the body as the locus and incarnation of perception, experience, subjectivism, "being-in-the-world," and "life philosophy."[65] Historians have as usual come late to flesh out this epistemological turn and place it in cultural context.

The End of History

History is always open to questions, but some historians, especially those seduced by theory, prefer closure. If the end of philosophy is ideology and the end of ideology (in the absence of Revolution) is passivity, what is the "end of history"? To say "liberal democracy" is to restore ideology, if not philosophy, but in fact myopia infects all these judgments from the standpoint of this book, since several questions remain. The idea of an end to history belongs to the philosophy or theology of history and not to historical inquiry. It is part of the medieval religious tradition of millenarian and apocalyptic prophecy conscripted into the service of social activism, especially in the wake of the Reformation.[66] Yet we still think anthropomorphically in terms of ages and stages, genesis and corruption, life and death, and we may well wonder where we stand in the evolutionary trajectory which historians have seen, imagined, or argued.

Historians have long been fascinated by periodization, especially by the ancient-medieval-modern convention,[67] and efforts to escape this secular trinity have only added to it — referring here to the new claim to an identity beyond history, namely, the postmodern. The term was first associated with Spenglerian pessimism, as in the work of Rudolf Pannwitz on "the crisis of European culture" of 1917 linking Nietzsche and his *Übermensch* with nihilism, decadence, and what Pannwitz called "postmodern humanity" (*postmodernen Menschen*).[68] Since then the word has spread through artistic, architectural, artistic, and literary discourse, becoming in the past generation an inescapable part of current philosophical and historical jargon. As a German critic has remarked, "The word 'postmodern' belongs to a network of 'postist' concepts and ways of thinking" — and so a new species of "-isms" for the young to throw in the face of the old, or the left to throw in the face of the right.[69] Can we speak of a "postmodern" turn, in the phrase of Steven Seidman, and is it in any sense a human turn? Postmodernism is supposed to be above, or beyond, the process of history (despite the temporal implication of the "post" affix). Chronology becomes irrelevant: in the words of Lyotard — who defined the "postmodern condition" but did not locate it in time — "the essay (Montaigne) is postmodern, and the fragment (the *Athenaeum* [of the Schlegels]) is modern."[70] Postmodernism is a beginning, as it were, that is defined as an ending; a historical category that affects to deny history. It is a sort of life of the mind after the death of the subject and the demise of the comforting metanarratives which used to give meaning — a single and stable meaning — to human life.

Many authors employed the term between the time of Pannwitz and Toynbee, who used it (with a question mark) to label the period following the modern age, beginning in 1875, which Toynbee thought opened a new chapter in the history of our civilization. His argument, formulated in 1934, was that industrialism and nationalism operated to build up the great powers before 1875 and then turned against them afterwards; but the term "postmodern" did not appear until the abridged version of his *Study of History* in 1946; and now usages of the term have increased logarithmically. "What are we calling postmodernity?" Foucault asked; "I'm not up-to-date."[71] For this question there is no "we," and my own is surely a minority opinion. In my view postmodernism is a product of the excesses of modernism, and it is hard to draw a line (or find a turning point) between the two, especially as the former resists the sort of historicizing definitions suggested by the first part of the term itself. Like St. Paul, postmodernism is all things to all men (and women), and so the ex-Marxist Seidman, on the basis of a personal turning point, associates it with gay liberation — and while it may be a useful and even inescapable term to suggest the predicament of the world in the early years of this millennium, it defines a turning point in only a most subjective or generic sense, or rather multiple turning points for a post-Marxist, post-Darwinian, post-Nietzschean, post-Freudian, post-historical, and even post-human age.[72]

To historians postmodernism is a process of unbuilding, of undermining foundations, and denial of metanarratives; but in this connection it seems less a new point of departure than a radical extension of such modernist and anti-foundationalist lines of thought as Heidegger's destruction of metaphysics, Niels Bohr's principle of complementarity, Werner Heisenberg's indeterminism, Hans Vaihinger's philosophy of "as if," Kurt Gödel's critique of metalogic, and new fashions in what has been called the "new scientific revolution" of chaos and complexity.[73] In this general perspective postmodernism may indeed be seen as a continuation of the negative aspect of the "Enlightenment project" — and what a modern philosopher calls the "modern project to rigor" from Descartes to Nietzsche — that is, skepticism, criticism, and metacriticism, which each generation takes up afresh.[74] Reason completed, the turn is to imagination, or history; memory and emotions exhausted, it is to science; positivism ineffective, to the human sciences; modernism spent, to postmodernism — and so what comes next? Where can we turn? Each generation has its turning, or returning, and its turning away, or turning against, or overturning, and who knows where and when the next turning point will appear, or who will take credit for it? We have come to the end, and now to the beginning, of a millennium, and maybe this is a turning point too, but from what and to what we are not yet in a position to say, though we continue to ask.

What seems clear is that this generation has seen an end to the ideologies generated and then discredited by the world war(s) of the first half of the past century. Communism and Fascism both had deep roots and were dominated by pathological personalities who imposed a personal agenda on a social and political program; and historians, even those not drawn to contemporary historiography, had to maneuver between these extremes, leaving behind a vast amount of contaminated literature fit only to become itself materials for diagnostic examination.[75] As medieval scholarship in Germany was infected with the excesses of anachronistic nationalism and racism, so French revolutionary historiography underwent a leftist revision in the light of the Russian Revolution, and of course twentieth-century history (*histoire contemporaine, Zeitgeschichte*) was caught in the maelstroms of ideology and postwar revisionisms that stirred professionals outside as well as inside state service. What survives, of course, are the nationalisms which color and distort the globalisms of the period after the disintegration of the Soviet empire, the formation of the European Union, and the rise of what much of the world sees as a new American imperialism. Daniel Bell's impression of an "end of ideology" seems even more appropriate than during the Cold War.

History is always past (as indeed is its writing), but does it have an end? In the imaginary realm of the postmodern the answer is perhaps yes (but with the further question, for whom?), and indeed more than one ending; for while the imagined master narrative not only does not end (the implication of Lyotard's argument) but does not exist, the fragmentary mini-narratives constructed in particular contexts and from particular points of view must all end and be supplanted — and supplanted, indeed, by another turn of "history." So if post-modern and post-human, then, why not "post-history," a term and concept which has indeed appeared, or reappeared, at our millennium's end?[76] This might seem to mark an end to turning points, but there is a history to "post-history," too. During the Nazi period Arnold Gehlen claimed to have taken the term "posthistoire" from Antoine Cournot, who (though the word does not appear in his work) in the 1860s assessed the late modern period transformed by science and secular reason. Gehlen associated "posthistory" with extreme secularization and the falling away from German idealism, a trend which he hoped to reverse, and indeed later in the century this neologism (like "post-modern" in its earlier usages) has been often been associated with decay and decline.[77] More recently it has acquired a more positive and indeed progressive appearance, though even so at millennium's end "posthistory" seems little more than a topos fashioned to evoke the special quality of the present age and perhaps the irrelevance of old historical perspectives and the old historicism. After 1989 Francis Fukuyama pontificated on "the end of history," and then commented ironically on "the end of history five years later," although he was only repeating a commonplace from Hegel, who saw his age as "the last stage of history, of our world, of our time."[78] But as T. S. Eliot put it, "In our end is our beginning."

But who is the "we" underlying "our" end and beginning? Have "we" encompassed the "other" sharing "our" globe? The first volume of this work began with the conceit of the two faces of the two foundational master historians, Herodotus and Thucydides, and approaching the end we may return to this symbolic distinction, this time to represent the difference between early and contemporary history — and also between global and local (national or ethnic) history. In his bibliographical appendix to his *Method of History* on the descending order of reading histories Jean Bodin had distinguished between universal historians and "universal geographistorians" and historians of particular religions (or superstitions) and nations, eastern as well as western, followed by biographies; and it seems to me that these categories, received into historical pedagogy in the eighteenth century, are still in place, as is the logical descent from the general to the individual. Formerly, "universal history" (*historia katholike,* a coinage of Polybius) was conceived as the sum of national or special histories, or more recently civilizations, and beyond the miscellany humanity has been conceived within different formal or informal organizational arrangements from empire (Rome and its emulators) to oecumene to modern "world systems"; but in an age of globalism, "meta-geography," and ecological history scholars try to give it a more distinctive shape, as usual with the help of other disciplines and methods and with attention to such international phenomena as migration, trade, disease, and cultural exchange.

Historical space has expanded enormously with the opening of extraterrestrial frontiers, and the same may be said about time, with the rise and retrospective development of prehistory; but here the "last frontier" remains the future, and here the Thucydidean rejection of "archeology" and focus on contemporary or near-contemporary events come into play — although writing "in the shadow of tomorrow," in Huizinga's phrase, brings the historian to confront the future, and "futurology" has not yet been received into the auxiliary sciences of history. Current history is defined in terms not only of time but also of utility, "interest," and practical relevance (in the tradition of the "pragmatic history" of Polybius), since earlier stages of human experience offer at best a reflective sort of wisdom or consolation, if not pessimism and despair. For scientific discovery there may be a "role for history," as Thomas Kuhn argued, but for political and social policy history seems less immediately relevant. But how can one interpret contemporary history in a general way except by projections from the past or artificial recourse to other disciplines and to theory? One way is to descend to the small horizons of the memoir or the autobiography and extend historical vision speculatively toward a vision of the world, as did Winston Churchill (who, as someone remarked, wrote his autobiography and called it *The World Crisis*), but this is a perspective denied to most humans, except in fiction, to which indeed many historians have been drawn as a superior way to invoke past experience.

As geographic horizons have expanded, so has the desirability of a synthetic world history above the level of conjectural biological evolution and demographic abstraction. Globalism rests on connections and encounters but not on any sort of unity which can inform the narratives of historians, although it does locate a field in which other human sciences can operate, and it suggest generalizations that cut across conventional political and economic categories. Global history may be an "intelligible field of study," in Toynbee's phrase, but only through the partial views afforded by particular disciplines and, perhaps, area studies, with comparative methods being attached not to history itself but to these disciplines (which is why I object to the misleading term "comparative history"). Otherwise history on a global scale must be conjectural or philosophical in essentially outmoded forms which have at best pedagogical value. It is not relativism, skepticism, or postmodernism but admission of intellectual humility in the face of a shifting pandemonium of states, economies, societies, and cultures that turns historians to the rejection of a single "grand narrative" and toward the notion of an endless number of stories that can be told about the human past from different points of view and cultural contexts.

To ask about the future is to ask the postmodern question about what comes after the end? Something strange no doubt, because not only the past but also the future is a "foreign country," and even more so, despite efforts of projection, prediction, and extrapolation from the familiar. I tend to follow the old historiographical convention that without traces of some sort, there is no history, but prehistory belies this in some ways, and so my answer to this question, what next? can only be, "more history"; and judging from what I have called "my times," which are almost past, it will be foreign indeed. Yet this foreignness will also be placed in perspective, set in linguistic contexts, domesticated philosophically, absorbed in historical narratives, and dissolved in that powerful reagent which people call historicism — and then, in large part, forgotten in the oblivion that grows along with the information overload which floods in now at a logarithmic pace, creating out of fragmentation the new sciences of chaos and complexity and multiplying the faces of history on our receding cultural horizons, with history still seen (according to the ancient topos) as in a mirror, but a rear-view mirror from a fast-moving vehicle.

What Europe experienced after that *annus mirabilis* 1989 after the collapse of Communism was a sort of re-Balkanization, with the revival of national movements and historiographies in Poland, Czechoslovakia (two traditions), Hungary, Romania, and Yugoslavia, with the latter itself fragmented after the death of Tito in 1980.[79] The false universalism created by the sovietization of historical writing was replaced by free inquiry into national traditions, with Western-style research and criticism encouraged by international contacts and conferences and the revival of old debates around national myths, for example, the notion of Romania's connections with the ancient Dacians of the Roman Empire, which turned on critical philology and archeology. But historiographically it was not business as usual, for scholars had also to confront recent traumatic experiences created by Fascism, Soviet Communism, the Holocaust, and other xenophobic phenomena of the past century, all of which generated further movements of "revision."

Globalism at the start of the third millennium has many implications that affect the practice and theory of history, beginning with the anachronism of the national state and the idea of international order which encompassed it in a borderless world in which environment and ethnic conflicts no longer figure as mere background.[80] Yet ethnic conflicts are themselves complicated by explosive population increase, especially in urban areas, by migrations ("pushed" or "pulled"), by economic interests and political manipulation; and old Western ideals of liberal democracy and the rule of law become even more remote in contemporary context. The world is shrinking as well as expanding, making not only travel and information exchange but also cultural imperialism and terror part of everyday life. These and other factors have brought to us—and "others"—by the all-encompassing media mark a kind of cultural homogenization but also an end to the possibility of grand narratives and a unified historical understanding.

So the problem of knowledge has taken a different form in this new millennium—the problem of knowledge in the sense not of epistemology (whose modern history was traced a century ago by Ernst Cassirer) but rather of the question of the organization and control of knowledge: how to preserve, arrange, retrieve, communicate, transmit, and interpret the accumulation of data overwhelming human memory since records have been kept. Of course I pursue this problem in the context of the "Gutenberg galaxy" (as Marshall McLuhan called it forty years ago); but more urgent these days is another revolution now in the making, which is that of electronic texts, in which, to the amusement of some of us, medieval practices of scrolling and hypertexts are restored. "Where," T. S. Eliot asked, "is the wisdom we have lost in knowledge?" Or to rephrase the question, how can we distill wisdom out of the vast and increasing superfluity of knowledge that descends on us? The fetishism of the book is embedded deep in Western tradition: "Blessed is he that readeth" is the first message of the Revelation of St. John, and many an honest librarian and author in search of an audience must echo this prayer. Yet as Solomon said, "Of making many books there is no end," and the proverb was repeated in the age of print by Sancho Panza, thinking of his poor deranged master, for whom books had replaced reality. Whence the primacy of interpretation, and as Montaigne wrote, "There is more ado to interpret interpretations than to interpret things, and more books upon books than upon any other subject; we do nothing but intergloss one another." If this is true of the canons of philosophy and literature, how much more is it for historians who keep repeating and revising one another?

As usual our epistemological predicament provokes further questions. Must we give our memories over to the false precision, vagaries, and serendipity of technological management? Must we, in an age of post-linguistic turning, frame our questions in—and bind our answers to—the language of computers? What will happen to narrative? Will it be taken over by fictional forms, which indeed, under journalistic impulse, are already overlapping with historical writing? Will undersimplification replace oversimplification as the major fallacy of historians? And how many readers will be around to care? It may be that print culture, which created the modern sense of history, is now, through its excesses and electronic extensions, producing a postmodern reaction to history in an old-fashioned scholarly mode — history based on the reading of old books and the writing of new ones. Is this the way that history will come to an "end," not with a bang or a whimper but with unreflective surrender to information overload? But even then, as Hans Blumenberg asks about the efforts to extirpate myth, "what if there were still something to say, after all?"[81]

Prospect

So, once more and for the last time here, what is history? My hermeneutically and anthropologically inspired answer has always been: history is what historians do — have done — and this led me (Euro- and egocentrically) from Acton to Vico, to the Renaissance "art" and the modern "science" of history and various "new histories," thence back, in a longer perspective, to a larger panorama of ancient and medieval ways of inquiry and more recently to modern and postmodern inheritors of this complex, contradictory, and many-layered legacy, with all their differing goals, methods, perspectives, and contexts. At the end of this pilgrimage I think of the reflection of Rilke, that:

> I live my life in growing orbits
> which move out over the things of the world.
> Perhaps I can never achieve the last,
> but that will be my attempt.[82]

So after these reflections what is history? For me the answer is still in the making.

But what about historiography in its latest modes? For some it is still in "crisis," though the arguments for this are entirely commonplace — a presentist topos which suggests myopia rather than perspective.[83] If nothing else, current conditions act to liberate younger historians from such methodological or ideological constrictions in the name of pluralism and freedom from "grand narratives," though also in the interests of self-indulgence, unencumbered interpretation, distractions by trivia, and the detachment of historical inquiry from its ancient authorities and literary habits. In the wake of that confused and commercialized surrender to modern or postmodern chaos the study of history in the third millennium has lost its innocence. By "loss of innocence" I mean not the disillusioning force of experience but rather insights gained through contact with other lines of inquiry, and by other lines of inquiry I do not refer mainly to the social sciences but rather to the humanities, especially philosophy, literary theory, and the history of science. Historians have, to be sure, learned from economics, sociology, political science, and anthropology; but in many ways these contacts have served to strengthen rather than to criticize the premises of conventional historical scholarship. It is mainly through the humanities that historians have come to understand the foundations and finer points of their projects and to discard some of their illusions and awaken from their professional dreams, however "noble."

I am not invoking here any of the celebrated innovations of current historical writing, such as the "new historicism" or the "new cultural history," nor do I mean to disinter complaints about the primacy of politics and "drum-and-trumpet history." Such laments — tired topoi of latter-day Moderns and Ancients — are as time-worn as the tradition of Western historiography; and we hardly need the impetus of anthropology to direct our attention to the cultural and private aspects of our lives. What I want to do instead in these concluding ego-historical reflections is to review a few of the elementary insights which by now we should have grasped and made axioms of our scholarly craft in practice as well as theory. To some degree I may exaggerate, since each of the terms, or concepts, which I call into question represents an oversimplified historiographical shorthand; the point is that we would do well to recognize their problematic and ultimately fictional character. I begin with a text from that wise and memorable old classic, *1066 and All That*: "History is not what you thought. *It is what you can remember*." This is good advice for students, but for writers of history it may be altered to read: "History is not what happened. *It is what you can find out about*." Let me elaborate on this assertion with a few assertions about the craft of history.

1. *There is no "past."* This is a grammatical oxymoron. There *was* a past, we assume, but the study of history is carried on in an eternal present (which immediately becomes a past). Here it is obvious that we are in the clutches of the tense structure of our language, and further that historians have long employed such structure in a rhetoric designed to express such pastness. The past we envision and debate is poised on the edge of an always-evanescent present between two inaccessible loci . In practice this point may not bear extended examination by historians, but must be content with happenings imagined — recalled or anticipated — from myriad, changing points of view. Human time itself, Paul Ricoeur suggests, is not psychological but a creation of historical narrative.[84]

2. *There are no "facts."* There *were* facts, no doubt; but all we have is their recollections, records, or remains; and again such evidence will be viewed differently by different historians. This is not a deeply epistemological argument, for if we can often establish that a particular event did occur, its histor-

ical presence remains a product of human imputation. In the forest the tree does not "fall" without an observer; the "fact" is meaningless, indeed nonexistent, without human apprehension.

3. *There is no "context."* There is no "social base" or cultural "climate," either, but only texts, works of art, artifacts, etc., in which historians see similarities and from which they construct categories of judgment to locate *zeitgeistlich* and *volkgeistlich* epiphenomena; but as Burckhardt said of the Renaissance, these appear differently to each eye — and, as experience shows, they will be argued over endlessly by scholars with different professional trainings and different points of view.

4. *There can be no historical "explanation."* Explanation is a matter of assigning causes, and in a strict and logical sense it is identical with prediction except for the positioning of time's arrow.[85] As Isaiah Berlin and Paul Veyne have argued, all that the historian can attempt is *retrodiction;* but in both cases the effort of explanation requires some sort of reductionism — something is really something else — or a selecting of causal factors which is tied to a particular point of view; and this seems to be inconsistent with an explanatory ideal.

5. *There is no historical "truth."* Even as scholars, we live and learn within our own small horizons. As Barry Allen has said of philosophers, "We cannot speak the truth; words cannot mimic the way the world is; language imposes subjects and predicates on a world that does not have stable, enduring units corresponding to its terms."[86] How much less can historians speak the truth of the way the world *was* — and its languages *were?*

6. *There is no historical or cultural "memory."* If we cannot trust our own recollections, how much less can we identify history with memory except as a rhetorical device that exploits the analogy between this faculty and tangible processes of institutional and cultural transmission? If autobiography is an imaginative effort, how much more so is the attempt to reconstruct a collective historical process? Indeed the term "reconstruct" is itself a sign of the sort of rhetoric camouflaging the historical effort of what is more precisely the work of imaginative construction.

7. *There is no "history."* I mean not just no past but no collective experience shared by the human species except its existence in a hostile natural environment within institutions of kinship. History cannot "speak" except through human ventriloquism, and (to invoke Lyotard's postmodernist criticism) there can be no "metanarrative" that captures the "nature and destiny of man." Such metanarratives we have, of course — founded on all sorts of ideologies and utopias — but as frameworks for human history they all sooner or later, I believe, come to grief.

These comments may seem to be symptoms of Hume's skeptical "malady" recurring in a particularly virulent form and leading to a radical relativism and what E. D. Hirsch has called "conceptual atheism." If I were a philosopher, I would probably admit the charge and welcome the consequences: if this be Relativism, then make the most of it. I am a historian, however, and have other business at hand; and so for practical purposes I shall retreat on all of the above points and move to a reprise and qualification of these assertions.

1. There is a past, then — but this past takes the form not of a tradition or a legacy but of a literary convention which refers to surviving records, testimony, and artifacts, and of a literary genre that assembles, arranges, and expresses this material through the devices of language and especially use of the past tense and conventional copulae. The past is the historian's *Ding an sich*.

2. There are facts — but these are not the noumena of conventional historiography but the inferences established, exchanged, and agreed upon by particular historians and are always subject to reverification and revision — and I might add that much of our store of received historical truth should indeed be reviewed in the light of how "facts" are given definition.

3. There is also context, or rather there are numerous contexts — but these are necessarily built from particular points of view by scholars; and they may take as many forms, diachronic and synchronic, as there are communities of agents and authors which have left traces for historians to interpret. But such contexts, when they are not the clichés of conventional historiography, are always the work of imaginative *assemblages* — or *bricolages* — of evidence assembled necessarily from texts.

4. There is explanation — but it takes the limited and reflective form of interpretation, and here the model is that of translation rather than the workings of a mechanical toy. Nietzsche's insistence on "the interpretive character of all that happens" should be a rule for even the most resistantly realistic of historians.

5. There is truth — but it is not the higher truth which, as Nietzsche said, has been "lying added" by certain philosophers; it is the human truth of appearances. That the so-called "true world" behind these appearances is useless, as Nietzsche taught, is a hard lesson which not every historian has learned but which through reflection and self-criticism, if arising only from the endless progression of revisionisms, should have become clear. That we must be content with "what passes for truth," as Allen says, seems a most appropriate rule for historians, if not for philosophers and theologians.

6. There is cultural memory — but it is a residue of innumerable traces whose meaning may or may not be retrievable, and so it is both flickering and

faulty. It is also a repository of many mythical creations which transcend and perhaps violate conventional standards of historical study.

7. And so history does exist—but only in particular forms representing particular points of view and derivative syntheses of these forms.

The wider the lens, the less reliable the picture. Biography is conjectural enough; the history of groups is almost metaphorical; with nations we enter the realm of law, politics, and war; and as for humanity we are still exploring and speculating. Universal history has been pursued for two millennia; but while it ostensibly employs historical evidence and conclusions, it rests on a mythical or metahistorical foundation far transcending horizons of historical study and falling short of the "autopsy" on which Herodotean inquiry was founded. History remains "local knowledge"—*et tout le rest est littérature* (if not "history" in a pejorative sense). Yet like Herodotus we are free to enter the realm of myth, conjecture, and speculation, so that, as Certeau said, "history is probably our myth"—perhaps even, contra Hans Blumenberg and philosophical dreams, our "last myth."[87]

Conclusion

Millennium

*But what if there were still something
to say, after all?*
                                   — Hans Blumenberg

So my trilogy on historical inquiry across the ages comes to an end: *Faces of History* placed the story of Western historiography in a long perspective and carried it down to the eighteenth century; *Fortunes of History* pursued an increasingly complex narrative from the Enlightenment down to World War I; and *Frontiers of History* surveys in a more personal manner, from the author's own self-examination and "point of view," from then down to the first decade of the new millennium. "A man sets out to draw the world," Borges wrote. "As the years go by, he peoples a space with images of provinces, kingdoms, mountains, bays, ships, islands, fishes, rooms, instruments, stars, horses, and individuals. A short time before he dies, he discovers that the patient labyrinth of lines traces the lineaments of his own face."[1]

Not that my drawing of the world is original, for it is based not on the world but on stories rehearsed many times before with recurrent, if not constant, patterns. At the start of the third millennium A.D. (according to the chronological scheme inherited from the Venerable Bede), as so often before, written history is poised between two poles — between fragmentation and synthesis, between analysis and narrative, between research and conjecture, between a vision of world unity and increasing Balkanization, between the forest and the trees. On the one hand there is a macro-quest for some sort of grand narrative (to adopt a postmodernist cliché), whether national or global, and on the other hand the myriad mini-voices and problems of particular groups and activities that flash and resound across our horizons. The alternation is between order and chaos, and it is further complicated by the intrusion of ideologies, which both distract scholars and give direction and coherence, at least temporarily, to their inquiries and interpretations. In the early part of the century Fascism and Communism as well as liberal democracy competed for attention and long-term historical meaning; these days the choice has turned — back — to national, ethnic, and religious interests, though still cast against a background of economic and political pressures, leaving historians trained in the realities of yesterday still searching for patterns and telling details.

The most troubling problems and major imperatives at the start of the twenty-first century are much the same as those which faced Herodotus in the middle of the first millennium B.C., and these are the mysteries of human space and time beyond the horizons of local experience. Herodotus could not begin to encompass these alien dimensions except by analogy and imagination, but even the most learned and well-traveled modern historian cannot draw much more than a tiny fraction into historical ken. Beyond a mid-twentieth-century and mid-American starting point I have been able to make only a few feeble forays into foreign languages juxtaposed to or overlapping with my Anglophone world and into that "foreign country" that is the past. Confronting the problem and the imperative of global history, I am unable to make contact with much of humanity within traveling range and virtually none beyond the civilized areas joined by transportation. As for probing the human past recognized by the technology of print and museum collections beyond my cultural zone, I find myself consulting dictionaries, encyclopedias, and companions to historiography, which is mainly to say bibliographies that provide lists of authors, texts, and other remains of human behavior in the past — and these, of course, in the major European languages. So far searching the Web can only be supplementary to such research (or so it seems to one of my generation). There are classic works in many languages, of course, but few translated or absorbed into mainstream historiography, for which the whole world is Scythia, if not Mars. In any case the impression is that history, which was born in "lists," is reverting to this ancient genre.

As for Western Europe, the story, aside from economic institutions and actions beyond the political sphere, continues to be that of consolidating and expanding nation-states encroaching on, or taking over, marginalized minorities, while in Central and Eastern Europe (one region or two?) the story has been that of competing and overlapping mini-nationalities subjected to the great powers, whether or not officially designated "empires."[2] Another problem was the lack of correlation between national or ethnic identity, as in the case of Balkan Muslims, who were recognized only as a religious group by Serbia and Croatia.[3] In any case the minor states wanted no longer to be "small fry," as Traian Stoianovich put it, but also "eagles," "bears," and "lions."[4] The last of the imperial structures, the Soviet Union, carried with it a vision of history that accompanied international Communism, but this vision did not really survive 1989, except in certain areas of social discontent. Beginning as a specter, Communism was a corpse, a shattered tower of Babel; and once again nationalism in various forms came to dominate the East European scene (most riotously in the Balkans but also in the Baltics), Africa, and Latin America. Political independence achieved, the smaller states could turn to ideological and social advance through Western-style historiography and the construction of national traditions — yet in a critical and professional mode that avoids both romantic and partisan excesses and yet remains open to the idea of a global community.

The Western model of national historiography has been imitated, or paralleled, by many cultural traditions on various levels of political achievement. Russia, China, India, Japan, Korea, Vietnam, Indonesia, Islam, Turkey, and other linguistic groups as well as the Anglophone areas of Canada, Australia, New Zealand, South Africa, and Polynesia have historiographical traditions which generally follow the progressive model, beginning with the collection and interpretation of myths, chronicles, poetry, and records, the identification of intellectual founders, usually associated with national revivals in the nineteenth and twentieth centuries, the establishment of scientific methods, professional organization (often invoking the paternal figure of Ranke), university teaching, the distortions of official and subversive ideologies, revisionist controversies, especially over origins, continuity, and periodization, and partial merging with international research and publications and efforts to find a place in global history.[5] The pattern is repeated by other groups, though in less focused ways, as Central Asian states, which often lack sources for the construction of traditions independent of China or Russia, or Africa, about which a recent author asks, "What History for Which Africa?"[6] This question can be asked of all the continents, which have been rendered problematical by the new discipline of "metageography."[7] The ultimate shaping factor, of course, remains the identification and employment of source materials.

History is a luxury of settled and organized peoples, while migrating and diasporic groups find it difficult to establish their roots or "invent" their nations. It is extraordinary to consider the range and number of linguistic groups and potential nationalities within our global framework. It has been estimated that there are well over 4,000 distinct languages, distributed into families (though relationships often remain problematical in the present state of historical linguistics, a field whose credit is not high these days), and—although languages die at a rate comparable to biological species—the question is whether this means there are an equal number of potential or incipient and intermingled as well as competing historiographies.[8] When the linguistic map is drawn, the contours and adjoined histories are further confused and hardly amenable to general interpretation, except perhaps a transplanted vulgar evolutionism,[9] and in human terms simplification means elimination in the interest of conjectural construction. This is the other side of the globalist coin, and it presents a growing challenge to the old conventions of narrative history.

So what next? History points to the past, but it occupies a continuum that is connected with the future, and the future, though inaccessible, may be anticipated and in some ways expected. Although history has a horizon structure and relies on a point of view, it is obvious that it has been radically globalized in the past generation or two (though building on much earlier effort) and is becoming used to the unfamiliar. Yet the effects of this globalization are more quantitative than conceptual, because of the need to accommodate peoples from hundreds of countries speaking thousands of languages, including those moving as immigrants or settled in diasporas in what, in a relic of our flat-earthly past, we still call the four corners of the world.[10] The materials of history have likewise been transformed quantitatively, as they have been placed On Line and gathered into plausible categories and searchable elements not of meaning but of information, which old-fashioned historians can rearrange as they see fit, with or without a story line but still according to canons of interpretation drawn mainly from languages not yet (despite the wonders of mechanical translation) accommodated to electro-exchange. This is a world becoming familiar to some but truly a foreign country to others even though conventional books, libraries, and publishers still support our practices of historical learning, at least for now.

Yet the present, too, is becoming a foreign country, and still, as it passes, invites Herodotean inquiry as well as Thucydidean analysis. What is appearing on our horizons of expectation? One time-honored way of accommodating the future is the cult of novelty, which arose in early modern times and which was reinforced by the Gutenberg galaxy and the trade in and advertisement of books, letters, pamphlets, and periodicals. Not until the sixteenth century could thinkers conceive of philosophy not merely as a legacy to be worked over and taught but as a project inviting novel (and better) departures.

New philosophy, new science, new history, and just plain "news" were all products of the expansion of print culture and harbingers of our present historical predicament and historiographical pandemonium. For Michel de Certeau history is a "fragmented god . . . , chatter[ing] incessantly — everywhere, in the news, in statistics, in polls, in documents . . . , thereby forming the tangled web of 'our' history."[11]

One result of innovation was the replacement or occultation of older works by newer (new and improved in commercial jargon) ones, with the result that ideas, arguments, and conclusions have continually to be reaffirmed as if newly discovered — producing, in the words of Sorokin, ever "new Columbuses," inadvertent copycats and plagiarists, setting out on voyages of discovery already made but then forgotten. By now we should have learned better; having been decentered by the Copernican, Darwinian, and Freudian revolutions, we should not be surprised to be marginalized and fragmented further by a sense of deep history. Thinking of the present moment as the climax of history is "one of the most destructive habits of modern thought," writes Foucault, who then adds, "One must probably find the humility to admit that the time of one's own life is not the one-time, basic, revolutionary moment of history, from which everything begins and is completed."[12]

Yet we cannot avoid the continual renewing, if not the uniqueness, of our perspective and both the impossibility of knowing enough and the disadvantages of knowing too much. In a little essay published in 1939 Jorge Luis Borges imagined an institution, which he called "the Total Library," which was both divine and hellish, utopian and absurd. His vision may have been inspired by the famous hypotheses of the team of monkeys that, given enough time. would eventually type out the complete works of Dickens; for he remarks in a note that, "strictly speaking, one immortal monkey would be sufficient." In any case Borges's Total Library, transcending the simian effort, would be of "astronomical size" and include absolutely "everything," not only the catalog of the library itself in all languages but also entries of infinite diversity, such as a detailed history of the future, the encyclopedia Novalis thought of assembling, the paradoxes Bishop Berkeley failed to publish, the proof of Fermat's theorem, the unwritten chapters of Edwin Drood, and trivia, real and possible, without end. This "subaltern horror," as Borges calls it, may haunt the imaginations of historians as well as poets; nor can any ingenious technology let us escape these flickering visions of what time conceals and what hominids can produce. Both truth and folly are the daughters of time.

Historians can no longer avoid the permanent condition of "information overload," which (unlike the expansion of historical sources in the nineteenth century) is a cause for alarm as well as celebration.[13] The center of "scientific" historical inquiry is no longer the archives but new forms of information technology, including a shift to electronic recording, storage, transmission, and exchange, which will arguably produce a decline in concern for literary judgment, style, and standards and a rise in repetition and the bookish offense of plagiarism, intended and unintended. Since the 1950s scholars have celebrated quantitative history and they have done so even more enthusiastically in the computer age, but usually as a way of enhancing conventional historical inquiry and with no concern about the epistemological effects of the new technologies and media, where Marshall McLuhan's insights about what he called "post-literacy" still apply.[14] Through war and peace traditional practices of research and writing will surely continue, as will writing long-hand and lecturing, but historical inquiry may be increasingly detached from teaching and reading. Some topics in world history will attract research in original sources, but larger narratives of national, international, and comparative history must rely on the growing stores of secondary, tertiary, and quaternary materials, shaped by conjecture and controversy for academic and popular reception. Or are these just modern, or postmodern and technologically enhanced, versions of the old and familiar predicament, which is that information is without limit and historians must always operate selectively within local horizons — intensified perhaps by the Balkan model of politics?[15]

With Marxism and other "metanarratives" in demise it is not surprising that the quest for economic sources of behavior has shifted to the surrounding material culture — as evident in the proliferation of topics brought by "cultural studies." For many historians, weary of the journalistic pursuit of politics, its spokesmen, its gossip, and its scandals, "political culture" seems a more challenging, if also more tangible, target, with structures and forces of power being reflected in domestic as well as public creations and displays. Some of this is a result of the turn to women's history; but of course there are deeper roots, as in the works of cultural historians going back at least to the eighteenth century. What Katherine Hayles argues about literature, that it cannot be separated from materiality and the surrounding media, may apply to history itself, especially as it shifts attention from words to things, as art historians have done for generations.[16] Meanwhile the "history of ideas," long set by some historians at the center of historical change, has in large part been relegated, explicitly or implicitly, to the histories of political, religious, and scientific thought and to literature, which is to say the languages of these disciplines.

The search for a science beyond the confusions and contradictions of life and language in the new millennium continues, and indeed the theories of chaos and complexity seem to be the sophisticated equivalents to the statistical science of the nineteenth century — still seeking to reduce local knowledge to global theory and to determine regularities, if not predictabilities behind the flux, though in nonlinear and fragmentary modes consistent, perhaps, with claims made for "cultural postmodernism."[17] For Hayles this condition of "orderly disorder" has been produced by the successive "denaturing" of language, context, and time, subjecting each to constructionist interpretation, separating time from sequence and causality, and anticipating the denaturing of the human itself. So history, in its classical form, is reduced to local and linear — and perhaps "complementary" — stories within a framework that undermines its temporal form and projects it into "systematic" modes of understanding and representation — that may suggest ways of building bridges between microhistory and macrohistory.[18] Yet much of this is carried out in the spirit of play — the postmodern "culture of fun" — which, as Huizinga pointed out, is more encompassing than seriousness, since the former includes the latter but not vice versa.

In some areas of historical study, of course, it is still business as usual. The history of the printed book, for example, is a very active line of research just as its future in conventional form is being put in doubt because of "information overload" and economic pressures. Not that the quantity of published books will decline in the near future, especially in the field of historiography, but the problems of coping with expanding discourse and accessing essential information make old-fashioned methods of research increasingly inefficient and irrelevant. The shelf life of printed books will be drastically curtailed, and while bibliographical searching will be easier, it will also become more arbitrary because of technical intermediaries between writers and readers. There will be changes, too, in the institutional environment, which will incline not to lecture or seminar room and desk with pen, typewriter, and paper but to computer space for reading, writing, and reverting, with a nice irony, to ancient scrolling techniques, hypertextual marginalia, and pre-print exchange — leaving print culture mainly for a wider reading public and the textbook market.

Yet the encyclopedic impulse continues, to the extent indeed that we seem to be moving into a new age of the medieval Summa, demonstrated by the proliferation not only of textbooks but also of dictionaries, encyclopedias, "companions," commentaries, and the like — many of them now likewise on line. Under these conditions there are no longer many "original sources" for historians to explore, only information (not individual facts but quantifiable "data") and apparatus processed by technicians, which add another complication to historical epistemology, as points of view and biases are already embedded in the sources on still another level. In sufficiently general terms and for pedagogical purposes this may not make a difference — and indeed may in some ways mark progress over earlier impressionism — but then where are

grounds for historical qualification and criticism beyond cultural common-
places and ideological forestructures? The hegemony of computer technology
threatens to change the very fabric of human time, so that, according to Arno
Borst, invoking the time-scholar J. T. Fraser, "the global networking of the
present . . . has destroyed more and more of the complexity of past temporal
orders, and narrowed the range of variations between the working day and
free time, youth and old age, biological, intellectual, and social development."[19] In our haste we are indeed "losing time."

Does "postmodernism" capture these conditions of modern historical
scholarship? This term, accepted widely and construed no less widely and as
yet showing no signs of passing. has become an umbrella for contemporary
intellectual fashions which seek identity beyond the intimidating and overused
label of "modernism," even in its most perverse excesses. In fact postmodernism follows the familiar generational pattern of revolt against tradition, but it
raises the stakes by questioning the conventions of temporality itself, lifting
itself above time. This is accomplished, of course, through rhetorical strategies
which themselves cannot be extracted from either language or historical experience; and the effect, if not goal, is to privilege imaginative interpretations
and — severing ties with questions of chronology and the authority of conventional historical scholarship — to elevate scholars and writers to the position of
judges, "cultural critics," and even prophets.[20] For non-theoretical historians
postmodernism is a fishing license for exotic targets and opinions, if not a new
way of injecting life into old subjects.[21] Of course there is nothing especially
new in this, either, and it is still left open to historians to "historicize" such
efforts as well as the label (I don't call it the concept) of postmodernism. Over
a century ago Nietzsche prophesied *"Our new infinite,"* meaning that "the
world has once again become infinite to us: insofar as we cannot reject the
possibility *that it includes infinite interpretations"* — and the corollary that "all
acting requires forgetting."[22] Is this an invitation to or resignation in the face
of endless opinionating and conjecture, an anticipation of "chaos theory" or a
denial that there can be any such thing?

Under these conditions what is the use of history? The ancient prescriptions
for truth, profit, and pleasure still apply, but in different forms in modern mass
society under conditions of technological change and the threat of Balkanization, which might indeed be "interpreted" under the catchall rubric of "postmodernism." Most striking perhaps is the plurality of perspectives available to
modern readers, that is, the multiplicity of pasts, historical and prehistorical,
which printed books yield and which are elaborated in electronic culture. The
eighteenth century saw the emergence of modern hermeneutics and the concept of "point of view," which was later incorporated in historical method and

which undermined the notion of a single narrative of human experience, whether providential or secularist. "To each eye," as Burckhardt began his great work on the Renaissance, "the outlines of a civilization [*Kultur*] present a different picture," and this impressionistic insight has become a defining premise of postmodern history. But "culture," too, has been pluralized and fragmented, and indeed a century before Burckhardt scholars were investigating not only high culture but also "material culture" and the concerns not only of ruling elites but also the history of the middle and laboring classes and subaltern groups, women, children, gays, the aged, disabled, criminals, animals, elements of material culture (including the book as commodity), and environment, and so on down the chain of human life. To this must be added the experience of "alterity," as contacts with the East and the new world have complicated Eurocentric history and undermined the old Adamic (and Evean) story. Of course the conventions of universal history, from the old biblical framework to evolutionism to more sophisticated philosophies of history, often joined to quasi-religious prophecy and utopian visions, continued to support grand narratives; but new explorations in both time and space have again undermined such visions of a unified history of humankind, past, present, or future, and neo-evolutionism has blurred the definition of a modern human "we."

Another inherited condition of modern historical scholarship is the centrality of debate and disputation. Of course scholarly quarrels were conventional in the ancient and medieval schools of philosophy and theology, but they were intensified and institutionalized in the age of printed exchange and learned journalism in the Republic of Letters, periodical literature, the growing practice of reviewing books, and authorial self-advertisement. This falls under the rubric of "criticism," the expansion of the ancient *ars critica,* whose modern form is the literary theory invading historical inquiry as well as literary interpretation. One by-product of this is the phenomenon which, in the past century and more, acquired the label of "revisionism" and which pits one school against another — often in the form of generational difference. Such revisionism has become a fixture not only in religious and social thought but also in historical studies — followed today (you won't be surprised to learn) by "post-revisionism." The positive side of this recurring disputatious pattern is the awareness that scholarly achievements are the product not of eurekan breakthroughs or arguments by individuals but rather of dialogue and cooperation in historical study, although this often becomes evident only in retrospect. In this connection consider the hardening and proliferation of genres, disciplines, and their attendant histories, keeping in mind that disciplines spawn sub-disciplines, producing, for example, not only the history of history as a special branch of literature (for example, Eduard Fueter's history of European historiography) but also (as in the recent work of Horst Blanke, dedicated to Fueter) histories of the history of history (*Historiographiegeschichte*, the Germans call it). This sort of accumulation, which was predicted long ago by Harry Elmer Barnes, will no doubt produce a sub-genre of a still lower order (the history of histories of the history of history) and so on, like the little man on the Quaker Oats box, which suggests that history, though perhaps nourishing, has not so much a substantial foundation as a vanishing point.

What seems certain is that there will continue to be "new histories" in one area or another, and that these new histories will draw, at least inadvertently, on older, perhaps forgotten, patterns without significant acknowledgment until historiography reveals constants, continuities, and repetitions. This is not to say that we will not experience and proclaim novelties, for historical knowledge is always new, and we are always on the frontier, looking ahead as well as back. The historian shares this with man (and, now it is necessary to add, woman) in general, about whom Pope aphorized,

> His knowledge measured to his state and place;
> His time a moment, and a point his space.[23]

No longer, however, can we pretend to be moving along a single line within a well-charted space (despite the efforts of modern map-makers), and the only constant is the curiosity that seeks new horizons and puzzles. Herodotus, if not Thucydides, would recognize the condition.

Notes

Chapter 1. Before the Great War

1. See Thomas Harrison, *1910: The Emancipation of Dissonance* (Berkeley, 1996).

2. Hugh Kenner, *A Sinking Island: The Modern English Writers* (Baltimore, 1987), 124.

3. Adams, *Selected Letters*, ed. Ernest Samuels (Cambridge, Mass., 1992), 526–27.

4. *Poems for the Millennium*, ed. Jerome Rothenberg and Pierre Noris, II (Berkeley, 1998), 23, 409.

5. *The Journal of Arnold Bennett* (Garden City, 1932), 402.

6. "The Eighth Duino Elegy."

7. *Friedrich Paulsen: An Autobiography*, tr. Theodor Lorenz (New York, 1938), 483–87.

8. *Diaries 1910–13*, ed. Max Brod, tr. Joseph Kresh (New York, 1948), 14, 15, 16, 18, 22.

9. *Modern and Modernism: The Sovereignty of the Artist 1885–1925* (New York, 1988).

10. *Revue de Synthèse* (1910), 204, 8.

11. *The Collected Poems of Wallace Stevens* (New York, 1980), 165.

12. *Soul of the Age: Selected Letters of Hermann Hesse 1891–1962*, tr. Mark Harman (New York, 1991), 103 (Nov. 1919).

13. See Kelley, *Fortunes of History* (New Haven, 2003), 314ff.

14. Heussi, *Die Krisis des Historismus* (Tübingen, 1932); Meinecke, "Von der Krisis des Historismus," in *Zur Theorie und Philosophie der Geschichte*, ed. Ebehard Kessel

(Stuttgart, 1959), 196–204; Georg G. Iggers, *The German Conception of History: The National Tradition of Historical Thought from Herder to the Present* (Middletown, Conn., 1982²), 124–73; Charles R. Bambach, *Heidegger, Dilthey, and the Crisis of Historicism* (Ithaca, 1995); and Wolfgang Bialas and Gérard Raulet, *Der Historismusdebatte in der Weimarer Republik* (Frankfurt, 1996).

15. See Franco Bianco (ed.), *Il dibatto sullo storicismo* (Bologna, 1978), and Bianco, *Storicismo e ermeneutica* (Rome, 1974); also Wilhelm Hennis, "A Science of Man: Max Weber and the Political Economy of the German Historical School," in *Max Weber and His Contemporaries*, ed. Wolfgang J. Mommsen and Jürgen Osterhammel (London, 1987), 5–58.

16. *Main Currents of Modern Thought*, tr. M. Booth (New York, 1912), 316.

17. See Hans-Georg Drescher, *Ernst Troeltsch: His Life and Work*, tr. John Bowden (London, 1992).

18. Gunter Scholz (ed.), *Historismus am Ends der 20. Jahrhunderts: Eine internationale Duiskussion* (Berlin, 1997), and see Brook Thomas, *The New Historicism and Other Old-Fashioned Topics* (Princeton, 1991), and Stuart Sim (ed.), *The Routledge Companion to Postmodernism* (London, 2001), fourteen topics not including history.

19. *The Problems of the Philosophy of History: An Epistemological Essay*, tr. Guy Oakes (New York, 1977), 61–68.

20. Breysig, *Der Stufenbau und die Gesetz der Weltgeschichte* (Stuttgart, 1917); and see Stefan Haas, *Historische Kulturforschung in Deutschland 1880–1930* (Cologne, 1994), 158–66.

21. Windelband, "Geschichte und Naturwissenschaft" (1894), *Präludien* (Tübingen, 1915), 136–60, and Rickert, *The Limits of Concept Formation in Natural Science: A Logical Introduction to the Historical Sciences*, tr. Guy Oakes (Cambridge, 1986) — but rejecting (184) the nomothetic *Kulturgeschichte* of Karl Lamprecht; also Guy Oakes, *Weber and Rickert: Concept Formation in the Cultural Sciences* (Cambridge, Mass., 1988).

22. Dilthey, *Introduction to the Human Sciences*, ed. Rudolph Makreel and Frithjof Rodi (Princeton, 1989), 117.

23. See Carlo Antoni, *From History to Sociology*, tr. Hayden White (Detroit, 1959), 3, and Fritz Ringer, *The Decline of the German Mandarins* (Cambridge, Mass., 1969). 336.

24. "On Understanding and Hermeneutics: Student Lecture Notes" (1867–68), in *Hermeneutics and the Study of History*, in *Selected Works*, IV, ed. Rudolph Makreel and Frithjof Rodi (Princeton, 1996), 233.

25. *The Formation of the Historical World in the Human Sciences*, tr. Rudolph A. Makkreel and Frithjof Rodi (Princeton, 2002); and see Larry Frohman, "Wilhelm Dilthey's Philosophy of History," *Journal of the History of Ideas*, 56 (1995), 263–88.

26. Dilthey *Introduction to the Human Sciences*, 76.

27. Steven Lukes, *Emile Durkheim, His Life and Work* (New York, 1972), 6ff., and Terry Nichols Clark, *Prophets and Patrons: The French University and the Emergence of the Social Sciences* (Cambridge, Mass., 1973); also Kelley, *The Human Measure: Social Thought in the Western Legal Tradition* (Cambridge, Mass., 1990), 272.

28. Steven Mithen, *The Prehistory of the Mind: The Cognitive Origins of Art, Religion, and Science* (London, 1996), though without reference either to Durkheim or to Lévy-Bruhl.

29. Spengler, *Letters, 1913–1936,* tr. Arthur Helps (London, 1966), 30, 59.

30. *Fortunes of History,* ch. 9.

31. See John Kenyon, *The History Men: Macaulay, Carlyle, Buckle, Acton, Stubbs, Namier, Tawney, Elton . . .* (London, 1983); Herman Ausubel et al. (eds.), *Some Modern Historians of Britain* (New York, 1951); Victor Feske, *From Belloc to Churchill: Private Scholars, Public Culture, and the Crisis of British Liberalism, 1900–1939* (Chapel Hill, 1996); and Elizabeth Chapin Furber (ed.), *Changing Views on British History* (Cambridge, Mass., 1966).

32. Bate, *The Burden of the Past and the English Poet* (Cambridge, Mass., 1970), 3, and Harold Bloom, *A Map of Misreading* (Oxford, 1975).

33. See discussions in my *Fortunes of History.*

34. Reginald L. Poole, *Chronicles and Annals* (Oxford, 1926).

35. *Selected Essays of F. W. Maitland,* ed. Helen M. Cam (Cambridge, 1957), 97; and see C. H. S. Fifoot, *Frederick William Maitland* (Cambridge, Mass., 1971).

36. Pollock and Maitland, *The History of English Law* (Cambridge, 1895), I, 65.

37. *The Divine Right of Kings* (Cambridge, 1896), 266, and *Political Thought from Gerson to Grotius: 1414–1625* (Cambridge, 1907), 40.

38. *The Collected Papers of Thomas Frederick Tout* (Manchester, 1932), I, 94, and *The Present State of Medieval Studies in Great Britain* (London, 1913); and see P. B. M. Blaas, *Continuity and Anachronism: Parliamentary and Constitutional Development in Whig Historiography and in the Anti-Whig Reactions between 1890 and 1930* (The Hague, 1978), 345–73.

39. *The Place of the Reign of Edward II in English History* (Manchester, 1936 [1914]), vi.

40. *England under Protector Somerset* (London, 1900), 323; and see Blaas, *Continuity and Anachronism,* 274–344.

41. *Henry VIII* (London, 1905), vii; *Somerset,* 338; Garrett Mattingly was careful to pass this warning on to his students.

42. *Henry VIII,* 352.

43. *Factors in Modern History* (New York, 1926), 30.

44. *The History of England: A Study in Political Evolution* (London, 1912), 225.

45. *The Evolution of Parliament* (London, 1926²), 3.

46. Ibid., 379.

47. David Cannadine, *G. M. Trevelyan: A Life in History* (New York, 1992)

48. *England in the Age of Wycliffe 1368–1420* (New York, 1963), 2.

49. *England under the Stuarts* (London, 1949), 186.

50. Ibid., 430.

51. Ibid., 821.

52. *The Ancient Greek Historians* (New York, 1958), 69–70, 81.

53. Ibid., 212.

54. *The Idea of Progress (London, 1932),* 352.

55. Ibid., 49.

56. *Ibid.,* 352.

57. For a new survey of aspects of professional history see Christian Amalvi (ed.), *Les Lieux de l'histoire* (Paris, 2004).

58. *A Political History of Europe since 1814,* tr. S. M. Macvane (New York, 1900), preface.

59. Robert Wohl, *The Generation of 1914* (Cambridge, Mass., 1979), 5–18, and Martha Hanna, *The Mobilization of Intellect: French Scholars and Writers during the Great War* (Cambridge, Mass., 1996), 26–49.

60. *Introduction to the Study of History,* tr. G. G. Berry (London, 1898).

61. *L'Histoire considerée comme science* (Paris, 1894); and see William R. Keylor, *Academy and Community: The Foundation of the French Historical Profession* (Cambridge, Mass., 1795), 116–21.

62. *Les Principes fondamentaux de l'histoire* (Paris, 1899), and Al. Zub, *L'Historiographie roumaine d'âge de synthèse* (Bucarest, 1983).

63. *Esquisse psychologique du peuples européens* (Paris, 1903²), and see James T. Kloppenberg, *Uncertain Victory: Social Democracy and Progressivism in European and American Thought, 1870–1920* (Oxford, 1986), 35–37.

64. *Etudes de politique et d'histoire* (Paris, 1934), 26–59 ("Les conditions practiques de la recherche des causes dans le travail historique" [1907]).

65. Ibid., 16.

66. Ibid. 56.

67. Ibid., 120.

68. Ibid., 54.

69. *The "Soul" of the Primitive,* tr. Lilian A. Clare (New York, 1928), 59; also *How Natives Think* (1909), tr. Clare (London, 1926), and *Primitive Mentality* (London, 1928).

70. Lévy-Bruhl, *Primitive Mentality,* 11 (preface of 1921). Lévy-Bruhl did not use the phrase *mentalité primitive* until his second book, since neither term had been current before the war. See also Jacques Le Goff, "Mentalities: A History of Ambiguities," in *Constructing the Past: Essays in Historical Methodology,* ed. Le Goff and Pierre Nora (Cambridge, 1985), 166–80.

71. *Anthropo-Geographie, oder Grundzüge der Anwendung der Erdkunde auf die Geschichte* (Stuttgart, 1882); and Günther Buttmann, *Friedrich Ratzel: Leben und Werke einer deutschen Geographen* (Stuttgart, 1977).

72. Nathalie Richard (ed.), *L'Invention de la préhistoire* (Paris, 1992).

73. Steven Lukes, *Emile Durkheim, His Life and Work: A Historical and Critical Study* (New York, 1972), 61.

74. Cited in ibid., 625.

75. D. R. Kelley, *The Human Measure,* 274.

76. *La Synthèse*(Paris, 1911), 24.

77. *La Synthèse* (ed. 1953), 308.

78. *Fortunes of History,* ch. 12.

79. *Mein Leben* (Berlin, 1926), 101; and see Kelley, *Fortunes of History,* 304–6.

80. *Die Aufgaben der Kulturgeschichte* (Leipzig, 1889); and see Peter Alter, "Eberhard Gothein," in *Deutsche Historiker,* ed. H.-U. Wehler (Göttingen, 1982), III, 40–55.

81. *Die Aufgaben,* 11.

82. Lamprecht, *Deutsche Wirtschaftsleben in Mittelalter: Unterzuchung über die Entwicklung der materiellen Kultur des platten Landes auf Grund der Quellen* (Leipzig, 1885–86), and *Deutsche Geschichte* (Leipzig, 1891–1909).

83. Eberhard Kessel (ed.), *Zur Geschichte der Geschichtsschreibung* (Munich, 1968), 321–30.

84. Heinrich Ritter von Srbik, *Geist und Geschichte vom deutschen Humanismus bis zur Gegenwart* (Munich, 1951), II, 1–32; Hans-Heinz Krill, *Die Rankerenaissance: Max Lenz und Erich Marcks* (Berlin, 1962), referring also to "Ranke-Epigonen," "Jungrankeaner," "Rankebewegung," "Neurankeanismus," etc.; and see Wolfgang Weber, *Priester der Klio: Historisch-sozialwissenschaftliche Studien zur Herkunft und Karriere deutsche Historiker und zur Geschichte der Geschichtswissenschaft 1800–1970* (Frankfurt, 1987).

85. Charles E. McClelland, "Berlin Historians and German Politics," *Historians in Politics*, ed. Walter Laqueur and George L. Mosse (London, 1974), 191–222.

86. *Lehrbuch der Historischen Methode und der Geschichtsphilosophie* (Leipzig, 1908⁶), 22.

87. J. H. J. Van der Pot, *De Periodisierung der Geschiedenis* (The Hague, 1951), and D. R. Kelley, "Periodization in the West" (forthcoming).

88. *Lehrbuch*, II, 750.

89. Quoted by Friedrich Meinecke, *Autobiographische Schriften*, ed. Eberhard Kessel (Stuttgart, 1969), 141.

90. *Anfänge deutscher Geschichtschreibung* (Amsterdam, 1938), 31.

91. *History of the Art of War within the Framework of Political History*, tr. Walter J. Renfroe, Jr. (Westport, 1995), I, 17.

92. Arden Bucholz, *Hans Delbrück and the German Military Establishment: War Images in Conflict* (Iowa City, 1985).

93. Meinecke, *Autobiographische Schriften*, 76.

94. *Ibid.*, 120.

95. *Ibid.*, 117; *Ausgewählter Briefwechsel*, ed. Ludwig Dehio and Peter Classen (Stuttgart, 1962), 15ff.

96. *Briefwechsel*, 12.

97. *Cosmopolitanism and the National State*, tr. Robert B. Kimber (Princeton, 1970), 93; and see Richard W. Sterling, *Ethics in a World of Power: The Political Ideas of Friedrich Meinecke* (Princeton, 1958), 32–102.

98. *Cosmopolitanism*, 19.

99. *Ibid.*, 197.

100. Lenz, *Kleine historische Schriften* (Munich, 1910), 391 ("Bismarck und Ranke" [1901]), and 475 ("Heinrich von Treitschke" [1896]).

101. *Cosmopolitanism*, 322.

102. *Ibid.*, 375.

103. *The Age of German Liberation, 1795–1815*, tr. Peter Paret and Helmuth Fischer (Berkeley, 1977); and *Briefwechsel*, 51 (to Alfred Dove, 4 Nov. 1914).

104. *Autobiographische Schriften*, 220.

105. *Ibid.*, 238.

106. Charles E. McClelland, *The German Historians and England: A Study in Nineteenth-Century Views* (Cambridge, 1971), 168ff.

107. *Autobiographische Schriften*, 259, 312.

108. See Otto Büsch and Michael Erbe (eds.), *Otto Hintze und die moderne Geschichtswissenschaft, ein Tagungsbericht* (Berlin, 1983).

109. *Die Hohenzollern und Ihr Werk: Fünfhundert Jahre vaterländischer Geschichte* (Berlin, 1915), 111, 202.

110. *Ibid.,* 685.

111. *Briefwechsel,* 19.

112. Lenz, *Kleine historische Schriften,* 383–408 ("Bismarck and Ranke" [1901]); Marcks, *Männe und Zeiten* (Leipzig, 1912), 3–29 ("Goethe und Bismarck); both eulogies for Treitschke; and see Krill, *Die Rankerenaissance,* 211–25.

113. *Das Bismarckjahr: Eine Würdigung Bismarck und seiner Politik in Einzelschilderungen* (Berlin, 1915).

114. Cited by Krill, *Die Rankerenaissance,* 213.

115. *Die deutsche Geschichtschreibung von den Befreiungskriegen bis zu unsern Tagen* (Munich, 1924).

116. *Ibid.,* 155.

117. *The History of the Popes from the Close of the Middle Ages drawn from the Secret Archives of the Vatican and Other Sources,* tr. Frederick Ignatius Antrobus (London, 1899), 20.

118. *Historische Kulturforschung,* 268.

119. *Kulturgeschichte also Soziologie* (Munich, 1950), 446.

120. Martin V. Pundeff, *Bulgaria in American Perspective: Political and Cultural Issues* (Sofia, 1993), 298.

121. Bernard Michel, *Nations et nationalismes en Europe centrale XIXe–XXe siècle* (Paris, 1995).

122. William H. Hubbard et al. (eds.), *Making a Historical Culture: Historiography in Norway* (Oslo, 1995).

123. See the national entries in Daniel Woolf (ed.), *A Global Encyclopedia of Historical Writing* (London, 1998).

124. Karl Dietrich Erdmann, *Die Ökumene der Historiker: Geschichte der Internationalen Historikerkongresse und der Comité International des Sciences Historiques* (Göttingen, 1987); Ulrich Muhlack, "Universal History and National History," in *British and German Historiography: Traditions, Perceptions, and Transfers,* ed. Benedikt Stuchtey and Peter Wende (Oxford, 2000), 34; and Gioacchino Volpe, *Storici e maestri* (Florence, 1967 [1925]).

125. See *An Historian's World: Selections from the Correspondence of John Franklin Jameson,* ed. Elizabeth Donnan and Leo F. Stock (Philadelphia, 1956), 248.

126. Minnie von Below, *Georg von Below* (Stuttgart, 1930), 143.

127. Leon Dominian, *The Frontiers of Language and Nationality in Europe* (New York, 1917).

128. For an up-to-date discussion see *Minor Transnationalism,* ed. Françoise Lionnet and Shu-mei Shih (Durham, 2005).

Chapter 2. Reevaluations

1. David S. Luft, *Robert Musil and the Crisis of European Culture 1880–1942* (Berkeley, 1980), 129; and cf. Roland G. Usher, *Pan-Germanism* (Boston, 1913), 1, with a bibliography of the already "appalling mass of literature on the subject."

2. *Reflections of a Nonpolitical Man*, tr. Walter D. Morris (New York, 1983), 33.

3. *Weimar Culture: The Outsider as Insider* (New York, 1968), 11.

4. Lucian Boia, *History and Myth in Roumanian Consciousness* (Budapest, 2001), 37; also Stelian Brezeanu, *La Continuité Daco-Roumaine: Science et politique* (Bucarest, 1984), and Alain DuNay and André DuNay, *Transylvania: Fiction and Reality* (Hamilton, 1997).

5. Brandenburg, *Die Reichsgründung*, (2 vols., (Leipzig, 1916), Vorwort.

6. Brandi, *Geschichte der Geschichtswissenschaft* (Bonn, 1952 [1922]), Vorwort (1 Nov. 1918).

7. Stefan Berger, *The Search for Normality: National Identity and Historical Consciousness in Germany since 1800* (Providence, 1997), 30.

8. *Reflections of a Nonpolitical Man*, 335.

9. J. Holland Rose, *Nationality in Modern History* (New York, 1916), 51.

10. And see Fritz Fischer, *World Power or Decline: The Controversy over Germany's Aims in the First World War*, tr. Lancelot L. Farrar, Robert Kimber, and Rita Kimber (New York, 1974).

11. *Germany and Europe* (London, 1914); cf. J. A. Cramb, *Germany and England* (London, 1915); also Stuart Wallace, *War and the Image of Germany: British Academics, 1914–1918* (Edinburgh, 1988).

12. "Nietzsche and Treitschke: The Worship of Power in Modern Germany," *Oxford Pamphlets* ([Oxford], 1914), 90.

13. *The Commonwealth at War* (London, 1917), 115 (April 1916).

14. *The Political Thought of Heinrich von Treitschke* (London, 1914), 287.

15. *Essays and Addresses in Wartime* (London, 1918), 65, 153.

16. *The Living Past: A Sketch of Western Progress* (Oxford, 1931), vii.

17. *Aimons la France: Conferences 1914–1919* (Paris, 1920), 22.

18. See Martha Hanna, *The Mobilization of Intellect: French Scholars and Writers during the Great War* (Cambridge, Mass., 1996), 86–90; also Robert Wohl, *The Generation of 1914* (Cambridge, Mass., 1979).

19. *"L'Allemagne au-dessus de tout": La mentalité allemande et la guerre* (Paris, 1915), appearing originally in the collection *Sur le vif*, to which Seignobos, Bergson, Boutroux, Durkheim, Lanson, Lavisse, and others contributed.

20. *La Guerre actuelle commentée par l'histoire* (Paris, 1916).

21. See Hanna, *Mobilization*, 78–97, and Fritz Stern, *Dreams and Delusions: The Drama of German History* (New Haven, 1987), 257.

22. *Deutschland und der Weltkrieg*, ed. Hintze, Meinecke, Oncken, and Schumacher (Berlin, 1915), with contributions also by Troeltsch, Delbrück, Marcks, Schmoller, Hampe, and others as well as the editors; Eng. trans. William Wallace Whitelock, *Modern Germany in Relation to the Great War* (New York, 1916); and see Michael Dreyer and Oliver Lembcke, *Die deutsche Diskussion um die Kriegsschuldfrage 1918/19* (Berlin, 1993).

23. *Deutschland und England in See- und Weltgeltung* (Leipzig, 1915).

24. "The Spirit of German *Kultur*," in *Modern Germany*, tr. Whitelock, 56.

25. *A European Past: Memoirs, 1905–1945* (New York, 1988), 33.

26. Cited by Peter Novick, *That Noble Dream: The "Objectivity Question" in the*

American Historical Profession (Cambridge, 1988), 115; see also Carol S. Gruber, *Mars and Minerva: World War I and the Uses of Higher Learning in America* (Baton Rouge, 1975), and Georg G. Iggers, "Historians Confronted the War," *Storia della storiografia*, 42 (2002), 3–22, with further bibliography.

27. Preface to *Conquest and Kultur: Aims of the Germans in Their Own Words*, ed. Wallace Notestein and Elmer E. Stoll (Washington, 1917), 7; and see George T. Blakey, *Historians on the Homefront: American Propagandists for the Great War* (Lexington, Ky., 1970).

28. *England: Its Political Organization and Development and the War against Germany*, tr. Helene White (Boston, 1918), 60, 64, 328.

29. *Britain* versus *Germany: An Open Letter to Professor Eduard Meyer, Ph. D., Ll. D., of the University of Berlin* (London, 1917).

30. *America's Relation to the Great War* (Chicago, 1916).

31. Hans Peter Hanssen, *Diary of a Dying Empire*, tr. Oscar Osburn Winther (Bloomington, 1955), 103 (20 May 1915).

32. *Delbrück's Modern Military History*, tr. Arden Bucholz (Lincoln, Neb., 1997), 169.

33. *The World in Revolt: A Psychological Study of Our Times* (New York, 1921), 21.

34. *Weimar Culture*, 91.

35. Morey Rothberg (ed.), *John Franklin Jameson and the Development of Humanistic Scholarship in America* (Athens, Ga., 2001), 129; and *At the Paris Peace Conference* (New York, 1937); also Charles Homer Haskins and Robert Howard Lord, *Some Problems of the Peace Conference* (Cambridge, Mass., 1920).

36. See Agnes Headlam-Morley, Russell Bryant, and Anna Cienciala (eds.), *A Memoir of the Paris Peace Conference, 1919* (London, 1972).

37. Hans-Georg Drescher, *Ernst Troeltsch: His Life and Work*, tr. John Bowden (London, 1992), 261ff.; and see Pietro Rossi, *Le storicismo tedesco contemporaneo* (Turin, 1971).

38. Krill, *Die Ranke Renaissance*, 214; and on Haller see Fischer, *World Power or Decline*, 1.

39. Drescher, *Ernst Troeltsch*, 271.

40. *Zur Geschichte der Geschichtsschreibung*, ed. Eberhard Kessel (Munich, 1968), 183ff.

41. *The Historical Essays of Otto Hintze*, ed. Felix Gilbert (Oxford, 1975), 266; and Otto Büsch and Michael Erbe (eds.), *Otto Hintze und die moderne Geschichtswissenschaft* (Berlin, 1983).

42. *Historical Essays*, 821ff., 305ff.

43. *Ibid.*, 372.

44. *Ibid.*, 417.

45. *The Absoluteness of Christianity and the History of Religions*, tr. David Reid (Richmond, Va., 1971; 3rd ed. 1929), 25 (foreword, 1901); and Robert J. Rubanowice, *Crisis in Consciousness: The Thought of Ernst Troeltsch* (Tallahassee, 1982).

46. *Religion in History*, tr. James Luther Adams and Walter F. Bense (Minneapolis, 1991), 16.

47. *History as the Story of Liberty*, tr. Sylvia Sprigge (New York, 1941), 78.

48. *The Idea of History* (Oxford, 1946), 9–10.

49. *The Rise of Historicism*, 492.

50. "Kausalitäten und Werte in der Geschichte," *Historische Zeitschrift*, 124 (1928), 23.

51. See Marc Raeff, *Russia Abroad: A Cultural History of the Russian Emigration, 1919–1939* (New York, 1990), 156–86.

52. *Specters of Marx*, tr. Peggy Kamuf (New York, 1994).

53. *Black Athena: The Afroasiatic Roots of Classical Civilization*, I, *The Fabrication of Ancient Greece, 1785–1985* (New Brunswick, 1987), which castigates Elliot Smith and other archeologists and classicists for "Hellenomania," racism, and antisemitism; with vol. II (1991) this sensationalist work has generated a vast and tendentious literature, on which see *Black Athena Writes Back: Martin Bernal Responds to His Critics* (Durham, 2001).

54. Robert Sole, *Les Savants de Bonaparte* (Paris, 1998).

55. Daniel, *The Idea of Prehistory*, 79ff.; and see D. R. Kelley, "The Rise of Prehistory," *Journal of World History*, 14(2003), 17–36.

56. *Histoire ancienne de l'orient jusqu'aux guerres médiques* (Paris, 1881⁹), I, 119, 208, 263.

57. *Die Bevölkerung der griechisch-römischen Welt* (Leipzig, 1886).

58. Maurice Oleander, *The Languages of Paradise: Race, Religion, and Philology in the Nineteenth Century* (Cambridge, Mass., 1992).

59. O. G. S. Crawford, *Man and His Past* (Oxford, 1921), 32–33.

60. *The Dawn of History* (London, 1911), 13.

61. *The Ancient History of the Near East: From the Earliest Times to the Battle of Salamis* (London, 1960¹¹), 589ff.

62. See Jean Bottéro (ed.), *Initiation à l'Orient ancien: De Sumer à la Bible* (Paris, 1992).

63. Suzanne L. Marchand, *Archaeology and Philhellenism in Germany, 1750–1970* (Princeton, 1996), 162ff., 182.

64. Ibid., 240.

65. Beat Näf, "Eduard Meyers Geschichtstheorie. Entwicklung und zeitgenössische Reaktionen," in *Eduard Meyer: Leben und Leistung eines Universalhistorikers*, ed. William M. Calder III and Alexander Demandt (Leiden, 1990), 292.

66. Paul Petit, *Guide de l'étudiant en histoire ancienne* (Paris, 1959).

67. *A History of Greece to the Death of Alexander the Great* (New York, n. d.), "preface to the 1913 edition" and "preface to the first edition," and 838.

68. *History of the Later Roman Empire from the Death of Theodosius I to the Death of Justinian* (New York, 1958), I, 1, 9.

69. *Characters and Events of Roman History from Caesar to Nero* (Lowell Lectures, 1908), tr. Frances Lance Ferrero (New York, 1909), 243; and *The Ruin of Ancient Civilization and the Triumph of Christianity with Some Considerations of Conditions in the Europe of Today*, tr. Ady Whitehead (New York, 1921).

70. Léon Homo, *Primitive Italy and the Beginnings of Roman Imperialism*, tr. V. Gordon Childe (London, 1927), 2.

71. Ferrero, *Characters and Events*, 3; cf. Glover, *The Conflict of Religions in the Early Roman Empire* (Boston, 1909), 3.

72. See his three volumes (1898–1926) on Roman imperial society.

73. *Geschichte des Untergangs der antiken Welt* (6 vols.; Berlin, 1895–1920), VI, 380.

74. *The Social and Economic History of the Roman Empire* (Oxford, 1957² [1926]), 532ff.; and see Marinus A. Wes, *Michael Rostovtzeff, Historian in Exile* (Stuttgart, 1990).

75. See J. G. A. Pocock's massive reassessment of Gibbon's work, *Barbarism and Religion* (Cambridge, 1999–2003), 3 volumes so far.

76. *Early History of the Christian Church from Its Foundation to the End of the Third Century* (1906–10), Eng. tr. (New York, 1909), I, 145.

77. Ibid., III, 469.

78. See J. G. A. Pocock's work on Gibbon.

79. *Poems for the Millennium*, ed. Jerome Rothenberg and Pierre Joris, I (Berkeley, 1995), 275.

80. W. M. Simon, *European Positivism in the Nineteenth Century: An Essay in Intellectual History* (Ithaca, 1963).

81. *Historical Philosophy in France and French Belgium and Switzerland* (New York, 1894); and see D. R. Kelley, "Robert Flint, Historian of Ideas," *Storiografia*, 27 (1995), 1–17.

82. *Grundriss der Historik*, 38, 49.

83. See Tagliacozzo, *The Arbor Scientiae Reconceived and the History of Vico's Resurrection* (Atlantic Highlands, N.J., 1993).

84. Kelley, *Faces of History* (New Haven, 1998), 223.

85. Lukács, *The Historical Novel*, tr. Hannah Mitchell and Stanley Mitchell (London, 1962), 285.

86. *The Materialist Conception of History*, tr. Raymond Meyer, with John Kautsky (New Haven, 1988); and see M. M. Bober, *Karl Marx's Interpretation of History* (Cambridge, Mass., 1927).

87. *History and Class Consciousness*, tr. Rodney Livingstone (London, 1971).

88. *The Unity of Western Civilization* (Oxford, 1915), 17.

89. *The Problems of the Philosophy of History: An Epistemological Essay*, tr. Guy Oakes (New York, 1977), 39.

90. Collingwood, *The Idea of History* (Oxford, 1993²), 171.

91. *Ideology and Utopia: An Introduction to the Sociology of Knowledge*, tr. Louis Wirth and Edward Shils (New York, 1952), 82.

92. Paul Kecskemeti (ed.), *Essays on the Sociology of Knowledge* (New York, 1952), 38.

93. *The Meaning of History*, tr. George Reavey (New York, 1936), based on lectures given in Moscow in 1919–20.

94. *Modern Historians and the Study of History* (London, 1955), 191 (1931).

95. *Geschichte also Sinngebung des Sinnlosen, oder die Geburt der Geschichte aus dem Mythos* (Hamburg, 1962 [1927]), 41, 93.

96. Breysig, *Der Stufenbau und die Gesetz der Weltgeschichte* (Stuttgart, 1927 [1905]), and see Bernhard vom Brock, *Kurt Breysig: Geschichtswissenschaft zwischen Historismus und Soziologie* (Lübeck, 1971); Alfred Weber, *Kulturgeschichte als Kultursoziologie* (Munich, 1960 [1935]).

97. See J. H. J. van der Pot, *De Periodisering der Geschiedenis* (The Hague, 1951).

98. *Der Historismus und seine Probleme* (Tübingen, 1922), and see Karl Heussi, *Die Krisis des Historismus* (Tübingen, 1932).

99. *History, Its Theory and Practice*, tr. Douglas Ainslie (New York, 1920); *What Is Living and What Is Dead in the Philosophy of Hegel*, tr. Ainslie (New York, 1915); *La Filosofia di Giambattista Vico* (Bari, 1911); *History as the Story of Liberty*, tr. Sylvia Sprigge (New York, 1941); and *Storia della storiografia italiana nel secolo decimonono* (2 vols.; Bari, 1920); and see David Roberts, *Benedetto Croce and the Uses of Historicism* (Berkeley, 1987).

100. *Creative Evolution*, tr. Arthur Mitchell (New York, 1911), 114.

101. *The Making of Europe: An Introduction to the History of European Unity* (London, 1946) and *Progress and Religion* (London, 1960), and see Stratford Caldecott and John Morrill (eds.), *Eternity in Time: Christopher Dawson and the Catholic Idea of History* (Edinburgh, 1997).

102. "Gnostic Politics" (1952), *The Collected Works*, X, *Published Essays 1940–1952* (Columbia, Mo., 2000), 227; and see *Autobiographical Reflections*, ed. Ellis Sandoz (Baton, Rouge, 1989).

103. *Man the Measure: A New Approach to History* (Cleveland, 1967 [1943]), 639.

104. *What Is History? and Other Late Unpublished Writings*, ed. Thomas A. Hollweck and Paul Caringolla (Baton Rouge, 1990), 1–2 (c. 1963).

105. *The Idea of History*, 63, 88.

106. *Autobiography* (Oxford, 1939), 37; and see William Dray, *History as Re-Inactment: R. G. Collingwood's Idea of History* (Oxford, 1995).

107. *The Origins and Diversity of Axial Civilizations*, ed. S. N. Eisenstadt (Albany, 1986).

108. *The Interpretation of History*, tr. M. A. Hamilton (New York, 1911), 2, and see Daniel Pick, *Faces of Degeneration: A European Disorder, c. 1848–c. 1918* (Cambridge, 1989), 24–25.

109. *Interpretation*, 102; and see Barth, "Die Philosophie der Geschichte als Soziologie," *L'Année Sociologique*, 1 (1896–97), 116–23.

110. *Interpretation*, 354.

111. *A Cultural History of the Modern Age*, tr. Charles Francis Atkinson, III (New York, 1933), 457, 467.

112. *The Concept of the Political*, tr. George Schwab (Chicago, 1996), 35, and see Gopal Balakrishnan, *The Enemy: An Intellectual Portrait of Carl Schmitt* (London, 2000); also Jeffrey Barash, *Politique de l'histoire: L'Historicisme comme promesse et comme mythe* (Paris, 2004).

113. "History as a System," *Philosophy and History: The Ernst Cassirer Festschrift*, ed. Raymond Klibansky and H. J. Paton (Oxford, 1936), 277–82; and see John T. Graham, *Theory of History in Ortega y Gasset: "The Dawn of Historical Reason"* (Columbia, Mo., 1997), 15, 39, 161, *A Pragmatist Philosophy of Life in Ortega y Gasset* (Columbia, Mo., 1994), and *The Social Thought of Ortega y Gasset: A Systematic Synthesis in Postmodernism and Interdisciplinarity* (Columbia, Mo., 2001); also Rockwell Gray, *The Imperative of Modernity: An Intellectual Biography of José Ortega y Gasset* (Berkeley, 1989).

114. *History as a System*, tr. Helene Weyl (New York, 1961), 216.

115. *The Revolt of the Masses*, tr. anon. (New York, 1950), 135.

116. *In the Shadow of Tomorrow*, tr. J. H. Huizinga (New York, 1936), 89.

117. Ibid., 109.

118. Ibid., 148.

119. *Truth and Opinion* (London, 1960), 15.

120. *The King's Peace* (London, 1955), 16.

121. *Everyman His Own Historian* (New York, 1935).

122. Joseph Schumpeter, *Capitalism, Socialism, and Democracy* (New York, 1950³), 5.

123. See Jacques Derrida, *The Spectre of Marx*, tr. Peggy Kamuf (London, 1994).

Chapter 3. After the Great War

1. *Four Quartets* (New York, 1943), 24.

2. *The Revolt of the Masses*, tr. anon. (New York, 1957), 194.

3. See Hugo Ott, *Martin Heidegger, A Political Life*, tr. Allan Blunden (New York, 1993).

4. *Delbrück's Modern Military History*, tr. Arden Bucholz (Lincoln, Neb., 1997), 192.

5. Renouvin, *The Immediate Origins of the War*, tr. Thomas Carnwell Hume (New Haven, 1928), 1.

6. *Priester der Klio: Historisch sozialwissenschaftliche Studien zur Herkunft und Karriere deutsche Historiker und zur Geschichte der Geschichtswissenschaft 1800–1970* (Frankfurt, 1987).

7. Hartung, *Deutsche Geschichte vom Frankfurter Frieden bis zum Vertrag von Versailles* (Leipzig, 1924²), 373; and *Jurist unter vier Reichen* (Cologne, 1971), 27.

8. Andreas, *Staatskunst und Diplomatie der Venetianer* (Leipzig, 1943).

9. Willi Oberkrome, *Volksgeschichte: Methodologische Innovation und Völkische Ideolosierung in der deutschen Geschichtswissenschaft 1918–1945* (Göttingen, 1993).

10. Kehr, *Economic Interest, Militarism, and Foreign Policy*, tr. Grete Heinz (Berkeley, 1937), intro. by Gordon A. Graig, and see Peter Paret, Introduction to Meinecke, *The Age of German Liberation*, xvi; also Hans Schleier, *Die bürgerliche deutsche Geschichtsschreibung der Weimarer Republik* (Berlin, 1975).

11. *Reflections of a Nonpolitical Man*, tr. Walter D. Morris (New York, 1983), 210.

12. Gilbert, *A European Past: Memoirs, 1905–1945* (New York, 1988), 83.

13. *History of Economic Analysis* (New York, 1954), 818.

14. *General Economic History*, tr. Frank H. Knight (New York, 1961), and on Schmoller and Sombart see Wolfgang J. Mommsen and Jürgen Osterhammel (eds.), *Max Weber and His Contemporaries* (London, 1987), 59, 99.

15. Georg von Below, *Die italienische Kaiserpolitik des deutschen Mittelalters mit besonderem Hinblick auf die Politik Friederick Barbarossas* (Munich, 1927).

16. *Die Wandlungen des grossdeutschen Gedankens* (Stuttgart, 1924).

17. Friedrich Schneider, *Die neueren Anschauungen der deutschen Historiker über die deutsche Kaiserpolitik des Mittelalters* (Weimar, 1940 [1934]); Gerd Althoff (ed.), *Die Deutschen und ihr Mittelalter: Themen und Funktionem moderner Geschichtsbilder vom*

Mittelalter (Darmstadt, 1992); Heinrich Hostenkamp, *Die mittelalterliche Kaiserpolitik in der deutschen Historiographie seit v. Sybel und Ficker* (Berlin, 1934); Raoul Manselli and Josef Riedmann (ed.), *Federico Barbarossa nel dibasttito storiografico in Italia e in Germania* (Bologna, 1982); and Patrick J. Geary, *Medieval Germany in America* (Washington D.C., 1996).

18. *European Literature and the Latin Middle Ages,* tr. Willard Trask (Princeton, 1973), 7.

19. Kantorowicz, *Frederick the Second, 1194–1250,* tr. E. O. Lorimer (London, 1931). See Robert L. Benson and Johannes Fried (eds.), *Ernst Kantorowicz: Erträge der Doppeltagung. Institute for Advanced Study, Princeton, Johann Wolfgang Goethe-Universität, Frankfurt* (Stuttgart, 1997): Kantorowicz, "Das Geheime Deutschland" (1933), 77–93; Yakov Malkiel in Arthur R. Evans, Jr., *On Four Modern Humanists* (Princeton, 1970); R. Howard Bloch and Stephen G. Nichols (eds.), *Medievalism and the Modern Temper* (Baltimore, 1996), including Otto Gerhard Oexle, "German Malaise of Modernity: Ernst H. Kantorowicz and his 'Kaiser Friedrich der Zweite,'" 33–56; Robert E. Lerner, "Kantorowicz and Continuity"; Eckhart Grünewald, "'Not Only in Learned Circles': The Reception of *Frederick the Second* in Germany before the Second World War," 162–79; and Alain Boureau, "Kantorowicz, or the Middle Ages as Refuge," 355–67; Robert E. Lerner, "Ernst Kantorowicz and Theodor E. Mommsen," *An Interrupted Past: German-Speaking Refugee Historians in the United States after 1933,* ed. Hartmut Lehman and James J. Sheehan (Cambridge, 1991), 188–205; Boureau, *Kantorowicz: Stories of a Historian,* tr. Stephen G. Nichols and Gabrielle M. Spiegel (Baltimore, 2001); Karl Hampe, *Kaiser Friedrich II in der Auffassung der Nachwelt* (Berlin, 1925); and Gunther Wolf (ed.), *Stupor Mundi: Zur Geschichte Friedrichs II von Hohenstaufen* (Darmstadt, 1966).

20. See Robert E. Norton, *Secret Germany: Stefan George and His Circle* (Ithaca, 2002), and Eckart Grünewald, *Ernst Kantorowicz und Stefan George* (Wiesbaden, 1982).

21. *Frederick II, 1194–1250,* tr. E. O. Lorimer (New York, 1931), 688.

22. "The Beginnings of the National State in Medieval Germany and the Norman Monarchies" (1936), *Medieval Germany, 911–1250,* ed. and tr. Geoffrey Barraclough (Oxford, 1948), 281–99.

23. "The State of the Dukes of Zähringen," in Barraclough, 175–202.

24. *The King's Two Bodies* (Princeton, 1957), and cf. Carl Schmitt, *Politische Theologie* (Munich, 1922) and *Politische Theologie II* (Berlin, 1970).

25. Albrecht Wirth, *Völkische Weltgeschichte 1879–1933* (Braunschweig, 1934), 531.

26. Fueter, *Geschichte der neueren Historiographie* (Munich, 1911), and see Horst Walter Blanke, *Historiographiegeschichte als Historik* (Stuttgart, 1991), dedicated to Fueter.

27. *Die deutsche Geschichtschreibung von der Befreiungskriegen bis zu unsern Tagen* (Munich, 1924), 159.

28. *The Epochs of German History* (London, 1930), 239; cf. *Wendepunkte der deutschen Geschichte* (Cologne, 1934).

29. Marcks, *Englands Machtpolitik: Vorträge und Studien,* ed. Willy Andreas (Stuttgart, 1940).

30. *Tausend Jahre deutsch-französischen Beziehungen* (Stuttgart, 1930).

31. See Michael Burleigh, *Germany Turns East: A Study of* Ostforschung *in the Third Reich* (Cambridge, 1988); W. Wippermann, *Der deutsche Drang nach Osten* (Berlin, 1981); Gerd Althoff, "Die Bedeutung des mittelalterlichen Ostpolitik als Paradigma für zeitgebundene Geschichtswertung," *Die Deutschen und ihr Mittelalter,* 147–64.

32. Hampe, *Der Zug nach dem Osten* (Leipzig, 1935³), 1921.

33. *Belgiens Vergangenheit und Gegenwart* (Berlin, 1916).

34. Brackmann (ed.), *Deutschland und Polen: Beiträge zu ihren geschichtlichen Beziehungen* (Munich, 1933).

35. Karen Schönwälder, *Historiker und Politik: Geschichtswissenschaft im Nationalsozialismus* (Frankfurt, 1992); Karl Ferdinand Werner, *Das N-S Geschichtsbild und die deutsche Geschichtswissenschaft* (Stuttgart, 1967); Bernd Faulenbach, *Ideologie des deutschen Weges: Die deutsche Geschichte in der Historiographie zwischen Kaiserreich und Nationalsozialismus* (Munich, 1980); Weber, *Priester der Klio;* Helmut Heiber, *Walter Frank und sein Reivchsinstitut für Geschichte des neuen Deutschlands* (Stuttgart, 1966); and Ursula Wolf, *Litteris et Patriae: Das Janusgeschicht der Historie* (Stuttgart, 1996).

36. See Douglas Tobler, "Walter Goetz: Historian for the Republic," *Historians in Politics,* ed. Walter Laqueur and George L. Mosse (London, 1974), 223–51.

37. Wolfgang Mommsen, "German Historiography during the Weimar Republic and the Émigré Historians," Michael H. Kater, "Refugee Historians in America: Premigration Germany to 1939," and Felix Gilbert, "The Berlin Historical Seminar in the Twenties," in *An Interrupted Past,* ed. Lehman and Sheehan, 32–66, 73–93, 67–72; also Geoff Eley, *From Unification to Nazism: Reinterpreting the German Past* (Boston, 1986).

38. *Man in the Modern Age,* tr. Eden Paul and Cedar Paul (New York, 1933).

39. Karl Dietrich Erdmann, *Die Ökumene der Historiker: Geschichte der Internationalen Historikerkongresse und des Comité des Science Historiques* (Göttingen, 1987).

40. *English Democratic Ideas in the 17ᵗʰ Century* (New York, 1959 [1898]), 304.

41. Frank Eyck, *G. P. Gooch: A Study in History and Politics* (London, 1982).

42. *Chapters in The Administrative History of Mediaeval England* (6 vols.; Manchester, 1920–33); see P. B. M. Blaas, *Continuity and Anachronism: Parliamentary and Constitutional Development in Whig Historiography and in the Anti-Whig Reactions between 1890 and 1930* (The Hague, 1978), 345–73, and F. M. Powicke, "The Manchester History School," in *Modern Historians and the Study of History* (London, 1955), 19ff.

43. Seligman, *The Economic Interpretation of History* (New York, 1902), 163; Toynbee, *Lectures on the Industrial Revolution of the Eighteenth Century in England* (London, 1928), 6.

44. See, e.g., William Ashley, "On the Study of Economic History," *Quarterly Journal of Economics* (Jan. 1893), 115–36.

45. *Economic Development of France and Germany, 1815–1914* (Cambridge, 1968⁴), 402.

46. Maxine Berg, *A Woman in History: Eileen Power, 1889–1940* (Cambridge, 1996). and Madeline R. Robinton, "Eileen Power (1889–1940)," *Some Modern Historians of Britain,* ed. H. Ausubel et al. (New York, 1951), 358–76.

47. *Medieval English Nunneries, c. 1275 to 1535* (Cambridge, 1922), xviii.

48. *Medieval People* (New York, n. d. [1924]), 15, 16, 36, 124.

49. *An Economic History of Modern Britain*, I, *The Early Railway Age, 1820–1850* (Cambridge, 1926), viii.

50. Victor Feske, *From Belloc to Churchill: Private Scholars, Public Culture, and the Crisis of British Liberalism, 1900–1939* (Chapel Hill, 1996).

51. *A History of the English Agricultural Labourer*, tr. Ruth Kenyon (London, 1920), vii.

52. *The Village Labourer: A Study of the Government of England before the Reform Bill; The Town Labourer, 1760–1832; The Skilled Labourer, 1760–1832* (3 vols. in 1; London, 1995); and see Stewart Weaver, *The Hammonds: A Marriage in History* (Stanford, 1997).

53. *A Short History of the British Working-Class Movement, 1789–1947* (London, 1948); and see Margaret Cole, *The Life of G. D. H. Cole* (London, 1971).

54. *The History of Trade Unionism* (London, 1920), 718.

55. Tawney, *The Acquisitive Society* (New York, 1948 [1920]); see Ross Terrill, *R. H. Tawney and His Times: Socialism as Fellowship* (Cambridge, Mass., 1973), John Kenyon, "Tawney and Social History," *The History Men* (London, 1983), 235–50, and W. H. Nelson, "R. H. Tawney," in *Some Modern Historians of Britain*, ed. Ausubel et al., 325–40.

56. *Religion and the Rise of Capitalism* (New York, 1953 [1926]), 230, 39.

57. See Harvey J. Kaye, *The British Historians* (London, 1984), on Dobb, Hilton, Hill, and Hobsbawm.

58. *The World Turned Upside Down: Radical Ideas During the English Revolution* (New York, 1972), 336.

59. *The Making of the English Working Class* (New York, 1963), 84.

60. Ibid., 195.

61. *Marxism and Literature* (Oxford, 1977), 16, extending his argument from *Culture and Society* (1958), *The Long Revolution* (1961), and *Keywords* (1976); and also *The Politics of Modernism: Against the New Conformists.* (London, 1989).

62. *The Coming of the French Revolution*, tr. R. R. Palmer (New York, 1957) and *The Great Fear of 1789*, tr. Joan White (New York, 1973).

63. Febvre, *De la Revue de Synthèse aux Annales: Lettres à Henri Berr 1911–1954*, ed. Gilles Candas and Jacqueline Pluet-Despatin (Paris, 1997), and Bloch-Febvre, *Correspondance*, ed. Bertrand Müller, I, *La Naissance des* Annales *1928–1933* (Paris, 1994), II and III (Paris, 2003).

64. *Pour une histoire à part entière* (Paris, 1962), *Combats pour l'histoire* (Paris, 1953), *Au Coeur religieux du XVIᵉ siècle* (Paris, 1957); and *A New Kind of History*, ed. P. Burke (London, 1973).

65. Peter Burke, *The French Historical Revolution: The* Annales School, *1929–89* (Stanford, 1990); Philippe Carrard, *Poetics of the New History: French Historical Discourse from Braudel to Chartier* (Baltimore, 1992); François Dosse, *New History in France: The Triumph of the* Annales, tr. Peter V. Conroy, Jr. (Urbana, 1994); and Traian Stoianovich, *French Historical Method: The Annales Paradigm* (Ithaca, 1976).

66. *A New Kind of History*, 11.

67. *Ibid.*, 145.

68. *Comment on écrit l'histoire: essai d'epistémologie* (Paris, 1971), 296.

69. *Combats pour l'histoire* and *Pour une histoire à part entière.*

70. *The Problem of Unbelief in Sixteenth-Century France: The Religion of Rabelais,* tr. Beatrice Gottlieb (Cambridge, Mass., 1982), 18.

71. See, e.g., Alan Charles Kors, *Atheism in France, 1650–1729* (Princeton, 1990), I, 9.

72. Carole Fink, *Marc Bloch: A Life in History* (Cambridge, 1989), and see Hartmut Atsma and André Burghière (eds.), *Marc Bloch aujourd'hui: Histoire comparé et sciences sociales* (Paris, 1990).

73. *The Royal Touch: Sacred Monarchy and Scrofula in England and France,* tr. J. E. Anderson (London, 1973), 243.

74. "A Contribution towards a Comparative History of European Societies," *Life and Work in Medieval Europe,* tr. J. E. Anderson (London, 1967), 47; from *Project d'un enseignement d'histoire comparée des sociétés européennes* (Strasbourg, 1933); and cf. Susan Reynolds, *Fiefs and Vassals: The Medieval Evidence Reinterpreted* (Oxford, 1994), 479, concluding, "First there is a need for comparison."

75. *La Société féodale* (Paris, 1949), II, 252: "D'autres sociétés ont-elles également passé par [cette phase de féodalité]? Et, s'il en a été ainsi, sous l'action de quelles causes, peut-être communes? C'est le secret des travaux futurs." And see D. R. Kelley, "Grounds for Comparison," *Storia della storiografia,* 39 (2001), 3–16.

76. *French Rural History: An Essay on Its Basic Characteristics,* tr. Janet Sondheimer (Berkeley, 1966), 247, 70.

77. *La Société féodale* (Paris, 1940), II, 257.

78. *An Historian's World,* ed. Elizabeth Donnan and Leo F. Stock (Philadelphia, 1956), 104 (letter of 31 Jan. 1907).

79. *Methods of Teaching History* (Boston, 1883), published in the "Pedagogical Library" edited by G. Stanley Hall.

80. *The History of Historical Writing in America* (Boston, 1891), 141; *An Historian's World,* 105 (letter to James Bryce, 17 April 1907); and Morey Rothberg and Jacqueline Goggin (eds.), *John Franklin Jameson and the Development of Humanistic Scholarship in America* (Athens, Ga., 1993), I, 166; also Ellen Fitzpatrick, *History's Memory: Writing America's Past, 1880–1980.* (Cambridge, Mass., 2002).

81. *An Historian's World,* 236 (letter of 31 March 1919).

82. Ibid., 302 (letter of 6 Oct. 1924).

83. Morey Rothberg (ed.), *John Franklin Jameson and the Development of Humanistic Scholarship in America* (Athens, Ga., 2001), III, 148.

84. See Lee Benson, *Turner and Beard: American Historical Writing Reconsidered* (Westport, 1960).

85. Lucy Maynard Salmon, *History and the Texture of Modern Life: Selected Essays,* ed. Nicholas Adams and Bonnie G. Smith (Philadelphia, 2001), 169ff.

86. *World Politics and Modern Civilization* (New York, 1930), 465–67; and see especially Arthur Goddard (ed.), *Harry Elmer Barnes, Learned Crusader* (Colorado Springs, 1968).

87. Rothberg (ed.), *John Franklin Jameson,* III, 205; and see D. R. Kelley, "The Prehistory of Sociology: Montesquieu, Vico, and the Legal Tradition," *Journal of the History of the Behavioral Sciences,* 16 (1980), 133–44.

88. *A History of Historical Writing* (New York, 1963 [1937]), 289.

89. *The Cultural Approach to History,* ed. Caroline Ware (New York, 1940).

90. *The Autobiography of James T. Shotwell* (New York, 1961), 69.

91. *History of the United States from the Compromise of 1850* (7 vols.; New York, 1892–1906); and see Robert Cruden, *James Ford Rhodes: The Man, the Historian, the Work* (Cleveland, 1961), 43.

92. *History of the People of the United States from the Revolution to the Civil War* (5 vols.; New York, 1883); and see Eric Goldman, *John Bach McMaster* (New York, 1943).

93. *The Rise of American Civilization* (New York, 1937 [1927]), II, 837.

94. *New Viewpoints in American History* (New York, 1922); cf. *In Retrospect: The History of a Historian* (New York, 1963), 36.

95. *A Century of Progress* (New York, 1932).

96. Gregory M. Pfitzer, *Samuel Eliot Morison's Historical World: In Quest of a New Parkman* (Boston, 1991).

97. Morison, *The Intellectual Life of Colonial New England* (New York, 1956), originally published as *The Puritan Pronaos* (1936).

98. *The Renaissance of the Twelfth Century* (New York, 1957 [1927]), 275.

99. *That Noble Dream: The "Objectivity Question" in the American Historical Profession* (Cambridge, 1988), and see Allan Megill (ed.), *Rethinking Objectivity* (Durham, 1994).

100. Novick, *That Noble Dream,* 161.

101. *The Gateway to History* (New York, 1938).

102. Louis L. Snyder, *Global Mini-Nationalisms: Autonomy or Independence* (London, 1982).

103. Dragoslav Jankovic, *The Historiography of Yugoslavia, 1965–1975* (Belgrade, 1975); and Ivo Banec, "The Dissolution of Yugoslav Historiography," *Beyond Yugoslavia: Politics, Economics, and Culture in a Shattered Community,* ed. S. Ramet and L. Adamovich (Boulder, 1995).

104. H. W. von der Dunk, "Pieter Geyl: History as a Form of Self-Expression," *Clio's Mirror: Historiography in Britain and the Netherlands,* ed. A. C. Duke and C. A. Tamse (Zutphen, 1985), 185–214.

105. Herbert Dachs, *Österreichische Geschichtswissenschaft und Anschluss* (Vienna, 1974); Günther Ramhardter, *Geschichtswissenschaft und Patriotismus österreichische Historiker im Weltkrieg 1914–1918* (Vienna, 1973).

106. Steven Bela Vardy, *Modern Hungarian Historiography* (New York, 1976), and for the Marxist line Tibor Erdey-Grúz and Imre Trancsényi-Waldapfel (eds.), *Science in Hungary* (Budapest, 1965), 161–78.

107. Lee Congdon, "The Moralist as Social Thinker: Oskár Jászi in Hungary 1900–1919," in *Historians in Politics,* 273–313.

108. See Peter Brock, *The Slovak National Awakening: An Essay in the Intellectual History of East Central Europe* (Toronto, 1976), and Horst Glassl, *Die Slovakische Geschichtswissenschaft nach 1945* (Wiesbaden, 1971).

109. See Marian Leczek (ed.), *La Science historique polonaise dans l'historiographie mondiale* (Wroclaw, 1990).

110. Frederick G. Heyman, "The Hussite Movement in the Historiography of the

Czech Renaissance of the Nineteenth Century," *The Czech Renaissance of the Nineteenth Century*, ed. Peter Brock and H. Gordon Skilling (Toronto, 1970), 224–38.

111. See William H. Hubbard et al. (eds.), *Making a Historical Culture: Historiography in Norway* (Oslo, 1995).

112. Al. Zub, *Alexandru Xenopol: L'Historiographie roumaine à l'âge de la synthèse* (Bucarest, 1983).

113. *History and Myth in Romanian Consciousness* (Budapest, 1997), and cf. George S. Williamson, *The Legacy of Myth in Germany: Religion and Aesthetic Culture from Romanticism to Nietzsche* (Chicago, 2004).

114. Kunigas Antanas Jusaitis, *The History of the Lithuanian Nation and Its Present National Aspiration*, tr. anon (Philadelphia, 1918), preface; and cf. Constantine R. Jurgéla, *History of the Lithuanian Nation* (New York, 1948), 13, with a "hope for a brighter tomorrow."

115. Snyder, *Global Mini-Nationalisms*, 21.

116. See Alan Dingdale, *Mapping Modernities: Geographies of Central and Eastern Europe, 1920–2000* (London, 2002).

Chapter 4. Modern Times

1. *The Waste Land*.

2. *Poetry, Language, Thought*, tr. Albert Hofstadter (New York, 1971), 91.

3. *Canto* LIII.

4. See among others John Higham, Leonard Krieger, and Felix Gilbert, *History: The Development of Historical Studies in the United States* (Englewood Cliffs, N.J., 1965); L. P. Curtis, Jr. (ed.), *The Historian's Workshop* (New York, 1970); Felix Gilbert and Stephen R. Graubard (eds.), *Historical Studies Today* (New York, 1972); *The New Cambridge Modern History*, XIII, *Companion Volume*, ed. Peter Burke (Cambridge, 1979); Michael Kammen (ed.), *The Past before Us: Contemporary Historical Writing in the United States* (Ithaca, 1980); Juliet Gardiner (ed.), *What Is History Today?* (Atlantic Highlands, N.J., 1988); Peter Burke (ed.), *New Perspectives on Historical Writing* (University Park, Pa., 1991); Maria Lúcia Palares-Burke (ed.), *The New History* (Cambridge, 2002); and Lutz Raphael, *Geschichtswissenschaft im Zeitalter der Extreme* (Munich, 2003)

5. *Honneur et patrie* (Paris, 1996).

6. Marc Bloch, Lucien Febvre, *Les Annales d'Histoire Economique et Sociale, Correspondance*, ed. Bertrand Müller, III, 1938–1943 (Paris, 2003).

7. *The Historian's Craft*, tr. Peter Putnam (New York, 1953), 8.

8. *Ibid.*, 13.

9. *Ibid.*, 178; cf. Varga, *Das Schlagwort von "Finsteren Mittelalter"* (Baden, 1932), and Peter Schöttler (ed.), *Les Autorités invisibles: une historienne autrichienne aux Annales dans les années trente* (Paris, 1991).

10. *The Historian's Craft*, 197.

11. *A Study of History*, IX (Oxford, 1954), 409.

12. See the two volumes commemorating the centenary of his death in 1986: Wolfgang J. Mommsen (ed.), *Leopold von Ranke und die moderne Geschichtswissenschaft* (Stutt-

gart, 1988), and Georg G. Iggers and James M. Powell (eds.), *Leopold von Ranke and the Shaping of the Historical Discipline* (Syracuse, 1990).

13. Gilbert, *History: Politics or Culture? Reflections on Ranke and Burckhardt* (Princeton, 1990).

14. See Georg G. Iggers, *Historiography in the Twentieth Century: From Scientific Objectivity to Postmodern Challenge* (Hanover, N.H., 1997), and *New Directions in European Historiography* (Middletown, Conn., 1984²).

15. See Massimo Salvadori, *Gaetano Salvemini* (Turin, 1963).

16. See Brunello Vigezzi (ed.), *Federico Chabod e la "Nouva Storiografia" Italiano dal Primo al Secondo Dopoguerra, 1919–1950* (Milan, 1984), and Eric Cochrane and John Tedeschi, "Delio Cantimori: Historian (1904–1966), *Journal of Modern History,* 39 (1967), 438–45.

17. See David D. Roberts, *Benedetto Croce and the Uses of Historicism* (Berkeley, 1987), 294.

18. *The Mind and Method of the Historian,* tr. Siân Reynolds and Ben Reynolds (Chicago, 1978), 1.

19. Braudel, *Ecrits sur l'histoire* (Paris, 1969), 11–13; and see Febvre, *Pour une histoire à part entière,* 176; also John A. Marino (ed.), *Early Modern History and the Social Sciences: Testing the Limits of Braudel's Mediterranean* (Kirksville, Mo., 2002).

20. *Ecrits,* 24.

21. Cited by Carole Fink, *Marc Bloch: A Life in History* (Cambridge, 1989), 50.

22. *The Identity of France,* tr. Siân Reynolds (New York, 1988), 17–18. See Pierre Daix, *Braudel* (Paris, 1995); and Marino (ed.), *Early Modern History.*

23. Private letter to Hexter (author's copy); and see Samuel Kinser, "Annaliste Paradigm? The Geohistorical Structuralism of F. Braudel," *American Historical Review,* 86 (1981), 63–105.

24. *Introduction à la France moderne: Essai de psychologie historique 1500–1640* (Paris, 1961).

25. *Elizabeth I and Her Parliaments, 1559–1581* (New York, 1952).

26. *1848: The Revolution of the Intellectuals* (London, 1944).

27. *In the Margin of History* (London, 1939), 26.

28. *England in the Age of the American Revolution* (New York, 1966 [1930]), 40; and see Linda Colley, *Namier* (New York, 1989).

29. *The Roman Revolution* (Oxford, 1960 [1939]), preface.

30. *George III and the Historians* (New York, 1959 [1957]), 211–13, 7, 198, etc.; and see John Kenyon, *The History Men* (London, 1983), 251–69.

31. *The Whig Interpretation of History* (New York, 1965 [1931]); and see C. T. McIntire, *Herbert Butterfield: Historian as Dissenter* (New Haven, 2004).

32. *The Englishman and His History* (Cambridge, 1944) and *Man on His Past: The Study of the History of Historical Scholarship* (Cambridge, 1955).

33. *The Englishman and His History,* 138.

34. *Man on His Past,* 205–6. Starting graduate school in 1955, I thought that La Popelinière was my discovery; see my "History as a Calling: The Case of La Popelinière," *Renaissance Studies in Honor of Hans Baron* (Florence, 1971), 771–89.

35. *Man on His Past,* viii.

36. *The Origins of History* (New York, 1981), 48.

37. Walter Carruthers Sellar and Robert Julian Yeatman, *1066 and All That* (London, 1931[15]), vii.

38. *The Struggle for Mastery in Europe, 1848–1918* (Oxford, 1954), xix, and see Robert Cole, *A. J. P. Taylor: The Traitor within the Gates* (New York, 1993).

39. *English History, 1914–1945* (Oxford, 1965), 600.

40. *Mediaeval Germany, 911–1250*, II, *Essays* (Oxford, 1948 [1938]), 281–99.

41. *The Origins of Modern Germany* (Oxford, 1947), 466.

42. *The Social Interpretation of the French Revolution* (Cambridge, 1964).

43. *What Is History?* (New York, 1961), 76.

44. *The Englishman and His History*, 82.

45. *An Introduction to Contemporary History* (New York, 1964), 23.

46. Kurt W. Forster (ed.), *Aby Warburg: The Renewal and Pagan Antiquity* (Los Angeles, 1999); Peter Alter (ed.), *Out of the Third Reich: Refugee Historians in Post-War Britain* (London, 1998).

47. Cited by David S. Luft, *Robert Musil and the Crisis of European Culture, 1880–1942* (Berkeley, 1980), 269.

48. *Kaiser, Rom und Renovatio* (Darmstadt, 1957 [1929]).

49. Franz Schnabel, *Deutsche Geschichte in neunzehnten Jahrhundert* (4 vols.; Freiburg, 1959[5]); and see Thomas Hertfelder, *Franz Schnabel und die deutsche Geschichtswissenschaft* (2 vols.; Göttingen, 1998).

50. Srbik, *Deutsche Einheit: Idee und Wirklichkeit vom heiligen Reich bis Königgratz* (4 vols.; Munich, 1935–42).

51. Richard Benz, *Geist und Reich um die Bestimmung des deutschen Volkes* (Jena, 1933).

52. *Europa und die Welt* (Hamburg, 1937).

53. *Reichsgründung* (2 vols.; Leipzig, 1916), II, 432, and *Von Bismarck zum Weltkrieg* (Darmstadt, 1939), 595; Eng. tr. *From Bismarck to the World War: A History of German Foreign Policy, 1870–1914*, tr. Annie Elizabeth Adams (London, 1927).

54. *I Will Bear Witness: A Diary of the Nazi Years, 1933–1941*, tr. Martin Chalmers (2 vols.; New York, 1998), I, 24, 64, 74, 77.

55. *I Will Bear Witness*, II, 12 (8 Feb. 1942).

56. Winfried Schulte, *Deutsche Geschichtswissenschaft nach 1945* (Munich, 1989).

57. See Peter N. Miller, "Nazis and Neo-Stoics: Otto Brunner and Gerhard Oestreich before and after the Second World War," *Past and Present*, 176 (2002), 144–86.

58. Stefan Berger, *The Search for Normality: National Identity and Historical Consciousness in Germany since 1800* (Providence, 1997).

59. *The German Catastrophe*, tr. Sidney B. Fay (Cambridge, Mass., 1950), 10, and see Dehio, *Germany and World Politics in the Twentieth Century*, tr. Dieter Pevsner (New York, 1959), 13.

60. Wolfgang Petke, "Karl Brandi und die Geschichtswissenschaft," *Geschichtswissenschaft in Göttingen*, ed. Hartmut Boockmann and Hermann Wellenreuther (Göttingen, 1987), 287–320.

61. Karen Schönwalder, *Historiker und Politik: Geschtswissenschaft im Nationalismus* (Frankfurt, 1992), 207.

62. *Die Dämonie der Macht: Betrachtungen über Geschichte und Wesen des Macht-problems im politischen Denken der Neuzeit* (Stuttgart, n.d.[5]).

63. *The German Problem: Basic Questions of German Political Life, Past and Present* (Columbus, 1965).

64. Wolfgang J. Mommsen, *The Return to the Western Tradition: German Historiography since 1945* (Washington, D.C., 1991), 8.

65. *Germany and World Politics*, 65.

66. *The Precarious Balance: Four Centuries of the European Power Struggle*, tr. Charles Fullman (New York, 1962).

67. Lothar Machtan, "Hans Rothfels and the Historiography of Social Policy in Germany," *Storia della storiografia*, 21 (1992), 3–24.

68. Winfried Schulze, *Deutsche Geschichtswissenschaft nach 1945* (Munich, 1989), 18.

69. *Einführung in das Studium der Geschichte*, ed. Walter Eckermann et al. (Berlin, 1978); but see Andreas Dorpalen, *German History in Marxist Perspective: The East German Approach* (Detroit, 1985).

70. See John Higham, *History: Professional Scholarship in America* (Baltimore, 1965).

71. On "the myth of consensus history" see Ellen Fitzpatrick, *History's Memory: Writing the American Past, 1880–1980* (Cambridge, Mass., 2002).

72. *The Progressive Historians: Turner, Beard, Parrington* (New York, 1968).

73. Gabriela Ann Eakin-Thimme, *Geschichte im Exil: Deutschsprachige Historiker nach 1933* (Munich, 2005), Hartmut Lehmann and James Van Horn Melton (eds.), *Paths of Continuity: Central European Historiography from the 1930s to the 1950s* (Cambridge, 1994), Catherine Epstein, *A Past Renewed: A Catalog of German-Speaking Historians in the United States after 1933* (Cambridge, 1993), and H. Stuart Hughes, *The Sea Change: The Migration of Social Thought, 1930–1965* (New York, 1975); also Peter Gay, *My German Question: Growing Up in Nazi Berlin* (New Haven, 1998).

74. See Lehman and Sheehan (eds.), *An Interrupted Past*.

75. *Prophets of Yesterday: Studies in European Culture 1890–1914* (New York, 1961).

76. Schorske, *Thinking with History* (Princeton, 1990), 24; and see Robin W. Winks, *Cloak and Gown: Scholars in the Secret War, 1939–1961* (New Haven, 1996[2]), 70–82.

77. See *Consciousness and Society, The Obstructed Path*, and *The Sea Change*; also *Oswald Spengler* (New Brunswick, 1992[2]).

78. *Freud for Historians* (New York, 1985), xi, 78.

79. "Psychohistory," *The Past before Us: Contemporary Historical Writing in the United States*, ed. Michael Kammen (Ithaca, 1980), 409.

80. Marcuse, *Eros and Civilization* (New York, 1962),

81. Lynn Hunt, "Psychology, Psychoanalysis, and Historical Thought," *A Companion to Western Historical Thought*, ed. Lloyd Kramer and Sarah Maza (Oxford, 2002), 337–56, and see Jacques Barzun, *Clio and the Doctors: Psycho-History, Quanto-History, and History* (Chicago, 1974).

82. *The Unbound Prometheus* (Cambridge, 1969), 545.

83. Peter Stearns, "Toward a Wider Vision: Trends in Social History," and J. Morgan Kousser, "Quantitative Social-Scientific History," *The Past before Us*, 205–30, 433–56.

84. *The Territory of the Historian,* tr. Ben Reynolds and Siân Reynolds (Chicago, 1979), 6, 54.

85. "Quantitative History," *Historical Studies Today,* ed. Felix Gilbert and Stephen Graubard (New York, 1972), 53.

86. Fitzpatrick, *History's Memory,* passim.

87. *The Gender of History* (Cambridge, Mass., 1998).

88. A. B. McKillop, *The Spinster and the Prophet: H. G. Wells, Florence Deeks, and the Case of the Plagiarized Text* (New York, 2000), 163.

89. These are the authors studied in Paul Costello, *World Historians and Their Goals: Twentieth-Century Answers to Modernism* (DeKalb, 1993); see also W. Warren Wagar, *Books in World History: A Guide for Teachers and Students* (Bloomington, 1973).

90. Andrew C. Isenberg, "Historicizing Natural Environments," *A Companion to Western Historical Thought,* ed. Kramer and Maza, 372–89; and see Jared Diamond, *Guns, Germs, and Steel: The Fates of Human Societies* (New York, 1999).

91. Janet Abu-Lugod, *Before European Hegemony: The World System, A.D. 1250–1350* (New York, 1989), and see William A. Green, *History, Historians, and the Dynamics of Change* (London, 1993).

92. Braudel, *Civilization and Capitalism,* III, *The Perspective of the World,* tr. Siân Reynolds (New York, 1984).

93. Stoianovich, *Balkan Lands: The First and Last Europe* (London, 1994), and Chaudhuri, *Asia before Europe: Economy and Civilisation of the Indian Ocean from the Rise of Islam to 1750* (Cambridge, 1990).

94. Jack Goody, *Food and Love: A Cultural History of East and West* (London, 1998), 222ff.

95. Dipesh Chakrabarty, *Provincializing Europe: Postcolonial Thought and Historical Difference* (Princeton, 2000).

96. Philip D. Curtin, *The World and the West: The European Challenge and the Overseas Response in the Age of Empire* (Cambridge, 2000); Alfred W. Crosby, *Ecological Imperialism: The Biological Expansion of Europe. 900–1900* (Cambridge, 1986); Jerry H. Bentley, *Old World Encounters: Cross Cultural Contacts and Exchanges in Pre-Modern Times* (New York, 1993); and various works of William McNeill.

Chapter 5. After the Good War

1. Rosenberg, *Bureaucracy, Aristocracy, and Autocracy: The Prussian Experience, 1660–1815* (Boston, 1966), and Wehler, *Bismarck und der Imperialismus* (1969).

2. *Land and Lordship: Structures of Governance in Medieval Austria,* tr. H. Kaminsky and J. Van Horn Melton (Philadelphia, 1992).

3. *Behemoth: The Structure and Practice of Socialism, 1933–1944* (New York, 1944²).

4. *Geschichte des Historismus* (Munich, 1992), 181.

5. *Geschichte als historische Sozialwissenschaft* (Frankfurt, 1973), and see Georg Iggers (ed.), *The Social History of Politics: Critical Perspectives in West German Historical Writing since 1945* (Dover, N.H., 1985) and Geoff Eley, *From Unification to Nazism: Reinterpreting the German Past* (Boston, 1986).

6. Alf Lüdtke, *The History of Everyday life,* tr. William Templer (Princeton, 1989); Andreas Dorpalen, *German History in Marxist Perspective: The East German Approach* (Detroit, 1985).

7. Stefan Berger, *The Search for Normality: National Identity and Historical Consciousness in Germany since 1800* (Providence, 1997), 165, and Lutz Raphael, *Geschichtswissenschaft im Zeitalter der Extreme* (Munich, 2003), 117ff.

8. *Klassengesellschaft im Krieg 1914–1918* (Göttingen, 1973), I, 138.

9. *Das deutsche Kaiserreich 1871–1918* (Göttingen, 1973), 238.

10. *Deutsche Geschichte 1866–1918,* I, *Arbeitswelt und Bürgergeist,* and II, *Machtstaat vor der Demokratie* (Munich, 1990).

11. *Preussen zwischen Reform und Revolution: Allgemeines Landrecht, Verwaltung, und soziale Bewegung von 1791 bis 1848* (Munich, 1989).

12. See Hartmut Lehmann and Melvin Richter (eds.), *The Meaning of Historical Terms and Concepts: News Studies on Begriffsgeschichte* (Washington, D.C., 1996).

13. "Begriffsgeschichte and Social History," *Futures Past: On the Semantics of Historical Time,* tr. Keith Tribe (Cambridge, Mass., 1985), 73–91; and see *The Practice of Conceptual History: Timing History, Spacing Concepts,* tr. Todd Samuel Presner et al. (Stanford, 2002).

14. "Perspective and Temporality: A Contribution to the Historiographical Exposure of the Historical World," and "On the Disposability of History," *Futures Past,* 130–55, 198–212.

15. *Le Origini della guerra di 1914* (Milan, 1942–43).

16. E. R. Piper (ed.), *Historiker streit: Die Dokumentation der Kontroverse und die Einzigartigkeit der national-sozialisten Judenvernightung* (Munich, 1987), 72.

17. Udo Wengst (ed.), *Historiker betrachten Deutschland: Beiträge zum Vereinigungsprozess und zum Hauptstadt Diskussion* (Bonn, 1992), and Rainer Eckert, Wolfgang Küttler, and Gustav Seeber (eds.), *Krise-Umbruch Neubeginn: ein kritische und selbstkritische Dokumentation der DDR-Geschichtswissenschaft 1989/90* (Stuttgart, 1992).

18. Berger, *The Search for Normality.*

19. Schulze, *Deutsche Geschichtswissenschaft nach 1945* (Munich, 1989), and see Uwe Uffelmann (ed.), *Identitätsbildung und Geschichtsbewusstsein nach der Vereinigung Deutschlands* (Weinheim, 1993).

20. *Geschichtsdenken im 20. Jahrhundert* (Berlin, 1991).

21. *A History of Historical Writing* (New York, 1962²), 399.

22. *Historiographiegeschichte als Historik* (Stuttgart, 1991).

23. In a vast literature see Georg G. Iggers, "Historicism: The History and Meaning of the Term," *Journal of the History of Ideas,* 56 (1995), 129–52.

24. "The Temple of Fame," 37–40.

25. Haigh, *The English Reformation Revised* (Cambridge, 1987), 9.

26. See Guy Burgess, *The New British History: Founding a Modern State, 1603–1715* (London, 1990).

27. Elton, *England: 1200–1640* (Ithaca, 1969), in a series edited by him titled "The Sources of History"; and cf. Charles Oman, *On the Writing of History* (London, 1939).

28. *The Parliament of England, 1559–1581* (Cambridge, 1986), 378.

29. Personal response to my question.

30. *The Practice of History* (London, 1967), 62.

31. In Robert William Fogel and G. R. Elton, *Which Road to the Past? Two Views of History* (New Haven, 1983), 84.

32. Ibid. 83, and see Elton, *Return to Essentials: Some Reflections on the Present State of Historical Study* (Cambridge, 1991).

33. J. G. A. Pocock, *Politics, Language, and Time: Essays on Political Thought and History* (Chicago, 1989), 11.

34. "The Concept of a Language and the *métier d'historien:* Some Considerations on Practice," *The Languages of Political Theory in Early-Modern Europe,* ed. Anthony Pagden (Cambridge, 1987), 19–40.

35. *Man on His Past,* viii.

36. See Philippe Carrard, *Poetics of the New History: French Historical Discourse from Braudel to Chartier* (Baltimore, 1992), 90.

37. *The Peasants of Languedoc,* tr. John Day (Urbana, 1974), 3–8; cf. Febvre, *Combats pour l'Histoire* (Paris, 1953), 18.

38. *History Continues,* tr. Arthur Goldhammer (Chicago, 1944), 48; Nora (ed.), *Essais d'ego-histoire* (Paris, 1987).

39. Gérard Noiriel, *Sur la "crise" de l'histoire.* (Paris, 1996), 123; and see Jacques Le Goff (ed.), *La nouvelle Histoire* (Paris, 1988), and Jacques Le Goff and Pierre Nora (eds.), *Constructing the Past: Essays in Historical Methodology* (Cambridge, 1985).

40. *The Three Orders: Feudal Society Imagined,* tr. Arthur Goldhammer (Chicago, 1980), 114.

41. *The Medieval Imagination,* tr. Arthur Goldhammer (Chicago, 1988).

42. Philippe Ariès and Georges Duby (eds.), *A History of Private Life,* tr. Arthur Goldhammer (5 vols.; Cambridge, Mass., 1987), I, viii.

43. *Montaillou: The Promised Land of Error,* tr. Barbara Bray (New York, 1979), 71; and see Giovanni Levi, "On Microhistory," *New Perspectives on Historical Writing,* ed. Peter Burke (University Park, Pa., 1991), 95.

44. *Remembrance of Things Past,* tr. C. K. Scott Moncrieff (New York, 1934), I, 33–34.

45. *On Collective Memory,* tr. Lewis Coser (Chicago, 1992).

46. Besides the volumes edited by Nora, *Realms of Memory* (New York, 1996–), see Jacques Le Goff, *Histoire et memoire* (Paris, 1988), and Richard Glasser, *Time in French Life and Thought,* tr. C. G. Pearson (Manchester, 1972).

47. *History as an Art of Memory* (Hanover, N.H., 1993).

48. *Les Lieux de mémoire,* I, *La République* (Paris, 1984), xx.

49. *The Creation of Mythology,* tr. Margaret Cook (Chicago, 1981), 37.

50. *Did the Greeks Believe in Their Myths? An Essay on the Constitutive Imagination,* tr. Paula Wissing (Chicago, 1983), 120.

51. *The Masters of Truth in Archaic Greece,* tr. Janet Lloyd (New York, 1996).

52. See Shapin, *A Social History of Truth* (Chicago, 1994), Peter Burke, *A Social History of Knowledge* (Cambridge, 2000), and Ian Hacking, *The Social Construction of What?* (Cambridge, Mass., 1999).

53. *L'Apparition du livre* (Paris, 1958).

54. *The History and Power of Writing,* tr. Lydia G. Cochrane (Chicago, 1994).

55. *On the Edge of the Cliff: History, Language, and Practice,* tr. Lydia G. Cochrane (Baltimore, 1997), 28; also *The Cultural Uses of Print in Early Modern France,* tr. Cochrane (Princeton, 1987), and *Cultural History,* tr. Cochrane (Ithaca, 1988).

56. *The German Idea of Freedom: History of a Political Tradition* (Boston, 1957), and see his contribution to John Higham (ed.), *History: The Development of Historical Studies in the United States* (Englewood Cliffs, N.J., 1965).

57. *The Enlightenment: An Interpretation* (2 vols.; New York, 1967); *Weimar Culture: The Outsider as Insider* (New York, 1968); *Freud for Historians* (New York, 1985); *Freud: A Life for Our Time* (New York, 1988); and see *My German Question: Growing Up in Nazi Berlin* (New Haven, 1998).

58. See, e.g., *German Encounters with Modernism, 1840–1945* (Cambridge, 2001), and *Art as History: Episodes in the Culture and Politics of Nineteenth-Century Germany* (Princeton, 1988); also "Crossing Borders," *Historically Speaking,* 4 (2002), 8–10.

59. *Fin-de-Siècle Vienna: Politics and Culture* (New York, 1981).

60. *Consciousness and Society: The Reconstruction of European Social Thought, 1890–1930* (New York, 1958) and *The Obstructed Path: French Social Thought in the Years of Desperation, 1930–1960* (New York, 1968).

61. *The Dialectical Imagination: A History of the Frankfurt School and the Institute for Social Research, 1923–1950* (Boston, 1973); *Permanent Exiles: Essays on the Intellectual Migration from Germany to America* (New York, 1986); *Downcast Eyes: The Denigration of Vision in Twentieth-Century French Thought* (Berkeley, 1993).

62. See, e.g., the festschrifts for Schorske and Gay, *Rediscovering History: Culture, Politics, and the Psyche,* ed. Michael S. Roth (Stanford, 1994), and *Enlightenment, Passion, Modernity: Historical Essays in European Thought and Culture,* ed. Mark S. Micale and Robert L. Dietle (Stanford, 2000).

63. Kermit Vanderbilt, *American Literature and the Academy: The Roots, Growth, and Maturity of a Profession* (Philadelphia, 1986); also Malcolm Bradbury and Harold Temperley, *Introduction to American Studies* (London, 1981).

64. In a vast and continuing bibliography see Neil Jumonville, *Critical Crossings: The New York Intellectuals in Postwar America* (Berkeley, 1991); also Arthur Schlesinger, Jr., *A Life in the Twentieth Century: Innocent Beginnings, 1917–1950* (Boston, 2000).

65. See Stanley Kutler (ed.), *American Retrospectives: Historians on Historians* (Baltimore, 1995).

66. Lynn Hunt (ed.), *The New Cultural History* (Berkeley, 1989).

67. *Fin-de-siècle Socialism* (New York, 1988), 17.

68. Richard M. Rorty (ed.), *The Linguistic Turn: Essays in Philosophical Method* (Chicago, 1992); Orr, "The Revenge of Literature," *Studies in Historical Change,* ed. Ralph Cohen (Charlottesville, 1992), 84–108; White, *The Content of the Form: Narrative Discourse and Historical Representation* (Baltimore, 1987); LaCapra, *Rethinking Intellectual History: Texts, Contexts, Language* (Ithaca, 1983); and Ankersmit, "The Linguistic Turn," *Historical Representation* (Stanford, 2001), 29–74.

69. "A Definition of the Concept of History," in *Philosophy and History: Essays Presented to Ernst Cassirer,* ed. R. Klibansky and H. J. Paton (Oxford, 1936), 6.

70. *A New Philosophy of History,* ed. Frank Ankersmit and Hans Kellner (Chicago, 1995).

71. See his *Poetics of the New History: French Historical Discourse from Braudel to Chartier* (Baltimore, 1992).

72. *Beyond the Great Story: History as Text and Discourse* (Cambridge, Mass., 1995).

73. Nancy Partner, "Historicity in an Age of Reality," *A New Philosophy of History*, ed. Ankersmit and Kellner, 23–39.

74. Alexander Demandt, *Endzeit? Die Zukunft der Geschichte* (Berlin, 1993).

75. *A Portrait of the Artist as a Young Man* (New York, 1948), 8.

76. *Sin and Fear: The Emergence of a Western Guilt Culture, 13th–18th Centuries*, tr. Eric Nicholson (New York, 1990).

77. Londa Schiebinger, *The Mind Has No Sex? Women in the Origins of Modern Science* (Cambridge, Mass., 1989).

78. Brown, *The Body and Society: Men, Women, and Sexual Renunciation in Early Christianity* (New York, 1988), and Bynum, *The Resurrection of the Body* (New York, 1995).

79. E.g., Rudi C. Bleys, *The Geography of Perversion: Male to Male Sexual Behavior outside the West and the Ethnographic Imagination, 1750–1918* (New York, 1995).

80. Ariès, *The Hour of Our Death*, tr. Helen Weaver (New York, 1982), and *Western Attitudes toward Death from the Middle Ages to the Present*, tr. Patricia M. Ranum (Baltimore, 1974), and Vovelle, *La Mort et l'Occident de 1300 à nos jours* (Paris, 1883).

81. E.g., Moishe Pontone and Eric Santner (eds.), *Catastrophe and Meaning: The Holocaust and the Twentieth Century* (Chicago, 2003).

82. *The Family, Sex, and Marriage in England, 1500–1800* (New York, 1977), 19.

83. *A History of Private Life*, ed. Ariès and Duby, III, *Passions of the Renaissance* (Cambridge, Mass., 1989), 609.

854. Jana Howlett (ed.), *Historical Anthropology of the Middle Ages* (Chicago, 1992), 26.

85. *Rabelais and His World*, tr. Hélène Iswolsky (Cambridge, Mass., 1968); and see also Samuel Kinser, *Rabelais's Carnival: Text, Context, Metatext* (Berkeley, 1990), and Walter Stephens, *Giants in Those Days: Folklore, Ancient History, and Nationalism* (Lincoln, Neb., 1989).

86. Marina S. Brownlee et al. (eds.), *The New Medievalism* (Baltimore, 1991), and cf. R. Howard Bloch and Stephen G. Nichols (eds.), *Medievalism and the Modern Temper* (Baltimore, 1996).

87. "Begriffsgeschichte and Social History," *Futures Past*, tr. Keith Tribe (Cambridge, Mass., 1985), 73–91; and see D. R. Kelley, "On the Margins of *Begriffsgeschichte*" (German Historical Institute pamphlet, 1996), 33–38.

88. *Futures Past*, 215; and see *The Practice of Conceptual History: Timing History, Spacing Concepts*, tr. Todd Samuel Presner et al. (Stanford, 2002), intro. by Hayden White.

89. Ross E. Dunn (ed.), *The New World History: A Teacher's Companion* (New York, 2000); and cf. Geary, *The Myth of Nations: The Medieval Origins of Europe* (Princeton, 2002), and Strayer, *On the Medieval Origins of the Modern State* (Princeton, 1970).

90. Richard Vann and Arthur Danto in *A New Philosophy of History*, ed. Ankersmit and Kellner, 40–88.

91. David Hackett Fisher, *Historian's Fallacies: Toward a Logic of Historical Thought* (New York, 1970).

Chapter 6. Circumspect and Prospect

1. *Of Time and the River*, II, vii, "Young Faustus."

2. 1959 must have been the heyday of early modern French history, since my Fulbright colleagues in Paris included Orest Ranum, Lionel Rothkrug, and Sam Kinser, who was then a collaborator in the field of historiography before he turned to greener fields.

3. See my "Garrett Mattingly, Bernard De Voto and the Craft of History," *Annals of Scholarship*, 2 (1981), 15–29.

4. *The Beginning of Ideology: Consciousness and Society in the French Reformation* (Cambridge, 1981)

5. *Historians and the Law in Postrevolutionary France* (Princeton, 1984).

6. *The Human Measure: Western Social Thought and the Legal Tradition* (Cambridge, Mass., 1990).

7. Elliott and Skinner have since moved back to England, where they became regius professors of history at Oxford and Cambridge respectively.

8. *The History of Ideas: Canon and Variations*, ed. D. R. Kelley (Rochester, 1990).

9. *History and the Disciplines: The Reclassification of Knowledge in Early Modern Europe* (Rochester, 1997). Inspired by Constance Blackwell, the seminar included Ann Blair, Ulrich Schneider, Martin Mulsow, Peter Miller, Ann Moyer, Paula Findlen, and Heikki Mikkeli, as well as visitors, including J. B. Schneewind, Donald Verene, Anthony Pagden, Anthony Grafton, Nicholas Jardine, and Londa Schiebinger.

10. *The Descent of Ideas: The History of Intellectual History* (London, 2002).

11. *Faces of History: Historical Inquiry from Herodotus to Herder* (New Haven, 1998) and *Fortunes of History: Historical Inquiry from Herder to Huizinga* (New Haven, 2003).

12. *On the Advantage and Disadvantage of History for Life,* tr. Peter Preuss (Indianapolis, 1980), 11.

13. Kurt Mueller-Vollmer (ed.), *The Hermeneutics Reader* (Oxford, 1986).

14. *The Will to Power,* tr. Walter Kaufmann and R. J. Hollingdale (New York, 1967), 327.

15. *Farewell to Matters of Principle,* German tr. (New York, 1981), 111.

16. See my article "Between History and System" in *Historia: Empiricism and Erudition in Early Modern Europe*, ed. Gianna Pomata and Nancy G. Siraisi (Cambridge, Mass, 2005), 211–37.

17. Stone, "The Revival of Narrative: Reflections on a New Old History," *Past and Present,* 85 (1979), 3–24; Nevins, *The Gateway to History* (New York, 1938).

18. Gay, *Style in History* (New York, 1974), 217, and see Hexter, "The Rhetoric of History," in *Doing History* (London, 1971), 15–76.

19. *Attitudes toward History* (Boston, 1937) and *A Rhetoric of Motives* (New York, 1950); also Robert Wess, *Kenneth Burke: Rhetoric, Subjectivity, Postmodernism* (Cambridge, 1996), and Ch. Perelman and L. Olbrechts-Tyteca, *The New Rhetoric: A Treatise*

on Argumentation (Notre Dame, 1969); also Ankersmit, *Historical Representation* (Stanford, 2001).

20. Ankersmit, *Narrative Logic, A Semantic Analysis of the Historian's Language* (The Hague, 1983), rev. by me *AHR*, 101 (1996), 447, and see his *Historical Representation*.

21. *Metahistory: The Historical Imagination in Nineteenth-Century Europe* (Baltimore, 1973) and *The Content of the Form: Narrative Discourse and Historical Representation* (Baltimore, 1987).

22. See the articles collected in *Storia della storiografia,* 24 (1993) and 25 (1994).

23. *Rethinking Intellectual History: Texts, Contexts, Language* (Ithaca, 1983) and later publications.

24. Kellner, *Language and Historical Representation: Getting the Story Crooked* (Madison, 1989).

25. *Journal,* II, 152.

26. Catherine Gallagher and Stephen Greenblatt, *Practicing New Historicism* (Chicago, 2000).

27. In *A New Philosophy of History,* ed. Frank Ankersmit and Hans Kellner (Chicago, 1995). and see Berkhofer, *Beyond the Great Story: History as Text and Discourse* (Cambridge, Mass., 1995).

28. *The Rhetoric of Representation: Three Narrative Histories of the French Revolution* (Cambridge, 1990).

29. See his *Poetics of the New History: French Historical Discourse from Braudel to Chartier* (Baltimore, 1992).

30. "'Grand Narrative' and the Discipline of History," *A New Philosophy of History,* 151–73.

31. See, e.g., Clive Gamble, *Timewalkers: The Prehistory of Global Civilization* (Cambridge, Mass., 1994), Peter James, *Centuries of Darkness* (New Brunswick, 1993), Steven Mithen, *The Prehistory of the Mind: The Cognitive Origins of Art, Religion, and Science* (London, 1996), and Jared Diamond, *Guns, Germs, and Steel: The Fates of Human Societies* (New York, 1997); also Bernal, *Black Athena Writes Back* (Durham, 2001), with a bow to Walter Burkert, *The Orientalizing Revolution: Near Eastern Influence on Greek Culture in the Early Archaic Age*, tr. Margaret C. Pinder and Walter Burkert (Cambridge, Mass., 1992).

32. Shrimpton, *History and Memory in Ancient Greece* (Montreal, 1997), Assmann, *Moses the Egyptian: The Memory of Egypt in Western Monotheism* (Cambridge, Mass., 1997), Coleman, *Ancient and Medieval Memories: Studies in the Reconstruction of the Past* (Cambridge, 1992), Geary, *Phantoms of Remembrance: Memory and Oblivion at the End of the First Millennium* (Princeton, 1994), and Carruthers, *The Book of Memory: A Study of Memory in Medieval Culture* (Cambridge, 1990), McKitterick, *The Carolingians and the Written Word* (Cambridge, 1989), and (ed.) *The Uses of Literacy in Early Medieval Europe* (Cambridge, 1990), and Van Houts, *Memory and Gender in Medieval Europe* (Toronto, 1999).

33. Jan-Werner Müller (ed.), *Memory and Power in Post-War Europe: Studies in the Presence of the Past* (Cambridge, 2002).

34. D. R. Kelley, "Something Happened: Panofsky and Cultural History," *Meaning in*

the *Visual Arts: Views from the Outside, A Centennial Commemmoration of Erwin Panofsky (1892–1968)*, ed. Irving Lavin (Princeton, 1995), 113–21.

35. Peter Novick, *That Noble Dream: The "Objectivity Question" in the American Historical Profession* (Cambridge, 1988), and Allan Megill (ed.), *Rethinking Objectivity* (Durham, 1994).

36. See Roger Chartier, *On the Edge of the Cliff: History, Language, and Practices*, tr. Lydia G. Cochrane (Baltimore, 1997), 19, 26; and Gallagher and Greenblatt. *Practicing New Historicism.*

37. See, e.g., Kathy Eden, *Hermeneutics and the Rhetorical Tradition: Chapters in the Ancient Legacy and Its Humanist Reception* (New Haven, 1997), Ruth Morse, *Truth and Convention in the Middle Ages: Rhetoric, Representation, and Reality* (Cambridge, 1991), and Rita Copeland, *Rhetoric, Hermeneutics, and Translation in the Middle Ages: Academic Traditions and Vernacular Texts* (Cambridge, 1991).

38. Marcel Detienne, *The Masters of Truth in Archaic Greece*, tr. Janet Lloyd (New York, 1996), and Christopher Gill and T. P. Wisemen (eds.), *Lies and Fiction in the Ancient World* (Austin, 1993).

39. *The Long Revolution* (Harmondsworth, 1961).

40. S. C. Humphreys, *Anthropology and the Greeks* (London, 1978).

41. *The Mirror of Herodotus: The Representation of the Other in the Writing of History* (Berkeley, 1988), and *Memories of Odysseus: Frontier Tales from Ancient Greece* (Chicago, 2001), both tr. Janet Lloyd.

42. Lorraine Daston and Katherine Park, *Wonders and the Order of Nature, 1150–1750* (New York, 1998).

43. See *The Cambridge History of Science*, VIII, *The Modern Social Sciences*, ed. Theodore M. Porter and Dorothy Ross (Cambridge, 2003).

44. *The Structural Transformation of the Public Sphere: An Inquiry into a Category of Bourgeois Society*, tr. Thomas Burger (Cambridge, Mass., 1989); Craig Calhoun (ed.), *Habermas and the Public Sphere* (Cambridge, Mass., 1992); Peter Uwe Hohendahl, *The Institution of Criticism* (Ithaca, 1982), ch. 7, "Critical Theory, Public Sphere, and Culture: Jürgen Habermas and His Critics" (tr. Marc Silverman); and James Van Horn Melton, *The Rise of the Public in Enlightenment Europe* (Cambridge, 2001).

45. Kelley, "Civil Science in the Renaissance: Jurisprudence Italian Style," *Historical Journal*, 22 (1979), 777–97; "Civil Science in the Renaissance: Jurisprudence in the French Manner," *History of European Ideas*, 2 (1981), 261–76; "Civil Science in the Renaissance: The Problem of Interpretation," *The Languages of Political Theory in Early Modern Europe*, ed. A. Pagden (Cambridge, 1987), 57–78.

46. Baron, *In Search of Florentine Civic Humanism: Essays on the Transition from Medieval to Modern Thought* (Princeton, 1988); *Crisis of the Early Italian Renaissance* (Princeton, 1966 [1955]), dedicated to Jaeger; Jaeger, *Paideia: The Ideals of Greek Culture*, tr. Gilbert Highet (New York, 1945), I, 436, "political humanism."

47. James Van Horn Melton, *The Rise of the Public in Enlightenment Europe* (Cambridge, 2001).

48. *Literary Language and Its Public in Late Latin Antiquity and in the Middle Ages*, tr. Ralph Manheim (New York, 1965)

49. *The Carolingians and the Written Word* (Cambridge, 1989), and (ed.), *The Uses of Literacy in Early Medieval Europe* (Cambridge, 1990)

50. *Vox Dei: Communication in the Middle Ages* (Oxford, 1990).

51. R. Scholz, *Die Publizistik zur Zeit Philippe des Schönen und Bonifaz VIII* (Stuttgart, 1903).

52. G. A. di Gennaro, *Respublica jurisconsultorum* (Naples, 1752).

53. Roberto Weiss, *The Dawn of Humanism in Italy* (London, 1947), and Kelley, *Renaissance Humanism* (Boston, 1997).

54. See the classic paper of Hans Baron, "The Memory of Cicero's Roman Civic Spirit in the Medieval Centuries and in the Florentine Renaissance," *In Search of Florentine Civic Humanism*, I, 94–133.

55. Cited in Brian Vickers, *In Defense of Rhetoric* (Oxford, 1998), 194.

56. Cited by Marc Fumaroli in James J. Murphey (ed.), *Renaissance Eloquence* (Berkeley, 1983), 255; and see Fumaroli, *L'Age de l'eloquence: rhétorique et "res literaria" de la Renaissance au seuil de l'époch classique* (Paris, 1980).

57. Eisenstein, *The Printing Press as an Agent of Change* (2 vols.; Cambridge, 1979).

58. See Sandra L. Hindman, *Printing the Written Word: The Social History of Books, circa 1450–1520* (Ithaca, 1991).

59. Sophia Menache, *The Vox Dei: Communication in the Middle Ages* (New York, 1990); and see Brendan Dooley, "From Literary Criticism to Systems Theory in Early Modern Journalism History," *Journal of the History of Ideas*, 51 (1990), 461–86.

60. *The Beginning of Ideology: Consciousness and Society in the French Reformation* (Cambridge, 1981), 213–52; Jack Censer, *The French Press in the Age of Enlightenment* (London, 1994).

61. *Le Modèle français et l'Italie savante (1660–1750)* (Paris, 1989).

62. *The Social History of Skepticism: Experience and Doubt in Early Modern Culture* (Baltimore, 1999).

63. See the articles of Ann Blair and others in *Journal of the History of Ideas*, 64, no. 2 (2003).

64. *The Gutenberg Galaxy* (Toronto, 1962), 278.

65. Merleau-Ponty, *Phenomenology of Perception*, tr. Colin Smith (London, 1962), 67ff.

66. See, e.g., Norman Cohn, *The Pursuit of the Millennium* (London, 1957), and Katharine R. Firth, *The Apocalyptic Tradition in Reformation Britain, 1530–1645* (Oxford, 1979).

67. See Krzysztof Pomian, *L'Ordre du temps* (Paris, 1984), and Kelley, "Periodization in the West" (forthcoming).

68. *Die Krisis der europäischen Kultur* (Nürnberg, 1917), 674.

69. Albrecht Wellman, *Zur Dialektik von Moderne und Postmoderne* (Frankfurt, 1985), 48.

70. *The Postmodern Explained* (Minneapolis, 1992), 15.

71. "Structuralism and Poststructuralism," *Telos*, 55 (1983), 204. In fact I am up-to-date–at least I checked the Web and found over 51,000 hits for the term "postmodern," and over 10,000 for "postmodern turn"–rather too much, I think, to constitute much of a novelty anymore.

72. See N. Katherine Hayles, *Chaos Bound: Orderly Disorder in Contemporary Literature and Science* (Ithaca, 1990).

73. See Mitchell Waldrop, *Complexity: The Emerging Science at the Edge of Order and Chaos* (New York, 1992).

74. Patrick Madigan, *The Modern Project to Rigor: Descartes to Nietzsche* (Lanham, Md., 1986).

75. See François Furet, *The Passing of an Illusion: The Idea of Communism in the Twentieth Century,* tr. Deborah Furet (Chicago, 1999).

76. Lutz Niethammer, *Posthistoire: Has History Come to an End?* tr. Patrick Camiller (London, 1992), and Francis Fukuyama, *The End of History and the Last Man* (New York, 1992), and "The End of History, Five Years Later," *History and Theory,* 34 (1995, Theme Issue), 27–43; also Gianni Vattimo, *The End of Modernity,* tr. Jon R. Snyder (Baltimore, 1988).

77. Niethammer, *Posthistoire,* and Vattimo, *The End of Modernity.*

78. *The Philosophy of History,* tr. J. Sibree (New York, 1944), 442.

79. See the six articles in "Historiography of the 'Countries of Eastern Europe,'" *American Historical Review,* 97 (1992).

80. See, e.g., Patrick O'Meara et al., *Globalization and the Challenges of a New Century* (Bloomington, 2002).

81. *Work on Myth,* tr. Robert M. Wallace (Cambridge, Mass., 1985), 636; and see Joseph Mali, *Mythistory: The Making of a Modern Historiography* (Chicago, 2003).

82. *Selected Poems of Rainer Maria Rilke,* tr. Robert Bly (New York, 1981), 13.

83. Gérard Noiriel, *Sur la "crise" de l'histoire* (Paris, 1996), and see Lutz Raphael, *Geschichtswissenschaft im Zeitalter der Extreme: Theorien, Methoden, Tendenzen von 1900 bis zur Gegenwart* (Munich, 2003).

84. *Temps et récit,* I (Paris, 1983).

85. Alan Garfinkel, *Forms of Explanation: Rethinking the Questions in Social Theory* (New Haven, 1981).

86. *Truth in Philosophy* (Cambridge, Mass., 1993), 46–47.

87. Certeau, *The Writing of History,* tr. Tom Conley (New York, 1988), 21; and cf. Blumenberg, *Work on Myth.*

Conclusion: Millennium

1. *Collected Fictions,* tr. Andrew Hurley (New York, 1998), 327.

2. Jenó Szúcs, *Les Trois Europes* (Paris, 1985), with a preface by Braudel.

3. Francine Friedman, *The Bosnian Muslims: Denial of a Nation* (Boulder, 1996), and Jean Forward, *Endangered Peoples of Europe: Struggles to Survive and Thrive* (Westport, 2001).

4. *Between East and West: The Balkans and the Mediterranean Worlds,* IV (New Rochelle, 1995), 84; and see Benedict Anderson, *Imagined Communities* (London, 1983), Eric Hobsbawm and Terence Ranger (eds.), *The Invention of Tradition* (Cambridge, 1983), and Mikuláš Teich and Roy Porter (eds.), *The National Question in Europe in Historical Context* (Cambridge, 1993).

5. See, e.g., W. G. Beasley and E. G. Pulleyblank (eds.), *Historians of China and Japan*

(Oxford, 1961); S. P. Sens (ed.), *Historians and Historiography in Modern India* (Calcutta, 1973); H. A. J. Klooster, *Indoniërs Schrijventum Geschiedenis* (Dordrecht, 1985); Sopedjatmoko (ed.), *An Introduction to Indonesian Historiography* (Ithaca, 1965).

6. Bogumil Jewsiewicki and David Newbury (eds.), *African Historiographies* (Beverly Hills, 1986), and Steven Feierman, "Africa in History: The End of Universal Narrative," *After Colonization: Imperial History and Postcolonial Developments*, ed. Gyan Prakash (Princeton, 1995), 40ff.

7. Martin W. Lewis and Kären E. Wigen, *The Myth of Continents: A Critique of Metageography* (Berkeley, 1997).

8. Bernard Comrie (ed.), *The World's Major Languages* (New York, 1990), 2; George L. Campbell (ed.), *Concise Compendium of the World's Language* (London, 1995); and Meic Stephens, *Linguistic Minorities in Western Europe* (Llandysul, Wales, 1976).

9. John McWhorter, *The Power of Babel: A Natural History of Language* (New York, 2003).

10. See, e.g., A. G. Hopkins (ed.), *Globalization in World History* (New York, 2002); John McWhorter, *The Power of Babel: A Natural History of Language* (New York, 2001).

11. *Heterologies: Discourse on the Other*, tr. Brian Massumi (Minneapolis, 1986), 206.

12. *Foucault Live (Interviews, 1966–1984)*, tr. John Johnston (New York, 1989), 251.

13. Michael E. Hobart and Zachary Schiffman, *Information Ages: Literacy, Numeracy, and the Computer Revolution* (Baltimore, 1998), and on "information overload" see the articles assembled by Ann Blair in *Journal of the History of Ideas*, 64 (2003), 1–72.

14. *The Gutenberg Galaxy: The Making of Typographic Man* (Toronto, 1962), 46.

15. See Stephen G. Meštrovič, *The Balkanization of the West: The Confluence of Postmodernism and Post Communism* (London, 1994).

16. Hayles, *Writing Machines* (Cambridge, Mass., n.d.), and see George Kubler, *The Shape of Time: Remarks on the History of Things* (New Haven, 1962).

17. In a vast literature see N. Katherine Hayles, *Chaos Bound: Orderly Disorder in Contemporary Literature and Science* (Ithaca, 1990), 266.

18. Arkady Plotnitsky, *Complementarity: Anti-Epistemology after Bohr and Derrida* (Durham, 1994).

19. *The Ordering of Time: From the Ancient Computus to the Modern Computer*, tr. Andrew Winnard (Chicago, 1993), 129, and Hobart and Schiffman, *Information Ages*.

20. See Elizabeth Deeds Ermarth, *Sequel to History: Postmodernism and the Crisis of Representational Time* (Princeton, 1992).

21. See Daniel Gordon (ed.), *Postmodernism and the Enlightenment: New Perspectives in Eighteenth-Century French Intellectual History* (New York, 2001).

22. *On the Advantage and Disadvantage of History for Life*, tr. Peter Preuss (Indianapolis, 1980), 10.

23. *Essay on Man*, 71–72.

Index

Aasen, Ivan, 40
Acton, John, Lord, 14, 41, 50, 67, 101, 102, 111, 145, 149, 238
Adams, Brooks, 71
Adams, C. K., 117
Adams, George Burton, 124
Adams, Henry, 5, 117, 121, 122
Adams, Herbert Burton, 117
Adams, J. T., 53
"Agathon," 23
Albertini, Luigi, 174
Alexander the Great, 66
Allen, Barry, 240, 241
Allen, J. W., 48
Altamira, Rafael, 118, 134
Anaximander, 122
Anderson, Benedict, 204
Andler, Charles, 50
Andreas, Willi, 91, 92, 95, 97
Ankersmit, Frank, 192, 193, 215, 216, 220, 221
Appleby, Joyce, 221

Ariès, Philippe, 114, 184, 186, 199, 200, 201
Aristotle, 21, 65
Ashley, William, 103
Assmann, Jan, 225
Aston, William, 108
Aubin, Hermann, 98
Auerbach, Erich, 149, 213, 228
Augustine, St., 31, 80, 82, 119
Aulard, Alphonse, 32, 50, 110, 186

Bacon, Francis, 22, 229
Bainton, R. H., 134
Bakhtin, M. M., 192, 202
Balbo, Cesare, 42
Balzac, Honoré de, 220
Bancroft, George, 42, 120, 121
Barker, Ernest, 48
Barnes, Harry Elmer, 90, 119, 123, 176, 212, 252
Baron, Hans, 70, 98, 139, 149, 159, 160, 209, 228

Baronius, Cardinal, 69

Barraclough, Geoffrey, 53, 142, 147, 148, 149

Barth, Hans, 41

Barth, Paul, 82

Barthes, Roland, 216

Bartok, Antonin, 40

Barzun, Jacques, 162

Bate, Walter Jackson, 14, 207

Baudelaire, Charles, 123

Bauer, Wilhelm, 95

Beard, Charles, 92, 120, 122, 123, 124, 134, 142, 144, 158, 162

Beard, Mary Ritter, 120, 122, 134

Becker, Carl, 87, 120, 134, 189

Bede, the Venerable, 211, 243

Beer, G. L., 52

Bell, Daniel, 191, 233

Beloch, Julius, 61, 65, 66

Below, Georg von, 29, 30, 32, 33, 37, 38, 42, 55, 95, 96, 99, 152

Bémont, Charles, 50

Bennett, Arnold, 6

Berdyaev, Nicolas, 71, 75, 76

Berger, Adolph, 159

Bergman, Gustav, 192

Bergson, Henri, 26, 28, 49, 79, 83, 212

Berkeley, Bishop, 247

Berkhofer, Robert, 193, 194, 221, 223

Berlin, Isaiah, 142, 160, 212, 239

Bernal, Martin, 60, 66, 224

Bernhardi, General, 48

Bernheim, Eduard, 24, 29, 30, 65, 117

Berr, Henri, 8, 9, 25, 28, 30, 66, 109, 110, 111, 112, 113, 114, 116, 118, 120, 134, 140, 141, 202

Binion, Rudolph, 161

Biondo, Flavio, 70

Bismarck, Otto von, 31, 32, 33, 34, 37, 38, 55, 84, 93, 94, 154, 155, 157, 171, 172, 175

Blackwell, Constance, 211

Blair, Ann, 229

Blanc, Louis, 82

Blanke, Horst, 175, 176, 212, 252

Bloch, Ernst, 71

Bloch, Gustav, 23, 68, 136

Bloch, Marc, 26, 109, 111, 112, 113, 114, 115, 116, 117, 136, 137, 138, 139, 141, 182, 183, 185, 200, 220

Blok, P. J., 41, 118

Blumenberg, Hans, 238, 242, 243

Bodin, Jean, 21, 26, 30, 56, 58, 71, 79, 82, 111, 114, 194, 200, 213, 234

Boeckh, P. A., 31

Bohr, Niels, 233

Boja, Lucian, 132

Bolton, H. E., 121

Boniface VIII, Pope, 229

Boorstin, Daniel, 158

Borges, Jorge Luis, 243, 247

Bossuet, J. B., 82, 200

Bourdeau, Louis, 113

Bourdieu, Pierre, 187

Boutroux, Emile, 26, 49

Brachmann, Albert, 91, 94, 95, 97, 98, 147

Bracton, William, 15

Bradley, F. H., 205

Brandenburg, Erich, 30, 32, 47, 53, 55, 59, 90, 91, 92, 95, 152, 153

Brandi, Karl, 47, 53, 55, 92, 93, 95, 98, 154, 155

Braudel, Fernend, 111, 113, 136, 139, 140, 141, 166, 171, 180, 183, 196, 202, 220

Breasted, James, 62, 63, 126

Breysig, Kurt, 9, 10, 30, 77, 94

Bridenthal, Renate, 208

Brinton, Crane, 125, 207

Brooks, Van Wyck, 126, 190

Brown, Peter, 184, 199

Brugsch, Heinrich, 62

Bruni, Leonardo, 70

Brunner, Otto, 15, 139, 153, 172

Bryce, James, 48, 66

Buckle, Henry T., 22, 117, 216

Buffon, G. L. I., 215

Bugge, Alexander, 131

Bull, Edward, 131

Burckhardt, Jacob, 7, 10, 29, 33, 58, 84, 85, 92, 124, 154, 156, 209, 216, 218, 220, 251
Burgess, J. W., 51, 119, 120
Burke, Edmund, 145, 182
Burke, Kenneth, 215
Burke, Peter, 212
Burleigh, Michael, 98
Bury, J. B., 20, 21, 22, 62, 66, 67, 79
Bush, Douglas, 207
Butterfield, Herbert, 13, 144, 145, 148, 182
Bynum, Caroline, 199

Caesar, Julius, 31, 128
Cam, Helen Maud, 207
Camus, Albert, 86
Cantimori, Delio, 134, 139
Cantor, Norman, 210
Carbomnel, Charles, 212
Carlyle, Thomas, 18, 20, 104
Caron, Pierre, 23
Carr, E. H., 142, 147, 148, 178
Carrard, Philippe, 194, 222
Carruthers, Mary, 225
Carter, Howard, 61
Cassirer, Ernst, 35, 236
Castro, Américo, 134
Catherine of Aragon, 210
Cavour, 19
Celan, Paul, 167
Cellarius, Conrad, 31
Censer, Jack, 230
Certeau, Michel, 242, 247
Chabod, Federico, 134, 139
Chakrabarty, K. N., 168
Channing, Edward, 120, 121
Charlemagne, 6
Charles I, King, 87
Charles V, Emperor, 31, 93, 96, 154
Chartier, Roger, 184, 187, 188, 201, 229, 230
Chateaubriand, René, 185
Chaucer, Geoffrey, 19, 104
Chaudhuri, K. N., 166

Cheyney, Edward P., 121
Childe, V. Gordon, 61, 68
Chladenius, J. W., 30, 173, 193, 203
Chrimes, Sidney, 16, 177
Churchill, Winston, 48, 235
Cicero, Marcus Tullius, 225
Claggett, Marshall, 210
Clanchy, M. T., 225
Clapham, J. H., 103, 105, 106, 107, 108, 151
Clough, Shepherd, 210
Cobb, Richard, 183
Cobban, Alfred, 142, 147
Cobbett, William, 106
Cochrane, Eric, 208, 212
Cole, Edward, 182
Cole, G. D. H., 84, 105, 106
Cole, Margaret, 105
Coleman, Janet, 225
Collingwood, R. G., 57, 72, 74, 80, 81, 163, 212, 213, 214
Columbus, Christopher, 123, 124
Commager, Henry Steele, 126
Commines, Philippe de, 31
Commodus, Emperor, 69
Comte, Auguste, 12, 21, 22, 28, 71, 77, 85
Conant, James Bryant, 207
Condorcet, Marqius, 21, 22, 31, 77
Constantine, Emperor, 12
Conze, Werner, 153, 171, 173
Coolidge, Archibald Carey, 52
Copernicus, Nicolaus, 2
Coulton, G. G., 104
Cournot, Antoine, 28, 234
Cowley, Malcolm, 122
Craig, Gordon, 56, 92
Crèvecoeur, J., 159
Croce, Benedetto, 9, 28, 30, 57, 58, 74, 78, 80, 81, 85, 96, 125, 139, 176, 193, 195, 212, 216
Cromwell, Thomas, 124, 177
Culler, Jonathan, 215
Cumont, Franz, 68
Cunningham, William, 103, 105, 106, 107

Curti, Merle, 126
Curtius, Ernst Robert, 35, 66, 94, 152, 202

Dahlmann, F. C., 41
Dante Alighieri, 67, 196
Darmstädter, Paul, 50
Darnton, Robert, 187, 210, 229, 230
Darwin, Charles, 22, 60, 61, 117
Daston, Lorraine, 227
Daunou, P. C. F., 22
Davis, H. W. C., 49
Davis, Natalie, 219
Dawson, Christopher, 79, 165
Deeks, Florence, 165
De Grazia, Sebastian, 210
Dehio, Ludwig, 150, 154, 156
Delbrück, Hans, 30, 32, 35, 48, 51, 52, 53, 54, 55, 90, 91, 92, 154, 156
Delumeau, Jean, 198
Dempf, Alois, 76
Den Boer, Pim, 212
Dennis the Menace, 18
Derrida, Jacques, 59, 187, 217, 223
Descartes, René, 22, 76, 78, 80, 185, 233
Detienne, Marcel, 186
De Voto, Bernard, 190, 210
Dickens, A. G., 181
Dickens, Charles, 209, 247
Diderot, Denis, 112
Diehls, Hermann, 35
Diggens, J. P., 191
Dill, Samuel, 68
Dilthey, Wilhelm, 8, 11, 12, 25, 33, 38, 75, 77, 79, 81, 86, 129, 156, 161, 212
Dionysius the Areopagite, 183
Dobb, Maurice, 106, 107, 142
Dodds, E. R., 161
Dolet, Etienne, 115
Döllinger, Ignaz von, 69
Domanovsky, Sándor, 129
Dominian, Leon, 43, 44
Dopsch, Alfons, 42, 109, 129, 137, 139
Dorn, Walter, 56, 160, 210
Dos Passos, John, 122

Dow, Sterling, 207
Dreyfus, Alfred, 23
Droysen, Johann Gustav, 6, 24, 30, 31, 34, 42, 55, 67, 72, 74, 85, 91, 160, 220
Duby, Georges, 183, 184, 201, 220
Duchesne, Louis, 69, 70
Duhem, Pierre, 26
Dumezil, Georges, 111, 183
Duncker, Max, 34, 62
Durkheim, Emile, 12, 25, 27, 28, 30, 50, 65, 66, 71, 111, 113, 115, 137, 140, 198, 225
Duruy, Victor, 62, 165

Edward I, King, 18
Edward II, King, 104
Edward III, King, 18
Egan, Maurice Francis, 133
Ehrenberg, Victor, 177
Einstein, Albert, 56
Eisenstein, Elizabeth, 187, 229, 230
Elias, Norbert, 187
Eliot, T. S., 89, 126, 234, 237
Elizabeth I, Queen, 97, 143, 178
Elliott, John H., 210
Elton, G. R., 16, 135, 177, 180, 221
Elwitt, Sanford, 210
Emerton, Ephraim, 117
Engel-Janosi, Friedrich, 160
Engels, Friedrich, 168
Erasmus, Desiderius, 19, 115
Erdmann, Karl, 98
Erikson, Erik, 161
Erman, Adolph, 62
Erskine, John, 123
Espinas, Georges, 42
Eucken, Rudolph, 10
Eusebius, 1, 3, 69
Evans, Arthur, 21, 61, 63, 67

Fay, Sidney B., 51, 124, 125, 174, 207
Febvre, Lucien, 26, 109, 110, 111, 112, 113, 114, 115, 116, 117, 136, 137, 139, 140, 141, 182, 183, 185, 187, 188, 200, 202, 203, 220, 229

Felix III, Pope, 70
Ferguson, Wallace, 134
Fermat, Pierre, 247
Ferraro, Gugliermo, 67, 68, 69
Fichte, J. G., 33, 48, 49
Ficker, Julius von, 93
Figgis, John Neville, 16, 84
Finke, Heinrich, 29
Finkel, Ludwig, 41
Firth, C. H., 155
Fischer, Fritz, 157, 172, 174
Fish, Max H., 208
Fisher, David Hackett, 205
Fisher, H. A. L., 102
Flacius Illyricus, Matthias, 69
Flint, Robert, 30,
Florovsky, George, 59
Ford, Franklin, 160
Ford, Guy Stanton, 51
Ford, Henry, 123
Foucault, Marcel, 157, 166, 186, 187, 192, 221, 230, 232, 247
Fouillé, Alfred, 25
Fournier, Jacques, 184, 185
Fowler, W. Ward, 68
Fox, D. R., 122
Frank, Tenney, 68, 69
Frank, Walter, 59, 99, 150, 151, 153, 155
Franklin, Alfred, 201
Franklin, Julian, 210
Fraser, J. T., 250
Frederick I, 96
Frederick II, Emperor, 84, 94, 155
Frederick the Great, 31, 36, 58, 155
Fredericq, P., 118
Freedman, Charles, 210
Freeman, Edward A., 14, 66, 67
Freud, Sigmund, 5, 74, 85, 89, 160, 161, 162, 200, 208
Freyer, Hans, 150
Friedell, Egon, 39, 84
Friedjung, Heinrich, 129
Friedländer, Ludwig, 68
Friis, A., 129
Froude, James Anthony, 14, 17, 18

Fruin, Robert, 41
Fry, Northrup, 216
Fueter, Eduard, 78, 95, 96, 152, 208, 212, 252
Fukuyama, Francis, 223, 234
Furet, François, 110, 163
Fustel de Coulanges, Numa Denis, 23, 27, 28, 49, 66, 112, 116, 137, 138, 141, 183

Gabriel, Ralph, 126
Gadamer, Hans-Georg, 8, 173, 186, 192, 200, 212, 213, 214, 219
Gallagher, Catherine, 221
Gandhi, Mohandas K., 161
Gardiner, Samuel Rawson, 14, 143
Garibaldi, Giuseppe, 18, 19
Gasquet, F. A., 19
Gay, Edwin, 103
Gay, Peter, 47, 52, 98, 159, 160, 162, 189, 215, 216
Geary, Patrick, 204, 225
Geertz, Clifford, 192, 210, 221
Gehlen, Arnold, 234
Geijer, E., 43, 129
Gelbart, Nina, 230
Genovese, Eugene, 210
George III, King, 145, 178
George, Stefan, 31, 94
Gerhard, Dietrich, 98, 156, 159
Geyl, Peter, 128, 134
Gibbon, Edward, 20, 66, 67, 68, 69, 70, 87, 126, 164, 195, 215
Gierke, Otto von, 15, 101
Giesebrecht, Wilhelm von, 42
Giesey, Ralph E., 210
Gilbert, Felix, 50, 51, 92, 98, 99, 139, 149, 159, 160, 209, 210
Gilmore, Myron, 207
Ginzburg, Carlo, 185, 229
Glotz, Gustav, 27, 66
Glover, T. R., 68
Gödel, Kurt, 233
Goethe, Johann Wolfgang, 13, 15, 37, 40, 56, 58, 59, 83, 151, 152, 153, 154, 156

Goetz, Walter, 30, 91, 99, 150
Goll, Jarislav, 41, 43, 130, 131
Gooch, G. P., 5, 53, 100, 101, 102
Goody, Jack, 167, 168
Gothein, Eberhard, 29, 94
Grafton, Anthony, 187, 229
Gramsci, Antonio, 87
Grant, Madison, 43
Green, J. R., 13, 14, 17, 19, 121, 122
Greenblatt, Steven, 215, 221
Gregory of Tours, 194, 200
Grimm, Jakob, 15
Gross, Charles, 41, 124
Grossi, Paolo, 212
Grote, George, 66, 67
Grundmann, Herbert, 91, 94
Guenée, Bernard, 185
Guerard, Albert, Jr., 207
Guicciardini, Francesco, 160, 218
Guizot, François, 40, 110, 116, 137, 195
Gundolf, Friedrich, 31, 94
Gurevich, Aaron, 202

Haas, Stefan, 39
Habermas, Jürgen, 174, 187, 227, 228
Haeckel, Ernst, 50
Haigh, Christopher, 177
Halbwachs, Maurice, 185, 200, 225
Halecki, Oskar, 130
Halévy, Elie, 104
Hall, H. R., 63
Haller, Johannes, 30, 53, 54, 92, 95, 96, 97, 98
Hallgarten, G. W. F., 171
Halphen, Louis, 116
Hamilton, Earl, 203, 208
Hammond, Barbara, 105, 106, 107
Hammond, J. L., 105, 106, 107
Hammond, Mason, 207
Hampe, Karl, 94, 95, 97
Handlin, Oscar, 125, 158, 207, 221
Hanotaux, Gabriel, 82
Hanssen, Georg, 93
Harnack, Adolph von, 57, 69, 101
Harrington, James, 70

Hart, A. B., 117, 122
Hartman, Ludo, 129
Hartog, François, 227
Hartung, Fritz, 59, 91, 92, 95, 98
Hartz, Louis, 158
Hasbach, W., 106
Haskins, Charles H., 42, 52, 53, 124
Hauptmann, Gerhard, 50
Hayles, Katherine, 248, 249
Hazard, Paul, 85
Headlam-Morley, J. W., 53
Hearnshaw, F. J. C., 48
Hecataeus, 21
Heeren, Arnold, 41, 42, 91
Hegel, G. W. F., 30, 33, 34, 49, 58, 71, 78, 80, 82, 85, 122, 188, 202, 218, 222, 227, 228
Heidegger, Martin, 85, 86, 90, 135, 160, 167, 168, 170, 198, 213, 214, 219, 220, 231, 233
Heisenberg, Werner, 233
Hellwald, Friedrich, 39, 165
Hempel, Carl G., 205
Henry VIII, King, 17, 18, 104, 178, 210
Herder, J. G., 11, 31, 40, 56, 58, 64, 71, 80, 81, 118, 126, 151, 154, 164, 192, 212, 213, 216, 224, 227, 231
Herodotus, 1, 2, 4, 21, 30, 60, 126, 165, 193, 194, 212, 213, 215, 216, 223, 224, 226, 234, 242, 244, 246, 252
Hesse, Hermann, 9
Heussi, Karl, 10, 57
Hexter, J. H., 17, 134, 141, 179, 181, 182, 210, 215, 222
Heyne, C. G., 91, 227
Hicks, Granville, 190
Higgs, Henry, 103
Higham, John, 158
Hildebrand, Emil, 43
Hill, Christopher, 73, 108, 142, 178, 179
Himmelfarb, Gertrude, 221
Hintze, Otto, 10, 29, 30, 32, 33, 35, 36, 37, 42, 50, 53, 54, 55, 56, 57, 92, 154, 160
Hirsch, E. D., 241

Hitler, Adolf, 37, 99, 147, 153, 154, 155, 156, 157, 161, 175
Hjärne, Harald, 131
Hobbes, Thomas, 17
Hobsbawm, Eric, 73, 179, 182
Hodgkin, T., 48
Hoetsch, Otto, 97
Hofmannsthal, Hugo von, 7
Hofstadter, Richard, 126, 158, 159, 191
Holborn, Hajo, 98, 99, 154, 159, 160, 189
Hölderlin, Friedrich, 135
Holdsworth, William, 14
Holl, Karl, 35
Hölzle, Erwin, 95, 98, 174
Hóman, Bálint, 129, 130
Homo, Léon, 68
Hotman, François, 210
Hughes, H. Stuart, 160, 161, 190, 207
Huizinga, Johan, 45, 71, 85, 86, 134, 193, 198, 199, 205, 213, 216, 220, 235, 249
Humboldt, Alexander von, 26
Humboldt, Wilhelm von, 33
Hume, David, 13, 75, 181, 198, 241
Hunt, Lynn, 191, 221
Huntington, E., 111
Hus, Jan, 131
Husserl, Edmund, 76, 85, 231
Hutton, Patrick, 186

Ibn Khaldūn, 164
Iggers, Georg, 176, 212
Imbart de La Tour, Pierre, 49
Iorga, Nicolae, 132
Isabella, Queen (England), 104
Israel, Jonathan, 210, 212
Ivinskis, Zenonas, 132

Jacobs, Margaret, 221
Jaeger, Friedrich, 171
Jaeger, Werner, 60
James, William, 5
Jameson, Fredric, 223

Jameson, John Franklin, 52, 117, 118, 119
Jan of Leiden, 153
Jaspers, Karl, 81, 86, 89, 99
Jászi, Oskár, 130
Jaurès, Jean, 110
Jay, Martin, 2, 190, 192
Jiriček, Constantin, 43
Joachim of Flora, 94
John, St., 237
Johns, Adrian, 229
Johnson, Samuel, 87, 179
John the Baptist, 72
Joinville, Jean, 31
Jones, Howard Mumford, 190, 207
Jonson, Ben, 206
Josephson, Matthew, 122
Joyce, James, 4, 5, 46, 194, 196, 197, 207, 213, 214
Julian, Emperor, 70
Jullian, Camille, 49, 66

Kafka, Franz, 7, 86, 135, 207
Kahler, Erich, 80
Kammen, Michael, 158
Kant, Immanuel, 8, 11, 71, 75, 77, 80, 82, 86, 227
Kantorowicz, Ernst, 94, 95, 98, 139, 150, 159
Karl, Friedrich, 7, 13
Karpovich, Michael, 59, 207
Kautsky, Karl, 73
Kazin, Alfred, 190
Kehr, Eckhard, 92, 98, 159
Kellner, Hans, 215, 219, 220, 221, 222
Kern, Fritz, 98
Keyser, R., 129
Kienast, Walter, 98
Kierkegaard, Søren, 160
Kingdon, Robert, 212
Kinser, Samuel, 208
Kisch, Guido, 159
Klee, Paul, 70
Klemperer, Victor, 153
Kliuchevskii, V. O., 42

Knape, Joachim, 212
Knowles, David, 142
Knowles, Lilian, 105
Kocka, Jürgen, 171, 172, 174
Köhler, Erich, 30
Koht, Halvadan, 10, 131
Korbzybski, Alfred, 125
Koselleck, Reinhart, 173, 203, 212
Kossina, Gustav, 64
Koyré, Alexandre, 26
Kramer, Samuel Noah, 63
Krieger, Leonard, 189
Kristeller, Paul Oskar, 149, 160, 209, 211
Kruus, Hans, 132
Kuhn, Thomas, 163, 171, 210, 235
Kurth, Godefroid, 41

Labrousse, Ernest, 110–11
La Capra, Dominick, 192, 215, 219, 220, 221
Lacombe, Paul, 25, 113, 140
La Croix, Paul, 201
Ladner, Gerhard, 160
Lamprecht, Karl, 8, 9, 10, 24, 28, 29, 30, 32, 33, 36, 37, 38, 42, 50, 55, 56, 58, 91, 92, 113, 118, 120, 122, 149, 150, 152, 161, 171, 220
Landauer, Carl, 159
Landes, David, 162
Langer, William L., 124, 160, 161, 174, 207
Langland, William, 104
Langlois, C. V., 22, 23, 24, 26, 28, 104, 113, 117, 137, 140
Lanson, Gustav, 50
La Popelinière, Henri de, 145
Laski, Harold, 84, 106
Laslett, Peter, 181
LaTour, Bruno, 2
Lavin, Irving, 210
Lavisse, Ernest, 22, 23, 24, 26, 41, 49, 50, 53, 97, 101, 118
Leavis, F. R., 216
LeBon, Gustav, 52

Lecky, W. H., 14
Lefebvre, Georges, de, 73, 110, 186
Lefranc, Abel, 112, 115
Le Goff, Jacques, 184, 185, 202, 220
Leibniz, G. W., 17, 137
Lenormant, François, 61
Lenz, Max, 29, 30, 32, 34, 35, 36, 37, 42, 53, 54, 55, 92, 156
LeQueux, William, 5
LeRoy, Louis, 21
LeRoy Ladurie, Emmanuel, 140, 163, 183, 184, 185, 196, 202
Lessing, Gotthold, 153
Lessing, Theodor, 74, 76, 77
Levin, Harry, 207
Levine, Joseph, 212
Levi-Strauss, Claude, 140
Lévy-Bruhl, Lucien, 12, 26, 27, 28, 114
Lewis, Wyndham, 6
Liebermann, Felix, 14
Lingard, John, 13
Lipsius, Justus, 70
Livy, 1, 21, 68, 127, 223
Löwith, Karl, 71
Lord, R. H., 52
Lorenz, Otto, 152
Loria, Achille, 118
Lot, Ferdinand, 53
Louis XIV, King, 96
Lovejoy, Arthur O., 50, 51, 188, 210, 211
Lowenberg, Peter, 161
Loyseau, Charles, 183
Luchaire, Achille, 23, 102
Lucian, 217, 218
Lucretius, 63
Luden, Heinrich, 91
Lukács, Georg, 73, 86, 87
Lukes, Steven, 27
Lunt, William, 52
Luther, Martin, 31, 37, 55, 112, 115, 154, 155, 161, 175
Lyon, Bryce, 207
Lyotard, Jean-François, 223, 232, 234

Mabillon, Jean, 104, 137
Macaulay, Thomas Babington, 14, 15, 17, 20, 42, 121, 122, 215
Machiavelli, Niccolò, 21, 31, 38, 58, 68, 70, 83, 139, 155, 160
MacKay, Donald, 125, 207
MacKechnie, William, 14
Mailer, Norman, 207
Maitland, Frederick William, 14, 15, 16, 18, 116, 124, 138, 143, 216
Mâle, Emile, 26
Malia, Martin, 207
Mandelbaum, Maurice, 205
Mandrou, Robert, 141, 187
Mann, J. S., 101
Mann, Thomas, 46, 92, 156, 207, 220
Mannheim, Karl, 10, 11, 57, 75, 85, 86, 122, 125
Marchand, Susan, 64
Marcks, Erich, 29, 32, 36, 37, 47, 50, 54, 59, 92, 95, 97, 98, 99
Marco Polo, 104
Marcusa, Herbert, 162
Marcus Aurelius, 69
Marquardt, Odo, 214
Marshall, Alfred, 105
Martin, Henri-Jean, 23, 187, 229
Marvin, F. S., 49, 74, 75
Marx, Karl, 31, 59, 69, 72, 73, 75, 80, 85, 87, 88, 92, 99, 106, 107, 108, 109, 113, 114, 117, 122, 130, 137, 139, 141, 157, 162, 165, 166, 168, 170, 179, 180, 186, 187, 191, 208, 209, 216, 223, 226, 227, 228, 248
Masaryk, Thomas, 130, 131
Maspero, C. G. C., 62, 63, 135
Maspero, Henri, 136
Massis, Henri, 23
Masur, Gerhard, 98
Mathiez, Albert, 110, 160
Matthiessen, F. O., 190, 191
Mattingly, Garrett, 134, 210
Maurer, Konrad von, 93
Mauss, Marcel, 28, 186
Mayer, Thomas, 95, 159

Mazlish, Bruce, 161
Mazzini, G., 139
McIlwain, C. H., 14, 124, 134, 182
McKitterick, Rosamond, 225, 228
McLuhan, Marshall, 230, 237, 248
McMaster, John Bach, 120, 121
McNeill, William, 81, 165
Megill, Allan, 193, 223
Meillet, Antoine, 111, 116
Meinecke, Friedrich, 10, 30, 32, 33, 34, 35, 36, 37, 50, 51, 52, 53, 54, 55, 56, 57, 58, 59, 79, 86, 92, 94, 95, 97, 98, 99, 139, 150, 151, 152, 153, 154, 156, 160, 171, 176, 187, 196, 209, 212, 220
Meiners, Christoph, 199
Melanchthon, Phillip, 229
Menache, Sophie, 228
Mencken, H. L., 51
Menéndez Pelayo, R., 42
Menéndez Pidal, Ramón, 134
Menger, Carl, 10, 57
Mentré, F., 75
Merk, Frederick, 125, 207
Merleau-Ponty, Maurice, 198, 231
Merriman, R. B., 124, 180
Metternich, Clemens, 129, 151
Mexia, Pedro, 70
Meyer, Eduard, 28, 42, 51, 53, 56, 62, 63, 64, 65, 81, 102, 178, 212
Michelet, Jules, 22, 23, 24, 42, 110, 114, 122, 141, 183, 185, 186, 195, 200, 202, 214, 216, 217, 218, 220, 221, 222
Mickiewicz, Adam, 98
Miller, Perry, 123, 125, 159, 190, 191, 207
Mills, James, 161
Mills, John Stuart, 161
Milton, John, 70, 181
Momigliano, Arnaldo, 1, 70, 134, 212
Mommsen, Hans, 174
Mommsen, Theodor, 6, 10, 20, 30, 32, 35, 42, 65, 67, 68, 91, 98, 159, 178, 216

Mommsen, Wolfgang, 172, 174
Monod, Gabriel, 22, 27, 28
Montaigne, Michel de, 232, 237
Montesquieu, Baron de, 22, 68, 114
More, Thomas, 155
Morgan, Jacques, 61
Morgan, Lewis Henry, 168
Morison, Samuel Eliot, 123, 124, 125, 134, 191, 207
Mortillet, Guillaume de, 27
Mosheim, J. L., 69
Mousnier, Roland, 184, 208
Müller, K. A., 150, 153
Mulsow, Martin, 212
Mumford, Lewis, 165, 190
Mundy, John, 210
Munro, Dana, 52
Munz, Peter, 212
Murdoch, Kenneth, 123, 125, 190, 191
Musil, Robert, 46, 149
Myer, Eduard, 62, 63, 67, 68

Namier, Lewis, 53, 81, 101, 120, 142, 143, 144, 145, 146, 148, 177, 178, 179
Napoleon III, 55, 60, 93
Naville, Adrien, 28
Neale, J. E., 101, 142, 143, 178
Needham, Joseph, 142
Neumann, Franz, 171
Nevins, Alan, 126, 215
Nicholson, Marjorie Hope, 210
Niebuhr, Barthold Georg, 68, 151, 195, 216
Niebuhr, Reinhold, 71, 72, 159
Nietzsche, Friedrich, 4, 9, 48, 65, 83, 84, 86, 160, 161, 170, 193, 198, 213, 214, 222, 233, 241, 250
Nipperdey, Thomas, 91, 172, 174
Nisbet, Robert, 79
Noah, 61
Nolte, Ernst, 170, 174, 175
Nora, Pierre, 183, 186, 214, 225
Nordau, Max, 82
Notestein, Wallace, 52

Novalis (G. F. P. Hardenburg), 3
Novick, Peter, 125
Nürnberger, Richard, 91

Oestreich, Gerhhard, 153
Olson, Charles, 5
Oman, Charles, 14
Oncken, Hermann, 37, 42, 50, 53, 55, 59, 90, 95, 98, 150, 155, 156
Orosius, 69
Orr, Linda, 192, 215
Ortega y Gasset, José, 9, 71, 84, 85, 89, 90
Otto of Freising, 3
Owen, David, 207
Owen, Robert, 100

Pagden, Anthony, 212
Pais, Ettore de, 68, 118
Palacký, František, 41, 43, 130
Palmer, Robert, 210
Panofsky, Erwin, 225
Panwitz, Rudolph, 60, 232
Paolo Emilio, 23
Pares, Richard, 148
Paret, Peter, 190, 210
Pareto, Vilfredo, 189
Park, Katherine, 227
Parrington, Vernon L., 123, 124, 126, 158, 190
Parsons, Talcott, 71
Partner, Nancy, 194
Pastor, Ludwig, 38, 39, 69
Patrizi, Francesco, 79
Paul, St., 232
Paulsen, Friedrich, 6, 7
Pausanias, 26
Pekař, Josef, 130
Perry, W. J., 61
Petit-Dutaillis, Charles, 14, 19
Petrarch, Francesco, 31
Pfister, Christian, 50
Phillip IV, King of France, 229
Phillip of Alexandria, 66
Phillip II, King of Spain, 111

Pico della Mirandola, 60
Piganiol, André, 68
Pirenne, Henri, 41, 109, 112, 115, 116,
    118, 128, 137, 207
Plumb, J. H., 148
Pocock, J. G. A., 70, 181, 182, 209, 212
Poe, Edgar Allen, 123
Poirot, Hercule, 212
Poktrovskii, M. N., 59
Pollard, A. F., 15, 17, 18, 48, 49, 101,
    102, 142, 143, 182
Pollock, Frederick, 15
Polybius, 21, 127, 164, 194, 212, 234,
    235
Poole, Reginald Lane, 14, 15
Pope, Alexander, 176, 252
Popkin, Jeremy, 230
Popkin, Richard, 210, 212
Postgate, Raymond, 107
Potter, David, 158
Poullain de la Barre, François, 198
Pound, Ezra, 135
Pound, J. H., 14
Power, Eileen, 104, 105, 142
Powicke, Maurice, 76
Prescott, William H., 124
Prothero, G. W., 53
Proudhon, P. J., 210
Proust, Marcel, 185, 186, 207
Ptolemy, 26

Rabb, Theodore, 210
Rabelais, François, 112, 115
Rachfels, Felix, 29
Raleigh, Walter, 49, 51
Rambaud, Alfred, 41, 43
Ramus, Peter, 159
Randall, Jr., John Herman, 210
Ranke, Leopold von, 6, 8, 10, 29, 30, 31,
    32, 33, 34, 36, 37, 38, 50, 52, 58, 62,
    66, 76, 91, 92, 96, 125, 127, 132, 145,
    146, 151, 152, 156, 157, 171, 172,
    176, 178, 195, 209, 216, 217, 218,
    219, 220, 221, 222, 223, 231, 245
Ranum, Orest, 208

Ratzel, Friedrich, 25, 111
Rawlinson, George, 62
Rawlinson, Henry, 63
Redlich, Josef, 129
Renan, Ernest, 22, 28
Renard, G., 63
Renouvier, Charles, 26
Renouvin, Pierre, 90
Reville, André, 19
Rhodes, James Ford, 120, 121
Richardson, H. D., 101
Rickert, Heinrich, 11, 28, 33, 38, 56, 76,
    77, 81, 85, 212
Ricoeur, Paul, 186, 192, 214, 239
Riegl, Alois, 75
Riehl, Wilhelm, 39
Rienzi, Cola di, 67, 153
Rigney, Ann, 222
Rilke, Rainer Maria, 6, 89, 238
Rimbaud, Arthur, 7
Ritter, Gerhard, 91, 139, 150, 154, 155,
    156, 157, 174, 187
Ritter, Karl, 26, 98
Ritter, Moriz, 53, 55, 95, 98, 152
Rivers, W. H. R., 61
Robertson, J. M., 51
Robinson, James Harvey, 9, 118, 119, 120
Roelker, Nancy, 212
Rogers, Thorold, 103
Romein, Jan, 134
Roosevelt, Theodore, 121
Rörig, Fritz, 98
Rorty, Richard, 192
Rose, J. Holland, 47, 48
Rosenberg, Arthur, 98, 159, 171
Rosenberg, Hans, 98, 99, 159, 171, 173
Rostovtzeff, Michael, 68, 69
Rothfels, Hans, 99, 157, 159, 172, 174
Rousseau, Jean-Jacques, 56, 217
Rowse, A. L., 148
Rudé, Georges, 73
Rüsen, Jörn, 176, 212

Sacy, Silvestre de, 61
Sagnac, Philippe, 23

Saint-Pierre, Abbé, 21, 22
Saint-Simon, C. H., 22, 185
Sallust, 21
Salmon, Lucy Maynard, 119, 164
Salvatorelli, Luigi, 134
Salvemini, Gaetano, 134, 139
Sánchez Albornoz, Claudio, 134
Sanchez-Alonzo, Claudio, 41
Sanctis, Gaetano de, 68
Sars, Johann, 43
Sarton, George, 134
Sartre, Jean Paul, 86
Saussure, Ferdinand de, 192, 193
Savigny, Friedrich Karl von, 15, 34, 210
Sayles, G. O., 101
Scaliger, J. J., 61
Schäfer, Dietrich, 29, 32, 33, 36, 42, 50, 53, 55, 91, 97
Scheler, Max, 85, 86, 156
Schelling, F. W. J., 71
Schevill, Ferdinand, 206
Schiemann, Theodor, 97, 132
Schlegel, Friedrich von, 31, 33, 71, 232
Schlesinger, Arthur M., 122, 123, 125, 207
Schlesinger, Arthur M., Jr., 125, 126, 161, 191
Schliemann, Heinrich, 61
Schlosser, F. C., 31, 91
Schlözer, A. L., 39, 91
Schmitt, Carl, 84, 85, 86, 95
Schmitt, Charles, 212
Schmoller, Gustav, 36, 51, 92, 93
Schnabel, Franz, 98, 150, 151
Schneider, Ulrich Johannes, 212
Schorske, Carl, 160, 190, 207
Schramm, Percy Ernst, 98, 139, 159
Schulze, Winfried, 174, 175
Schumpeter, Joseph, 87, 93
Scott, James, 52
Scott, Walter, 20
Seeck, Otto, 68, 69, 83
Seeley, J. R., 117
Seidman, Steven, 232

Seigel, Jerrold, 210
Seignobos, Charles, 8, 22, 23, 24, 25, 26, 27, 28, 49, 111, 113, 117, 133, 137, 140
Selden, John, 182
Seligman, Edwin, 103
Seraphim, E. and A., 43
Shapin, Steven, 186
Shaw, George Bernard, 107, 135
Shepard, William R., 121
Shorter, Edward, 200
Shotwell, J. T., 53, 119, 120
Shrimpton, Gordon, 225
Sieyès, Abbé E. J., 110
Sigonio, Carlo, 70
Simiand, François, 25, 28, 111, 113, 114, 140, 196
Simmel, George, 5, 10, 11, 74, 75, 77, 81, 82, 85, 86, 212
Šišić, Ferdo, 133
Skinner, Quentin, 181, 210, 211
Sleidan, Johann, 218
Smith, Bonnie, 164, 208
Smith, G. Elliot, 61
Soboul, Albert, 73, 110
Soll, Jacob, 229
Solomon, 237
Sombart, Werner, 93, 107, 122, 156
Somerset, Protestor, 17
Sorel, Georges, 101
Sorokin, Pitrim A., 71, 165, 247
Spencer, Herbert, 21
Spengler, Oswald, 13, 55, 56, 58, 60, 65, 71, 74, 75, 76, 80, 81, 83, 84, 85, 86, 99, 122, 160, 165, 212, 232
Spiller, Robert, 190
Spitzer, Leo, 153
Srbik, Heinrich von, 93, 95, 98, 129, 139, 149, 151, 152, 154
Stadelmann, Richard, 91, 95, 98, 156
Stalin, Josef, 108
Stanojeviç, Stanoje, 43
Stearns, Peter, 163
Steenstrup, Johannes, 43, 131
Steinhausen, Georg, 30, 39

Stephenson, Carl, 207
Stern, Fritz, 160, 189
Stevens, Wallace, 8, 185
Stoianovich, Traian, 113, 166, 245
Stone, Lawrence, 147, 163, 178, 180, 192, 200, 210, 215
Strabo, 114
Strayer, Joseph, 204
Stubbs, William, 14, 15, 19, 102, 105, 124, 143, 182, 216
Šusta, Josef, 130
Sybel, Heinrich von, 32, 82, 91
Syme, Ronald, 144
Szeckfü, Gyula, 129, 130
Szilágy, Sándor, 43, 129

Tacitus, 21, 30, 31, 67, 68, 125
Tagliacozzo, Giorgio, 72, 212, 213
Taine, Hippolyte, 25, 28, 140, 216
Tarde, Alfred de, 23
Tardieu, André, 53
Tawney, R. H., 103, 105, 106, 107, 142, 147, 206
Taylor, A. J. P., 129, 142, 146
Taylor, Henry Osborn, 124
Teggart, F. J., 81
Teilhard de Chardin, Pierre, 71, 79, 165, 204
Tellenbach, Gerd, 91
Temperley, Harold, 53, 98, 101
Terence, 141
Thackeray, William Makepeace, 223
Thienemann, Theodor, 129
Thierry, Augustin, 222
Thiers, Adolphe, 82
Thomas, Keith, 178, 182
Thompson, A. H., 104
Thompson, E. P., 73, 108, 144, 179, 221
Thompson, James Westfall, 118, 212
Thorndike, Lynn, 134
Thou, J. A. de, 208
Thucydides, 1, 4, 11, 21, 29, 30, 81, 113, 194, 212, 217, 224, 234, 246, 252
Tito, 133, 236
Tocqueville, Alexis de, 216

Tolstoy, Leo, 5, 223
Tönnies, Friedrich, 86
Tout, T. F., 14, 16, 48, 102, 177
Toynbee, Arnold, 13, 53, 71, 80, 81, 85, 106, 138, 142, 148, 149, 165, 168, 195, 205, 232, 235
Toynbee, Arnold (the elder), 103, 106, 107, 108, 206
Traill, H. D., 101
Treitschke, Heinrich von, 29, 30, 32, 33, 34, 35, 37, 38, 42, 48, 49, 52, 54, 58, 82, 90, 92, 101, 150, 151, 216
Trevelyan, George Macaulay, 15, 17, 18, 19, 20, 87, 101, 106, 118, 142, 146, 215
Trevelyan, George Otto, 18
Trevor-Roper, Hugh, 142, 146, 147, 179, 189
Troeltsch, Ernst, 10, 11, 33, 35, 50, 53, 54, 55, 56, 57, 58, 65, 71, 77, 78, 92, 107, 160
Troie, Hans, 212
Trollope, Anthony, 223
Tunstall, Cuthbert, 19
Turner, Frederick Jackson, 52, 118, 120, 121, 122, 125, 158, 159, 165, 207
Twain, Mark, 5
Tyler, Moses Coit, 126, 190

Ukert, F. A., 42
Ullmann, Walter, 139
Unamuno, Miguel de, 160

Vaihinger, Hans, 125
Valentin, Veit, 98, 99, 159
Valla, Lorenzo, 38, 192
Van Coch, Vincent, 160
Van Hout, Elizabeth, 225
Vann, Richard, 222
Varga, Lucie, 137
Veblen, Thorstein, 171
Verene, Donald, 212
Vergil, 94
Vernadsky, George, 59
Veyne, Paul, 113, 184, 186, 239

Vico, Giambattista, 4, 64, 71, 72, 76, 78, 80, 81, 82, 83, 85, 109, 126, 160, 185, 192, 200, 212, 213, 219, 222, 227, 238

Victoria, Queen, 146

Vidal de la Blache, Paul, 23, 26, 111, 114

Vilar, Pierre, 73

Vincens Vives, Jaime, 134

Vinogradoff, Paul, 14, 15, 49

Violet, Paul, 102

Visagier, Jean, 115

Voegelin, Erich, 71, 80

Voltaire, François, 22, 31, 71, 118, 126, 137, 164, 195, 217

Von Martin, Alfred, 98

Vossius, G., 30

Vossler, Kurt, 149

Vovelle, Michel, 187, 199

Wachler, Ludwig, 91, 152

Waitz, Georg, 15, 41, 91, 116

Wallerstein, Immanuel, 166

Waquet, François, 230

Warburg, Aby, 149

Ward, A. W., 48, 102

Weaver, Stewart, 106

Webb, Beatrice, 105, 106, 107, 108

Webb, Sydney, 105, 106, 107, 108

Weber, Alfred, 39, 77, 86, 94

Weber, Max, 11, 39, 59, 65, 71, 86, 92, 107, 123, 171

Weber, Wolfgang, 91

Wedgwood, C. V., 86, 87, 154

Wegele, F. X. von, 152

Wehler, Hans Ulrich, 99, 171, 172, 175

Wells, H. G., 57, 71, 85, 165, 206

Wendell, Barrett, 5

Westerman, William, 52

White, Andrew Dickson, 117

White, Hayden, 187, 192, 215, 216, 217, 218, 222

White, Morton, 205, 210

Willamowitz-Moellendorf, Ulrich von, 65, 67

Williams, Raymond, 108, 109, 221, 226, 227

Williams, William Appleman, 159

Wilson, Edmund, 122

Wilson, Woodrow, 44, 52, 119, 120, 133

Winckler, Henry-August, 172, 174

Windelband, Wilhelm, 11, 33, 38, 76, 77, 81, 212

Wittgenstein, Ludwig, 86, 192

Wittke, Raxane, 209

Wolf, Eric, 168

Wolf, F. A., 91

Wolf, Gustav, 55

Wolfe, Thomas, 206, 207

Wooley, Leonard, 61

Woolf, Virginia, 5

Wundt, Wilhelm, 50

Wycliffe, John, 19

Xénopol, Alexandre, 25, 28, 43, 132

Zagorin, Perez, 108, 179

Zimmern, Alfred, 53